THE IDEA OF PEACE
IN ANTIQUITY

THE IDEA
IN

GERARDO ZAMPAGLIONE

OF PEACE
ANTIQUITY

TRANSLATED BY RICHARD DUNN

UNIVERSITY OF NOTRE DAME PRESS

NOTRE DAME   LONDON

Published as *L'Idea della pace nel mondo antico,*
© 1967 by Eri-Edizioni Rai Radiotelevisione Italiana, Turin, Italy

Library of Congress Cataloging in Publication Data

Zampaglione, Gerardo.
The idea of peace in antiquity.

Translation of L'idea della pace nel mondo antico.

1. Peace. I. Title.
JX1941.Z3513   327'.172   72-3505
ISBN 0-268-00470-6

Printed in the United States of America by
NAPCO Graphic Arts, Inc., New Berlin, Wisconsin

CONTENTS

II. PEACE IN ROMAN THINKING AND IN LATER HELLENISTIC SPECULATION

III. PEACE IN THE OLD TESTAMENT

ACKNOWLEDGMENTS

Grateful acknowledgment is made to the Harvard University Press for permission to use excerpts from the Loeb Classical Library translations of the following works:

Hesiod, *Works and Days,* trans. Hugh G. Evelyn White.
Hesiod, *Theogony,* trans. Hugh G. Evelyn White.
Thucydides, *History of the Peloponnesian War,* trans. C. F. Smith.
Xenophon, *Oeconomicus,* trans. E. C. Marchant.
Xenophon, *Hiero,* trans. E. C. Marchant.
Xenophon, *Ways and Means,* trans. E. C. Marchant.
Xenophon, *Cyropaedia,* trans. Walter Miller.
Isocrates, *On the Peace,* trans. George Norlin.
Dio Cassius, *Roman History,* trans. E. Cary.
Tacitus, *Life of Agricola,* trans. Maurice Hutton.
Polybius, *Histories,* trans. W. R. Paton.
Lucretius, *De rerum natura,* trans. W. H. D. Rouse.
Cicero, *De officiis,* trans. Walter Miller.
Cicero, *Pro P. Sestio,* trans. R. Gardner.
Virgil, *Aeneid,* trans. H. R. Fairclough.
Virgil, *Eclogue IV,* trans. H. R. Fairclough.
Horace, *Odes,* trans. C. E. Bennett.
Ovid, *Fasti,* trans. Sir James G. Frazer.

Seneca, *Epistola ad Lucilium,* trans. R. M. Gummere.

Seneca, *De otio,* trans. John W. Basore.

Seneca, *De vita beata,* trans. John W. Basore.

Seneca, *De ira,* trans. John W. Basore.

Pliny the Elder, *Natural History,* bks II & X, trans. H. Rackham; bk. XXVII, trans. W. H. S. Jones.

Dio Chrysostom, *Discourses XL & XLVIII,* trans. H. Lamar Crosby.

Plutarch, *On the Fortune or the Virtue of Alexander,* trans. F. C. Babbitt.

Marcus Aurelius, *Meditations,* trans. C. R. Haines.

Philo, *On the Creation,* trans. F. H. Colson & G. H. Whitaker.

Philo, *On the Change of Names,* trans. F. H. Colson & G. H. Whitaker.

Philo, *On the Special Laws,* trans. F. H. Colson.

Philostratus, *Life of Apollonius of Tyana,* trans. F. C. Conybeare.

Plotinus, *Enneads,* trans. A. H. Armstrong.

Julian, *To the Uneducated Cynics,* trans. Wilmer Cave Wright.

Julian, *II Panegyric of Constantius,* trans. Wilmer Cave Wright.

Augustine, *City of God,* bk. XIV, trans. Philip Levine; bk. XIX, trans. W. C. Greene.

INTRODUCTION

The End of the Myth of War

We live in a time of great change due to the progress of science and technology and to the consequent adoption of new ways and standards of thinking. The forces challenging man are no longer those of a short while ago, and they tend to develop in patterns and along lines which are difficult to predict and classify in advance. The ever increasing pace of progress entails constant adjustment.

Man's aspirations are changing while new myths determine his actions—myths created by technology, the mass media, and the relentless quest for material welfare. To some extent, a new morality is being forged by the widespread conviction, characteristic of our time, that man can find in himself, solely through the diligent channeling of his own will, a response to the difficult problems raised by the need to advance and to seek betterment.

War and intolerance have unfortunately not disappeared.[1] Brotherly dedication, love, the humility preached by the Gospels, and mutual understanding are certainly not what count most in community life. A glance at any newspaper is enough to show that conflict, rebellions, and aggression still hamper the progress of mankind. And yet the rules of good conduct are moving increasingly toward principles excluding intolerance, boastfulness, and arrogance. Gone is the time when the German Kaiser William II could hand out photographs of himself in warlike pose with the caption: "My hour will come." The age is past when an Adolf Hitler could assure his armies that in Germany's hour of need—the need for *Lebensraum*—the God of War would not let her down. This mythology has fortunately collapsed under the pressure of changes which have taken place in the entire human condition.

1

The fact that statesmen can no longer resort—overtly at least—to such expedients, but must justify themselves in the face of public opinion before they can take up attitudes liable to lead to war, is evidence that real progress has been made and that new ideas and more modern critical judgments have taken the place of outmoded ways of thinking. Despite a very widespread restlessness, *Angst,* and sense of instability, the abandonment of certain willfully bellicose attitudes and the adoption of others based on the view that peace must be defended at all costs are symptomatic of change, even though the danger of war is still present.

The rhetoric of peace[2] is, in the last analysis, preferable to that of war. For example, it is not insignificant that at the most critical moments of the cold war,when a new world conflict seemed imminent, the USSR should have supported a peace movement, proclaiming the need to mobilize public opinion in order to secure the banning of nuclear armaments and maintain peace between the powers. It may be objected that this was almost certainly a stratagem adopted by a great power to play off the naive, the young, and the most optimistic of all countries against its enemies, in order to achieve a psychological advantage. Even if this were so, the circumstance would prove what a deep change has taken place in contemporary society: Something has stirred man's awareness and replaced the pressures toward violence to which he was traditionally exposed. One begins to understand the stark contrast between the achievements of scientific research and industrial organization on the one hand, and moral principles firmly rooted in sterile prejudices and conventional wisdom on the other.

Crisis in the Nation-State

It is worthwhile investigating the causes of this change. Why, in a world divided by ideological struggle—the modern counterpart of the religious wars—a world in which men in every walk of life, be it public or private, make no attempt to hide their mutual distrust and animosity, has such an important development nevertheless taken place? Why are the countries of the world now called upon to adopt an attitude at least apparently conciliatory, even when they are secretly hostile and possibly planning acts of aggression? How has the ideal of peace succeeded to some extent in superseding that of war, regarded for millennia as an honorable and indeed sublime activity? The answer is in part that new ideas have prevailed among men, ousting the old ones, too long regarded as immutable.

Although the quest for a rational explanation of war has for centuries been the favorite exercise of thinkers and philosophers in the service of states, it is mainly during the last four hundred years that the Western world has developed its own doctrine of war, its causes and its effects. This philosophy owes much to the birth of nationalism.

It was nationalism which strengthened the state in its claim to embody all powers—heavenly and secular—and which supplied it, through the doctrine of divine right, with the justification for physical violence. The abdication of the individual before the state yielded its bitter fruit in a succession of European wars. All were due partly or wholly to the conviction held by monarchs that they were the evangelists of an imperious and inalienable gospel of expansion, the victims of which were other peoples. Millions of individuals were relegated to the status of robots at the mercy of a new Leviathan, the nation-state. And while the new states fought wars just as ferocious as those fought in earlier centuries, the old universal outlook which had been one merit of medieval society was abandoned.

It is therefore not surprising that new myths were born fostering ideas similar to those they claimed to oppose. Nationalism was at least partly responsible for the hostility that developed among the masses and the classes in several countries, and for the subsequent consolidation, through philosophic romanticism and Hegelian idealism, of an unfortunate form of worship of the state of which "jingoism" was a natural concomitant. All this left Western society divided and weakened, and the outcome in the twentieth century was tragedy.

This kind of worship of the state is partly accounted for by the intense forces of irrationality to which man is subject and to his need to seek outside himself a key to "all this unintelligible world." The nation-state, of limited horizons, took the place of wider approaches to the problem. A boundless arrogance, an unrelenting quest for happiness on earth, and a tendency to view the way mankind developed in relation to one's own national interest bound men to the state. The cult of war emerged strengthened from this transposition of activities and of ideals.

It is easy to understand, then, why we have suffered so much in modern times from the insanity of war and why people have come to believe that the state should be the highest form of human organization, since it fulfills entirely their aspirations, hopes, and expectations. Though its teaching had rarely achieved the results expected, Christianity had preached for centuries a message of equality, justice, and peace, in the attempt to unite all men as brothers, with equal rights to eternal salvation. A society focused on the state, on the other hand, encouraged hierarchies, entailing, by definition, inequality. Each class sought to monopolize these power patterns, coveting the right to legislate and establish codes of behavior for others. War had always been the inevitable corollary of this.

The present crisis of the nation-state has altered the situation. The Second World War was not only yet another fearful reminder of the heavy tribute of blood which the state is forced to claim from men, but also demonstrated its inability to cope with the new human environment and with the new prevailing ideas. Progress and the resulting social and political advances (decolonization, new independent states, the broadening of the electorate, the spread of new doctrines, mass political parties and movements, etc.) have made glaringly obvious the fragility of the traditional state and the vanity of its preten-sions to be the perfect and unexcelled expression of man's social nature.

People have felt that the response made by the state to the challenge and the expectations of modern individuals is more and more disappointing, that the elaborate choreography which used to lend some kind of elegance to the trappings of power has often merely blurred the issues and created a barrier to progress and tolerance. It has been understood that other forms of com-munity life (states on a continental scale, for example, or indeed a world state) could usefully take its place, that sovereignty, understood in the exclu-sive and extreme terms of the past, will be increasingly curbed by the con-trols and interference of new world agencies like the United Nations and the other bodies which the needs of men will certainly engender. It has been un-derstood—as Bertrand Russell has pointed out[3]—that peace must be the sup-porting pillar of tolerance. And though the primeval urges of the past linger on, though some states, whether old or new, still allow themselves to be se-duced by sterile memories and harmful myths, in the background we can now detect more and more clearly a new pattern of attitudes which is a great deal less friendly to war.

This explains why, at a time of transition like the present one with most people longing for a peaceful society, all statesmen—even the least idealistic—discern the need to avoid, at least in the external aspects of their policies, tub-thumping, "my-country-right-or-wrong" arguments, and to express them-selves as apparently convinced advocates of peace. Peace as a popular ideal has come into its own.

Vitality of Pacifist Thinking

Yet, even in the centuries during which the state was worshipped unreserv-edly, not all European thinking was based solely on the exaltation of the unity and power of the state or on the individual's wholehearted accep-tance of the military mystique. Even then European society included men who sought ways and means of discouraging an attitude to life having obvi-ously harmful implications. They hoped therefore that man would succeed in freeing himself from the atmosphere of *Angst* into which he was forced by in-sufficient economic organization and the existing relations between commu-nities for whom war seemed to constitute the foundation of every decision and the ultimate objective of every act.

This group of enlightened forerunners included not only philosophers and theologians but also men of action and statesmen, all equally aware of the danger caused by aggressive intolerance. They proposed to remove all obsta-cles to progress and to the elimination of war. They believed that peace was essential to all religious and civil faith and must necessarily govern any valid ethical system. Avoiding the temptations of empty magniloquence, they ar-gued the urgency of rejecting everything inimical to the peaceful needs of man.

Underlying their conduct and their thinking there was not only a profound religious feeling, seeking a more ordered life and a less dramatic conception of the destiny of man; there were also certain fundamental principles of rationalism, which had reached the same conclusions by other routes. The forerunners, who challenged the absolute state and the almost sacred cult of which it was the center, based their attitude on the Gospels and on reason. In the European society of the seventeenth and eighteenth centuries, a group of thinkers were arguing, almost covertly, and certainly without the publicity essential if their ideas were to win general acceptance, against warlike rhetoric.

Acting in the name of ideals having the same basis even if presented under different forms, the forerunners looked ahead to the day when mankind would finally shake off the chains of intolerance. They attacked the European society plagued by innumerable inhibitions, enslaved to the most humiliating compromises, committed to the maintenance of a system which sought no changes or reforms of any kind. Yet their attitude was regarded by the governing classes as wrong and ridiculous.

We may take as a remarkable example of this the various attempts made by the Abbé de Saint-Pierre to persuade the European monarchs of the first half of the eighteenth century to examine his "Projet de Traité pour rendre la Paix perpétuelle entre les souverains chrétiens," and the complacency larded with sarcasm with which this wandering apostle of a political ideal was received at the courts, where every proposal to consolidate peace was regarded as folly.

The rebellion of outstanding minds is the distinctive mark of the successive eras of history, the mainspring of human progress, and the expression of constant and fruitful endeavor. What was the Christian revolution if not the revolt of a suffering society, long humiliated and held down by a utilitarian vision of human destiny, but finally raised up by moral forces of overwhelming strength, such as the journey of Christ on earth and the message of the Gospel? In the Middle Ages, the religious sects, often fired by a genuine and burning attachment to the Gospels, were really reacting to the process of fossilization of the Christian message in forms which they believed lacked vitality. In modern times, new economic factors like the birth of industry and the advent of more advanced ideas with regard to community life are closely linked with the revolt of the working classes against current economic relationships and an unfair social framework.

The Forerunners

Who were the forerunners and how can they be classified? We have seen that the key periods of human development are anticipated by enlightened men and women, who, in thought and action, foreshadow and influence the progress of the body politic. Through their work they stimulate individuals and communities toward more civilized forms of life. Their mission is seldom immediately crowned with success. Almost always their contemporaries ac-

cuse them of irresponsibility and exact a heavy price for their reforming enthusiasm. But without the forerunners and their "fine frenzy," mankind
would stand now perhaps where it stood a thousand years ago. Each generation, certain of having achieved the final goals of human ambition, would settle down complacently in the positions reached.

The forerunners may be classified in two main categories. Firstly, there are
those who concentrate their thirst for knowledge and action on the natural
world and its laws and its utilization. These are the scientists, the captains of
industry, the organizers in general. Secondly, there are those who fix their
prophetic scrutiny on the life of the spirit and who feel the call of a sublime
and mysterious vocation. These are the philosophers, the theologians, the reformers of morals and law. Their view of the community is colored by the
need to find new routes and better means of development. They are not in
the habit of simply waiting passively for an extraordinary but uncertain
change in society. They regard accepted attitudes in this respect as owing
more to mental indolence and credulity than to cold reason. Though discerning in the succession of events convincing evidence of the existence of God
(they are often pious), they reject comfortable but sterile ideas that He will
help those who fail to help themselves. They are not convinced that the world
in which they live is the best of all possible worlds nor that attempts to make
good its deficiencies should be condemned. Their faith and their enthusiasm
generally provoke hostility: Men do not like being disturbed in their traditional way of life. The classes who have a vested interest in the maintenance
of the social status quo believe it right to oppose by every means the spread
of new ideas, and, since the easiest way of resisting them is to suffocate them
in violence, through the centuries the powerful have generally used persecution in their endless vendetta with the innovators.

The Pacifist Ideal of Community Life

This seems to be confirmed by the fate of the pacifist message. Seldom has
an idea been propagated with greater enthusiasm and sincerity, but equally
seldom has an idea met more relentless opposition. If mankind were once re-
lieved of the frightening prospects of recurring wars, there would be a fundamental change in social priorities. Nothing could be more disconcerting for
the members of the "establishment." The warning was for them and it made
them feel that human relations were about to move into a phase fraught with
unknown difficulties. It could hardly be expected that they would renounce
the possibility of using violence, the only means believed appropriate to overcome enemy resistance. In their age-old political systems, the art of government was based essentially on the energetic use of force to silence opponents.
Nothing could be further from their intentions than to allow, much less to encourage, closer cooperation between nations and social classes. If the existing
form of society was to be maintained intact, governments must have the
means to impose their will on those opposing them. Hence their distrust—

witness the many examples recorded in history—of anyone bearing a message of tolerance.

The pacifism of the early Christians and of the later sects was attacked because it was based on a religious experience isolating people from practical life. Pacifists were constantly accused of having failed to give their message a political framework, leaving it wholly in the field of pure abstraction.

In the seventeenth and eighteenth centuries pacifism ceased to be religious expectation linked with the prospect of a coming Messiah, and it eventually found room for the contributions of philosophy. Having entered into the heritage of the Enlightenment, it began to acquire some of the prestige gained during the eighteenth century by rational activity. This was not enough, however, to pierce the thick blanket of distrust which enveloped it, preventing it from influencing the decisions of the governing classes.

In the nineteenth century, leagues and congresses were an effective way of disseminating the ideas of peace and brotherhood thrown up by the liberal revolution. The pacifist ideal rose above its former inferior status but was not yet accepted as one of the group of key ideas which were to govern future society. Although it became the object of erudite study, it still did not escape scorn and persecution. The term *pacifist* was used pejoratively, suggesting an enemy of the established order whose behavior was unlikely to do much harm, though, as a matter of principle, it must be opposed. The opposition was, indeed, understandable, since European governments, despite the new wind of liberalism, had by no means abandoned the state's traditional approach to war.

The twentieth century saw the first direct attempts to give an institutional framework to the results of intellectual research, and a crusade of persuasion began, guided by a mature awareness of man's needs. Though convened in an atmosphere of general skepticism and against fierce resistance, the Hague Conferences of 1899 and 1907 did make some practical progress, setting up a Permanent Court of International Justice to review certain disputes between states. There followed the League of Nations and later the United Nations, bold attempts to come to terms with the past and build a brighter future using agencies empowered to intervene in the affairs of states in order to end wars.

The formation of institutions designed to consolidate peace in the world did not put an end to speculative activity. In fact, seldom as much as in recent years has the pacifist ideal interested philosophers and writers and inspired so many noble adventures in thought. From the philosopher of action Maurice Blondel to the neo-Thomist Jacques Maritain, from the romantic pessimist Romain Rolland to the existentialist Karl Jaspers and the empirical optimist Bertrand Russell, from the champion of bourgeois rationalism George Santayana to the pioneer of proletarian palingenesis Vladimir Lenin, from mystics like Leo Tolstoy, Gandhi, and Albert Schweitzer to the physicists of the nuclear age like Albert Einstein and Frédéric Joliot-Curie, we have seen a remarkable succession of gifted philosophers. Though tackling the same problem from differing angles, they have helped by their authority to bring the problem to the attention of a wider audience.

How can this flow of ideas, which has moved on from mysticism to rationalism and then to an institutional and scientific approach, be denied the importance and status of a discipline? The United Nations is now the axis on which relations between states revolve. It has acted as a catalyst in the process of the establishment of new countries and as a vehicle for their entry into the community of nations. Why then should one contest the value of the intellectual and moral movement from which they sprang?

Pacifism as a Science

Those who imagine pacifism to be the outcome of an illusory and absurd mental exercise, believing that they are thus emphasizing its subordination to other more essential intellectual activities, cannot ignore its influence on certain recent developments of mankind. In the nineteenth century a number of scholars devoted themselves to the problems of peace, making a critical catalogue of precious contributions. If pacifism had not yet achieved the dignity of a genuine science, if the evolution of morality had not yet proved its urgency and the need for it, why did famous economists like John Stuart Mill[4] and distinguished jurists like Johann Kaspar Bluntschli[5] take it as a subject of their teaching? Further evidence of its importance as a force in civilized society is found in the controversies it aroused: Those nineteenth-century writers who extolled war and its alleged moral primacy were compelled to defend themselves more vigorously precisely in order to stem the growing influence of their opponents. These were the years in which the doctrines of Joseph-Arthur de Gobineau[6] and his followers, who preached the biological and intellectual superiority of a given race over others, were very much in vogue. At the same time Friedrich Nietzsche was teaching that mass morality is servile and that it is not wrong to treat peoples as slaves and cannon-fodder. Such men argued with a ferocious obstinacy which bore eloquent witness to the violence of their animosities and the fanaticism of their beliefs. Pleading the inevitability and the necessity of war, they seemed unable to contain their passions, and all too often the result was disaster.

War itself was thus scarcely more irrational than the doctrine attempting to explain it. The arguments expounded by leading theorists (Treitschke, von Clausewitz, von Moltke, Nietzsche, von Bernhardi, etc.) were useless as material for a dialogue with the peace-lovers. The aim was to justify the custom of the centuries, arguing that violence was a response to rational and ethical principles. There have always been thinkers ready to defend with elaborate arguments outworn and barbaric institutions. Both torture and slavery have had their distinguished champions.

It was inevitable that the ideas used should prove threadbare. Their dissemination had coincided, historically, with a phase of human development during which Europeans—outstripping the rest in technical progress and expansive energy—had assumed the right to subjugate territories and peoples of every other continent. The glorification of military virtues seemed to be a feature of the European governing classes and, in particular, that of the German Empire, which had been built up in 1870 in an atmosphere charged with war fever. The fervor of thinkers and scholars, around which a substantial part of German university life turned for decades, led to the aberrations of racism and Nazism. Presented more as moral precepts than as scientific arguments, these doctrines were not confined to providing an erroneous explanation of history. They were also an attempt to protect the hierarchical order existing among countries, as if this order were a necessity.

The Enemies of Pacifism

The rift between pacifists and their opponents grew wider and wider: For the latter, war was a legitimate weapon of diplomacy; the former saw peace as the greatest good, uniting and enhancing man's virtues, opening a path to the triumph of a common ethic. For the pacifists the final objective was therefore the happiness of man, a state which was regarded as attainable provided he curbed his aggressive and militaristic impulses. Peace was thus identified with a condition tending toward perfection.

The enemies of pacifism believed that the natural instinct of men justified violence and intolerance. In support of their argument they cited—not implausibly—the public enthusiasm which often marks the beginning of a war. An interesting example from recent history is the entry of Italy into the First World War. Some historians contend that the country was compelled by popular demand, which was heavily on the side of the *Entente,* to switch alliances and oppose the Central Powers, with which it had long been associated. In fact, the event, treated as the effect of the will of the majority, was the result of the explosion of the emotions of an active minority misled by propaganda and thus encouraged to demonstrate for war. In the inaccurate logic of a particular brand of patriotism, this active minority was mistaken for the Italian people and was believed to interpret their will. There is no evidence whatever that the millions of peasants and workers inveigled into the war in this way had ever genuinely desired to don a uniform.

When it is not actually the result of the unforeseen and uncontrollable caprice of a single person, war is usually the result of the desire for political hegemony nurtured by a small number of people in key positions. Italy's entry into the Second World War, forced on the country by Mussolini, is an example of how one man can commit his country to disaster.

The continuity of the pacifist ideal, with its objectives unchanged despite the upheavals which have taken place in society, goes far by itself to weaken the argument that man is by nature a warrior. Another important point is that prominent men, responsible in various ways for contributions to progress, have sympathized with the appeal to pacifism and have sought to give it a rational framework and to interpret its moral message.

The message of the Gospel is also highly relevant. The need to condemn violence is implicit in the teaching of Christ and it seemed so serious and important that war is singled out in the Gospel as a sign that the kingdom of man is coming to an end.[7] The early Christians faced the problem of reconciling the profession of arms with their metaphysical convictions. Could one be a Christian and a soldier at the same time? The question was eventually answered in the affirmative, but at the cost of hard-fought compromise. To this day it is kept alive by the conscientious objectors and the supporters of unilateral disarmament, who believe that the spirit and the letter of the Christian message should prevail over all other considerations.

One argument against the pacifist ideal and its consolidation in institutional forms is that efforts to encourage pacifism have so far achieved no useful results. The fact that the appeal to peace has always gone unheard and has failed to eliminate the danger of conflict is used to show that it runs against the fundamentally aggressive nature of man. This argument is fundamentally weak. The fact that the pacifist ideal has been ignored and derided for centuries is no reflection on its importance, much less proof of its falseness.

What *is* surprising is that despite persecutions there have always been gifted individuals who have worked, as part of an effort to achieve moral improvement, to develop the peace-loving aspects of human nature. The hostility of the opponents of pacifism never had a moral content such as that which has always informed pacifism. No one, not even God, the pacifists said, could claim to be the protector of the arms of one nation against those of another, nor to be the guarantor and interpreter of the interests of a single people. Henry V's famous appeal "O God of battles! steel my soldiers' hearts" is a cry in vain, for there *is* no god of battles.

The warmongers argued that war was an expression at the international level of the struggle for existence. The pacifists believed that the causes of war were generally to be found in circumstances having precious little to do with the genuine interests of ordinary people. How else could one explain wars generated by the ambition of a dynasty, or hereditary disputes, or by religious causes? Even the wars that nations had won had seldom brought them real benefit. In the last analysis, the only advantages were prestige for the heads of state and for the governing classes. Almost always victors and vanquished alike returned from the war exhausted, their treasuries empty, their families bereaved, their economies crippled.

Thus the idea that wars had entailed a selection of the species, bringing forward the fittest and eliminating the weakest, was no less specious. In fact the opposite had happened: War cut down in their prime those who were physically and intellectually best endowed, selecting, if anything, the worse for survival.

Man the Peace-Lover

War violates the nature of man, involving him in behavior conflicting with his true propensities: What does the ordinary individual long for, other than a normal and serene existence, a comfortable standard of living and progress in his work in an atmosphere of wholesome rivalry? A spirit of conservation governs and guides his choices. War and its preparation force other choices on him, manifestly conflicting with his nature. His distaste for violence is more than offset by considerations of honor and prestige and by a desire to dominate which lacks a rational foundation. Killing, which should fill men with total horror, becomes an acceptable act, so that the personality is spurred on toward an objective which normally he would have to reject.

Nowadays we have a fuller understanding of how the individual and collective will can be manipulated by skillful propaganda. Those who can organize and maneuver public opinion cleverly enough can overcome views to which normally the individual would cling as he would to life itself. Politicans have always known this, and this is how they have elicited obedience and submission from those under their control in matters of warfare. History is a long chronicle of man's cruelty to man, due more to coercion than human nature. Many arguments can be used to prove that man is born bellicose, but how many more convincing arguments can be adduced to prove the opposite! For who can sincerely deny that there is a latent solidarity among men uniting them on the road to material and spiritual betterment?

The essence of community life is not war but the quest for brotherhood and the practice of love, humility, and mutual respect, summarized by the Christians of the first centuries in the term *peace*, and by later philosophers in the expression of *tolerance*. This is why, despite the outbursts of ferocity to which he gives way when his reasoning capacities are blunted and his moral restraints broken down, it must be conceded that man has an inborn longing for peace and serenity.

Nor can it be denied that man's victory over the distances which will still separate individuals, his ability to communicate through instruments working at the speed of light, the television transmission of images, supersonic aircraft, space flights, nuclear physics, and so many other remarkable discoveries will widen horizons far beyond the frontiers which have so far confined and restricted his curiosity and his keen sense of rivalry. It is no accident that the first dissemination of pacifist ideas took place at the time when information first began to circulate swiftly in Europe, following the invention of printing. There is every reason to believe that the means of communication now available, and those which science and technology will certainly make available in the future, can only speed up, extremely rapidly, the spreading of pacifism as an ideal.

A Change in Thought and Behavior

That pacifism has not yet been a universal success does not prove—as we have seen—that it is wrong: The difficulties to overcome have been immense. The wall of prejudice, vested interests, hates, and ambitions consolidated over millenia and tricked out with absurd literary conceits could not—cannot—be demolished overnight.

Every attempt to reform customs, morality, and the law is obstructed, as we have noted, by distrust and suspicion. This has not prevented the work from making substantial headway over the years. Men nowadays reject practices and prejudices once obstinately defended. But they have still not succeeded in conquering the age-old blight on human existence which is war. Starting from this fact and summarizing in terms of destruction and grief the balance-sheet of every conflict, the pacifists claim that there is a need for reform of the human condition and that pacifism must be the foundation of any such reform. This should help to banish false ideals and certain conventions and pharisaical "truths" by means of which war has made itself not only acceptable but also respectable.

The use of force merely reflects our ignorance of reality. Matters once regarded as essential have lost much of their importance, to become secondary aspects of the constant flow of man's affairs. It is not too far from the truth to say that if certain present-day problems were ignored they would simply go away, that it is *because* we attach importance to them that they would have become important. For example, how much significance should really be attributed to frontier disputes, the cause of so many wars, now that man has to all intents and purposes conquered the force of gravity?

What is the use of seeking to possess the territories of others when, through technological progress, matter itself has proved an inexhaustible source of energy?

Still less than material arguments can ethical and religious arguments be used to justify war. In an age in which freedom of conscience and its defense are written into almost every constitution (though not always respected in practice), the fierce religious and ideological conflicts of the past are seen to be as foolish, outmoded, and harmful as the trial of a person for a sin or thought. The premise on which every war of religion has been based is that those taking part in it know the truth and feel that it is their mission to defend it. But who has nowadays so much certainty in matters of faith and philosophy? Even men of science, though equipped with extraordinarily sophisticated techniques, are well aware of the fragility of their theories and the wide margins of error affecting their results. No scientist, no contemporary thinker would dare to claim that he had achieved final truths and that no one else could amplify or, for that matter, reverse the results he had obtained. The arrogant certitudes of only a few generations ago now seem ridiculous.

Meanwhile politics has emerged as the science of the means of improving the human condition through choices and measures adopted in relation with the collective benefit. It can therefore no longer be used solely as the preparation for war. Disagreeing with writers like Joseph de Maistre, who defined war as a divine experience,[8] we see it as a yardstick of human foolishness.

There is a symptomatic analogy between the ideas of the pacifists and those of internationalism, if we include in this term every doctrine attacking the principle of national sovereignty. In this way, the aspiration for peace is being given an institutional framework. The aim of internationalism is to create a network of obligations and controls which, by curbing the freedom of action of states, will compel them to submit to a binding order. Universal peace is one of its objectives, but it is not the only one and not even the most important. In certain circumstances, especially in the case of sanctions to be imposed on a state which has infringed existing rules, the internationalists do not rule out the use of war, provided it is declared and waged in compliance with certain principles and certain firm rules. Ceasing to be a factor of disturbance, war would then become an instrument legally accepted by world order. Internationalism and pacifism are thus complementary doctrines but are distinct from each other, reflecting the various nuances of human feeling and the differing natures of those who have attempted, through philosophical speculation and practical action, to put an end to armed conflict.

The Four Pacifisms

A systematic historical study of the doctrine of peace leads us to a classification of the analogies found in the works of its most representative exponents. As he examines each contribution, the scholar should ask: "Why did this author write this discourse? Why was he a pacifist?" The replies would, in my opinion, reveal four fundamental forms of pacifism. The first derives from a propensity to humility which is congenital in man. It covers the attitudes of the early Christians, of the religious sects, of certain peace societies, of the conscientious objectors and of the peace walkers, of Leo Tolstoy and Romain Rolland, and of those who call for unilateral disarmament. This we may call mystical pacifism.

Others have seen pacifism as a part of a philosophical doctrine. Their main objective here has been to make the pattern of pacifist rules part of a wider system of rules of conduct. We are referring to thinkers like Seneca, St. Augustine, Erasmus, Leibnitz, the Abbé de Saint-Pierre, Kant, and in our own time, Jacques Maritain, Maurice Blondel, Max Scheler, Bertrand Russell, William James, and John Dewey. Though differing in many ways in their ideas, they adopted much the same approach to the problem of peace and war, searching for reasons and remedies. We shall call this philosophical pacifism.

The nineteenth century saw the birth of a new science, "sociology," a neologism introduced by Auguste Comte which has apparently come to stay. This science studies social phenomena and their development. It is hard to imagine a human activity qualifying better for the description "social" than warfare. In its causes and effects it touches the whole of a people and brings with it the deepest and most revolutionary changes. From this angle, the problem of peace has been examined by economists and sociologists such as Cobden, Leroux, Fourier, and Saint-Simon and by workers' peace societies. This is sociological pacifism.

Lastly, peace and its place in society have been studied by statesmen such as George of Podebrad (King of Bohemia), Maximilien de Béthune duc de Sully, Cardinal Julius Alberoni, Alexander I of Russia, and by theoreticians of political science like Pierre Dubois. All treated peace as the ultimate objective of every sensible government. This is political pacifism.

The Way Ahead

The points I have made above are strong evidence that a longing for peace will become the key factor governing the conduct of men and their leaders. In recent decades old-fashioned institutions and outworn forms of dependence resting solely on the consolidated practice of centuries have been challenged and overthrown. In Western society the narrow confines in which individuals have lived for millenia have been broken open and the individual has been at least partially emancipated from the thraldom of the state. The masses, backed by the great political, religious, and trade-union movements, have found a place, and an ever higher place, in the hierarchy of society. The consequence has been a change in attitudes to community life and in the obligations of individual loyalty to the state. Men are compelled to acknowledge peace, its practice and its propagation, as what matters most in their time. The great pacifists of the past are now studied for their message of faith and their clear guidance. Society faces the following alternatives: Either to surrender supinely to an outworn idea of community life, or to accept bravely the challenge of liberation from fear, as the pacifists did in the past. There can be no hesitation as to what choice must be made.

Every reform is a function of men's faith in its justice and in its success. But faith in peace is no longer a minority idea kept alive by a few men scorned or ignored by the rest. It is penetrating further and further into every class of society, affecting the decisions of influential individuals and groups, compelling them to obey the still, small voice of conscience rather than the trumpets of war. Everyone must work to make known this situation to the leaders of the community and to the masses, who have now taken over the leading roles on the stage of history.

Through total dedication to truth and rejection of a sad heritage from the past, by refusing the easy path of acquiescence, men can break through the inhibitions which prevent them from escaping the weight of ancestral serfdom and can free themselves from fear to live in peace. They are asked to support and strengthen the peaceful elements of community life, to respect rules favoring unity and concord, and to reject customs which have sustained and protected the primacy and the cult of war.

In this book I have attempted to illustrate the continuity of the idea of universal peace and I have roughed out a tentative history. I have therefore examined systematically a number of literary and philosophical works of ancient times in an attempt to establish whether the desire to consolidate peace among peoples forever was a constant theme or not. Where I have found interesting clues, I have studied them critically. The results of my research have brought me to the conclusion that the problem of universal peace was posed, sometimes overtly, sometimes less so, at the center of classical and ancient Christian thought, sometimes also influencing artistic and literary invention. On the other hand, it exerted much less influence on the decisions of those exercising political power.

One of my difficulties arose from the fact that discourses devoted wholly to this problem were rare in early antiquity and only a little commoner at later periods. Exceptions are Book XIX of the *De civitate Dei* of St. Augustine and Kant's essay "Zum ewigen Frieden." Generally contributions to the subject are inorganic in form and are part—often a subordinate part—of more comprehensive doctrinal or literary works. Sometimes a vaguely pacifist line of thinking emerges from an intellectual attitude or from a political program from which it cannot be isolated. It was, for example, always present in the cosmopolitan ideas of community life, such as those favored by the Stoics.

Pacifism sometimes underlies a humanitarian approach or an exhortation to mercy, charity, and understanding of one's neighbor. Every form of mysticism, every ascetic voice, every genuinely religious message, every appeal to justice which is abiding because it is independent of the will of men and subject to that of a just God, must necessarily entail a favorable attitude toward peace, its attainment, and its sustenance.

I feel that I have carried out a fairly complete critical survey of the ancient world, using sources and works in the main libraries in Europe and in the United States.

I should like to conclude by expressing the hope that this book, the fruit of several years' research, may stimulate the interest in the beginnings of a form of speculation which is bound to exercise a strong influence on the future of mankind.

THE IDEA OF PEACE
IN GREEK CIVILIZATION

What the West Owes to Greek Civilization

When writers embark on a systematic study of any problem relating to Western civilization, particularly if the subject is connected with history or development of human knowledge and thought, they usually begin with the ancient Greeks. To go further back is a complex undertaking and indeed not always possible, for the sheer lack of records and evidence from earlier times may force the historian to proceed by mere conjecture. But underlying the conventional approach to the study of history is acknowledgment of the fact that Western civilization derives directly from that of Greece, whose beginning can be placed very roughly somewhere halfway through the second millennium B.C. This chronological break-off point at once simplifies and complicates research. It has the advantage of setting clear limits; but it complicates the work of the historian in that it makes Greek history seem a good deal more self-contained than it was. Nevertheless, we may be certain of one thing. However much Hellenic culture and thought was dependent upon cultures which flourished in the Mediterranean basin or elsewhere, however intense the influences felt, the Greeks were endowed with such formidable intellectual powers as to enable them to give new form to, and breathe new life into, the cultural tradition bequeathed to them by previous civilizations. This is why it is right to speak of a Greek creative experience, so comprehensive was the process of absorption and transformation to which the Greeks subjected the knowledge passed on by others, and so fertile and versatile was their inventive spirit. This led them to create philosophical currents and establish moral principles which still influence the development of society and, in particular, that fraction of society now known as the West.

Certain values regarded as essential and unchallengeable in our civilization, even though they may be thought ephemeral if they are cherished at all in other cultures, owe their very existence to the Hellenic genius. The idea of justice sustained by respect for the law, progress understood and the propulsive force of existence, acknowledgment of the individual's faculty for penetrating reality beyond any limits set by what is clearly demonstrable (on all of which we base our moral system and our methods of scientific research) link up with principles which asserted themselves in the Hellenic world and with the thinking of its most eager and vigilant minds. It is mainly to the credit of the Greeks—and here they broke completely new ground in the history of civilization—that the individual was deemed personally responsible for his acts and thoughts and that freedom and authority were reconciled through institutions which defined the rights and duties of the citizen and of the community, surrounding these rights and duties with clear guarantees and limits. The human framework in which this stupendous germination of ideas took place unfortunately developed a tendency to break up into a large number of separate states, from which the natural inventive and reflective capacities of the individual received a further stimulus. The Greek world was subdivided not only into tribes but also into city-states, each of which was driven by its own ambition to achieve hegemony. These were tiny territorial areas which in a different geographical context would have tended to unite. If Greece was eventually united, it was as a result of the military campaigns of Philip of Macedonia and of his son, Alexander the Great. For centuries, however, no experiment of this kind was to prove feasible, although one or other of the cities did exercise in turn a supremacy or actual hegemony over the others. Small as the city-states were and complex as their economic, political, and military problems turned out to be, they were always jealous of their own autonomy; though not infrequently driven to the brink of anarchy, they always fought hard for the independence of their homes.

Despite the lack of political unity, the sense of belonging to the same ethnic group, enjoying a common origin, religion, and language, never waned, either among the communities of the Balkan peninsula and of its island extensions, or among those communities established in Asia Minor, in Italy, on the shores of the Black Sea and of the Mediterranean. The fact of being able to boast of belonging to the same stock—different from that of the barbarians, so far removed in mentality and propensities—helped to diffuse those general ideas and conceptual abstractions which were characteristic of Greek thought. A civilization of small towns, scattered in a confusion of philosophies, ambitions, and experiences, was politically weak since it was disturbed by centrifugal forces as well as by an uneasy awareness of its own geographical dispersion. It would revert to cohesion only in times of danger and even then not completely. The sense of unity was reestablished around values like religion, language, art, culture, sport, philosophy; political reality was identified on the other hand, with dissension and a keen spirit of emulation, and these were bound to favor war. In order to strengthen their strategic and military positions and to extend their power over others, the city-states, although they had reached summits of critical sophistication and discovered speculative principles which are still valid today and which were often at the root of their constitutions, based their mutual relations on intolerance. Save on rare occasions, the states therefore failed to attain any political cooperation or to combat the use of war as a means for settling disputes. Even the Athenian system, the prototype of wise government—of which Thucydides exclaimed in admiration, attributing the remark to Pericles, "Its administration favors the many instead of the few; this is why it is called a democracy"[1] —had no peaceful approach to the external problems of the community.

Greece was therefore noted for a propensity for war, both in the ancient period and in subsequent centuries until the time of the Alexandrian empire and of the Hellenistic monarchies. Greek literature has preserved for us a record of these conflicts in poetry and prose of sustained and compelling quality.

Ferocity and Humaneness in the Homeric Poems

It could be inferred from this that the Greek people lived in an atmosphere of constant readiness for battle. Although situations of this kind did in fact occur—for example in Sparta, whose efforts to increase and maintain the efficiency of its military potential were proverbial in the ancient world—in many cases war was seen as a harsh, if inevitable, calamity. Although they judged it a legitimate instrument for settling disputes between communities, the Greeks were in no doubt that it was a *painful* necessity.

From the most ancient times their attitude to war had derived from opposing viewpoints. Homer's poems are adequate evidence of all this. They were written when ways of life were extremely primitive and when the cultural unity of the Greeks was still not complete. This is why an episode in the Greek colonization of the Anatolian coast—for this is what the Trojan campaign was in fact—gave birth to an extraordinary popular legend and to an illustrious national epic, in both of which a natural poetic bent was discernible.

Because of its nature, the world of the Homeric heroes was dominated by a conception of life which was essentially warlike. Whatever the event, whatever the change, conflict in one form or another was always close at hand. Religion often assumed violent overtones, as for example in the recurrent irruptions of supernatural powers into the earthly sphere. The main objective of economic activity, dependent, especially in the *Iliad*, on crop and pastoral farming, was the satisfaction of war needs. The society's leaders belonged to an armed aristocracy whose principle occupation was prosecuting the current campaign or preparing for the next one. Towns and villages were planned for easy defense, which explains why they were often built on a rock surrounded by a system of fortified walls and other passive defenses.

Although its background is a society obstinately clinging to its heroic identity, the *Odyssey* has a more sophisticated tone, open to the influence of the arts and the life of the mind, accustomed to more refined ways of life, dependent on new economic activities like commerce and handicrafts. The attitude of the authors of the *Odyssey* to conflict is not so violent or crude.

However, neither of the two poems directly condemned war, which remained a solemn and majestic social pursuit to which all other activities were related. Some passages of blood-chilling cruelty in the *Iliad* show that the spiral of violence was considered the key to the behavior of men. We may take as an example the episode concerning Menelaus, the Greek, who gets the better of the Trojan Adrastus in a battle and is about to slay him. But the young man begs the hero to spare his life. Menelaus has practically given way to the other's prayers when Agamemnon, commander of the expeditionary corps, arrives on the scene and without hesitation dispatches the Trojan, uttering these terrible words: "No; we are not going to leave a single one of them alive, down to the babies in their mothers' wombs—not even they must live. The whole people must be wiped out of existence, and none be left to think of them and shed a tear."[2] Another example of cruelty is found in Book XXII of the *Iliad*, which gives a description of the funeral rites celebrated by Achilles for the dead Patrocles. The funeral degenerates into an appalling massacre. Vendetta and human sacrifice lie at the heart of the poem, dominating the course of events. Even in the less-turbulent *Odyssey*, forgiveness is sometimes seen as an insult to the memory of the dead: "The disgrace of it will echo down the generations should we fail to punish the murderer of our sons and kinsmen."[3] Other passages in the two poems also prove that the characters in the vivid and moving narrative shared a fierce culture in which human relations were all too apt to lead to bloodshed.

But it should not be forgotten that the Homeric epics are composite poems and the authors used popular sagas and legends written by bards of earlier generations which were dominated by a sense of impending doom. Violence loomed large in the imaginations of these poets. Hence, the Homeric verses yield some information on the beliefs of earlier ages. In this poetic material war was the background which the singers could not and would not have wished to ignore. The objective of every conflict was, in their view of life, the annihilation of the enemy rather than the achievement of a compromise. It was permissible for a warrior to ill-treat and mutilate the corpse of an enemy soldier killed in battle, denying him the last rites, stealing his weapons, spiking the head on the outer ramparts of the enemy walls and leaving the body to crows and vultures. The treatment meted out to the vanquished by a conquering army sometimes came very close indeed to sanguinary dementia. Conquered cities were usually razed to the ground, warriors were butchered in front of their wives and children, their corpses thrown to the dogs. Such unrelenting hatred against the remains of the dead was an even greater manifestation of cruelty than it would be today, for the Greeks believed that outrages of this kind would seriously affect the fate of the dead. Women were sold into bondage and sent to toil in far-off lands; children also became slaves or were mercilessly exterminated. This was the embattled civilization of which wandering poets and minstrels had handed down a record.

The overall picture is undeniably true, but it is not unlikely that the authors of the Homeric poems themselves—no less than the civilization of which they were an expression—underwent a process of refinement. Particular emphasis should be given to the social aspect of the problem. The violence which was such a marked feature of the oldest lays or ballads reflected the way of thinking of professional soldiers, of the aristocrats in arms, of the minor despots of the city-states, whose only accomplishment was war. Relentless warlike ferocity and thirst for blood were justified because they were a way of life. But we may properly inquire if their attitude was shared by others, for example by those tilling the fields, to whose labor the entire Homeric civilization owed its means of subsistence. Were the peasants also moved by so much merciless intransigence? Did they share Agamemnon's opinion that the enemy should be cut down to the last individual?

Agamemnon's obstinacy was what one would expect of a great prince, but the peasant well knew that the same single-mindedness on his part would have brought him only mourning, poverty, and desolation. Intransigence in the face of the enemy might appear fascinating and necessary to those who judged human existence in terms of struggle and the imposition on others of one's own will, but simple souls did not reason like this. They preferred to pocket the enemy's ransom and let him go. The authors of the Homeric poems were not insensitive to these suggestions and recognized the need to adapt to changes which had taken place in contemporary society. This approach is discernible in the words of Menelaus: "People tire of everything, even of sleep and love, sweet music and the perfect dance, things that take far longer than a battle to make a man cry out 'Enough!' But these Trojans are not normal men; they are gluttons for war."[4]

Although respect for tradition and the texts prevented the process of refinement being taken to extremes, traces of it may be detected in the unusual moderation of certain passages. Some expressed a doubt as to whether slaughter might not be a form of madness and whether the Trojans might not have been wiser had they returned their ill-gotten gains to the Greeks, thus putting an end to hostilities. This was the view of Antenor: "Let us have done now, and give Argive Helen back to the Atreidae, along with all her property. By fighting on as we are doing, we have made perjurers of ourselves. No good that I can see will ever come of that."[5] Similar thoughts occurred to Hector shortly before his combat with Achilles. The lines in which they are expressed could not have remained without effect on the feelings of the public for whom they were written.

In other passages, war no longer justified the indiscriminate use of any means, even the harshest, to achieve victory. Certain methods deemed unduly cruel were already being condemned. In the *Odyssey*, for example, the warriors eventually agreed to ban the use of poisoned arrows. The treatment of those conquered in battle also became more humane. The enemy was killed if the impetus of the struggle carried the warriors away, but captured alive he could be ransomed. Those who begged for their lives were often spared as a tribute to Zeus, who was honored as the protector of the defeated. The views of Ajax, son of Telamon, concerning the treatment of the enemy were in marked contrast with those of Agamemnon. It was better to accept material compensation and not to shed blood. The refusal to show mercy in this way began to be regarded as an impious and sacrilegeous act. "After all, even in cases of murder it is quite common for a man to accept blood-money for a brother or maybe a son. The killer does not even have to leave the country if he pays up to the next of kin, whose pride and injured feelings are appeased by the indemnity."[6]

The opinions of Agamemnon and Ajax could, then, hardly have been wider apart. Blind intransigence on the one hand, a conciliating spirit ready to compromise, on the other. The attitude of the first reflected the views of the pre-Homeric generations and, in particular, of the belligerent aristocracy. The mildness of the latter was in line with the way of thinking of succeeding generations, especially of the more humble classes.

Homer's heroes suffered no uncertainty as to the final outcome of the military operations in which they were engaged, while grave doubts were felt by the ordinary soldiers, to whom war would bring no advantage. Their spokesman was Thersites, the deformed enemy of the sovereigns, whom he accused of pure self-interest. In the episode of which he is the protagonist, the poet writes of the malaise and disappointment felt among those taking part in the Trojan enterprise, who could not understand, especially when the operations were stagnating in the vain wait for something definite to happen, why they were fighting.[7] Partly protected from reprisals by his deformity, Thersites boldly challenged the commander of the expedition, speaking out loud, for all to hear, the whispered gossip of the camp. He reflected the opinion especially of the humble rank-and-file, who judged war the worst of all ills and would have preferred to abandon undertakings of doubtful outcome rather than persist doggedly in the hope that luck would come their way.

Other passages in Homer confirm a more humane influence when they emphasize the contrast between the duties of the soldier and those of the other occupations regarded as more useful to life and society. The work of the doctor, for example, began to be regarded as more necessary than that of the warrior: "A surgeon who can cut out an arrow and heal the wound with his ointments is worth a regiment."[8] Judgments and viewpoints of this kind, infrequent in the *Iliad*, become more common in the *Odyssey*. Ulysses, the main character, seemed to embody sophisticated tastes and the tendency of man to gain in refinement and to appreciate the more elegant ways of living, witness his disarming advice to Nausicaa: "May they give you a husband and a home, and the harmony that is so much to be desired, since there is nothing nobler or more admirable than when two people who see eye to eye keep house as man and wife, confounding their enemies and delighting their friends, as they themselves know better than anyone."[9] The characters of the *Odyssey* in general avoided the foolish bragging which professional soldiers were so fond of and which was deemed particularly odious when it concerned the killing of a man. For "it is an impious thing to exult over the slain."[10]

Religion had a bearing on this change. Homer's Olympus was inhabited by gods who participated actively in the Trojan war, favoring now one side, now the other. Despite the disequilibria produced by these irruptions of the supernatural into earthly things, the gods seemed to be in agreement in condemning war. Ares was the most despised of the gods. Zeus himself spoke his mind in the following words: "Most hateful to me art thou of all gods that hold Olympus, for ever is strife dear to thee, and wars and fightings."[11] The views and actions of Ares were unpredictable; he was always bent on evil, ever active spreading suffering and death. The god of Fear, he delighted in the pain of men. His allies among the divinities included Terror, Combat, and Defeat.

The process of refinement of customs seems to be reflected in certain legal rules and in a code of honor backed by religious sanctions. The principle of the sanctity of the truce—such as the one which brings the *Iliad* to an end—began to gain ground. In Homer's conflicts an armistice was always a pause for breath which the warriors granted each other, particularly at a time when the outcome of operations seemed uncertain. It was useful as a time to bury the dead, as a breathing space during which the leaders could instill new courage into their men, when the heroes could face each other in a single combat, thus staking on a single duel the final result of the collective struggle. For this reason the breach of a truce was regarded as an offence grave enough to lead to the immediate resumption of hostilities.[12]

Other semilegal rules suggesting more humane feelings had already gained acceptance. These included the privileged status of the guest, respect due to the stranger, the compulsory nature of commitments sworn to or assumed by mutual agreement. The *Iliad* ends with a truce, but the epilogue to the *Odyssey* closes with an actual invitation to peace, as if from so much suffering and vicissitude there was to emerge a warning to men to "let the mutual goodwill of the old days be restored, and let peace and plenty prevail."[13]

The need to regulate the conduct of war lay behind such rules, which were not unlike those in modern international law. Homeric society, like the society before it, comprised various tribal groups whose reciprocal relations were mainly based on war. To control these relations meant reaching agreement on certain principles. Thus the right to send legations—which was increasingly acknowledged—was placed under the direct protection of Zeus. A man who, like Antimachus, advocated the murder of the ambassadors sent by the Achaeans to Troy was guilty of sacrilege because he would violate a principle regarded as sacred. Links of patronage and affiliation obliged adversaries to spare one another in battle.[14] This process of refinement revealed how radically attitudes to war and life in society were changing.

Particularly in the *Odyssey*, the change of psychology was expressed in another manner: by emphasis on the ills engendered by war and its intrinsic absurdity. One passage discusses the brevity of human life: "Man's life is short enough. A churlish fellow with no idea of hospitality earns the whole world's ill-will while he is alive and its contempt when he is dead. . . ."[15] Another extract speaks of the fear of death. The dead Achilles tells Ulysses that he would be happy to go back as a serf to some landless man on earth rather than be king of the dead.[16] This new poetic theme bore witness to the widening of the life in society and to the influence exercised by classes once barred from any say in government.

Nonetheless, the unfolding of this great poetry still hinged on military campaigns, on calamitous bursts of anger and ruinous vendettas, the fruit, according to case, of emotional excesses or wise tactical stratagems. The atmosphere remained that of the heroes guided by elemental impulses and admirers of force. In the composite structure of the *Iliad* and the *Odyssey*, however, it is possible to distinguish the more recent sources of inspiration from the older ones. The latter, as we have sought to show, were instinctively inclined to consider violence as the yardstick of human conduct; the former show a desire to resist this blind exaltation and to approve a pattern of behavior informed with a certain respect for justice, moderation, and peace.

Hesiod and the Myth of the Golden Age

Even the earliest Greek literature, then, was sensitive to man's longing for a greater degree of tolerance in mutual relations and evidenced a timid desire to achieve forms of cooperation and understanding between peoples of varying origins. Were there other literary compositions in which the problem of peace was tackled more directly?

A field of inquiry is offered us by literary works of religious content. Mythology tells us that the ideal of a peaceful existence, from which war would be totally banished so that man could develop without conflict, inspired the myth of the Golden Age. Despite the endemic state of war, myths and legends still maintained the memory of a distant time when men were moved only by a spirit of peaceful emulation and the essentials of earthly life were abundance of material goods, simplicity of customs, and goodness. Such an idealized concept of primeval humanity gives evidence of a link between mythological inventions and collective hopes, since peoples tend to seek and find in the past, filtered through their own imagination, what they most long for in the present.

Expressed in the form of reminiscence, something of this longing is discernible in Hesiod's poetry. Like Homer before him, he paints war in somber colors, obviously intended, not to exalt, but to arouse revulsion and fear. War is pictured escorted by Death, Struggle, Tumult, Terror, Fear, all mythological personifications of the ills which it brings with it. In the *Shield of Heracles* —a short poem tentatively attributed to Hesiod—alluring descriptions of rural and urban peace contrast with the horror caused by conflict and slaughter.[17] In *Works and Days* the poet sketches out in idyllic terms the picture of a happy epoch when worry and pain were unknown to man. At that time sweetness and serenity dominated existence; men "lived like gods, without sorrow of heart, remote and free from toil and grief."[18] When they died, it was as though they were overcome with sleep, so that their lives came to an end without suffering. Love of the gods resolved itself in material prosperity and in the granting of every legitimate desire. So much comfort could not last, however, because of the perverse behavior of man. The Ages of Silver and of Bronze had succeeded the Golden Age. The last age—that of Iron, during which the poet himself was writing—was dominated by cruelty, terror, and venality. During this period the gods were pursuing mortals to punish them for their wickedness and had aroused ambition, envy, and war. The outlook for the future was bleak:

> Men will dishonor their parents as they grow quickly old, and will carp at them, chiding them with bitter words, hard-hearted they, not knowing the fear of the gods. They will not repay their aged parents the cost of their nurture, for might shall be their right: and one man will sack another's city. There will be no favour for the man who keeps his oath or for the just or for the good; but rather men will praise the evil-doer and his violent dealing. Strength will be right and reverence will cease to be.[19]

War was therefore born of treachery and hate. The only way to forestall it and defend oneself against it was to be guided by a sense of justice backed by firm moral principles. Such behavior would also ensure the prosperity of the cities and of men. Hesiod's picture of the contemporary world, with the emphasis on the prospect of peace, was due in part to the popular character of his poetry. The identification of happiness with peace had poetic and moral overtones. Another component of his poetry was the terror aroused by mysterious forces, operating in the world in the form of piercing passions. For Hesiod, as for Homer, the real fruit of war was suffering. Peace, situated poetically in a legendary past, expressed itself in the individual's abandoning himself to forces that would favor his serene development. It was the true reward for good men who respected the dictates of justice. "But they who give straight judgements to strangers and to the men of the land, and go not aside from what is just, their city flourishes, and the people prosper in it: Peace, the nurse of children, is abroad in their land, and all-seeing Zeus never decrees cruel war against them."[20]

In the Iron Age the gods had turned their backs on man and the consequences were felt everywhere, as gradually the rules of brotherhood, hospitality, and friendship lost their force. This judgment of the contemporary scene and of ways and means of repairing it reflected the swing-of-the-pendulum effect in human affairs, making a prelude to a return to happiness which men would be able to achieve through their own efforts. An optimistic vein was expressed in Hesiod's poetry: If men returned to respect for moral law, their certain recompense would be the reestablishment of peace.

His poetry was addressed to simple folk, to inculcate in them notions of life and moral principles within the framework of a mythology commonly known and accepted. But he also emphasized the primacy of the ideas nourished by the Greek people, whose noble genius and sense of emulation he saw as the fount of material prosperity and intellectual progress. For this reason he appealed to his audience to show understanding of the needs of peaceful life in society: "Listen to right and do not foster violence; for violence is bad for a poor man. Even the prosperous man cannot easily bear its burden, but is weighed down under it when he has fallen into delusion. The better path is to go by on the other side towards justice." And again: "Lay up these things within your heart and listen now to right, ceasing altogether to think of violence. For the son of Cronos has ordained this law for men, that fishes and beasts and winged fowls should devour one another, for right is not in them; but to mankind he gave right which proves far the best."[21]

Above all Hesiod was anxious to stimulate men and to promote productive activity, which alone could create wealth. Hence he was against enrichment that was the fruit of robbery, or war, and favored emulating those who work. This view enabled him to make a distinction between armed combat and productive competition.

> So, after all, there was not one kind of Strife alone, but all over the earth there are two. As for the one, a man would praise her when he came to understand her; but the other is blameworthy: and they are wholly different in nature. For one fosters evil war and battle, being cruel: her no man loves; but perforce, through the will of the deathless gods, men pay harsh Strife her honour due. But the other is the elder daughter of dark Night, and the son of Cronos who sits above and dwells in the aether, set her in the roots of the earth: and she is far kinder to men. She stirs up even the shiftless to toil; for a man grows eager to work when he considers his neighbours, a rich man who hastens to plough and plant and put his house in good order; and neighbour vies with his neighbour as he hurries after wealth. This Strife is wholesome for men. And potter is angry with potter, and craftsman with craftsman, and beggar is jealous of beggar, and minstrel of minstrel.[22]

Thus peace was anchored in economic prosperity, the bearer of serenity if it was acquired through work, whilst it was the cause of misfortune if it was obtained by violence.[23] This is an opinion which modern man can only approve.

If *Works and Days* contained practical warnings and urgings to reason, Hesiod's other long poem, *The Theogony*, included the personification of peace in a list of Greek divinities. This was Irene, one of the Horae (Hours), daughters of Zeus and Themis, the sister of Eunomia (Order) and of Diké, a figuration of legal order and of justice. Opposite them stood Athena Tritogeneia, the awful, the strife-stirring, avid for spoil and human blood, the queen who delights in tumult and wars and battles, and Ares, the sacker of towns, the father of Panic and Fear, the origin of confusion among men.[24] The descendants of Strife were legion. "But abhorred Strife bare painful Toil and Forgetfulness and Famine and tearful Sorrows, Fightings also, Battles, Murders, Manslaughters, Quarrels, Lying Words, Disputes, Lawlessnesses and Ruin, all of one nature, and Oath who most troubles men upon earth when anyone wilfully swears a false oath."[25]

For Hesiod and his readers the price of blood and suffering imposed by war seemed out of all proportion to the achievable results. The myths based on the exaltation of warlike heroism lost ground in the face of a view of life in society that was more practical and at the same time less narrow. The ancients saw as clearly as we do the progress made by his poetry in comparison with that of Homer. For example, the sophist Alcidamas, of the fourth century B.C., the author of a poem entitled *Museum*, thought more highly of Hesiod than of Homer because the former had celebrated the life of the fields and condemned war.[26]

Etymology and Meaning of the Word Εἰρήνη. Development of Greek Religious Feeling

Various theories have been put forward concerning the etymology and the meaning of the word *Irene* (εἰρήνη), the Greek equivalent of the word *peace*, but research has not yielded a conclusive answer to the question of etymology.[27] According to one theory, the word would seem to be related to the verb ἀραρίσκω (I conjugate, I confirm, I order, etc.). If this theory is correct, it would prove that the term did not originally refer to peace in the legal sense but to repose and serenity, to reestablishment of concord in the family and the community. According to another theory, in the earliest times the word stood for a divinity, to whom later generations attached the personification of an abstract idea.

Another question that has been asked is whether the term referred to a state of fact (peace already achieved, the absence of disorder, the prevalence of tranquillity) or to the circumstances likely to lead to peace as well. In the case of two states, should εἰρήνη be taken to mean the situation produced at the end of a war or should it also extend to the legal act on the basis of which an agreement was concluded and ratified?

It now seems certain that originally the word merely referred to the opposite of war and was not meant to cover the complex set of promises, pledges, and commitments enabling peace to be achieved. Other terms, particularly σπονδαί, were used to indicate these. The word therefore probably lacked legal associations and did not have the idea of constraint and obligation, which only later became part of the concept of a peace treaty. In the Peace of Antalcidas, made by the Persians and the Spartans in 386 B.C., the word would appear to be used in the sense of a binding commitment recognized by the parties who undertook to comply with the terms negotiated. We find it used in the same sense in the text of the treaty of alliance between Athens and Chios (384-383 B.C.) and in that of an epigraph praising Dionysius the Elder, Tyrant of Syracuse, and his sons (369-368 B.C.).[28]

This change of meaning may well be related to historical development. In Hesiod's poetry the implications of the word were mainly religious, so much so that peace was also the name of a divinity dispensing blessings and prosperity. At a time when man's main occupation was tilling and husbandry, it was natural that peace should be identified with bountiful harvests. In the passage in which Hesiod asserts that Zeus is willing to ensure serenity for those who walk in the paths of justice, he gives a definition of the concept of peace in a primitive economy:

> Neither famine nor disaster ever haunt men who do true justice; but light-heartedly they tend the fields which are all their care. The earth bears them victual in plenty, and on the mountains the oak bears acorns upon the top and bees in the midst. Their woolly sheep are laden with fleeces; their women bear children resembling their parents. They flourish continually with good things, and do not travel on ships, for the grain-giving earth bears them fruit.[29]

Here is a description of a simple civilization bound to the values of the land, seeking to express a profound longing in terms of day-to-day life. But the ancients had still not succeeded in giving a "local habitation and a name" to what was still no more than a vague longing. Peace was represented as a minor divinity in Hesiod's *Theogony* and was identified with the hope of material well-being and agricultural prosperity in *Works and Days*. What really mattered was the satisfaction of elemental needs, a sufficient supply of grain and livestock, the continuity of the race. A vision of this kind could not survive long in times of speculative ferment. The Greek ideal was soon to assume a deeper meaning.

In the fourth century B.C., the word had assumed, even in respect of the associations surrounding it, the same meaning as its English equivalent, *peace*. It meant the conclusion of peace negotiations, the treaty of peace itself with its clauses, the relevant written document, the condition of peace, the period of peace. This transition from the restricted meaning of the archaic time to the wider meaning of later centuries had been a steady trend gathering momentum in later years. The following data illustrate the change. In the archaic period, as we have said, εἰρήνη meant a condition of fact; σπονδαί, the legal mechanism determining peace itself. If the two terms are checked by the elementary test of frequency of occurrence, it is found that Thucydides uses the first 38 times and the second, including compounds, 219 times. Therefore the change of meaning had not yet taken place. In the writings of Demosthenes, who lived some two generations later than Thucydides, the situation was reversed. Εἰρήνη was used 206 times and σπονδαί only seven times. The case of Isocrates is also significant, for the great Athenian orator lived to be nearly a hundred (436-338 B.C.), a long lifetime coinciding with the great crisis of the Greek world, during which this and other linguistic changes occurred. In his writings the word εἰρήνη is found 57 times and σπονδαί only once.

Religion began by inspiring a new and more mature interpretation of the concept of peace, fitting it into a context in which the emphasis was not on material benefits but on the certainty that divine protection was concentrated on a given community, ensuring peace for it, peace being first and foremost the certainty of enjoying the favor of the gods and the grace dispensed by them. This did not mean that peace should not also procure material advantages (such as prosperity), but these were lesser achievements compared with the main one, associated with peace of mind. No longer interpreted in the narrow terms of Homer and Hesiod, the word was identified with a specific condition of divine goodwill, bringing spiritual and material advantages stemming from the gods, whose love men should strive to deserve.

But the development went further than this. Greece was to become the cradle of philosophic inquiry, in which the manifestations of faith (whether primitive myths, mystery, and esoteric beliefs or the self-conscious experiences of a more sophisticated type of mystical feeling) were to prepare the way for a formidable extension of the reasoning process. Eventually the mythology of Hesiod was rejected by more mature minds, whose curiosity and thirst for intellectual progress could be satisfied only by arguments acceptable to reason. Those based on feeling or presented in a confused and uncertain manner, either through the Olympian religion or by the poets who, like Hesiod, had become its interpreters and heralds, underwent a process of elaboration and of refinement. What the pre-Socratic philosophers tried to do was to explain critically what had for so long been accepted through mere intuition.

Greek Unity and the Polis. *The Milesian Philosophers*

The development of Greek civilization was dominated from earliest times by the city-states, in which the natural and indomitable individualism of the inhabitants found expression. This form of state was perhaps the result of the transition from a tribal structure to a territorially based society. An agreement between two or more neighboring tribes, bound by common interests, in either the military or the economic field, and by parallel experiences in matters of religion and language, created the need for an organization of the inhabitants in groupings possessing similar political and administrative structures. This development was probably a consequence of circumstances common to all of Greece, such as the pressure exerted by invaders. Its very nature accounts for the failure of any single city-state to impose a lasting hegemony over the others. Even when the survival of Greek civilization hung in the balance (for example, during the Persian invasions), unity was not achieved and forces of dissension hindered common defense efforts.

Having created political constitutions which seemed immutable and indispensable, the Greeks, sustained by extraordinary self-assurance and confidence in everything Greek, came to regard the *polis* as the best possible order for their society. They believed that in the polis, more than in any other organizational form, the natural abilities of their society could find fulfillment. They even came to feel that the polis was a pattern desired by the gods, since it was a microcosm—and a perfect microcosm—of the harmonious structure of the universe. "The single city belongs to its citizens in common" claimed Aristotle,[30] thus giving a hint of a principle of collective ownership which may conceivably have lain at the origin of the institutions.

Material interests had an important part to play in the birth and development of the city-states and went far to explain their reluctance to federate: The whole Greek world was divided into closed areas, surrounded by protectionist-type barriers. Economic history has since taught us that there is nothing more conservative and difficult to eradicate than monopolies which have become the vested interests of people settled in a specific area. Artisans and peasants, particularly when living near subsistence level, tend to seek shelter in restricted areas, protected from the cold wind of outside competition. This, combined with other moral and psychological factors, accounts to some extent for the conservatism of the city-states, their tendency to claim a god or an epic hero as their founder, their obstinacy in defending, even at the price of violence and war, prerogatives and rights on a scale no larger than parish politics in our time. The pressure toward monopoly also explains the opinion widely held among the ancients that the polis enjoyed a special vitality because it was small. They were unwilling to abandon the original pattern of a group of dwellings forming the nucleus of a farming area which provided food for the inhabitants, in favor of larger combined units comprising several towns. It became an established and resolutely defended principle that each and every polis must protect its independence and that any policy tending toward the union of the Greek cities was by the same token a threat to their hallowed rights.

If Greek civilization is examined it is possible to understand how the polis could provide the crucible for this extraordinary human experience. Everything which, to this very day, holds men in thrall to Greek ideals was then given its first impulse. In the development of human thought and of artistic and literary creation, there is no finer and more striking example of a desire for individual betterment and enhancement in imaginative terms; their achievement over the space of a few generations would seem indeed impossible had it not actually occurred. Among the conquests of the Greeks, the most worthwhile and the most enduring was the systematic discipline which it imposed on the modes of thinking of the individual and of mankind. When a civilization is broken up into so many small inward-looking units, determined to maintain their prerogatives and their freedom safe and intact and willing to make any sacrifice for these objectives, mobilizing their intellectual resources and capacities to the utmost, it is not in the least surprising that outstanding results in the field of thought should be obtained. Moreover, the Greek polis as a political experiment is by no means unique in history. There have been the free cities of Flanders, the Italian communes and the *signorie*, the warring states of China of the fifth to the third centuries B.C., always squabbling among themselves, always a prey to internal strife, unable to achieve any kind of political unity but all impelled by a powerful surge of imaginative energy and the clash of creative potential.

Although the Greek world reflected a situation of permanent dissension both within and between the city-states, this does not mean that no one sought conciliation. Factors of cohesion impelled the Greeks, if not toward political union, at least toward activities reflecting the genius of the race as a whole, its common matrix of ideas in no way obscured by the diverging historical backgrounds of the various ethnic families. Above all else, there was a shared longing for higher forms of spiritual and intellectual organization.

Religion provides plenty of relevant evidence here. On the one hand the city-states boasted their own local divinities, of which they were jealous and proud; on the other, they felt themselves bound by the cults of the national gods, common to all the tribes—Zeus, Apollo, Artemis—potent factors of cohesion and unity. We shall see later that after Alexander the Great, under the impact of new forces, there was a tendency to extend even further the number and the influence of such gods, identifying them with those of non-Greek peoples as part of a syncretistic movement reflecting on the religious level the conquests of Alexander and what the philosophers, particularly the Skeptics and the Stoics, had attained in the speculative field. The cult of the ancient national gods had always been a factor of unity among the Greek tribes. Feasts and ceremonies in their honor were so many opportunities for meetings between the peoples, most of whom were otherwise held apart by varying interests and aggressive emulation. Sanctuaries and sacred places, the objects of pilgrimages and of piety throughout the whole of Greece, were protected by privileges and immunities every infringement of which constituted a crime universally condemned. It was primarily the members of a single tribe who treated a given sacred place as a meeting place for their religious ceremonies. These cults, given their geographical location, were to lead to special sacred associations known as the amphictyonies, to which we shall return later.

The most important festivities common to all the Greeks were those celebrated every four years at Olympia in honor of Olympian Zeus. The inhabitants of the peninsula, of the islands, and of the *diaspora* all flocked to this famous meeting. Various immunities were connected with these ceremonies and the athletic games which were the main attraction. Truces were proclaimed to allow people to attend in large numbers; embassies and delegations were allowed to travel without let or hindrance even over the territories of warring states. The games themselves, if only because of the fame which they brought to those who pitted wit and muscle against one another, were a further spur to cohesion and unity. These regular encounters provided not only an opportunity for sporting events and literary competitions but also served to activate trade flows, the exchange of ideas, and a deeper understanding among diplomats, men of affairs, and people of culture.

Also linked to religious life were the oracles. The sanctuary of Delphi was the national center to which Greeks of all social classes turned to invoke the aid of the supernatural. Provided liturgical forms were observed and the necessary offerings made, the oracle gave replies to all, dispensing without fear or favor, in words of many meanings, the information solicited. Rich and powerful vied with offerings and alms for the favor of the priestess of Apollo, but the poor too were vouchsafed a glimpse into the future. The oracles in general, and in particular that of Delphi, offered an effective and convenient point of focus for the people's aspirations and fears. Though emigrating in large numbers and constantly at war among themselves, the Greeks became steadily more aware of the bonds that made them one.

Their feeling of solidarity, for which Plato was later to provide a theoretical basis,[31] led to the conclusion that war between Greek cities should be waged according to different rules from those governing war against the barbarian. It engendered a number of customary principles and rules recognized by all the Greeks as binding, so that any violation of them was regarded as a crime. War began to be accepted by all as the right instrument for regulating interstate controversies, a weapon of pressure to resolve major problems when agreement could be reached in no other way. It became almost a necessity, surrounded by legal and religious safeguards. As their scope widened, the rules derived to protect the sanctuaries during these violent struggles matured into laws consistently complied with. Thus war tended to be distinguished from the confused alarms and disorders of the Homeric poems and changed gradually into an activity governed by known principles. For example, the declaration of war had to be announced by heralds, almost in the form of the modern ultimatum; aggression without warning was condemned.

Military customs, even tactics and strategy, became more standardized. Even the behavior of the victors gradually adapted to certain standards. After the battle the opposing forces would grant each other a truce so that the dead could be buried and the wounded cared for. Every violation of this rule was regarded as a sacrilege and a crime. The acts of violence and brutality described in Homer's poems were tempered because of the great value the Greeks attached to human life and their desire to mitigate the sufferings caused by war. A beginning was made in disciplining actual combat by rules intended to curb its cruelty and to transform war itself from a form of collective bestiality into a legitimate instrument of pressure.

Other factors favored cohesion among Greeks, not so much in the form of political unity (which would not come before the end of the Macedonian adventure and the empire of Alexander), as in that of a growing feeling of solidarity. For example, links between colonies and founding cities led, especially in periods of crisis, to cooperation and active coordination. Horizontal links were also forged between city-states, paradoxically as a result of the struggles within them. The various social classes succeeded one another in the government of the states by maneuvers and stratagems that bore a remarkable similarity from state to state. If the same class (for example, the aristocracy) dominated in several cities at the same time, there would be a rapprochement between them, which often led to political and military agreement: The aristocrats of a given polis would feel a certain degree of solidarity with the other Greek communities governed by the same class. The same applied between the working classes struggling against oligarchy. Social conflicts, no less than religious ones, often engendered ideological alignments going beyond the confines of the states.

Even the emergence of the tyrannies—at first sight an element of disunion, since tyrants are usually unscrupulous autocrats ensuring no great measure of stability—became a factor of cohesion and rapprochement. Their courts were the resorts of prominent Greeks. Poets, artists, philosophers, intellectuals in general, athletes, adventurers, mercenaries arranged to meet there, helping to enhance the fame and the prestige of their hosts. Always on the move from place to place, from court to court, they strengthened by their presence and their work the conviction that the Greeks shared a common and glorious destiny.

Commerce itself was favored, since together with ideas and men, merchandise was also shipped throughout the Greek world. Pan-Hellenism, a sense of belonging to the common Greek stock—which was to become a factor of ideological expansion at the beginning of the fifth century B.C. and which Alexander the Great was to use to justify his claim to universal hegemony—was at least partly due to this intellectual and mercantile commerce.

According to the sources in our possession, the word *Hellenes* was used in its present meaning of "all the Greeks" from the time of Hesiod and of the lyric poet Archilochus (seventh century B.C.).[32] As we recalled in connection with Hesiod, the sense of Greekness was expressed mainly as the idea of being different from those who did not understand the language and the culture. These were the barbarians, for whom the Greeks never concealed their contempt.

The needs of politics and commerce, combined with that of keeping alive the dialogue between states linked by bonds of blood and culture, helped to engender a network of contacts maintained through the *proxenos* (πρόξενος), an official who represented the interests of a foreign polis, facilitated the establishment of its citizens, defended them from abuse of power and assisted them before the courts. Later his powers were extended to fields in the public arena, such as supervising the execution of treaties. The function of the *proxenos* lay halfway between that of an ambassador and a consul. This embryonic form of permanent diplomacy helped to attenuate some differences and to forestall a number of minor crises. Similarly, the use of arbitration to end less serious conflicts between cities was also to exert an influence.[33]

Despite the unifying forces at work in the polis, Greece was torn by violent aggressive impulses which from time to time dragged its people into sharp and bitter conflicts. A paradoxical situation emerged: On the one hand, the city-states were the expression of one of the most splendid experiments in civilization of all time; on the other hand their citizens utterly failed to discern the tragic implications of their quarrelsomeness and of the political divisions. The two phenomena were by no means as incompatible as might appear at first sight. Necessity being the mother of invention, war was often an incentive to progress and to a deeper, more thorough examination of problems and techniques which would otherwise have been neglected. In spite of the endemic strife and the endless conflicts, the civilization of the polis reached unsurpassed heights in artistic creation and intellectual activity. In the long pageant of human endeavor probably nothing was as important for the future of civilization as this period of Greek history.

The philosophic research pioneered and popularized by the Greeks has never ceased to yield profits. From it has stemmed a systematic treatment of abstract concepts and an ordered approach to speculation, without which the world of the mind would be a chaotic and amorphous congeries of uncoordinated sensations and intuitions. The discipline of reason, the quest for causalities that could explain the purpose of existence and provide a guide to men in their day-to-day behavior, the singling out of principles and rules which allow of an uninterrupted osmosis and succession of values and views were all conquests of the Greek spirit, spurred on by a restlessness and an anxiety nurtured in the polis.The work of the Greek philosophers, initiators of the great Western speculative movement, is accordingly our point of departure in examining opinions and attitudes concerning the problem of peace in the ancient world.

Hellenic thought began with the pre-Socratic schools, which flourished in the fifth and sixth centuries B.C. They prepared the ground and stated the premises for the great synthesis of ideas carried out by Socrates. Under their influence new methods of study and of criticism were adopted. Their work therefore took the form of a movement of emancipation from a particular way of viewing reality: The attempt to understand the nature of things was not only the fruit of a bold essay in scientific inquiry but of a general dissatisfaction with the old mythological apparatus through which Olympian religion had sought to explain these same problems.

Information concerning the earliest Greek thinkers is fragmentary and unreliable. The classical writers who described the work of these philosophers often distorted the earlier teaching to support their own systems. For this reason they were incapable of bringing to life the mystical and almost dreamlike atmosphere in which the pre-Socratics lived and worked. Little has survived of these works, which were often written in verse, almost as if the poetic rhythms would aid the individual to understand the problems they were dealing with. But they helped to bring about a revolution: Research into the nature of things and the problems of existence led them to doubt mythology and to mold it to ends other than those pursued by generations of believers to whom the ancient traditions had been represented as unchallengeable truths.

The first pre-Socratic school was that of Miletus, with which are linked the names of Thales, Anaximander, and Anaximenes. These precursors identified the primal substance with water, the universe, and air, respectively. Their teaching flourished in Asia Minor, where the Greek community lived in contact with foreign nations. Constant pressure from outside often had to be resisted by force. Thales is said to have worked as a military engineer for Croesus, the sovereign of Lydia. He was once asked how one could best sustain adversity, and made the following rather tart reply: "By realizing that the enemy is even worse off than we are."

Given the physical conditions in which they lived and the fact that these three thinkers were mainly interested in the nature of things and in the physical principle on which the world was based, it has been inferred that they showed little interest in ethics and consequently could not consider the problem of peace. But there is evidence that they did in fact devote some thought to this matter (Thales is believed to have fathered the scheme for federating the Greek cities of Ionia in a single state with its capital at Teos).[34] The attempt to derive from a single principle everything that had so far been the object of fragmentary study also proved their need for synthesis and their desire to reconcile opposing forces. This spurred them to seek unity in the ceaseless "becoming" of things, to explain and eliminate contradictions recorded by the senses and asserted by reason. The Milesian philosophers could not fail to consider the need to found community relations on a single rule of conduct valid for all men on earth. It was realized, therefore, that the laws in force in the individual states could be referred to a moral principle which was universally valid because it was determined by human nature.

Anaximander was keenly aware of the burden borne by mankind and the inanimate world because of obscure and hostile forces which were powerful in a world without justice. Since justice cannot exist without morality, he was compelled to condemn all violent striving designed to suffocate the will and the liberty of others. This appears also from the sense of expiation inherent in his thinking. In words bearing mystic overtones, Anaximander emphasized the anomalies produced by the human condition, acknowledging the existence of moral imperatives which nobody could escape "according to the ordering of time," that is, in application of the principle under which sooner or later everything must be paid for and nobody can sidestep destiny.

Pythagoras

Heraclitus of Ephesus (ca. 540-ca. 475 B.C.), was an isolated and vehement thinker who strongly believed in war. His philosophy is in striking contrast to that of Pythagoras (ca. 585-ca. 500 B.C.) and the Pythagoreans, who attributed precise cause-and-effect relationships to numbers and their combinations. They cited the unity of the cosmos as evidence of a hierarchy of commanding wills, at the heart of which they located the Creative One. Pythagoras' cosmogony took the form of preestablished and closely linked harmonies, and war was certainly considered the major cause of disturbance and disorder. Study of the heavenly bodies led him to the conclusion that the universe was governed by preordained periods and by cyclically recurring dates. Such exact repetitions must be related not only to cosmic phenomena, it was felt, but also to day-to-day events and to relationships of community life.

Those teaching a philosophy based on mathematical rules partly derived from celestial movements, seeing numbers not as symbols or as random, shifting relationships but as the essence of reality, were bound to look askance at war, the enemy of consolidated values and the negation of the basic laws of community living, particularly those governing brotherhood and hospitality. The Pythagoreans worked for a progressive and purifying enhancement of life, and it was for this that the master had set up a school in Croton, where he initiated deserving young people into the joys and the trials of the speculative life. At this school the slightest discord—were it only in music—was thought intolerable. How then can it be imagined that his attitude with regard to war, especially wars of conquest, could be other than one of severe condemnation? Pythagoras was often regarded as a reformer. His school was seen as an association of scholars and his research as in fact a series of attempts to renew the religious heritage. He must have seen peace of mind, peace within the cities, peace between peoples and nations as the corollaries of mathematical laws on which the universe was based.

Not without reason Pythagorean philosophy became a tradition which subsequent philosophers refused to discard, regarding it as essential to its time. Many centuries after the death of the "Weeping Philosopher," the pagan world, threatened by Christianity, set about refurbishing its image by stressing mystic and human values similar to those which had enabled the religion of Jesus to infiltrate so successfully the power centers of the Roman empire.

As thinkers scoured ancient tradition for a message of humanity and of peace, they turned to Pythagoras and to Plato, and transformed them, by a process of idealization, into the precursors of a moral renaissance. The biographies of Pythagoras compiled toward the end of the classical epoch by Porphyry and Iamblichus showed little critical insight, depicting the master against the background of a society impatiently awaiting a great spiritual event, but they did reflect a line of thinking corresponding to reality and not the mere product of fertile imaginations.

Pythagoras' rules of conduct were not fundamentally different from those already widely accepted by the Greek world. They included submission to the gods and to the laws of the state, respect for friendship, humility in relations with one's neighbors, personal purity, and temperance. What really set them apart was a greater and more tolerant humaneness. The moral system was handed on to the followers of the school in the conviction that these comprised not only the present audience but, by virtue of a sort of universal communion, all mankind. Among the teachings of the time, that of Pythagoras, having universal overtones, thus prompted an approach to ethics which later influenced other philosophies, such as those of the Sophists, the Cynics, and the Stoics. The Pythagorean doctrine of the transmigration of souls—the belief that the earthly journey of a living being would continue in the life of another, not necessarily belonging to the human species—implied in itself the interweaving of the fate of living beings for which only the universe could offer an adequate framework.

The fact that Pythagoreanism was organized from the very outset as a confraternity spreading to southern Italy and Sicily and then throughout the rest of the Hellenic world suggests that the doctrine would have nothing to gain from stressing the concept of individual citizenship. Because it was a closed group, dedicated to esoteric research and to the study of mathematics and astronomy, the school was bound to form a body with close-knit structures not easily broken into. The idealization of an experience of which life on earth was believed to be merely an episode tended to weaken the bonds between the individual and the state, an institution prone to fits of cruelty and irrationality. Contemporaries felt that the school escaped the control of the state and vied with it in the ideological sphere. This explains why Pythagoreanism was persecuted after the death of the master so that it disappeared for a time in southern Italy as a philosophic teaching, if not as a center of mystery practices. The nationalism fermenting in each community obviously could not come to terms with a conception of frontiers much wider than the conventional ones.

And the influence of the school reached even beyond the Hellenic world. The list of the early Pythagoreans handed down to us by Iamblichus includes a Hyperborean, that is to say a man originating from the legendary country of doubtful geographic location, usually placed by the ancients at the confines of the inhabited world.[35] The disciples, of such different ethnic origin, were united in a common speculative experience whose fundamental character was a desire to overcome earthly confines and obstacles. The law of divine harmony, from which Pythagoras derived the essence of physical reality and the informing principles of community life, was therefore realized in the cosmos and not in the state or the community.

Although he urged the individual to comply with the laws of the state, the master required them, first and foremost, to search in cosmic reality for the guiding rule to man's behavior, his aim being to free the individual of the commitments of the earthly city, which could never offer real security or hope. There is other evidence in the life of this philosopher of a leaning toward solidarity and hostility to violence. He left his native Samos, which had fallen into the hands of a tyrant, life having become, according to Porphyry, "more than a free man could endure."[36] His aversion to violence did not exclude violence toward animals. "So much did he hate killings and killers," wrote Porphyry, "that not only did he refuse to eat the meat of slaughtered animals but he avoided the company of cooks and hunters."[37] He devoted himself with enthusiasm to the education of the young (girls as well as boys), believing this to be vital to the progress of the community.

The episode of the destruction of Sybaris must be mentioned. The war against this city, supported, according to tradition, by Pythagoras himself, was said to be imposed by the need for compliance with a moral principle. Sybaris, the scene of a political revolution, claimed the restitution of five hundred citizens who had taken refuge in Croton, where they had asked for and been granted political asylum. To hand them back to their government would violate the principle of hospitality and ensure their certain deaths. Hence it seemed right to ignore all considerations of security and accept a necessary war.

Empedocles: The Principle of Love and Strife

Another important pre-Socratic was Empedocles of Agrigento (ca. 490-ca. 430 B.C.). He is partly a legendary figure, but we possess a number of fragments of two basic works, *Of Nature* and *The Hymns of Purification*. His thinking was imbued with the conviction that love was the key to being and hate that to its destruction. On the basis of "Eleatic" premises—deriving from the Eleatic school of Magna Graecia, which argued that reality is immutable and the eternal being indestructible—he analyzed the universe in terms of the association and dissociation of four elements: earth, water, air, and fire. Their infinite permutations and juxtapositions were determined by attraction and love, while hate was the cause of dispersion and death. The cosmic cycle was therefore broken down into four phases: the first dominated by love, the second by the conflict between love and hate, the third by the triumph of hate, and the fourth by the recovery of love. At this point the cycle began all over again. The underlying object of the system was therefore conciliation.

It is not surprising that this philosopher laid some emphasis on the myth of the Golden Age, in which he saw proof of the existence of an era in history ruled by love and peopled by a peace-loving community free of the anxieties of war. During the Golden Age there had been no hate, no envy, no pain, no inequality. Indeed—the conclusion must have seemed blasphemous—when serenity and concord reigned, nobody needed gods:

> Nor had they any Ares for a god nor Kydoimos,[38] no nor King Zeus nor Kronos nor Poseidon, but Kypris the Queen. . . . Her did they propitiate with holy gifts, with painted figures and perfumes of cunning fragrance, with offerings of pure myrrh and sweet-smelling frankincense, casting on the ground libations of brown honey. And the altar did not reek with pure bull's blood, but this was held in the greatest abomination among men, to eat the goodly limbs after tearing out the life.[39]

The narrative reveals a way of understanding reality, with a bias toward tolerance. Set in the half-historical, half-fabled past, this view of the world urged contemporaries to accept a program of moral betterment.

The elegiac atmosphere created by the words of Empedocles was sweetened with humaneness and with a pronounced sense of faith in a moral world for whose rebirth it did not seem absurd to hope. Helping to impel it on was the conviction that all living beings, not only men, should enjoy peace and serenity. The love of animals, which Empedocles shared with Pythagoras, was an important influence in his thinking, no less than his aversion to cruel sacrifices and the eating of meat: In the history of human thought, those who have loved and worked for peace have often espoused these two moral precepts, feeling that gentleness and humane feeling should not stop short at the barrier between man and the lower beings. The practice of virtue and of gentleness toward the animal kingdom, Empedocles argues, had also proved of considerable usefulness to men, for a vital factor throughout the Golden Age had been the complete humility of the animal world. "For all things were tame and gentle to man, both beasts and birds, and friendly feelings were kindled everywhere."[40]

It is clear that Empedocles appreciated the similarities which strengthen bonds between man and the wisdom of refraining from encouraging differences of opinion and disputes. If strife caused certain physical changes, if it recurred cyclically, all this had implications not restricted to a single event, to a single city, to a single nation. The cyclical recurrences, like the physical and social events caused by them, could not be other than universal. Their influence on earthly life allowed of no exceptions, since mankind, though much divided, had a single origin. Although quarrels and dissension seemed to be characteristic features of human society, this was no more than a semblance, since the underlying objective of community life as in the world of nature was the achievement of the dominion of love. During the Golden Age men had acted as brothers born of the same stock, and war had become a crucial factor in community life at the very time when the sense of natural consanguinity had been lost.

Empedocles had no doubts as to the universal scope of moral laws. "But that which is lawful for all extends continuously through the broad-ruling Air and through the boundless Light."[41] The singleness of the rule and its universal scope were evidence for him of the equality of men and of the absence of natural differences between the inhabitants of a single city, as between Greeks and barbarians. Two fragments from the philosopher manifestly condemn violence, though their poetic and declamatory tone does not enhance their clarity. "Will ye not cease from this harsh-sounding slaughter? Do you not see that you are devouring one another in the thoughtlessness of your minds?" And again:

> The father, having lifted up the son, slaughters him with a prayer, in his great folly. But they are troubled at sacrificing one who begs for mercy. But he, on the other hand, deaf to [the victim's] cries, slaughters him in his halls and prepares the evil feast. Likewise son takes father, and children their mother, and tearing out the life, eat the flesh of their own kin.[42]

Criticism of ritual sacrifices? Reference to events now belonging to the world of legend? Condemnation of religious intolerance and of an archaic liturgy judged irreconcilable with the evolution of customs? For lack of other evidence, we shall never know exactly how the warnings of this thinker should be interpreted.

Nonetheless it is obvious that, once the decisive function of love in the working of natural phenomena is recognized, Empedocles' philosophy must have an impact on social events as well. This must be so if fragment no. 135, which anticipated the principle of noncontradiction, is to fit into Empedocles' overall thinking. In ethical terms, the principles of Empedoclean physics implied condemnation of everything in human conduct which conflicted with the law of brotherly love.[43]

Cosmopolitanism of the Atomistic School

The atomistic school, founded by Leucippus but made famous by Democritus of Abdera (fifth-fourth-century B.C.), propounded theories which sought to explain organically the problems of being and knowing by deriving all interpretation of physical and moral realities from a single principle. For Democritus "being" was identical with fullness and "not being" with emptiness, but the first was broken down into infinite particles, called atoms, and from their combinations sprang natural phenomena. Corresponding to this mechanistic vision of the world were a general ethic which saw in man the true object of universal rules. Man's acts were therefore judged in relation to these rules and consonant with the basic principle of Democritus' physics.

What is attractive in his thinking is the vision of the universe and its identification with the principle of harmony, in which physical and moral laws are fixed and immutable. Even the individual soul was seen as something corporeal, made up of atoms lighter than those present in matter and destined, after death, to rejoin the universal circle. This led to a vision of happiness, to be achieved only through a pattern of behavior more in conformity with human nature and designed to overcome all weakness while striving for peace and harmony. The aim of existence remained that of increasing the scope for enjoyment, limiting suffering to a minimum. The concepts of happiness and pain were not, however, understood in the material sense, as one would have expected, but as an exaltation of the spiritual qualities of the individual: Happiness (εὐδαιμονία), lay not in wealth but in serenity and peace of mind. The problem of community life was accordingly presented in terms having cosmopolitan overtones, designed to overcome the confines of the polis, in relation to a world without frontiers in which the wise man was the man who moved most freely. "To a wise man, the whole world is open; for the native land of a good soul is the whole earth."[44]

The ultimate aim was knowledge, and knowledge was a function of the level of education. In this field Democritus' beliefs are extremely modern. Upbringing, especially that part of it which is the responsibility of parents through the example they set, became the cornerstone in preparing the individual for his entry into the community of men. To learn meant to raise oneself above the sensory world and enter into possession of the truth. This universal message was also addressed to men lacking philosophy, who were urged to observe the laws of the state but to prefer democratic constitutions, since "poverty under democracy is as much to be preferred to so-called prosperity under an autocracy as freedom to slavery."[45]

Although no precise and documented evidence can be drawn from the original works of Democritus, one may safely conclude that war was condemned as alien to a system based on tolerance and mutual understanding. "All bellicosity is foolish; for in studying the disadvantage of one's enemy, one loses sight of one's own advantage."[46]

The Decline of the Fatherland as Ideal

Under the pressure of historical and environmental circumstances, the panorama of Greek life was soon to change. A gradual refinement of creative activity in the fields of culture, philosophy, art, and politics was largely due to the conclusions reached by the pre-Socratics as to the nature of the world. They had overthrown many beliefs which had for centuries been treated as matters of faith and therefore as an ultimate frontier beyond which the probing mind of man might not venture. Precisely because of these beliefs, all research relating to peace and the need to ban war and violence from human relations had been carried out principally in terms of a re-evocation of the Golden Age, just as all speculation was presented as an effort to understand more fully religious truths enjoying common acceptance. The idea of peace was therefore being rediscovered, not invented.

Although developed along extremely primitive lines, pre-Socratic research had helped to sharpen the critical faculties of the Greeks. The thinking individual, once regarded as the slave of reality, thus came close to being its master. The change in attitude engendered Sophistry, a philosophic approach which refused to submit passively to authority and was to lead to a method of analysis regarded as perpetually inconclusive because it was constantly fed by dissatisfaction. This philosophy hinged on the new position achieved by the individual, for whom it claimed complete emancipation so that he could become the center of all intellectual activity. The problem of knowledge and of judgment was thus moved to a level at which individual thought reigned supreme. In declaring that "man is the measure of all things," the Sophist Protagoras was not only stating that all philosophic research is vain but also suggesting a method of inquiry based on the certainty that nothing is provable, since the essence of things is a relative datum, varying from individual to individual. This approach to the problem of knowledge led to the identification of the thinking subject with the object thought of. Taken to its extreme logical conclusion, this concept led in turn to the doctrine of Gorgias, who maintained that nothing existed but if anything did exist, it could not be perceived, and even if it were perceived by any one man, he could never communicate his knowledge to others.

The spread of the teaching of the Sophists was facilitated by a number of historical circumstances, including, in the first place, the crisis of the polis, whose extreme fragility had been cruelly exposed during the Persian wars. Resistance to the aggressor had been possible because the cracks of discord had been roughly papered over, but once the danger was passed, the age-old rivalries broke out anew, leading, with the Peloponnesian War, to the most bloody of civil conflicts. The war shattered the values on which the polis had been built. Where it had once been a tenet of faith that the city states were of sacred origin it now dawned on the Greeks that not the gods but men, with their virtues and their vices, had designed their administrative and political institutions, which had therefore never been breathed upon by god and were in no way perfect nor were they likely to become perfect. In their speculation, the Sophists popularized the view that free men (some even went so far as to include slaves and foreigners) were born with equal claim to power. The transition from the aristocratic regime to democracy, which occurred—in many cases not without violence—during the fifth century B.C., was partly du to this critical and stimulating attitude.

The advent of democratic governments favored the development of political eloquence. For centuries the orator's art had been primarily of a ceremonial and ritual character. Now it was transferred to public political meetings and harnessed to the achievement of material objectives. By means of words cleverly used, unproven "truths," whose authority derived solely from tradition, were refuted. It was believed that all things could be doubted and discussed, because reasons for uncertainty lay in all things. The Sophists were thus the inventors of the new eloquence, in which all too often the quickness of the tongue deceived the listener's reason and the verbal skirmish became more important than the arguments to be tested. Among the casualties were certain beliefs—the sanctity of religious institutions, for example—which had once been regarded as established and immutable. These had had significance when people had believed in the divine origin of the state, but they lost it as soon as the Sophists began to question these assumptions. Why should the state work for justice and equality for the citizens if it was then recognized that men were not subject to the rules which their will refuted? The Sophist Thrasymachus had argued in this connection that justice is nothing other than the interest of the stronger.

The challenge was not only to the divine origin of the polis, its underlying principles, and its traditional rules, but also to its capacity to ensure the protection and the progress of the citizens. The city-state stood accused of favoring municipal selfishness and of exalting it as a sublime manifestation of patriotism and civic virtue: The polis, it was alleged, was in no position to defend its citizens from the aggression of powerful enemies while it was the cause of the fragmentation of Greek life, the sharpening of differences of opinion and their rapid degeneration into war. Armed conflicts broke out where, in other circumstances, a peaceful arrangement could well have been found.

How did the followers of the new line of thought see the problem of war? Their abrasive minds could hardly have ignored this chronic feature of Greek history. In line with the opinions once widely held concerning the origins of the institutions and their oligarchic nature, war had at one time enjoyed a religious and heroic status. But the cruelest of man's activities was bound to be judged harshly by thinkers who gauged the realities of the world in terms of the interest of the individual.

However, the plight of the Greek world, which had never suffered so much as during the Peloponnesian War, was not the only reason the Sophists disliked war. They were sometimes influenced by other practical considerations and by cosmopolitan ideas which they felt disproved current views on the obligations toward the fatherland. In contrast to previous philosophers, the Sophists were not heads of schools living in a given place and thus involved in local politics. Most of them were itinerant masters, accustomed to moving from one city to another, avoiding as far as possible any fixed residence in a single center. This aspect of their teaching led them to deny that city institutions were unchangeable and eternal. When a man travels regularly from one country to another, he is apt to consider the state as the main cause of the difficulties (frontiers, tolls, tariffs, fees, etc.) hampering the free movement of persons, goods, and ideas. He then becomes instinctively cosmopolitan and sees the state as an artificial creation designed to limit the potentially unlimited freedom of movement of men. To be cosmopolitan means to regard one-self as a citizen of the world and not of any single state, to regard all men as having a single origin. A fragment from Antiphon the Sophist is significant in this connection:

> In this we are, in our relations with one another, like barbarians, since we are all by nature born the same in every way, both barbarians and Hel-lenes. And it is open to all men to observe the laws of nature, which are compulsory. Similarly all of these things can be acquired by all, and in none of these things is any of us to be distinguished as barbarian or Hel-lene. We all breathe into the air through mouth and nostrils. . . .[47]

We must be familiar with the opinions which had dominated the Greek world so far if we are to grasp the revolutionary impact of statements of this kind, which showed that custom was changing and that a new ferment was undermining the hallowed traditional institutions. These changes justified the remark attributed by Aristotle to the Sophist Alcidamas: "Philosophy is a machine for attacking the laws."[48]

The enthusiasm for war, regarded during the heroic centuries as the mea-sure of the stature of men and of states, yielded place to the conviction that it was a painful madness which man should seek to avoid whatever the cost. The skepticism immanent in the teaching of the Sophists, based on the cer-tainty that truth cannot be known, seemed to allow of an exception in re-spect to war. If every event was justified only in terms of its usefulness, war, as the cause of poverty and suffering, must be condemned. Moreover, if, as the Sophists consistently asserted, the practice of good could not be made de-pendent on the admonitions of religion, nor on the prescriptions of the civil power, since these were apt to vary in time and place, and for this reason, too, war should be shunned.

The Greeks suffered from another weakness: internal disagreement in the polis, which, as Thucydides tells us, was very serious, especially in its impact on day-to-day life.[49] So keen and widespread was the desire for concord with-in the communities as to make it appear the most urgent and worthy objec-tive of every effort. The end of the internal struggles between factions was considered at times as an aim even more urgent and necessary than peace be-tween the city-states. Thus the longing spread for ὁμόνοια, i.e., for concord in the sense of internal calm, for shared objectives, for the banishment of civil strife. The quest for this goal was to form the background to a body of litera-ture with a moral basis. Antiphon the Sophist and the Stoic Chrysippus were both authors of essays, now lost, entitled *Of Concord* (Περὶ Ὁμόνοιας). Eight centuries later, when Hellenic philosophy was aroused from its slumber by the threat of Christian doctrine, the Neoplatonic philosopher Iamblichus wrote an essay on the same subject, with the same title. This second way of understanding the idea of peace was to accompany Greek speculation until it waned. The desire for serenity and concord was also to be applied to family life. Elimination of domestic disputes represented the third stage of a journey which, starting with the widest form of community living, ended with the smallest.

For lack of original writings, it is impossible to form a complete view of the Sophists' teaching. The information available comes from the few fragments which we possess and from what has been handed down to us by writers like Plato who were admittedly not well disposed toward the school. However, there can be no doubt as to the basically peace-loving character of the Sophists, though the intensity and the extent of such attitude must have varied considerably from author to author.

The Teaching of the Sophists

The moral and political program of Protagoras was a direct attack on the concept of the polis. It is probable that in one of his works, called "Refutatory Arguments," he struck at the traditional ideas of the state and of war and urged his contemporaries to seek activities other than those pursued within the circle of the city's walls. Such a dislike of war and the development of a viewpoint wider than the narrow small-town interests were, in the last analysis, worthwhile attitudes if men forsook parish patriotism in favor of a loyalty to mankind. But this approach does not seem in accordance with the fragmentation of the cognitive process taught by Protagoras. Perhaps, then, the traditional interpretation of Protagorean thought is wrong. Perhaps it was not the individual who, in the opinion of Protagoras, was the measure of all things, but mankind as a whole. According to Plato, Protagoras believed that the gods were the origin of the principles of justice and of duty, which controlled moral conduct.[50] His subjectivism therefore allowed of an exception in the field of politics, the aim of which might ultimately be the elimination of war.

Gorgias believed that only between the Greeks could a condition of peace be achieved, war with the barbarians being unavoidable. Peace in the Greek world he saw as a precondition for stability and the basis for any resistance to aggression from outside. To attain this very objective, he urged that his compatriots put an end to their ancient and ill-starred feuding and reach concord, within and without the cities. This argument lay behind a speech made by Gorgias at Olympia and now lost, but of which Philostratus has left us a record.[51] The position of Gorgias was perhaps close to that assumed in the Renaissance by thinkers who advocated that European sovereigns end their secular wars to prepare themselves for a crusade against the Turks.

Hippias of Elis (fifth century B.C.) was certain that a spontaneous attraction brought men together, and, like other Sophists, he supported humanitarian and conciliatory attitudes. With Hippias, on the other hand, the distaste for organized society appeared to be stronger because he regarded the need for harmony as imperative and was certain that the principle of universal brotherhood was too often forced into second place behind the laws of the state. His was the logical conclusion of a system hinging on the exaltation of the human person and on the conviction that human beings are all born equal. A consequence of equality, of its application in nature and law, was that the individual was accorded a wider field of action, no longer limited to the polis but extended to the entire world, beyond frontiers artificially imposed by men. Thus the quest for a perfect social organization was to guide men in overcoming the limitations of city politics with a view to the attainment of the universal state. The political and military situation being what it was, this message did not fall on deaf ears. The Peloponnesian War was well under way and the hope of an early peace was uppermost in everyone's mind. These ideas were therefore well received and gained increasing numbers of converts. Thinking people became more amenable to principles like the natural equality of men, the need to eliminate discrimination between Greeks and barbarians, and the primacy of unwritten rules which complied with these principles over man-made laws.

Callicles (fifth century B.C.) adopted an even more extreme position. He believed his anarchic views were an appropriate answer to the ancient conflict between nature and law around which Sophistic speculation had turned for some time. His reasoning started from the fact that the strong were bound to exercise power in a community. Unable to escape dependence, the weak had sought to check the strong in the meshes of a net of laws. These were therefore the defense of the weak, but, being artificial, could rightly be ignored. All rebellion against the powers that be was right, since man had a duty to free himself from serfdom. The ultimate end must be the establishment of the natural order violated by the legislators. Such an extreme view, conflicting sharply with the conventional morality, is not substantially different from that of the anarchists of our own time, whose purpose is the destruction of society but who fail to state what arrangements, if any, should replace those discarded. Callicles seemed to sense this difficulty and to seek a solution in the person of a superman capable of leading a protest movement, of destroying the existing structures, and, once the "formulas, and spells, and charms, and all our laws which are against nature" were trampled underfoot, of replacing them with an order genuinely inspired by nature.

It is the ultimate aim of this system which interests us most because of its markedly cosmopolitan character, hostile to governments and to states with their paraphernalia of regulations, restrictions, and taxes. Most of the Sophists, probably including Callicles, adopted an aggressive stance and took up speculative arms against the state in order to put an end to the endemic disorder troubling Greek life. The disappearance of the state system would reduce the opportunities for conflict.

Callicles was not the only thinker to preach anarchy and social subversion. Thrasymachus, for example, pushed further in this direction, denying the possibility of basing community life on justice and arguing that the absence of all legal constraints could lead to a regeneration of society.

> Thus, Socrates, injustice on a sufficiently large scale is a stronger, freer, and more masterful thing than justice, and, as I said in the beginning, it is the advantage of the stronger that is the just, while the unjust is what profits a man's self and is for his advantage.[52]

So much subversive fury could be justified only by the fact that the doctrines of Thrasymachus and of the other Sophists echoed a feeling of the society in which they lived. Despite its anarchic approach, the teaching of the Sophists fitted into the evolution of contemporary morality. The abolition of war because of the recognition of the natural common identity of peoples and of their single origin was a necessary corollary to this approach.

A challenge to Callicles and Thrasymachus came from the anonymous author of the Sophistic work which has been discovered in an essay called *Protrepticus* [Exhortation to philosophy], by Iamblichus, the fourth-century Neoplatonist. Scholars have argued about the identity and the work of this anonymous writer for decades. He seems to have disapproved of the anarchical approach of the two Sophists and thought that the weak had a mission to fulfill in the effort to abolish war, as is evidenced in the following passage: "War, producer of the greatest evils, bringing disaster and slavery, is undertaken rather by the lawless than by the law-abiding."[53]

War therefore was caused, or at least encouraged, by illegality and other ills like social inequality. This was seen against the background of a plan for regenerating society in the name of tolerance. According to the unknown author, it was not necessary to let oneself be guided by violence, nor to believe that the defeat of one's neighbor was a form of virtue or compliance with the laws a sign of cowardice.

In Critias (ca. 460-403 B.C.) the keynote is one of skepticism with an illuministic bias. The aim is to overthrow religious tradition, which is written off as an invention of the first statesmen, who imposed respect for the law and spread fear of the next world. This thinker took the campaign to destroy the institutions of Greek society a step further, arguing in favor of the common ownership of goods and a form of collective management of wealth akin to communism.

Lycophron (rhetorician and thinker of the fifth-fourth century B.C.) denied that the law could have any function not linked with the interest of the citizens and the protection of their rights. The state, in its role as guardian of the social order, was reduced to a mere administrative machine set up to protect property and ensure respect for the conditions of equality. But the rational dismantlement of the institutions was taken to the furthest point by Alcidamas, author of a poem already mentioned in connection with Hesiod. The ethical and political values on which the institutions rested were heavily criticized.

Under the impact of Sophistic thinking, the old legacy of the Greek world was proclaimed an illusion, a sort of historical confidence trick. In the throes of crisis, the civilization based on the polis was reorientated along universal lines discovered and championed by the Sophists. The trend toward human brotherhood in the conviction that distinctions of race and nation are pointless—which Alexander the Great later catalyzed and Stoic teaching promoted tirelessly—thus had precursors in the Sophists. Their method of relentless criticism justified the impression that Sophist teaching was in fact based on paradoxical premises, the fruit of rhetorical expediency and not of reasoning, from which could be derived no real solution to problems. The Sophists themselves may well have discerned the weak points of their case; nobody can escape the necessary implications of his own logic. Hence, even when they were explaining their idea of justice, their main business was to attack and score points. The distinction between just and unjust was obscured or was made in terms so artificial that they were bound to weaken or even nullify the value of the arguments put forward.

In respect to the problem of peace, the dangers inherent in this position are obvious. Every doctrine based on an awareness of the relativity of things and of human relationships and on a presumption that no single criterion of knowledge can be preestablished is liable to lead to aberrant and conflicting conclusions. In view of this, attitudes hostile to war and cosmopolitan conceptions of community life were evidence of a general and vague feeling, not of hard conviction. From a pessimistic vision of life which took man as the yardstick of reality and the common denominator of all things, the Sophists inferred a distaste for war. But they were all too ready to retreat from this point of view as soon as the interests of man were threatened or seen in a different light: The points made by Gorgias in the Olympic oration and in the speech paying tribute to the Athenian citizens who had fallen in battle show that there was no plough to which Sophistic relativism could not be harnessed, no axe it could not grind—and that of the warrior was no exception.

Socrates and Virtue as Knowledge

With all its paradoxes and facile cleverness, Sophistic speculation was nevertheless a bold attempt to emancipate man from the state of intellectual serfdom in which he had languished for so long. It radically changed a system which, making man the center of a physical condition and a cosmogenic reality, had held him in thrall to an enduring compulsion and an inescapable fate. It also gave man the merits and capacities of a real thinking being. He was no longer at the mercy of forces over which he could exercise no influence; it was from him that all other existence stemmed and in relation to him that it should be judged. A revolution on such a scale was too important to be lost behind showy dialectic concerned with dazzling the sophisticated. It was to find a champion who carried the movement to its logical conclusions. Following the road mapped out by the Sophists and drawing together the jagged edges of a fabric which, in an orgy of destructive fury, the Sophists had torn in two, Socrates (470-399 B.C.) made it his task to free thought from the fetters which had so long held it down, pressing it forward in the speculative adventure, guided not by the immediate and vulgar suggestions of the senses, but by rational abstractions. This was the real achievement of the great philosopher, to whom Western thought is still in debt. To accomplish this, Socrates disciplined himself severely, withdrawing from all interests not directly linked with the object of his research and questioning many fellow citizens who were induced by him, through the dialectical method, to seek out truth for themselves. This insistent questioning bore witness to his certainty of reaching universally valid truths but also to a spirit of moderation which rejected the extreme positions others had reached. A similar approach governed his ethics. Here, the cornerstone was his belief in the identity of virtue and knowledge, which brought him to the view that goodness is the outcome of a process of upbringing. If one knew what virtue is, he could not fail to lead an honest life, while whoever failed to comply with the dictates of virtue was certainly an ignorant man. Knowledge became a factor that could restrain man's acritical excesses and his emotive impulses, guiding him in the practice of virtue.

Enlightened in this way, human behavior would escape the trap of the passions and serenity could be achieved. A state of happiness and tranquillity was therefore the ultimate objective. It stands to reason that a thinker basing his teaching on the identification of knowledge with virtue should come out against war, emphasizing its absurdity. But no direct condemnation seems to emerge from Socratic doctrine, as handed down to us in the writings of Plato and Xenophon. The reason for this is perhaps that the problem of war, no less than that of the cult of the gods, constituted a limit beyond which—despite the ample freedom of teaching accorded the philosophers in Athens—it was not permitted to go.

By his tragic death, Socrates was to show how serious were the risks run by those who assumed unconventional attitudes toward problems on which either public opinion or the authorities were still intransigent: The participation of the citizens in military campaigns imposed by the state constituted an obligation sanctioned by the law, and those who failed to comply could be severely punished. For the very reasons to which we have referred, Socrates' system, too, was to induce an aversion to war, the tragic consequence of an explosion of worldly passions.

In his speculative activity Socrates tried to get closer to his fellow human being, guiding him along the road to truth and supplying him with the necessary enlightenment. He spent his whole life educating his fellow citizens through personal contacts and conversation. The problem of participation in wars would naturally be stated in terms other than the traditional ones. What could be more irrational than the behavior of a state which had taken the field merely out of greed for dominion or thirst for vengeance? The only campaigns meeting the Socratic ideal of virtuous action were defensive ones, such as the wars fought against the Persians.

Now that ethical values had been given a universal setting, man's ambitions, hopes, and opportunities could no longer be realized within the polis. For all philosophic thought, by the very fact of posing human problems on a universal basis, distinguishing them from instincts and elemental appetites, was to help to bring individuals closer together and to make evident the vanity of their strife. Hence, Socratic doctrine was colored with a cosmopolitan light, essentially pacifist. A general love for fellow human beings and a natural propensity toward compromise and moderation flowed from his discoveries. And this is true although Xenophon points out that on at least two occasions the master showed that he could be tough with opponents.[54] However, not all the ancient sources were in agreement on this point. Plato, for example, although he gives the news of Socrates' participation in the battles of Pontidaea, Delium, and Amphipolis,[55] reports that he showed great humanity toward the enemy.[56] Cicero, too, in a controversial passage of the *Tusculan Disputations,* attributed to him cosmopolitan leanings and the feeling of being a "citizen of the world."[57] This was confirmed by other authors, such as Diogenes Laërtius and Arrian.

Despite the lack of direct evidence, then, it may be inferred that peace within and between the Greek cities was, in Socrates' view, the catalyzing element of unity and of Hellenic civilization. It would be bound to lead—and on this Socrates invited his listeners to meditate—to a renaissance of the Greek world and the reestablishment of a genuine and peaceful community life. Let us follow him in an argument preserved for us by Xenophon. Shorn of the literary ornamentation which is Xenophon's own, it reveals an attitude informed with humility, serenity, and love for orderly equilibrium, unfailing attributes of any system well disposed toward the quest for peace:

> Among rulers in cities, are you not aware that those who do most to make the citizens obey the laws are the best, and that the city in which the citizens are most obedient to the laws has the best time in peace and is irresistible in war? And again, agreement is deemed the greatest blessing for cities: their senates and their best men constantly exhort the citizens to agree, and everywhere in Greece there is a law that the citizens shall promis under oath to agree, and everywhere they take this oath.[58]

The passage proves that in the Socratic system the usual claim of Sophistic ethics—which began by praising man and ended by denying that moral precepts were of any value—underwent a radical transformation, based on real human needs. Civil law was no longer an expedient always opposed to the natural law but the instrument of a process of moral betterment designed to regenerate mankind and to eliminate all conditions of anarchy harmful to his peace of mind.

Socrates' view of the state was wholly new and quite different from that of the Sophists. The state and politics, factors of the greatest importance, should serve—and this was Socrates' innovation—the well-being and the happiness of citizens. The duties of the men engaged in government, as Xenophon recalled, were comparable to those of a shepherd protecting his flock.[59] This was the first formulation of a line of thought destined to influence the development of subsequent systems (for example those of the Cynics and the Stoics), based on the conviction that men, being brothers, must act in accordance with feelings of humanity and concord.

A number of factors peculiar to the Greek, indeed to the Athenian, mentality also affected the thinking and attitudes of the philosopher. For Socrates, the individual's membership in a given polis was the premise governing, and the yardstick for assessing, all political and civil behavior. This explains his conduct during the famous trial, when prosecuted by the Athenian authorities. Here he proclaimed his faith in the supremacy of the spirit and in the freedom of the individual. Although he could not stoop to compromise or meet the hostile judges halfway, he confirmed his submission to the state, whose rulings he accepted, even though he knew them to be unjust. His death would serve to teach posterity a lesson in internal discipline and to prove, through personal example and sacrifice, the vanity of intolerance. War and violence could not escape this condemnation, as is shown in these words attributed to him by Xenophon:

> But I hold that they who cultivate wisdom and think they will be able to guide the people in prudent policy never lapse into violence: they know that enmities and dangers are inseparable from violence, but persuasion produces the same results safely and amicably. . . . It is not, then, cultivation of wisdom that leads to violent methods, but the possession of power without prudence. Besides, many supporters are necessary to him who ventures to use force: but he who can persuade needs no confederate, having confidence in his own unaided power of persuasion. And such a man has no occasion to shed blood; for who would rather take a man's life than have a live and willing follower?[60]

The Socratic Schools: Cynics and Cyrenaics

Among the schools deriving from that of Socrates, two are of particular interest to us: the Cynic and the Cyrenaic. The Cynics relied more directly on Sophistic teaching, which, as we have seen, was impatient of heroic attitudes of all kinds and was to make a significant contribution to the development of Greek thinking on peace and the brotherhood of mankind.

The founder of the Cynic school was Antisthenes of Athens (ca. 436-ca. 366 B.C.), in his prime a disciple of Socrates, though he had once followed the Sophists. His speculative system owed something to both parents, and in it the Socratic discoveries clashed with the essentially anarchic character of Sophistic thinking.

With regard to the theory of knowledge, the Cynics were inclined to rela-tivism, which the Sophists had already defended and against which Socrates had reacted sharply. On the other hand, they followed Socrates on ethics, where they too considered virtue as the ultimate objective of all human be-havior and its practice as the quintessence of all real wisdom. Antisthenes be-lieved that virtue by itself would make men happy, whereas knowledge was not only quite useless but actually harmful. Hence the contempt of his school for science, which was considered a distraction from the practice of the vir-tues, especially justice, the most necessary of all to life in society. Since the only riches were spiritual ones, the traditional empirical distinction between good and evil was restated in relativistic terms. Poverty, shame, dishonor, dis-ease, even slavery were not evil in themselves, but were judged in relation to the reactions produced in the individual. If they succeeded in stimulating the will and the capacity to act, they could even lead to good. On the other hand, other realities regarded as useful by men could well be harmful if they were not transmuted into vehicles of spiritual edification. An approach based on the relativity of human actions, to be regarded as good or ill not for them-selves but in relation to the ends which could be achieved through them, led the Cynics to reject social institutions and conventions as being all too liable to divorce the individual from the development of his moral program. War, obedience to the state, the actions, interests, conditions and bonds imposed by membership of a certain community were seen by the Cynics as a complex of emotions and disturbances from which the individual should seek to es-cape. Anything opposed to the good of the soul (wealth, power, pleasure) or that which did not contribute to its edification should be rejected out of hand. Starting from these premises, the Cynics logically advocated the prac-tice of asceticism. Those like Diogenes of Sinope (ca. 412-323 B.C.) and Crates of Thebes (fifth-fourth century B.C.) and a number of their disciples became actual mendicants, itinerant lay apostles spreading a message of high mystic content. To deny oneself the superfluous and to follow an extremely severe rule of life became for them a form of moral edification and a means of drawing attention to the vanity of the things of this world. Among such things, the state with its pomp, its pretensions, its traditions, and its power hierarchies was the apparatus which always lay between man and his goals, ready to suffocate him in the name of principles seldom linked with the prac-tice of virtue.

Although the obstacle was a formidable one, it was not so imposing as to dissuade the Cynics from their desire to remove it: They challenged the limi-tations and the barriers imposed by the state with the argument that the com-munity should be governed not on the basis of written rules, the fragility of which was linked to their all-too-human origin, but by the rule of virtue ap-plied by wise men and taken to its furthest conclusions. Hence the formula-tion of a cosmopolitan ideal which saw the individual as a citizen of a universal city called the "cosmopolis" (a neologism attributed by Diogenes Laërtius to Diogenes of Sinope).[61] This was the natural consequence of the Cynics' unconcealed reluctance to submit themselves to the accepted order of things, appealing for rules spontaneously accepted. The practice of virtue could not be a matter of geography or local politics, but imposed on all universally valid duties. It is in this context that the judgment on Diogenes by Diogenes Laërtius should be read: "He would ridicule good birth and fame and all such distinctions, calling them showy ornaments of vice. The only true commonwealth was, he said, that which is as wide as the universe."[62] The idea of a citizenship covering the inhabited world did not imply legal or administrative arrangements. Denying any need for submission to the historical states, the Cynics were bound to oppose membership of a universal state. Rather, their idea reflected the desire for brotherhood and peace, linked with their reflections on the folly of war and on the pernicious character of hatred between cities and of quarrels between men.

But what was the point of considering oneself a citizen of the world? Because this was the way to achieve serenity, otherwise unattainable. This idea was present in the mind of Diogenes when he claimed that through the practice of philosophy he had achieved absolute peace of mind. The same may be said for "philanthropy," that is, for the love of humanity, one of the virtues preached by the school and dictated more by a desire to live in peace with human beings than by a genuine love for them.

The Cynics showed mercy and humanity toward their contemporaries but were convinced of their own superiority and made no attempt to hide this. Hence the attitude of teachers and educators toward the public in general and the powerful in particular—witness the famous meeting between Diogenes and Alexander the Great*—and their claim to be reformers of customs and guides on the difficult path of virtue. Their modest circumstances—they often lived on charity—did not prevent them from assuming a contemptuous and haughty attitude, supported by the belief that they were alone in possessing wisdom, wisdom being liberation from earthly worries, for the Cynics were proud of differing from those who constantly yearn for an impossible happiness foolishly linked with the possession of material goods and with external opulence. Their vision of life was a blend of faith in their own moral authority, the ability to resist pomp and splendor, and the ambition to guide others by providing a higher code of conduct.

Their conception of politics was also strange and inconsistent. Sometimes they seemed to favor an enlightened monarchy and at other times anarchy. Moreover, when they studied relations between men, they convinced themselves that no people and no state could legitimately aspire to supremacy over

---

*When the young conqueror asked Diogenes if there was any favor he could confer, Diogenes answered, "Yes, you can stand out of my light."

others, since all were equally free to express their personalities in the way indicated by their ambitions and experience. The condemnation of violence was a natural corollary: War conflicted with the teaching of the Cynics since it was a distortion which tended not only to prevent the dissemination of their message but to halt the process of moral improvement based on a bond of universal brotherhood.

Their condemnation of war naturally included that of political power when supported by force. Historical events which occurred during the period when the Cynic school flourished had much to do with this attitude. The Greek cities were still in the throes of the fierce struggles which gave the Macedonian dynasty its opportunity to impose a hegemony. Though the conquests, one after the other, of Greece, Asia Minor, and the Near and Middle East were to lead to the unification of most of the known world and to offer a means of dissemination of Hellenic civilization, the events of the time justified the view of the Cynics and their rebellion against a society whose moral objectives they rejected. These reflections inspired Crates' poem *Pera,* in which he urged the isolation of man from society to enable him to escape war and its consequences. In the poem, now lost, the life of an idealized Cynic community was described. Its inhabitants, cutting themselves off from the rest of the world, were governed by the rule of tolerance and love. It was one of the first examples of utopian literature, which was to enjoy a considerable vogue in later ages.

The teachings of another Cyrenaic school are also relevant to our inquiry: it was founded by Aristippus of Cyrene (fifth-fourth century B.C.), a thinker who moved from Africa to Athens in order to attend Socrates' lessons. Like Antisthenes, he had also followed the lectures of the Sophists. This fact explains the mingling in his thought, as in Cynic philosophy, of elements drawn from two different speculative sources. Under the Sophistic influence, the general orientation of the school was mainly concerned with perceptible experience and with the negation of everything outside perception. The result was a hedonistic view of life, in which pleasure represented the only possible good and pain the sole evil. Aristippus' successors provided a more complete explanation of the pleasure-pain relationship, identifying it with a state of grace generating happiness and serenity.

A hedonistic approach to human relations and ambitions, whether in the original form chosen by the founder of the school or in a form developed by certain disciples, was, of course, hostile to all obstacles to pleasure. A special object of aversion was war. The Sophistic notion of the contradiction between natural and man-made law was given a new lease on life. The world was seen as a stage on which man was free to emancipate himself from the oppressive heritage of the past and from the taboos fostered by ancient habits and traditions. In other words, the sad heritage of the misguided teaching imparted in youth was jettisoned and man was carried forward by an impulse—

almost Freudian in nature—of liberation from complexes. A principle of universality was implicit in the hedonistic orientation of the school, but this did not mean that the fatherland must coincide with the inhabited world. A position of this kind would have led to a cosmopolitanism similar to that taught by the Cynics; the vision of the Cyrenaics was a good deal less noble. The fatherland was the geographical locality in which it was possible to satisfy one's own desire for pleasure. *Ubi bene, ibi patria.* The fatherland could be anywhere, since there was nowhere where the Cyrenaic could not provide for the satisfaction of his own appetites. But war, being a source of pain, had no place in his concept of the happy life.

Plato on Peace

Protest against a civilization in thrall to war was implicit in Cynic teaching, but we shall seek in vain for attitudes as precise as this in the work of Plato (ca. 428-ca. 348 B.C.), the leading disciple of Socrates and his spiritual heir. It is no easy matter to condense his thinking, in this any more than in other fields: His ideas are spread over a considerable number of dialogues, the legacy of a literary career extending into his extreme old age, containing many inconsistencies, restatements of particular ideas, and actual changes of opinion. Thus it has been possible to argue that there is no genuine Platonic system. Efforts to give unity to his scattered intuitions and reflections are no more than so many attempts to straitjacket them in fixed patterns. Plato must be judged above all on his devotion to things of the spirit, his untiring quest for the essence of problems through persistent research: In his dialogues thesis balances antithesis, each viewpoint put forward by a different person, one of whom always predominates but can never make headway in the discussion without the critical cooperation of the others. The speculative enterprise therefore develops through a series of attitudes of mind emerging from a succession of comments on a specific subject, and no firm conclusion is necessarily arrived at.

This sort of pendular movement through which Platonic thought advances and gains in complexity does not facilitate full understanding, and his thought on peace is no exception. It must be emphasized, first, that politics was for Plato an essential field of inquiry. Plato's man was a social being whose personality and behavior were determined by identifiable community instincts. As a result the state was idealized and with it that part of the individual soul which is expressed through the state. While the problem of war and peace—that is, of the relations between human societies—was well to the fore, the use of the dialogue form precluded any clear-cut statement of attitude by Plato himself. At certain moments he discerned the conflict between war and a harmonious development of the collective soul, of which the state was the practical expression; at others, war was seen as a fact on which life and the development of the community depended. Hence he defined the art of war as part of the art of government.[63]

These ideas, insofar as they were linked to the political situation of Greece, had probably already lost their actuality when Plato was discussing them. His vision of the state was by no means new. Despite the brilliant presentation and the imaginative impetus which informs his writing, the ancient polis was always his model of a perfect organization. Neither the advent of the democratic regimes, nor the continuing struggles for hegemony, nor the Peloponnesian War seem to have affected the thinking of the great Athenian. He remained attached to conventional patterns and perhaps failed to understand the changes made by the new generations, longing to move outside the confines of the small but ferocious cities to scan wider horizons. Nor could he resolve the conflict between the position thus assumed and the reality of the times by formulating his ideas in utopian terms.

The exercise of justice, which is the source of concord and agreement,[64] can tend toward a unifying objective only if an overall vision of it is sought and if this vision is derived from immutable moral and legal premises. But experience taught, then as now, that there is room for diametrically opposed opinions as to the nature of justice. In a state governed by a military caste (Sparta, for example), the definition of justice differed from that accepted in an environment informed by feelings of humanity and tolerance. In Sparta anything serving the purpose of war was deemed "just." Elsewhere, justice was seen as a means of facilitating peaceful agreements, of bringing together divergent points of view and making compromise possible. The practice of this virtue was a state of mind as well as a rule of conduct and it enabled man to overcome his passions and curb his appetites. Plato failed to discern the conflict between points of view and assumed a wait-and-see position hardly reconcilable with the principles of equity and harmony on which he based his idea of the state and of good government.

By arguing that the reasoning part of man was divine in origin, Plato offered man a route for his earthly journey which would lead him to a perfection having two components. The first, which derived from a vision—in some respects a mystic vision—recognizing in the soul-body duality the poles of a permanent conflict, urged man to adopt superior models of life inspired above all by love, the quality which led men to perform good acts.[65] To this element, which some writers felt foreshadowed the Christian message, there was added a second one, based on the ideal of Hellenic life and therefore centering on the body, whose instincts were not considered as the origin of all guilt. This second element represented part of the cult of physical beauty and of the aesthetic ideal of the classical world. Through the continual interweaving of the two lines of thought, Plato proposed in *The Republic*, a plan for the organization of community life and of the perfect state.

There is no clear statement of hostility to war in this famous treatise. The ideal state was, in fact, capable of waging war, and was required to train soldiers for external defense. The fifth book of *The Republic* advocated the severest sanctions for deserters and for those who fell, even through no fault of their own, into the hands of the enemy. Again, since the brave must be rewarded if they were to give their best, they should be welcomed with special tributes; they should be crowned with garlands, and no one whom they "had a mind to kiss should refuse to be kissed" by them.[66] This paradoxical line of thought concealed the desire—apparently in no way prompted by a love of peace—of ensuring privileges for the warrior caste.

But perhaps with the intention of balancing such excesses, in Plato's state it was not the soldiers but the wise men who bore the highest responsibility of government. The "guardians," as they were called, must obey only the dictates of reason and moderation and shun temptations contrary to equity and justice.[67] The warriors thus came under an authority determined to safeguard the governance of the commonweal from the precarious fluctuation of all things human. Here, clearly, Plato had no illusions as to the harmful nature and origins of war, though he had described it as a "fine thing" in the *Protagoras.*[68] In a famous passage of *The Republic* he wrote: "Then, without determining as yet whether war does good or harm, this much we may affirm, that now we have discovered war to be derived from causes which are also the causes of almost all the evils in states, private as well as public."[69] A passage in the *Phaedo* shows war as a harmful exercise: "Whence come wars, and fightings and factions? Whence but from the body and the lusts of the body?"[70] For peace is not for the sake of war, but war for the sake of peace. "And therefore, as we say, every one of us should live the life of peace as long and well as he can."[71]

Being recruited among the wise men, the guardians were required to pursue harmony and equilibrium at all times. This could be done only through the exercise of self-control, and thus their behavior was bound to be moderate. The discipline the guardian imposed on himself was, as it were, the link between the social and the political world, and at the same time it enabled man's instincts to be tempered. This had been considered in *The Republic* but in *The Laws,* the political study written late in Plato's life, it was treated as a decisive factor for all public action. Here Plato asserts that wisdom should condition the work of the ruler but points out that wisdom can be of benefit and can aid equilibrium only in the serenity provided by harmony. Self-discipline was seen as the fundament not only of political virtues, but of virtues in general, like courage, temperance, and justice.[72]

Exercised unreservedly, self-control would generate order and harmony, making a free organism of the state, harmonious and open to an understanding of the world.[73] Its function was not only internal to the polis but essential, too, in relations with the outside. If it prevailed, together with moderation and brotherly understanding, peace and not war would be fostered. Starting from this premise, Plato regarded constitutions modeled on that of Sparta, designed for the preparation and conduct of war, as mistaken and unnatural.

In working out and describing the ideal state, to illustrate it to rulers and founders of constitutions and to promote harmonization of the citizens' rights and duties with those of the community, Plato, as we have seen, was guided by the actual situations existing in his own time. This aggravated the inconsistencies, for alongside moderate and calm statements are to be found passages of bewildering intransigence and severity. What are we to make, for example, of Plato's refusal to allow the citizen to follow a calling other than that allocated by fate, leaving it to the state to deal with any attempt to escape the law of destiny? How are we to judge the principles which the warriors were required to teach their sons? Besides keeping fit at all times, they were asked to train their children in handling arms, taking them to the battlefields so that they could acquire direct experience of combat. The poor pedagogic value of the spectacle, intended to increase the natural bellicosity of youth, did not seem to worry Plato, who was apparently concerned only with the dangers these practices might entail for the physical safety of the young.[74] Nor, indeed, were women exempt from military training, which was to be carried out even in time of peace.[75]

And yet even these rules should not be examined separately but should be seen in a wider context. Despite certain harsh and paradoxical passages, Platonic thought is based on the awareness that war is always a source of grief. This is inferred from *The Laws,* in which many earlier exaggerations were tempered by Plato's more mellow understanding of reality, suggesting that experience and the years had taught the author prudence and understanding for the changes which had taken place in Greek thought. The problem of peace and war is treated more humanely in *The Laws* than in *The Republic.* The myth of the Golden Age reemerges, a myth which had inspired Greek civilization from the earliest times. The legend, which in Hesiod's story was given the status of a religious allegory, is treated by Plato as historical certainty. Whereas Hesiod was concerned with moral considerations and used the myth as an instrument of edification and warning, Plato revives the allegory to plot the course of an ideological journey by appealing to past realities.

Without departing too much from the traditional story, the philosopher describes the legendary age following the great flood, celebrating the men of that time and their ways of life. Those who had escaped the natural catastrophe had, he says, taken refuge in the mountains, where they organized a new community in which wealth and poverty were unknown. In this idyllic environment no wars were fought. Men loved one another and did all they could to help one another. They had clothes, blankets, houses, and utensils. Fertile pastures provided them an ample supply of milk, meat, and game. So much prosperity generated noble sentiments neutralizing aggressive ambitions and incentives. Men knew their duty, and this completed a perfect situation, rendering a government superfluous. Alas, the situation changed as soon as man moved down to the plain, abandoning his mountain refuges. Then his self-discipline failed him, and toil and corruption—the causes of war and endless difficulties—began.[76]

The story would have been incomplete if the philosopher had not examined whether propensity to violence was an essential trait of human nature. This subject was also tackled in *The Laws*. Here, Plato, having accounted for the Cretan custom of eating meals together by the need to practise, even in time of peace, habits likely to facilitate the conduct of warlike operations, then put the following words into the mouth of one of his speakers: "For what men in general term peace is in fact only a name; in reality every city is in a natural state of war with every other, not indeed proclaimed by heralds, but everlasting."[77] In a most famous passage of *The Republic*, Plato had stressed the supremacy of the intellect, likening mankind to a group of prisoners chained in a cave or den, to whose eyes light came glimmering through an opening. They could achieve knowledge only after a difficult process of adaptation to incoming light.[78] It is amazing that he should express himself so differently in the case of war, for here he offers man no comparable means for overcoming darkness. Plainly the bonds which bind the individual to the authority of the state, operating in an atmosphere of underlying conflict or open war, seemed to him of such importance as to preclude man's shaking himself free from them, substituting concord for the old habits and primitive fatalism of the warrior.

A passage in *The Republic* already foreshadows this attitude. It examines the relations of the Greeks among themselves and with the barbarians. The Greeks had traditionally placed themselves above other peoples, seeing themselves as a privileged race to whom the gods had vouchsafed talent and critical capacity in a measure superior to the average. The barbarians were relegated to the status of inferiors. The current ideas on war and on the relations among peoples accepted the "race gap," which nothing, it was felt, could bridge. Plato endorsed these ideas when he explained the difference between "discord" and "war": The first term stood for a controversy between peoples belonging to the same race (for example, between Greeks), the second between peoples of different races. In the case of a contest between Greeks, the adversaries, although using armed force, should concentrate not on the enemy citizenry, but on "only [the] few at any time [who] are their foes, those, namely, who are to blame for the quarrel."[79] Military pressure was to be used until it provoked a civil uprising sufficient to force those governing the opposing city to withdraw from the fight. In the case of non-Greeks, however, they were to have recourse to total war.

The distinction between the ways of waging war showed that although Plato regarded the fragmentation of Greek civilization in small states as necessary, he eventually conceded the existence of an underlying solidarity among people of Hellenic stock. In this way he formulated implicitly a moral judgment on war. Thus, in the *Gorgias,* the dialogue on rhetoric, Plato described with compassion the human predicament, for man is a prey to violence and recklessness, condemned ever to wander from the path mapped out for him by those having his best interests at heart. What was important, he warned, was not external serenity but peace of mind, which could be won by those whose conduct was balanced and honest and who preferred to suffer an injustice rather than to commit one. He pitied Archelaus, who had become the sovereign of Macedonia after a long series of crimes: He was wrongly thought fortunate and happy by his contemporaries, whilst in fact he was the most miserable of men because he had despised the fundamental rule of honesty.[80]

Plato's output was large, and he was not always consistent. Yet his dialogue must be examined and judged as a whole. A passage in *The Laws* relating to the harmful consequences of soldiering for the education of the citizen is exactly counterbalanced in *The Republic* by a passage in which warriors are advised to use the battlefield as a stage on which to educate the young in their atrocious trade. However they should be judged, these passages bring us to consider what is the most genuine and inspired source of Platonic thought and thus to move more rapidly through the contradictions between the objectives of the philosopher and those of the legislator. And this is true although it is difficult to distinguish how much of his system is an effort to overcome the traditional concept of war along bold idealistic lines and how much is the consequence of his acceptance of certain aspects of community life. Plato was prepared to condemn war as the cause of many disasters, but he did not delude himself that it was in his power to transform the entire Hellenic conception of power. His aim was not submission, the destruction of traditional modes of life, nor did he wish to be seen as a visionary lost on the paths of utopia. To escape the tragic dilemma, he would have needed a faith or a mystic impetus sufficient to regenerate the political and military tradition of Greek society and to guide it toward completely new ethical and religious attitudes.

His attempt to persuade the Greeks that war should not be the supreme care of the state was by itself a bold enterprise. He advocates in *The Laws* that rulers should be most concerned with peaceful activities.[81] Peace was not only the final aim of human existence but also the reward for virtuous conduct. Men lived happily if they abstained from all unjust conduct and if they sheltered themselves from that of others. The same could be said of the state. "And cities are like individuals in this, for a city, if good, has a life of peace, but if evil, a life of war within and without."[82] An underlying harmony was what gave the behavior of men and of groups a noble completeness. Plato thus sought to achieve the unity of a world torn by discord, corroded by the lust for power, tormented by primeval appetites and urges, for he believed that man must bend, despite everything, to the imperatives of reason.

Because the system lacked any real religious light, these ideas were not taken to their furthest logical conclusions and remained side issues. Only a message of charity like that of Christianity could, centuries later, interpret effectively man's longing for peace.

Aristotle and the Choice between Peace and War

The works of Aristotle (384-322 B.C.)—in particular, the *Politics*, in which he set down his thoughts on the organization of the state—contain no precise statement on the problem of peace. In his system, the behavior of man and society was the basis of community morality, the function of which was to show man the right behavior in personal relations and in those maintained with society and its institutions. A keen observer of man and all his works, Aristotle concentrated mainly on the dynamics of the contemporary state. In this field, too, his teaching was very fruitful, both when he described the peculiar characteristics of each nation and when he sought to establish general rules and the teachings inferred from observation. He wished to avoid neglecting the reality of his time and to shun the paths of utopia, which had proved so tempting to other philosophers. His careful analysis of the present, his intimacy with working statesmen, and his anxiety to steer clear of paradox compelled him to accept certain institutions, imperfect though they might be, which had evolved from community life, and to refrain from proposing reforms which he felt could not be enforced.

In his system the state was the framework within which man must find fulfillment and in which his aspirations must become specific actions and choices. According to his famous definition, man is a political animal, naturally inclined to associate with his own kind, abhorring isolation. Community life is not only a response to the dictates of nature, but it enables the individual to give of his best, since it creates a context of legality and justice, outside which man's savagery knows no bounds.

Aristotle's approach to the problems of community organization is more realistic than Plato's: He is more respectful of institutions and acquired experience, less anxious to change the whole world in obedience to abstract principles worked out without warmth and perhaps originating in a certain distrust of the group instinct. It was precisely the warnings of experience which led him to challenge some of Plato's proposals for solving community problems: sharing of women and of goods, the rigid separation between social classes, the imposition by the state of heavy burdens on the citizens. He was bound to find these objectives unattainable and in conflict with the nature of man, a political animal, it is true, but also a creature endowed with a sensitivity and a critical capacity could not be neutralized or silenced. There is nothing rigid or burdensome, then, in his vision of the state, but a tendency to idealize it, while assigning it a specific function with regard to its basic and indispensable unit: the individual. The ultimate objective of the state was the happiness of the citizens. In this, too, he deviated from Plato. He replaced the just state, founded on immutable, abstract principles, by a more elastic concept, with a doctrine more sensitive to historical realities.

However, Aristotle's vision of the state did not go beyond the Greek polis, which he saw as the ultimate form of political organization. But the polis, given its limited geographical and environmental scope, offered no soil suitable for the germination of the ideas on peace then fermenting in the Greek world. These ideas needed much wider horizons. While conceding that peace was the ideal condition for the progress of any community and advising statesmen to encourage its consolidation,[83] he was incapable of establishing a systematic approach to the problem without denying some postulates of his political thought. Among these we may recall his claim, scarcely credible for a thinker of his calibre, that the rights of the Greeks were fundamentally different from those of the barbarians, since between them there could not exist relations based on equality but only on the subjection of the latter to the former. From this he derived his famous justification of slavery. And in a society permanently fragmented into so many states, war was sure to survive.

> Hence even the art of war will by nature be in a manner an art of acquisition (for the art of hunting is part of it) that is properly employed both against wild animals and against those of mankind who, though designed by nature for subjection, refuse to submit to it, inasmuch as this warfare is by nature just.[84]

Since he advocated a constitution modeled on the historic experience of Greece, Aristotle saw war as a legitimate instrument for settling disputes. In his opinion, it was right to be prepared for war, although this did not make fighting praiseworthy in itself, much less the ultimate goal of community life: *Peace* is the ideal condition toward which mankind must work. "War," he said, "must be for the sake of peace, business for the sake of leisure, things necessary and useful for the sake of things noble. . . ." This led him to condemn the deformed habits of mind of the professional soldier: " . . . a man should be capable of engaging in business and war, but still more capable of living in peace and leisure; and he should do what is necessary and useful, but still more what is noble."[85] Therefore those constitutions which made conquest and military activity in general the fundamental aim of the state were erroneous. Peoples governed in this way would live in misery. The final goal of the state was in fact to ensure happiness for its inhabitants and to see that the army was trained not to enslave neighbors nor to throw into bondage those who were free:

> For we do business in order that we may have leisure, and carry on war in order that we may have peace. Now the practical virtues are exercised in politics or in warfare; but the pursuits of politics and war seem to be unleisured—those of war indeed entirely so, for no one desires to be at war for the sake of being at war, nor deliberately takes steps to cause a war: a man would be thought an utterly bloodthirsty character if he declared war on a friendly state for the sake of causing battles and massacres.[86]

These words illustrate Aristotle's aim of distilling his experiences into lessons for the holders of power. They also reveal his feeling that it is important to plan ahead against the dangers and unexpected developments that issue from conflict. He felt that every type of state must comply with its own rules, and within the elaborate nexus of international relations the needs and problems of each community and the choices of its rulers must meet, though they were not bound to clash. That war was to be undertaken only with the aim of peace implied that if peace was obtainable by other means, war should no longer be the final arbiter.

As we have seen, Aristotle had no time for plans which could not be implemented. It should not be forgotten that he had taken active part in public life, first supporting Hermias, tyrant of Atarneus, then training the young prince who was to be known to posterity as Alexander the Great, and lastly acting as adviser to Antipater, regent in Macedonia during the absence of Alexander. His lack of enthusiasm for theory was partly due to his opinion that men were not equal, not only because some were born free and others not, but also because the Greeks enjoyed a privileged position.

At the same time Aristotle gave no support to the type of nationalist extremism to which any too eager and immoderate compliance with the principle of inequality would inevitably have led. In particular the ruler—and here again Aristotle speaks as a tutor—should oppose the idea of a political utopia. He should control his own impulses, resisting the temptation to increase the hegemonic pressure of the state whose fate was in his hands.

On the question of the exercise of power over subject peoples, Aristotle inclined toward tolerance.

> Yet most people seem to think that despotic rule is statesmanship, and are not ashamed to practise towards others treatment which they declare to be unjust and detrimental for themselves; for in their own internal affairs they demand just government, yet in their relations with other peoples they pay no attention to justice.[87]

Here he advocated the same fair treatment for the foreigner which the citizen demands of his own government. If it adopted the opposite rule, applying violence and intolerance, seeking an inordinate degree of power, society risked forfeiting what it had legitimately acquired.

Nor was military activity to be regarded as a valuable means of training, as Plato had argued. Day-to-day experience showed that communities devoted to the preparation of war, being too busy in the practice of military training, were severely handicapped when it came to organizing a peaceful existence. "Most military states remain safe while at war but perish when they have won their empire; in peacetime they lose their temper like iron. The lawgiver is to blame, because he did not educate them to be able to employ leisure."[88] These words derive from a careful observation of history and attachment to moral principles, the indispensable guides of any society. The idea that the legislator and the statesman should concern themselves with the instruction of the citizens shows the maturity of Aristotle's thinking. The education rule applied to all the constitutions, among which he judged that of Sparta the worst, since that state's authorities were constantly engaged in waging or making ready for war. He felt there could be no weaker or more one-sided approach than this, since it caused dangerous disequilibria and left unbridgeable gaps in time of transition from war to peace:

> In Sparta the entire system of the laws is directed toward one part of virtue only, military valor, because this is serviceable for conquest. Owing to this [the Spartans] remained secure while at war, but began to decline when they had won an empire, because they did not know how to live a life of leisure, and had been trained in no other form of training more important than the art of war. And another error no less serious than that one is this: They think that the coveted prizes of life are won by valor more than cowardice, and in this they are right, yet they imagine wrongly that these prizes are worth more than the valor that wins them.[89]

The general bias of Aristotle's thinking is unmistakable in these passages and is manifestly colored by a preference for peace. They stress man's natural inclination toward moderation and tolerance, toward the liberal arts and the activities that only peace can favor and which war necessarily hampers and disrupts. The objective must be to forestall war, if possible.[90] The philosopher was to serve as guide in the state, his job being, so to speak, that of throwing light on the work of the rulers, especially in the sectors related to the spiritual life and the training of the individual. This responsibility should be discharged on the basis of principles of humanity and with the aim of a kind of moral improvement which would concern not only one state and one community, but should embrace them all, since it referred to an attitude of mind. The question was not one of a choice between violence and tolerance; Aristotle argued that one should reject the first, as contrary to the nature of man, or because it was unlikely to ensure serenity for those who desired it. A universalist bias was therefore implicit in his teaching, which started with an approach much more widely based than that traditionally circumscribed by the polis and was extended to embrace the entire Greek world and perhaps, by implication, other peoples.

There was in all this a seed destined to grow in other teachings. For the moment it was unclear, because it was still bound by the attachment to the polis and the alleged supremacy of the Greek people. This explains why the idea of peace and war as mutual alternatives, although present in the thinking of Aristotle, never became an object of separate autonomous analysis for him and never provided the basis of a doctrine. Had he examined the problem more carefully, he would, perhaps, have made a complete reappraisal of war, developing systematically those findings and opinions which in his writings have only an episodic value. If an essay by Aristotle on the subject had come

down to us, the doctrine of peace would have gained much, were it only because it was supported by his authority. This seems all the more true in view
of the fact that, unlike Plato, Aristotle considered the opinion of the majority
as the basis of the will of the state. He could not therefore ignore the absurdity of war, the cause of disasters for the population of a state and, in particular, for that middle class to which he allocated essential tasks in maintaining
the equilibrium of society.

Peace and Lyric Poetry

Do poets express the feelings and emotions, the ambitions and the yearnings of their contemporaries? Are they in a position to reveal the human soul
to itself, enabling it to rise above the gray day-to-day world? The controversy
on the essence and nature of art is as old as man himself, and there are no
signs that a solution is being found. Aristotle has something to contribute on
this, when, in attempting to pinpoint the difference between poetry and history, he says that the former records universal ideas and the latter particular
events.[91] This was an approximate breakdown of the respective tasks performed by the historian and the poet. Art, and especially poetry, expresses
man's anxiety to escape the rule of mediocrity, to rise toward heights from
which the mind may range over reality, grasping what is important. The poets,
therefore, can help us to understand whether a certain disposition became effective at a particular time and whether it affected the manner of thinking of
their time.

Our inquiry began with Homer and Hesiod, in whose verses we found more
than a hint of the desire for peace, even if at times—especially in Homer—it is
overlaid with warlike passion and unrestrained animosity and desire for vengeance. Passing to the pre-Socratics, we emphasized that a full understanding
of their speculative activity has been made difficult not only because we
know very little about them and what we do know is fragmentary, but also
because it is almost impossible for modern students to journey back into the
atmosphere of dreamlike detachment from reality in which they lived and
wrote.

The loss of the works of the pre-Socratic thinkers is only one aspect of
the dispersion of the body of Greek writings. How can we ascertain, then,
with so little to go on, whether the earliest poetry was receptive to the message of peace and humanity which some of the philosophers sought to propo-
gate? How can we know that the spontaneous ferocity found in some passages of Homer and, as part of the myth of the Golden Age, echoed in the
work of Hesiod and Plato had no supporters among the lyric poets? Could
they ignore in their works the opinions of contemporaries and the fatality
which compelled men, in the exalted atmosphere of the city-state factions, to
fight for a hegemony that would always escape them? There is evidence that
they could not, and did not, do so. However, these are only indications, suf-
ficing perhaps to prove the actual existence of a point of view but definitely

not enough to tell us exactly what the poets were thinking and what were the limits beyond which they would not go. It is very probable that the lyric poets—who were, no less than the epic and tragic poets, an expression of the lively genius of the Greek race—also sang of the yearning for peace. With very little in the way of sources to guide us, let us seek out some evidence.

We must concern ourselves first and foremost with the elegiac poets, since the elegy marked the transition from epic to lyric poetry. Once the military and brutish enthusiasm which lay beyond Homer's work was spent, the Greeks made much use of the elegy (alternate hexameters and pentameters). The form and balance of the elegiac couplet lent itself to reflections on civic virtues and comments on relations between the individual and the state. At least in the beginning, it often celebrated sacrifices made for the community and to safeguard a society founded on the polis. The fatherland was generally seen as the goal toward which all efforts were aimed. But this form of poetry also sometimes preached the value of peace, urging the citizen to practise not only the virtues of heroism and abnegation but those of concord and union as well. The emphasis of elegiac poetry, therefore, tended to vary, sometimes appealing to warlike sentiments and sometimes seeking to calm them down, as part of a general attitude encouraging harmony.

The genre varied in content according to the inspiration of the poet. The poems were tranquil and meditative, serene and balanced, free of violence or restlessness—like a broad river which flows placidly toward the coast, noble, grandiose, unhurried. These were features shared by elegiac poetry and epic poetry, for the former derived from the latter. We are speaking of the elegy as it appeared at the beginning of Greek literary history, intended for declamation with musical accompaniment; only later was it to become a song of love and gaiety.

The earliest elegiac poet was Callinus of Ephesus (seventh century B.C.), who flourished at the time of the Cimmerian invasions of Asia Minor. He used poetry as a weapon to encourage his fellow nationals to resist the enemy. His writing is warlike in tone, but its aim is not a demented lust for power but the defense of hearth and fatherland: "The land is full of war ... purpose ye to sit in peace? ... When, young men, will ye show a stout heart? Have ye no shame of your sloth before them that dwell about you? ... When a brave man dieth the whole people regretteth him, and while he lives he is as good as a demi-god."[92] While his poetry sounds an epic note, it is very different in character from Homer's. Here there are none of the outbursts of rage so frequent, in act as well as word, among the ancient heroes. We are in the presence of two quite different mentalities: On the one hand, there is the war of expansion, the cause of death and destruction; on the other, defense against external aggression, conducted in order to ensure community life and the safety of the fatherland. In Callinus' poetry, peace is the ultimate objective of the city's efforts.

The same spirit informs the work of Tyrtaeus (seventh century B.C.), who lived in Sparta and wrote verses for the Spartan warriors appealing to the feelings of honor and pride that reward sacrifices made for the collective good.[93] His writing is governed by a civic morality and resists an unbalanced thirst for dominion. In the *Exhortations,* of which some elegies and fragments have survived, he seems to draw the moral that war generates unparalleled pain. Even so, there are occasions which force men to fight: "For 'tis a fair thing for a good man to fall and die fighting in the van for his native land."[94]

A sense of mysticism blended with fatality pervades these poems. This we should seek in vain in Homer. So far as we can infer from the fragments which have reached us, Tyrtaeus did not tackle the problem of the origins and motives of war, since he believed it to be inevitable. But even when they urged the Greeks to take up arms, his poems showed an awareness of the sacred character of life, of the need to spare mankind torment and pain unless they were imposed by special obligations. In any case, concord as a determinant of the equilibrium of individual and collective existence ranked high in his scale of priorities. Of his collection of elegies entitled *Eunomia* [Orderliness], a few fragments have survived. We know definitely that its intention was to revive in its readers a spirit of emulation based on respect for the human personality, on the orderly submission to law, and above all on concord.

The distress caused by invasions—which frequently brought about serfdom for the Greek cities of Asia Minor, since they were too divided to bury their differences in unyielding opposition to the enemy outside—prompted reactions of various kinds: On the one hand it added to the cities' capacity to resist, strengthened by a poetry designed to put fresh heart into the citizens, and on the other it awakened a desire for pleasure. This latter was the reaction of Mimnermus of Colophon (second half of the seventh century B.C.), who was writing when most of the Greek cities of Asia Minor languished under the direct or indirect domination of the kingdom of Lydia. Refusing to participate in public affairs, the poet sought refuge within himself, and preached a way of life devoted solely to pleasure. His poetry had nothing to say about rebellion against the foreign dominator; it did not even lament the sadness of the times and made no suggestion that the Greeks should adopt an attitude of warlike dignity. Its message was total abandonment to the cult of the activities dear to Aphrodite, with regret for the brevity of life, which allows only fleeting enjoyment and all too soon forces on us the burden of old age.

The poetry of Mimnermus shows how the manner of reacting to the drama of existence had changed and illustrates the prevalence of an hedonistic adaptation to circumstances which men no longer hoped to change. This attitude recurs in the thinking of the Greeks and in their conduct. Despite their efforts to rise to a level of high spirituality, they always yielded to a reality from which there was no escaping. Mimnermus' viewpoint had much in common with the Cyrenaic and Epicurean systems, and the same line of thinking inspired another elegiac poet, once credited with the foundation of the Eleatic philosophic school: Xenophanes of Colophon, who flourished in the second half of the sixth century B.C. Although born in the same city as Mimnermus, he had reacted differently to another foreign domination (that of the Persians): by abandoning Asia Minor.

The loss of the poem *On Nature*, in which Xenophanes developed his ideas on the essence of things, has deprived us of important evidence which may well have included attitudes toward military adventures and war in general. Nonetheless two elegies have survived in which his mind and his critical sensitivity reveal a profound understanding of problems related to peace. Thus in one of the elegies, he recommends that his listeners show reserve in convivial meetings, fleeing the celebration of heroic enterprises and preferring, in their place, praises sung to the gods.[95] He showed a certain disdain for the cult of might and of physical dexterity, so highly thought of in the Hellenic world, and preferred chaacter-building virtues and the practice of wisdom.

Solon (seventh-sixth century B.C.) was both a statesman and a poet. In his elegies he is always concerned to entice his fellow citizens along the road to civic virtue. In at least one of his works he praises unity and concord, giving a graphic description of the plight of the cities disfigured by strife and immorality and exhorting their inhabitants to follow an ideal of harmony.[96]

The most popular of the elegiac poets of the Greek world was Theognis of Megara (sixth century B.C.), who certainly knew the implications of war and discord, since he was himself their victim. Forced to abandon his city of birth after the victory of a hostile political party, he wandered through the Hellenic world, bearing with him the burden of unforgotten rancor. Convinced that his experiences should serve as a warning to his fellow citizens, particularly the young, he wrote a number of moving elegies, generally dedicating them to friends who shared his opinions. One of these was the young Cyrnus, whom he endeavored to guide by providing him with a compendium of exhortations and advice. Although the poet, embittered by grief, was primarily concerned with his own rehabilitation in civil life, he may nevertheless have voiced his inspiration in terms of tolerance and brotherly love. There was no organic doctrine, the poetry taking the form of episodic manifestations of kindness and harmony.

Two lines, the authenticity of which, unlike others, is not generally challenged, indicate Theognis' attitude. "May Peace and wealth possess the city, so that I may make merry with other men; I love not evil war."[97] These words, colored by a measure of hedonism, show how much he regrets that men should so seldom prove capable of tackling a problem that is obviously and dramatically absurd but whose thraldom they cannot escape. The problem of peace was once again linked with that of injustice and betrayal, the parents of strife. The poet felt that there was no bond between the moral behavior of the individual and the advantages he enjoyed. The wicked, as experience had shown him, were rewarded rather than punished for their actions, and the good were oppressed by disaster. This universal guilt, so difficult to escape, should have induced men to meditate seriously on their afflictions. "But it would be dishonorable for me not to mount behind swift steeds and look lamentable war in the face."[98] Since war, discord, and ingratitude dominated human relations, to die young was no tragedy. This would be a way of evading disappointment and pain and of generating a spirit of solidarity for which it would otherwise have been madness to hope. "Ah, blessed and happy and fortunate is he that goeth down into the black house of Death without knowing trouble, and ere he hath bent before his foes, sinned of necessity, or tested the loyalty of his friends."[99]

The favorite themes of the elegiac poets were political and community life. Their poetry abounded in exhortations to citizens to fight bravely when the interests of the fatherland were at stake and to cultivate virtues like concord and tolerance, the exercise of which would benefit the community. Their poetry was called "gnomic" or "sententious," because of its moral and edifying objectives. Elegiac poetry was born, then, with this property, which was maintained intact for several generations, until it evolved toward a sentimental and amorous genre. Because of their nature, elegiac verses were often quoted as proverbs and maxims, put together in collections passed from hand to hand among the public and bequeathed like heirlooms from generation to generation. The titles of the poems are evidence enough of their deliberately edifying nature. Though some acknowledged the importance of military activity and sang "of arms and men," this was done in moderate terms. The poets assumed maturity and experience in their readers, describing war as a hard necessity, not as an inspiring game into which the soldier could throw himself with unreserved enthusiasm.

The attitudes underlying iambic poetry were different. Convivial in nature, it indulged the taste of the hearer, surprising him and inspiring him through the incisive rhythm of the strophes and their sensual content. Because of its greater immediacy, it lent itself to mockery and derision, to attacks on groups of citizens or unpopular persons, to the exaltation of emotions. The first exponent of the genre was Archilochus of Paros (seventh century B.C.), who established the archetypes and was much imitated in antiquity. He was for a time a soldier of fortune, having little sense of discipline, and much readier to take the field in a fit of pique or anger than to fight for an ideal.

Mocking, enthusiastic, mordantly witty (Simonides of Amorgos, who was much concerned with human unhappiness, was one of the few exceptions), iambic poetry was ill-suited to celebrate peace and concord. It urged the reader to make the most of life without attempting to improve the condition of mankind. In the last analysis, men deserve nothing and must be accepted as they are. Ideas of this kind could well form an incentive not only to the extremist forms of hedonism but also to a contempt for activities (war in particular) irreconcilable with a utilitarian philosophy. Iambic poetry carefully avoided anything engendering torment or fear or involving the sensitive and painful side of life.

Unlike the elegy, which had a ceremonial and almost educative character, and the iamb, mainly devoted to satire, melic poetry lent itself better than any other form to expressing the fullness of the poet's feelings, as well as the passions and the innermost longings of the hearer. It was often sung to the accompaniment of music and dancing, together with a sort of stage show. In general the melic poets, at least as far as we can tell from that part of their work which still exists, were not concerned with problems of peace and war or, for that matter, with political problems of any kind. They sang of the pleasures of life, love, wine, and dancing. Theirs was a gay, utterly unmartial type of poetry, as can be seen in the poems of Sappho of Lesbos (seventh-sixth century B.C.) and Anacreon of Teos (sixth century B.C.). The very nature of the poetry—joyous and convivial—meant that it was bound to despise war, the exact opposite of all that the melic poems praised. We may take as an example a fragment by Anacreon in which he condemned war as evil since it robbed society of its bravest sons while allowing the craven to live.[100] Warlike rhetoric was anathema to him, and he made no secret of his disdain for those who dwelt on "tales of strife and lamentable war," preferring those who devoted themselves to "mingling the Muses and the splendid gifts of Aphrodite."[101]

Of the melic poets who wrote in Doric dialect, we must not omit Alcman, the earliest of all (eighth century B.C.). He may not even have been Greek, since he was born in Sardis, capital of Lydia. Brought in slavery to Sparta, he won renown for his skill in interpreting and recording popular traditions and for his choral poems written for choruses of Spartan girls and dealing mainly, of course, with subjects attractive to the popular imagination, such as love, pleasure, and peace. At the basis of his poetry, it would seem, lay a joyful ethic, receptive to pleasure, foreign to any expression of warlike brutality, as summarized in the following words: "Happy the man who lightly weaves the fabric of his days, and sheds no tears."[102] Sparta soon underwent a change to become a state permanently established on a war footing, famous for its rigid system of military organization, but the fact that within its walls at least one man called upon the citizens to enjoy life and to throw off the burdens created by their unrestrained, but restrainable, bellicosity seems significant.

A more organic treatment of the problem may be found in the most famous of Greek lyric poets, whose work—partly because more of it survived—greatly influenced ancient culture. Pindar (518-438 B.C.) was in his prime at the time of the Persian War. Of special interest is one of his collections of epinicia, that is, poems written in honor of victors in gymnastic games and belonging therefore to a literary genre given to exaltation of the warrior type and to praise of strife. But we would search in vain here for the enthusiastic celebration of military victories and Greek valor found in the poetry of Simonides of Ceos (556-ca. 468 B.C.).

There is a note in Pindar's poetry urging the reader to meditate the gravity of war and resist its flattery, and this corresponded to his inclination, at times, to melancholy and his concern with solving problems of community life. In a famous fragment, plainly written in a mood of humility and tolerance Pindar yielded to pessimistic thoughts as to the nature of human actions, too often spoiled by inexperience; the inexpert might allow themselves to be seduced by the exaltation of war, but those who had been through it sorely feared its approach.[103] In another fragment he praised the advantages of serenity and of peace, recalling the ills produced by faction "that bringeth poverty, and is an ill nurse of youth."[104] The same reflections are present in *Olympian Ode IV*, lines 12-16: "May Heaven be gracious to his further prayers, for I praise one who is right ready in the rearing of coursers, one who rejoiceth in welcoming all his guests, and one who in pure heart devoteth himself to Peace that loveth the State."

The poet's sensitivity was supported by the sound common sense of the ordinary man. He saw armed encounters as the fruit of ignorance and emotive fervor, which would be bitterly regretted at the first sight of bloodshed; no sooner the first defeats suffered, no sooner the initial enthusiasm spent. Viewed against this desire for peace "that maketh cities great,"[105] the many wars fought by the Greeks must be seen as so many obstacles to the completion of fruitful work.

The ideal solution was perhaps to be found in a return to the Golden Age, when war was unknown. This perfect condition of life survived, the poet claimed, among certain primitive populations who, because of their simplicity, repudiated violence and lived in peace.[106] When, then, was the ideal climate for a community achieved? When "within her walls dwelleth Law, and her sisters, the firm-set foundation of cities, with Justice and Peace. Fostered beside her are those guardians of wealth for man, the golden daughters of Themis, who excelled in counsel."[107]

Bacchylides of Ceos (fifth century B.C.), a contemporary of Pindar, also showed a markedly gentle humility, considered the indispensable premise for the attainment of prosperity. The anthology of Strobaeus has preserved for us one of his brief compositions in which we find the following message: "Moreover, great Peace bringeth forth for men wealth and the flowers of honey-tongued songs, and for Gods the yellow flame of the burning of the thighs of oxen and fleecy sheep upon fine-wrought altars, and for the young a desire for disport of body and for lute and festal dance." At this point, the poet takes over from the moralist: "Meanwhile in the iron-bound shield-thong hang the warps of the brown spider, headed spear and two-edged sword are whelmed in an ever-spreading rust, and the noise of the brazen trumpet is not;

nor is reft from our eyelids that honey-hearted sleep which soothes the spirit towards dawn. The streets are abloom with delightful feasting and the hymns of children go up like a flame."[108] A "purple passage," then, designed to impress the reader, and bring home to him the weight of painful fatality.

A hedonistic note was also present, as in the verses of Theognis, but it was tempered by greater moral refinement. Men were called upon to take a realistic view of life, to realize how great are the disasters caused by war and to accept the need to put an end to the insane absurdities that made of them robots, victims of a pitiless destiny. The benefits of peace were praised, not only because of the sufferings spared to the humbler classes but also because of the material progress peace ensured for all mankind. This led to a discussion of the mystery of human choices. Why must the individual succumb to the tragic inevitability of conflict when he could just as well live in peace with his neighbor, increasing his moral and material wealth? Why did the individual have to abandon himself to war, which only made human misery more serious and enduring?

Peace and the Tragedians

Tragedy was the literary genre in which the religious feeling suffusing Greek life and the Greeks' profound sense of inescapable fate found their finest expression. In his *Poetics* (VI,2), Aristotle said that tragedy is "a representation of an action that is heroic and complete." By arousing pity and fear, "it effects relief to these and similar emotions." The success of an author, apart from his creative versatility, was rooted in his ability to relate his drama to the expectations and ways of thinking of the public. He should therefore take account of the feelings felt by the majority, like love, fame, the fear of death, and disturbances of an ideological type. The Greek soul was suffused with a sense of dark and inexorable fatality, from which man could free himself only through a long and painful process of atonement. To meet this melancholy characteristic, the tragedians took as their themes ill-starred and unnatural loves, family vendettas worked out over generations, calamities befalling innocent protagonists, feats of war on which hinged many lives. Their warning could have been summarized thus: No joy can be drawn from existence, for in this life there is no depth and all is vanity. Let no one dare to resist destiny, which is in essence pain. Euripides makes the following admonition:

He should err not, who named the old singers in singing
Not cunning, but left-handed bards, for their lays
Did they frame for the mirth-tide, the festal in-bringing
Of the wine, and the feast, when the harp-strings are ringing
To sweeten with melody life's sweet days,
But the dread doom of mortals, the anguish heart-rending—
Never minstrel by music hath breathed on them peace,
Nor by song with his harp-notes in harmony blending,

Albeit thereof cometh death's dark ending
Unto many a home that is wrecked by these.[109]

Faced with the need to explain the cause of pain, the tragedians often found it in the importance enjoyed by injustice in the aberrant worldly relationship between good and ill. Their sensitivity led them to condemn the perverse desire for domination which was peculiar to man, and consequently to the gods, to whom they attributed human qualities and defects. If the religious feeling underlying Greek tragedy is examined carefully, one can detect a steady evolution toward maturer forms which draw their vitality not from external religious manifestations but from the aspirations and the uncertainties of the human soul. It is therefore right to inquire whether the gods often referred to in the tragedies were the same as those to whom citizens and authority turned in the Greek cities when, in the sacrifices and the religious ceremonies, they called for divine protection for the success of absurd conflicts and perverse adventures. In the writings of Aeschylus, Sophocles, and Euripides, this process of refinement and almost sublimation of religious feeling was an unyielding quest for a higher moral and metaphysical life.

This is true even for the work of Aeschylus (524-456 B.C.), father of Greek tragedy, although there is no lack of the epic touch in his plays and although he was inspired, according to the ancients, by Ares and not the muses, as is indicated by his pleasure at the successes which his favorite characters achieve in battle. Nonetheless, there is evidence in the plays of a faith in a reality beyond the world, a reality no longer conditioned by petty earthly interests but disciplined by a transcendent commitment to do good. *The Suppliant Maidens* shows us a Zeus who comes close to personifying a moral will which is the mediating force for the achievement of happiness and serenity. The destiny of men appears plunged, on the one hand, into cruel and fratricidal combat and, on the other, elevated through the quest for a higher justice capable of reuniting what men in their madness have cruelly torn asunder.

Even in the earliest of the tragedians—the most receptive to the heroic suggestions of tradition—traditional mythology was mitigated by new experiences which threw a new and softening light on the monstrosities of war. We can feel in Aeschylus the influence of a morality based on the longing for lasting justice, which was to be given even fuller recognition by Euripides. In *The Persians,* constructed around the theme of resistance to the invader, Aeschylus highlights the sufferings caused by armed conflict. Although at times the pride of the victor might seem legitimate to him, as in the case of the Greek victory over the Persians, nothing could induce him to forget the tears this success had cost.

The Persians showed the impact of war on a defeated people. Hence, were it only for theatrical and poetic reasons, it was bound to stress the theme of unhappiness and pain. The *Agamemnon* makes the ironical point that there is no victory even for the victor. The Aeschylean chorus reaches a peak of dramatic intensity in its mourning description of the battle.[110] The pain suffered by those who had stayed at home, aggravated by the uncertainty of the fate of their loved ones, also had to be remembered. In *The Persians* the warriors' mothers and wives, who, "shuddering at the lengthening delay," had counted the days separating them from the return of their men, were to receive a bitter message of pain and death.[111] Their position was made worse by the defeats suffered by the armies of their country.

In the *Agamemnon* the same problem was seen through the eyes of the woman deprived of the company and aid of her husband, forced to bear alone, in tears, the heavier responsibilities of the family.[112] One feels, in Clytemnestra's words, the bitter certainty that war, source of so many disasters, is useless to solve the problems which have caused it. Problems well beyond the ken of the ordinary man—as, in the extreme case of the war of Troy, the love of a prince for a married woman—are shown in all their tragic futility.[113] Only victory could make the sacrifices tolerable and give meaning to the harrowing and often vain vigil of mothers and wives. After a defeat there was not even the comfort that the exhaustion, the anxiety, the long separation, the upheaval of the families had brought an advantage to the community. All was desolation, suffering, and dramatic fatality, rendered more acute by the realization that the great effort had served no purpose.

In the story told by Aeschylus, the pain generated by war could not be seen as meritorious expiation, a fee paid to ensure success and to guide humanity toward good. This idea, which occurs in certain fragments of the lyric poets—for example in Theognis—would at least have been associated with a process of elevation of mankind, speeding up the attainment of a preordained destiny through suffering. But in the writings of Aeschylus, as for most of the tragedians, this was not the salient note. War was merely an aspect of inexorable and capricious destiny which struck hardest the innocent and the purer spirits, punishing those who least deserved reproach. In no circumstance could their pain be offset by a benefit for the community: There was no atonement by the innocent for the sins of the guilty. In *Seven against Thebes* the poet paints a dark picture of the city in the event of defeat: The warriors would be dead, the children abandoned to themselves would perish, the virgins would be violated, and hard serfdom would be imposed on the few survivors.[114]

An unmistakable feature of Aeschylus' work was, then, his conviction that war throws its own shadow on the cities, poisoning their existence and hampering their progress. The problem is dealt with not only from the angle of the pain caused to individuals, but also from that of the hardships caused to the communities as a whole, robbed of their young men. Though at times the poet condemned those who neglected their duty to defend the fatherland and though he despised the coward, he realized how dangerous was the loss in war of the flower of the race.[115] This explains why the chorus in *The Suppli-*

ant Maidens beseeched Ares to renounce the sacrifice of the youth of Argos.[116] Yet, when the need was to defend the community from enemy aggression, Aeschylus felt that men could be called upon to sacrifice their lives, and he himself took part in the battles of Marathon and of Salamis. As an old man he had introduced into his own epitaph words which proved how much greater weight he attached to his conduct on the battlefield than to his work as a writer. His patriotic vein breaks through in the *Eumenides,* when he depicts Athena promising glory and reward for the soldiers.[117] Despite all this, his tragedies are essentially orientated toward peace, understood as the crowning achievement of a moral world, of which justice is the yardstick and the principal component. His final objective was a society freed from anguish and conflict and restored to purity and happiness, elevated by conscious religious feeling.

The work and the personality of Sophocles (496-406 B.C.), the second of the three great Attic tragedians, must be considered against the background of political and military events which marked the fifth century B.C. Sophocles was already established at the time of the struggle for hegemony between Athens and Sparta prior to the Peloponnesian War. There were already clear signs that the animosities which so severely eroded Greek political life would prepare the ground for the lordship of Macedonia. Compared with the writings of Aeschylus, those of Sophocles (he wrote about 120 plays during his long life but only a few are now extant) reveal a more marked detachment from the traditional characters of popular mythology and more studious care in emphasizing the psychological motives guiding the actions and thoughts of the protagonists. Aeschylus had found material for poetic expression in mythology, which he had colored with warlike rhetoric, achieving what sounded sometimes a rather facile glorification of military exploits. Sophocles, on the other hand, has a more alert and sensitive mind, gives a more intimate refiguration of the myth, and makes a more careful analysis of the psychological and mental storms caused by major events in the Greek world.

His women are figures of grief. Following other models of ancient poetry, woman is depicted as the slave of man and subject in equal measure to his appetites and to his follies. And man is naturally inclined to dominion and violence. Sophocles' aim is to bring the spectator to meditate on human vicissitudes, on their dependence on catastrophes caused by violence, deriving their dramatic character from it. This was a way of drawing public attention to the faults and weaknesses of a society which preferred to squander vital energy, teaching evil, cultivating megalomania, and making a mockery of the virtues of wisdom, equilibrium, and humanity. It was not easy to assume a resolute attitude in this field. The authorities of Athens would not have allowed it, for the government was committed to a policy of hegemony and thus opposed to any propaganda designed to thwart the military and patriotic enthusiasm of the people. Besides, Athenian public opinion, especially in Sophocles' earlier period, had not yet been subjected to the influence of the Sophists and of the other philosophic schools. Audiences were probably little inclined to approve an attitude conflicting with the heroic attitude of life handed down by their ancestors. Sophocles himself was involved in economic and political activities which were difficult to reconcile with any profession of pacifism. His father had been an armaments manufacturer and he himself was given an important war mission in the naval campaign (441-439 B.C.) against the island of Samos, which had rebelled against Athens.

Yet it is significant that in his tragedies he rarely refers to war and that when he is forced to, he does so in a tone betraying his natural aversion to violence and its unhappy consequences. Sometimes his poetry reflects views which may well have been common among the people (views very common in Aristophanes) that war generally cuts down the best, so that all the individual can do is save his life, perhaps even by running away and thus risking being branded as a coward: "War never slays an evil man by choice, But still the good."[118]

Like Aeschylus, Sophocles seldom took opposition to war far enough to form the basis of a moral system. At most, he emphasized the weariness of the warriors, exhausted by long years of fighting, no longer reacting to the collective fervor which nourishes nearly all conflicts. In *Ajax* the task of describing the grief and exhaustion caused by the war and of cursing the memory of the first mortal who taught men the use of arms falls to the chorus of Greek warriors.[119] As already in Aeschylus, an important element of the play is the sympathy generated by the fate of women in general, and in particular those belonging to the defeated nation, left without defense and reduced to serfdom under the victor. They will remain "fatherless, homeless, in an alien land."[120] The accumulation of pain, the counterplay of frenzied passions, the squandering of wealth and human life combine to generate an attitude to war which, though not quite that of open opposition, should induce to moderation when the fate of a whole people hangs in the balance.

It would be too much to infer that this is an author convinced of the superiority of a doctrine concerned with attaining peaceful objectives and that he is committed to their support through his writings. At most, a philosophy of popular type colors Aeschylus' works, guiding the characters toward a certain way of thinking. The same philosophy still prevails in the public opinion of certain countries: People do not dare to challenge openly conventional attitudes to war because it is regarded to some extent as being bound up with traditional values. They lament individual ills and tragedies, grieving for young men cut to pieces in the prime of life, wealth lost, energy squandered. This is an empirical pacifism, which does not derive from a moral way of thinking, but from the practical disadvantages. It is the instinctive reaction of unfortunate people for whom war is an uncalled-for calamity and who, unable to rebel, have no remedy but complaint.

For a logically more justifiable conception of the problem and above all a fuller awareness of its consequences, we must turn to Euripides (480-406 B.C.), the third great Greek tragedian. Although roughly a contemporary of the other two, Euripides was guided by quite a different vision of life. He was the most "speculative" of the Greek tragedians, and dramatic invention gave him an opportunity to comment critically on the nature, the virtues, and the vices of men. Sophistic philosophy, seeking to liberate Greek life and culture from the chains of aristocratic tradition and the religion of the Olympian gods, won over Euripides and led him to abandon the "mythological" patterns and attitudes to which other authors were so attached. The poet came to the conclusion that relationships not guided by a firm desire for peace would do irreparable harm. Under the influence of the Sophists he came out firmly against war, even if it might sometimes be seen as a well-merited and perhaps salutary punishment for men.

Euripides' plays show that his aim was to cut down the characters of legend to human size, so that they lost much of their aura of grandeur and resembled the ordinary man. This approach was not perhaps to the taste of Athenian audiences, who in the annual drama competitions often preferred Sophocles. It was those who came after, rather than his contemporaries, who first discerned in Euripides the penetrating critical capacity and psychological insight which he used to dismantle myths and bring the world of fables down to the level of real life.

What *was* real life? It was certainly more tragic than the "reality" handed down by mythology. For the myths, although they told of an endless series of wars and disasters, set reality against the background of a completely imaginary life. The earthly world of Euripides was that of conflict between Greek peoples, of hegemonic struggles exacerbated by the boundless foolishness of rulers incapable of understanding that only concord could save the polis, otherwise sure to perish under Macedonian imperialism. When Euripides brought the characters of mythology down to the level of day-to-day reality, he was using a method well-fitted for an appraisal of the essence of evil. But by the same token it forced his audiences to recognize and understand the origin of the behavior of men and to dismiss any illusion as to the possibility of improving it beyond certain limits. As a result, Euripides' plays reflect a very personal vision of the world. In his system evil and war heavily overcast the destinies of mankind, contaminating every success achieved through force.

Euripides saw peace as something more immediate and concrete than Aeschylus and Sophocles. For them, it was relegated to the field of mythological legends. For him the feeling of tragic and inexorable fatality arose through awareness that so much grief derived from the madness of men apparently bent on their own destruction. "Oh, vanity of men. You draw the bow too far, and are rightly punished, and yield only in the end, not to the wisdom of friends but to the force of circumstance. And you, the cities, which could overcome your feuds by agreements, prefer to fight it out in the field."[121] This was madness not only because of the pain generated by war, but also because life was too short to allow of the relentless pursuit of animosities on this scale. "Luckless mortals! Why does war ever have to break out and why must you exterminate one another? Give up this quarreling and stay at home in peace. Leave others in peace, too. Life is short. Try to live away from pain, if you can. Avoid these troubles."[122]

In *The Suppliants,* Euripides is concerned with another illusion: the warmonger's blind confidence that only the other side is liable to suffer in a conflict, while his side will always emerge unharmed and victorious. Peoples and rulers seldom perceive that fate portions out disasters equally and even the victor must suffer. The herald of Euripides confirmed this idea:

> When a community votes in favor of war, no one thinks of the possibility of his own death. Everyone is quite sure that only others can be killed. But if the real implications were properly realized, nobody would ever succumb to the temptation to fight. And yet we can all choose between the two decisions, distinguish good from evil, appreciate the advantages of peace over war. Peace, dear to the Muses, enemy of the Furies, friend of fecundity and of wealth: these are the blessing we forego, fools that we are! We rate war higher than these benefits, to enslave the weak to the strong, one state to another, one man to another.[123]

Comments of this kind occur quite frequently. We find similar ones in *The Daughters of Troy,* lines 95-97: "Fool, sacking towns, laying temples waste, desecrating tombs, the sanctuaries of the dead! He who sows destruction shall reap destruction"; and in *Helen,* lines 1151-1160: "You senseless beings, athirst for glory among death-dealing weapons, believing, in your ignorance, that you will find some remedy for the misery of men. If blood is to be the arbiter of peace, strife between men will know no end; it is strife that brought the sons of Helen low and made them guests in subterranean kingdoms."

These passages are not to be seen as individual statements of views or outbursts of pain and irritability, used to achieve certain dramatic effects. Euripides is concerned with something more complex, the outcome of a renewed philosophic and moral outlook, challenging the entire traditional religious system handed down by previous generations. This is why he does not spare those established values, even the gods themselves, that are responsible for many disasters, wars in particular. Apparently accepting a kind of fatalism but in fact attacking sharply the personality conventionally attributed to the divinities, he lays at their door responsibility for the catastrophes that had befallen Greece and her inhabitants. Precisely when he perceived that the Trojan conflict was the expression of Zeus' desire to relieve the world of its excess population, to destroy Troy and punish Greece while offering its most deserving sons an opportunity to cover themselves in glory,[124] the poet, with great insight, formulated a judgment on a whole religion, convicted by him of having neglected the best qualities of man and having favored the harmful ones and of representing the gods as incapable of rising beyond any worldly, and thus rudimentary and oversimplified, idea of existence.

He voiced the anguish of a generation which owed much to philosophy and was less disposed to take at face value the impositions and deceits of politicians who had a vested interest in persuading ordinary citizens to bear arms. Though he very effectively described the horror of some of his contemporaries and of their Sophist-trained guides at the bloodshed caused by war, Euripides remained a man of his time and was by no means insensitive to the ordeals of which Athena was the tragic protagonist. While his city was involved in wars which would determine its survival as the focal point of civilization, was it right that a successful writer should take refuge behind an attitude of consistent and direct opposition, helping to spread the feeling of discontent and rebellion? All pacifists have faced a dilemma of this kind, torn between loyalty to their principles and loyalty to their country at war. Some have behaved like Romain Roland, who went into voluntary exile in a neutral state and devoted himself to helping the victims of the First World War. This is the attitude of the intransigent, for whom aversion to violence inspires clear-cut choices. For others a severely consistent line of conduct which would oblige them to leave their homeland, perhaps without the hope of return, is not in their nature. They are inclined to accept the policy of their country, were it only because they do not know how to cope with the uncertainties of underground life and a struggle against civil authorities. This is the case of authors, like Euripides, whose pacifism is sincere although they are not ready to sacrifice everything for it. In their works some passages of a definitely pacifist type are to be found, but other passages seem to echo and encourage opinions already favored by the public.

While retaining his basic view that war is perversion, Euripides sometimes allows himself a measure of admiration for those who have given their lives for the fatherland. Without betraying his preference for peaceful solutions or abandoning his moral vision, he urged that prizes and honors be awarded to those who had fallen or who had distinguished themselves in battle, as reflected in these lines (400-404) from *The Daughters of Troy*:

> To avoid war is the duty of every wise man. But if he is forced to fight, it is wrong to refuse him the crown for having laid down his life for his community. To die in an ugly cause brings only dishonor. So mother, do not weep for thy country or for thy bed.

Euripides sought to show in a favorable light characters willing to go calmly to their deaths in the certainty that they would be rewarded in the grateful memory of men and by the generous benevolence of the gods. An example is given by Creon in the *Phoenician Maidens* (lines 995-1005), when he praises the brave and rejects a cowardly course of action suggested to him by his father.

This one might forgive in age; but I could ask for no forgiveness if I were to betray the fatherland to which I owe my life. Therefore, be certain of one thing. I shall save the city and give my soul to death for my people. There would only be shame for me if men, constrained by no oracles, nor bound by fate, should stand shoulder to shoulder and look death in the face, fighting outside the walls for their city, while I, betraying father, brother and country, should run like a coward from my own land! Wherever I should wander thereafter, people would look on me only with contempt.

A similar sentiment is expressed in *Iphigeneia at Aulis,* when the protagonist offers herself spontaneously as sacrificial victim to make the divine auspices propitious. What is the genesis and what are the limits of Euripides' painful vision of existence? To understand him, we must follow a psychological analysis (the filial drama and paternal drama, personal feelings linked up with the future of the community) and also seek to understand the deeper mission of one who feels keenly the drama of war and is prepared to sacrifice himself for the good of all.

If they are examined carefully, it will be seen that these and other passages in Euripides' plays do not conflict with his general view of life and his criticisms of religion and politics. Assessing the reality of existence and the fickleness of human behavior, he felt that certainties and firm attitudes were no more than shadows bound to disappear at the first breath of wind and that men were mad when they insisted on fighting among themselves over petty issues. We have already seen that among the Greek philosophical systems, those which denied all importance to worldly events, arguing that truth does not exist, or if it does exist, cannot be known, opposed the warmongers, who justified their behavior only through blind faith in their own opinions. So it was with Euripides, whose Sophistic training often led him to question truths apparently confirmed by the senses. He doubted even life and death, their essence and their limits, and he could find no frontier between the initial reality and the final reality which mark off the course of existence. In the *Gorgias,* Plato refers to these profound uncertainties in Euripides' philosophy when he puts the following words into the mouth of Socrates: "For I tell you, I should not wonder if Euripides' words were true, when he says: 'Who knoweth if to live is to be dead,/And to be dead to live?'"[125] Although no trace of these lines has been found in the writings of Euripides which have come down to us, they are obviously of Sophistic origin. Inspired by a penetrating spirit of observation and a gift of reflection on man and god, in particular the important problem of the last ends, they were certainly intended to underline the difficulty of distinguishing truth from falsehood. They are an attack on the frontier, whatever its nature, between life and death, showing that the motive elements of being are in a cyclical relationship and that the constant contact and impact of this life on life beyond the grave are the key facts governing human existence.

It might be inferred that Euripides came close to anticipating the Christian message in the form of an existence reborn, in which every contamination suffered in the worldly life because of sin was atoned for in a spiritual world. But this would be a hasty conclusion. He was probably recounting a reminiscence, relived and made immediate by recent Sophistic experiences. All this nonetheless confirms the poet's orientation, a degree of relativity in his moral attitude to individual destiny and the organization of the state. If, as a result, the key problem of life was also called into question to such an extent that the dividing line between existence and nonexistence became difficult to discover, then so many other generally accepted values—for example, the sacrifice of life on the altar of the fatherland—were of negligible significance and doubtful validity.

The unreliability of traditional values is emphasized in a number of passages, the poet's aim being the regeneration of the state through different institutions and rules from those deemed final and immutable by Greek tradition. Euripides sought to raise his argument to a level much higher than that set by the Sophists and to bring out the lasting contrast between the real interests which touch the individual in his material and spiritual life and those often fictitious and imaginary ones imposed by the holders of religious and civil power. He gave the rulers a lesson of humility, explaining that it was wrong for them to place objects of aggrandizement and worldly glory at the top of their list of objectives, but that they should concentrate on wisdom and humanity, to the benefit of all men and not only the citizens of their states.

The same criticism applied for the generals. They sought glory at all costs and were indifferent to the fate of the soldiers, who had little prospect of earning glory and every prospect of suffering in the terrible encounters of war.

> Alas, what evil customs hold in Greece? When armies rear trophies over vanquished enemies, the credit goes not to those who have suffered; the general reaps the glory. Although he is only one man among ten thousand wielding their swords, although he has done no more than the others, he is the one to be praised. Sitting in proud authority, such men scorn the city's common folk, although they have no virtue of their own. The others are infinitely more competent than they are; and would prevail if wisdom had authority for an ally.[126]

And again:

> Later when you led the Argives all to war, while seers brought you heaven's warning, you despised them, flouted the gods and so ruined thy state. Young men led you astray. It was they, in their thirst for honor, who dared ignore what is right, multiplying wars, the bane of the people! The one thirsts for command, the other longs for power to satisfy his passions. Yet another pursues riches. But none is concerned with the suffering people.[127]

The reference to the internal politics of Athens is obvious. This last passage is followed by eight lines which have been regarded as a later interpolation, although both in concept and language they seem completely Euripidean. They exalt the "just mean," that is, the middle class which keeps well inside extremisms. The rich, busy increasing their fortunes, take no interest in general questions of state, and the poor, who have nothing to lose and nothing to fear from change, since it cannot worsen their plight, fall easy prey to troublemakers and agitators. The best citizens are therefore those belonging to the middle class, loyal to the institutions if only because they have a vested interest. Comments of the same kind (Aristotle held a similar view) are present in other writings of Euripides and show that he had a natural inclination toward compromise, so necessary in the internal life of a city.[128] It is not only a personal inclination but also the result of study. One cannot reach an objective unless he desires to do so; he must be realistic, stand up to adversity, overcome the inevitable obstacles if a solution is to be found and a reform program effectively implemented. With this aim in view the ground must be cleared of the vices which weigh so monstrously on the nature of men and cause so many disasters. Among these the most harmful is ambition, in the service of which politicans and generals unhesitatingly subordinate the lives of their fellow citizens and the fortunes of the country.

> Why, my son, are you guided by ambition, the worst of the gods? Resist her temptations! She is a goddess beyond the law. In many happy houses **and cities** her arrival and departure have brought disaster for her followers. She makes them mad. It is far better, my son, to honor equality, which forever unites friends with friends, cities with cities, allies with allies.[129]

Euripides was not content, however, to emphasize certain feelings and truths with ill humor and to reprove rulers for being too often the slaves of lower instincts and bereft of wisdom and moderation. The passages quoted—and others as well—almost without exception express, on the one hand, a deep love of peace, based on the certainty that only in this way can serenity and prosperity be ensured for men, and on the other hand, a vigorous repudiation of a dogmatic view of life and of relations between peoples. In all his work—in this respect, more committed than that of the earlier tragic poets—the moral awareness of the Greek people, matured by war and the abrasive force of the new philosophy, rebels against mythology and the traditional concept of duty and honor, which made power, and particularly armed power, the key to the rulers' choices and the yardstick of success. The lesson to be drawn from the writings of Euripides is that it is not force which should be considered as a prerogative of divinity but mercy and goodness, virtues of which man stand in ever greater need.

By attacking mythology—stories which had shown the gods in an all-too-human light as warmongers and war-lovers almost above all else—Euripides built up an opposition to war, showing it to be not so much the unavoidable necessity imposed by the gods as a catastrophe that human will could avoid or mitigate.

It is not possible for us to assess how far Euripides' poetry influenced the thinking of his contemporaries and affected their decisions. But subsequent developments in Greek politics suggest that his message went unheard—probably because, with his professions of Sophistic faith, his general mood of pessimism, and with the imprecations he placed in the mouths of his protagonists, the great tragedian denounced a harmful reality without proposing solutions. His was a moral attitude, not a political approach, and it was to have little effect or to be lost among the deceiving clichés which rulers use to dispose of poetic predictions.

Aristophanes' Comedies and the Yearning for Peace

Perhaps the right way to tackle the problem of peace was from the satiric point of view, stressing the contradictions between appearances and reality, between the noble-sounding claims of the politicians, ready at any time to risk other people's lives with the familiar argument that their own honor is at stake, and the actual facts of existence in a world in which such attitudes so often brought nothing but disaster.

Of the Greek city-states, Athens was the one whose citizens had the strongest inclination for controversy, and where writers were freest and best able to express their aversion to war. The vicissitudes of the Peloponnesian War, which broke out in 431 B.C., revived a spirit of violent criticism of the institutions, for it was clear from the outset that the war could lead to nothing but political serfdom. The longing for peace, naively formulated as expectation of the return of the Golden Age or more dramatically in the harrowing verses of Euripides, was expressed in Athens through the medium of comedy. The public favored this literary genre, as a welcome distraction from the sufferings caused by the struggle with Sparta.

Because it guaranteed freedom of speech and judgment for all, the democratic regime of Athens encouraged the development of comedy, the expression of sophisticated intelligence and critical insight. The comedy-writer—at least initially—was free to explore recesses in the human soul which, among other peoples, were shrouded in an aura of reverence and almost sacred respect. The liberty which allowed them to pillory even the most highly placed politicians generated not only an expression of original art of which the modern theater is the direct descendant, but facilitated the maturing of ideas which soon became part and parcel of the Greek legacy. Comedy-writers were not content to ridicule a few aspects of the lives of the citizens and the communities, but brought the weapon of words to bear on underlying motives and pronounced features of Hellenic civilization and life in general. And if the exigencies of the performance forced authors to treat problems of overall significance in an empirical manner, this did not mean that they ignored the major currents of contemporary thought. Peace and war and their implications for society could not escape what was often a destructive and always an acute examination in Attic comedy. An idea of the incidence of this problem is given if we reflect that three of the eleven extant comedies of Aristophanes (ca. 448-ca. 385 B.C.) concern the need to end the Peloponnesian War.

And yet, though Athenians were free to say and write what they wanted, it must not be forgotten that precisely in Athens, because of the economic situation and because of Pericles' imperialist policy, citizens were more susceptible to the romance and fascination of war than elsewhere. For this reason the Periclean age is now seen as that of the greatest flowering in art and culture but also of the most flagrant manifestations of aggressive intolerance. The Athenians' disposition and education made them at one and the same time appreciative of the pleasures of intellectual activity and an easy prey to the most vulgar appeals to violence. In a famous passage, Thucydides emphasizes these specific traits of character as he reports a speech made by the representatives of Corinth before the Spartan people calling on them to take up arms.

> For they [the Athenians] are given to innovation and quick to form plans and to put their decisions into execution, whereas you are disposed merely to keep what you have, to desire nothing new, and, when you do take action, not to carry to completion even what is indispensable. Again, they are bold beyond their strength, venturesome beyond their better judgment, and sanguine in the face of dangers; while your way is to do less than your strength warrants, to distrust even what your judgment is sure of, and when dangers come to despair of deliverance. Nay more, they are prompt in decision, while you are dilatory; they stir abroad, while you are perfect stay-at-homes; for they expect by absence from home to gain something, while you are afraid that, if you go out after something, you may imperil even what you have. If victorious over their enemies, they pursue their advantage to the utmost; if beaten, they fall back as little as possible. Moreover, they use their bodies in the service of their country as though they were the bodies of quite other men, but their minds as though they were wholly their own, so as to accomplish anything on her behalf. And whenever they have conceived a plan but fail to carry it to fulfillment, they think themselves robbed of a possession of their own; and whenever they go after a thing and obtain it, they consider that they have accomplished but little in comparison with what the future has in store for them; but if it so happens that they try a thing and fail, they form new hopes instead and thus make up the loss. For with them alone is it the same thing to hope for and to attain when once they conceive a plan, for the reason that they swiftly undertake whatever they determine upon.[130]

Probably this description is partly from imagination and partly based on hearsay. Nonetheless it gives a fair idea of what the other Greeks thought of the Athenians, their empire, and their determination to defend it and add to it.

The outbreak of the Peloponnesian War was followed by the invasion of Attica by the Spartans. The country-folk fled to Athens, where they lived in dire poverty and in crowded conditions. The Athenians had planned for a long war of attrition to wear down the resistance of the enemy and enable the Athenian navy to engage in offensive action in the Peloponnesus. If the strategy was to be effectively applied, firm unity of policy was essential. But the critical situation around the city strengthened feeling against Pericles, who was dismissed from office and impeached for peculation. Rehabilitated soon afterwards and reelected *strategus,* he died of the plague in 429 B.C.[131] His death encouraged the rise of the extreme wing of the democratic party, which expressed the resentment and discontent of the more modest classes and the refugees, who were longing to go home. This was the time of the demagogue Cleon, ruthless, ambitious, and unsubtle, who dominated the Athenian stage for some years.

The situation became more confused after a second invasion of Attica. There followed a change of heart among the refugees, who began to hanker for peace. Perhaps, after all, the price of foregoing revenge against the invading Spartans was not too much to pay. Although Cleon had been their spokesman at the time of the death of Pericles, they began now to question his "total war" policy. Feeling ran high and opinions clashed, creating an atmosphere charged with bitterness. Deeper quarrels caused by the economic and social situation added to the general war-weariness. For one thing the rich were divided among themselves; some of them had done well out of the war and increased their wealth by trading in army supplies; the land of others had suffered irreparable damage and they were reduced to a pittance. Then there was the city proletariat, whose eyes had been opened by the complaints and demands of the refugees to new social and political horizons, so that discontent intensified.

With disorder everywhere few citizens were in a position to decide exactly where their interest lay and what side they should take in the quarrels. As always in time of crisis, people tended to confuse cause and effect. The speculators were blamed for the shortage of necessities, but then it also appeared that the shortage of necessities favored speculation. Many people believed that the arms manufacturers were fostering a continuation of hostilities. In many passages in Aristophanes, particularly in the *Peace,* dislike of arms manufacturers and profiteers is undisguised.[132]

This is the context in which we should consider the plays, particularly the *Acharnians,* produced in 425 B.C., during one of the most critical periods in the Peloponnesian War. In the play Dikaiopolis, an Athenian farmer forced to leave the land and seek refuge in the city, has succeeded in concluding his own private treaty with Sparta. He thus escapes military service, while the Athenians, who had rejected his proposals for an immediate peace, must go on fighting. Accused of treason by charcoal burners of the Attic deme of Acharne (hence the title of the play), he saves himself from execution by donning a tragic actor's costume lent to him by Euripides and making a speech in his own defense. In the course of a succession of amusing scenes, he ensures for himself, despite the general poverty, a comfortable and peaceful existence.

The *Acharnians* belongs to the pacifist literature of all time. It is of little importance that accidental circumstances led to its composition and that its comic vein may seem inappropriate to its ideological message, since valid contributions to human progress—not infrequently the result of accidental circumstances—have often been conveyed through satire. The comedy betrays the influence of the Sophists, of whom Aristophanes himself, a few years later, was to make fun in *The Clouds.* Nevertheless they always affected his thinking, as they did that of Euripides. We can see this, in particular, in the behavior and the ways of reasoning of his characters. Dikaiopolis aligns his conduct on a moral rule conflicting with that of the fatherland. The fact that in a democratic assembly the people had voted for the continuation of the war was in his view in no way binding and he believed himself entitled to take independent decisions. This is evidence of the decay of the traditional principles of the polis: Dikaiopolis had nothing but contempt for the principles, because he was convinced that the soldiers and politicians were motivated solely by ambition and lust for power. Arbitrary judgments and personal interest govern the words and the actions of the characters. The once unchallenged duty committing every citizen to fight and, if necessary, lay down his life for his country, faded and was replaced by an ethical concept having a wider horizon than the polis and based on a principle of utility. Moreover, the ideological apprehensions of the Sophists concerning politicians seemed to be confirmed by the conduct of Cleon, at the time the most powerful man in Athens, who was determined to continue the hostilities; his obstinacy in this matter is well testified by Thucydides.[133]

But it would be a mistake to imagine that the *Acharnians* is merely an episodic representation of contemporary events and does not interpret wider feelings and deeper ideas. The banality of the accidents which lead to war, though demonstrated in humorous and satirical terms, is brought home in all its tragic reality—a warning the relevance of which has perhaps never been fully understood.[134] Audiences were compelled to acknowledge the madness of politicians, whose choices owed much more to impulse and anger than to reason. Aristophanes makes an important and subtle point when he says that war, however and for whatever reason declared, brings out the pettiest impulses in man, impelling him to commit acts of injustice and abuse.[135] The conclusion from this was that even if the case for war seems sound, it is, as a matter of principle, always preferable to avoid it, since there is no way of foreseeing the outcome and men are always carried away by their worst instincts. The passage also forces the reader to reflect that although it is customary to blame the enemy for the conflict, responsibility often lies in fact with the one who claims to be the victim. Usually the blame should be equally allocated between the two sides, because of their inability to achieve an agreement or a compromise.

The performance of the *Acharnians* was certainly not enough to win back peace. The tragic harvest of destruction and sorrow continued unabated. Cleon's obstinacy was matched by that of the Spartan Brasidas, also a zealous supporter of war. But the citizens and the soldiers were weary beyond measure, mainly because they felt that only the ill will of politicians stood in the way of peace.

In the *Knights,* a comedy first performed in 424 B.C., Cleon was accused by Aristophanes of wishing to pursue the war in order to keep the population crowded together in the city in a state of unparalleled promiscuity and poverty. His real aim was to consolidate his power and distract public opinion from social and economic abuses by making the most of the issues connected with war. Aristophanes was not the only man to make these severe criticism; Thucydides, who was perhaps not wholly impartial, spoke of Cleon as an obstinate warmonger: "He thought if quiet were restored he would be more manifest in his villainies and less credited in his calumnies."[136]

In the years between 427 and 423 B.C. the fortunes of war swayed to and fro, with victories and reverses on both sides. Cleon distinguished himself in the conquest of the island of Sphacteria, which led to the capture of four hundred Spartan hoplites and an upsurge in Athenian prestige. But the Spartans, led by Brasidas, also achieved successes. Then at last came the violent clash of Amphipolis (423 B.C.), in which both Cleon and Brasidas lost their lives. It therefore became possible in 421 B.C. to negotiate the peace of Nicias, named after the leading Athenian plenipotentiary. Both sides were tired of the war and realized they could never achieve dominance over the other.

When the conclusion of peace seemed imminent and a change in the general outlook was already evident, Aristophanes staged *Peace,* a drama of considerable comic and poetic power. Desiring to end the hostilities, Trygaios, the protagonist, decides to ride to heaven on a gigantic beetle. He discovers that the gods, disgusted with the quarrelsome Greeks, have abandoned their heavenly quarters to Polemos, the war god. Having imprisoned Irene, the goddess of peace, in a well, Polemos is preparing to crush the Greek cities. Aided by the chorus, Trygaios seeks to liberate the goddess and her companions, and after two fruitless attempts their efforts are eventually successful. In the epilogue the poet expresses the people's gratitude to Trygaios, who, having reestablished peace, can at last celebrate his own wedding. The comedy ends with praise of the peaceful life and of the joyful serenity of the fields.

Seldom has a literary composition been influenced to such an extent by current events, known to the spectators. References to the condition of Greece are legion. With an obvious allusion to the responsibility of the two captains, Polemos, when preparing to bray the Greek cities in the mortar, observes that he has no pestle following the deaths of Cleon and Brasidas, and

Trygaios issues a famous appeal to feelings of brotherliness, designed to convince the Greeks of the need for unity:

'Tis now, O Greeks, the moment when, freed of quarrels and fighting, we should rescue sweet Peace and draw her out of this pit, before some other pestle prevents us. Come, laborers, merchants, workmen, artisans, strangers, whether you be domiciled or not, islanders, come here. Greeks of all countries, come hurrying here with picks and levers and ropes! 'Tis the moment to drain a cup in honor of Good Fortune.[137]

Enthusiasm elicited an equally enthusiastic response. The coryphaeus, praising the spirit of Hellenic solidarity, responds (lines 301-302): "Come hither all! Quick, quick, hasten to the rescue! All peoples of Greece, now is the time or never, for you to help each other. You see yourselves freed from battles and all their horrors of bloodshed."

Thus the spiritual unity of the Greeks is an unmistakable objective of Aristophanes' comedies. His work expresses again and again the conviction that war is the great corrupter of man, over whom it throws a deep shadow. Every greatness born of war was therefore poisoned from the outset. In these plays a longing for serenity and peace recurs as a leitmotif whose magic seemed to enchant both protagonists and spectators. On several occasions the plays refer to the pacifying spirit which should regulate human relationships but all too often, is banned from them. There is a constant appeal to the life of the fields. Since farming favors prosperity born of work, it enables the citizen to appreciate the advantages of the life of the mind and gifts like "odor of sweet fruits, of festivals, of the Dionysia, of the harmony of flutes, of the comic poets, of the verses of Sophocles, of the phrases of Euripides."[138]

But the experience gained and the pain suffered proved insufficient to prevent the Greeks from falling again into the same errors. The peace of Nicias proved little more than a truce, scarcely long enough to allow the two sides to refit before taking the field with unabated violence. As before, fierce rivalry between generals, especially between the Athenian strategians, Nicias and Alcibiades, lay at the root of the conflict. The events that followed were to culminate in the expedition to Sicily, which resulted in the defeat of the Athenian navy and of the death of 50,000 soldiers (414 B.C.). Once again poverty and pain were reflected in the poetry of Aristophanes, this time in the *Lysistrata,* performed in 411 B.C. The plot may be summarized briefly: Since women are the ones who suffer most from wars imposed by men, the women of Athens, guided by one of their number, Lysistrata, decide to force continence on their husbands until a really lasting peace has been achieved. They therefore leave the men and withdraw to the Acropolis. The Spartan women have also, and for the same reasons, deserted the marital bed. Hence a series of comic incidents, some lewd, concerning the reestablishment of peace between the Athenians and the Spartans. The comedy was both funny and effective. It diffused what was in fact a political message, by making it accessible to a vast public.

Fourteen years had gone by since the performance of the *Acharnians*. The situation of Greece had grown worse, for the conflict became chronic and was costing more and more lives. The folly of civil war was clear beyond all possible doubt. Speaking out for Hellenic solidarity, Aristophanes sees the war for what it is. Of particular importance was the psychological context in which he assesses the problem of war and its consequences. The *Acharnians* had found its justification in the drama of the refugees; now the plot was dominated by the no less painful plight of women abandoned by the men who had left for the front.

Certain idealistic elements already noted in earlier plays of Aristophanes achieved greater importance in *Lysistrata*. The story was a mere literary device to illustrate the argument that if the Greeks wished to survive the dangers immanent in their geographic and political situation, they would have to bury their differences and acknowledge the bonds between them. Aristophanes was concerned not only with Athens, but with all Greece, as a historic and moral unity, the noble sponsor of an unfolding civilization capable of defending itself from external stresses and dangers and of becoming the source not only of its own renewal but of that of non-Greek peoples as well. A definite pan-Hellenic ideal was discernible: "And now, dear friends, I wish to chide you both, that related by blood, all brethren sprinkling the selfsame altars from the selfsame laver, at Pylae, Pytho, and Olympia, and many others, that, with barbarian foes armed, looking on, you should fight and destroy Hellenes!"[139] In other passages of the *Lysistrata*, it was still the immutable popular wisdom which prompted condemnation of the war as the cause of bereavement and disaster and which appealed to peace of mind as the source of joy and prosperity.[140] All was sublimated in the wider vision of real community interests and in the conviction that these could not be served by war.

Any judgment of the works of Aristophanes must be made in the context of the "old comedy," a style of mordant satire reflecting contemporary Athens, where everybody knew everybody else and political life, like the religious, philosophical, and literary debates, often took on an anecdotic and personal character. Therefore the theater became useful as a means of pressure at the disposal of the parties in an election campaign, as well as a means of forcing an enemy into exile. Authors sought to indulge the popular tastes and inclinations of the moment. There were no religious or moral barriers since every subject was open to criticism. This explains why Aristophanes' plays have been regarded as having no moral content and he is alleged to have intended only to entertain the public through puns and facile theatricality. He was also often considered the enemy of innovation and the paladin of the conservative party in the struggle against democracy, especially democracy as represented by Cleon.

In fact the problem was more complex. As a comic poet, Aristophanes was entitled to jibe at society's crimes and follies, which in the case in point were supplied to him by the democratic regime in power. But this did not make him its absolutely uncompromising foe. He also attacked the Sophists, although he appreciated their dialectical ability and the message immanent in a few key ideas. Evidence of his favorable attitude to democracy is his failure to take part in the oligarchic Athenian revolution of the years 411 and 402 B.C. Above all, in his literary work his leaning to pacifism went well beyond the mere episodes from which it started and took the form of an actual moral commitment. He disliked cheap rhetorical attitudes. In the contest between Sparta and Athens he saw no reason to side with his fellow-citizens when he felt they were in the wrong. In fact, he could show considerable impartiality and resist the emotive pressures so prevalent in time of war. That this was possible is a tribute to the liberal atmosphere of Athenian democracy.

Aristophanes was deeply aware that the man and the artist must inevitably give way to common interests. These were related to the needs of individuals, with their modest anxieties and modest aspirations. The characters of his comedies are humble folk—artisans, farmers, workers—people who had everything to lose and nothing to gain from war and for whom the great men of the earth, the politicians and the generals, seemed to have precious little concern. They often voice their desire for a simple but serene life, free of intellectual complications, a life in which the basic necessities are given proper recognition and are not sacrificed to false values. We must penetrate deeply into this spirit in order to understand his concept of society. The Peloponnesian War—so went his reasoning—had lasted for years without ever reaching a decisive solution, though the countryside had been depopulated and the villages had fallen in ruins. Refugees were crowded together in Athens, the victims of epidemics, hunger, and the demagogy of the politicians. There *must* be some way of putting an end to so much misery. Most of the characters in the three comedies we have considered believed that they could act directly breaking off from the rest of the community, ignoring the voice of common sense. The result was a sort of practical philosophy, of the type appreciated in times of crisis by simple souls who cannot see beyond the narrow world of their interest and pain. Hence the various paradoxical situations described through the actions of persons for whom the persistence of the war was the major obstacle to the achievement of a happy life: a life linked to the alternation of the seasons, the regular return of harvest-time, compliance with ancestral customs, the mythical intervention in earthly happenings by the gods, whose defects and virtues reflected on a hugely magnified scale the defects and virtues of men.

To achieve their objectives, Aristophanes' characters resorted to expedients typical of people unaware of the existence of a higher justice and treating relations between men and gods as a matter of pure self-interest. The poet sometimes advised them to take personal initiatives and to impute to others the responsibility for the plight of man. In general, there is no evidence here of any intent to establish a moral order governed by equity. But at other times the poet showed sympathy for the psychological and moral changes which had occurred in those very years and which led some observers to look beyond traditional religion for the satisfaction of their longing for justice. His vision of the calamities caused by the war was often expressed in terms of the new approach worked out by the Sophists.

Peace and the Greek Historians

The ability of the Greeks to record the events of their times in literary compositions remarkable for profundity of research, for richness of information, and for an outstanding gift of exposition was a major feature of their civilization. The earliest historians were concerned mainly with legends in which the gods played an important role in worldly events; we have very little reliable information on these writers and only a few fragments of their work have survived. We shall therefore proceed immediately to a consideration of Herodotus of Halicarnassus (ca. 484-425 B.C.), rightly styled the "father of history."

Herodotus, too, failed to shake off the feeling that man's affairs were governed by the will of the gods. He is much concerned to read a moral lesson into the events he records and uses them to illustrate his faith in a superior avenging justice, which is often applied out of all proportion to the gravity of the offense. Hence, he believed that the punishment of guilty men was sometimes visited on their children and that of the individual on the whole community. A sense of obscure fatality pervades his narrative, impairing its critical value and leaving it a mere chronicle of events handed down by word of mouth and accepted unselectively, in relation to certain political objectives. Herodotus held no specific views as to the good or ideal society. He favored democracy and liberty, rather than aristocracy and despotism, but offered no justification for this preference. The lack of formal unity and of any specific ideological approach in his writing makes it difficult to discern the guiding line of his thought on ethical problems. His approach is pragmatic for he refuses to be bound by any law of consistency in judging men and their conduct. Rather he examines them case by case, sometimes considering only certain aspects, sometimes their behavior only at certain times.

The particular situation of the Greek communities of Asia Minor, constantly threatened by the Persian empire, went far to justify his attitude. He shows a kind of agnosticism with regard to the ideological struggles which ravaged the communities of the Hellenic peninsula, since these struggles did not often involve cities of the Greek *diaspora*, some of which—as in the case of Halicarnassus, his birthplace—were in fact subject to foreign sovereignty or influence. He himself was born a Persian and had lived in the paralyzing atmosphere of Oriental despotism. Greek ideas with regard to democracy and liberty had little or no significance for a society ignorant of their value and importance. When he moved to peninsular Greece and from there set out to explore the Mediterranean world, Herodotus absorbed the lines of thinking and the political principles which were, so to speak, the foundation of Hellenic life. But his experiences as a curious traveler, engaged perhaps in trading and therefore obliged to maintain good relations with the authorities in the places visited, aggravated rather than corrected his eagerness to compromise. This explains his reluctance to judge individuals and events and his inclination to leave it to the reader to form a conclusive opinion. Obviously, he saw his role as that of a collector of the chronicles, often contradictory, circulating in the Hellenic world, not as a precursor or a reformer from whom a critical judgment could be expected.

His moral principles were much too simple, based as they were on a diffuse pessimism and on the certainty that selfish motives determined the conduct of men. Perhaps the situation of contemporary Greece, a myriad of miniature states constantly squabbling among themselves, prevented the formation of any pan-Hellenic mentality. Too often it happened that a Hellenic city appealed for the military support of non-Greek powers, particularly the Persians. In a significant passage Herodotus explains that the Argives remained neutral during the Persian War because of their desire to maintain their own forces intact in case of a war against the Spartans and their inability to agree on a commander for the combined military forces. This is Herodotus' conclusion: "At that—say the Argives—they deemed that the Spartans' covetousness was past all bearing, and that it was better to be ruled by foreigners than [to] give way to the Lacedaemonians."[141]

There were then some Greeks who preferred subjection to the foreigner to the discipline imposed by the feeling of belonging to a common fatherland. Herodotus did not criticize their attitude. He saw men as individuals motivated solely by selfishness. They sought only to increase their wealth and power, ignoring, if need be, any criteria of justice or liberty. Sin, moral poverty, insensitivity to the pain of others were therefore the keys to human conduct. So much pessimism led him to pour scorn on any policy pursued as a matter of principle.

In regard to war, what could be the attitude of a writer so skeptical as to the qualities of the individual and free of illusions as to the possibility of regenerating society? It is wise to distinguish his views according to whether the matter considered is one of personal or of collective ethics. In the first case his judgment regarding war arises from concern for the interests of the individual and distaste for the sufferings generated by every conflict. The following reflection—Croesus is speaking to Cyrus—confirms the point: "No man is so foolish as to desire war more than peace: for in peace sons bury their fathers, but in war fathers bury their sons."[142] He believed war between peoples of the same race, especially between Greeks, to be monstrous. Expressing a personal judgment, he writes: "Civil strife is as much worse than united war as war is worse than peace."[143] Only one instrument could settle the quarrels between the Greeks: arbitration. "Yet, speaking as they do the same language, they should end their disputes by the means of heralds and messengers, and by any way rather than fighting."[144]

In terms of a collective code of behavior, Herodotus thought war the lowest form of human conduct, the consequence of a state of madness. It was typical of communities incapable of self-control, who adopted their decisions in response to emotive impulses and not after reasoned assessment. Peoples take up arms—this appears to be his teaching—when they are immersed in a state of mental confusion which prevents them from weighing calmly the facts of a situation. And wars between the Greeks were the fullest expression of total insanity. Herodotus could not avoid condemning an attitude which weakened his compatriots, sapping their power to resist the barbarians. When he examines their relations with other peoples, he leans toward compromise and against what we should now call cold-war "brinkmanship," to which the Greeks of Asia Minor, victims of an emotive state of mind peculiar to peoples living in border areas, were particularly prone. Perhaps because of his experiences and his education, he believed that an understanding with the Persians was desirable. His idea of the wise ruler was Callias, who negotiated the peace which was given his name (448 B.C.). The peace of Callias established a *modus vivendi* between the Persian empire and the Greek communities of Asia Minor. Herodotus' attitudes led him to reject out of hand wars imposed by the quest for prestige or glory.

How did he judge the intransigence of the Greeks at certain crucial moments in their history? Did he approve of the decision of the inhabitants of Phocaea to refuse an agreement with the Persian Harpagus? Although threatening them, Harpagus apparently wanted only a token act of submission; an agreement might have saved them from being compelled to abandon the city.[145] Some Greek attitudes were bound to appear to him foolish in that they brought little or no real advantage. He found the obstinacy of the Ionians, when they refused to negotiate with the Persian generals, utterly inexplicable.[146] We shall seek in vain in Herodotus for praise of the bold feats so warmly admired by other writers. He could have regarded the insurrection of Ionia (499 B.C.), fomented by Aristagoras (already the tyrant of Miletus), as a noble manifestation of patriotism and one of the Greeks' "finest hours." In fact he wrote it off, not without a touch of asperity, as the direct cause of "new miseries," for it led to the first Persian War. And the decision to send the Athenian fleet to support the rebels, apparently a valuable initiative since it was imposed by the ideal of Hellenic solidarity of which he was an avowed supporter, is dismissed coldly as "the beginning of troubles."[147]

It is difficult to say whether this restraint was a matter of policy or of a moral judgment that all war—even that undertaken to resist a foreign invader—was wrong. If we accept the second alternative, the extraordinary conclusion could be reached that one should forego defense against the aggressor and prefer compromise at all costs. Obviously Herodotus was not interested in military and civil glory, just as he seemed to attach no importance to civil liberty. His attitude toward the great events of Greek history is that of the cautious onlooker, concerned only to set down the facts for posterity. Plutarch points out that in the description of the battle of Salamis, between the Greeks and the Persians, it is the Persians who win most of his admiration.[148]

Herodotus seems sometimes to have taken a perverse pleasure in emphasizing the paradoxical aspects of certain situations. Famous exploits, blown up by popular rhetoric and literature, were cut down to size in his *History*, as for example in his description of the cautious strategy of the Greek and Persian fleet, crossing each other's tracks at safe distance and reluctant to come to a confrontation.[149] Thus Amompharetus, a Spartan officer, is depicted as a hotheaded braggart eager to get at the opponents, despite the order for withdrawal received from Pausanias. It is odd how easily he allows himself to be talked into withdrawal when he finds himself alone.[150] These episodes are clear evidence of a specific mental attitude in Herodotus, who had nothing but contempt for explosions of useless enthusiasm in so serious a matter. But he was no more than a child of his time when he attributed decisive importance to supernatural influence on events and treated life on earth as reflecting decisions made by wills superior to those of human beings. It may be that this was a formal tribute paid to the tradition of the Greek world. His cautiousness in judging events was perhaps prompted by awareness that his real views, clearly expressed, would have led him too far from those fostered by his contemporaries, who were still lost in the facile worship of heroism for its own sake.

Thucydides (ca. 455-ca. 400 B.C.) belonged to the generation succeeding that of Herodotus. He was without question the most complete historian of antiquity, for he combined critical acumen with a gift of synthesis and no mean literary talent. His vision was that of a mature man made for public affairs, fully capable of recognizing what, in the documentary material at his disposal, was the fruit of the imagination and must be treated with caution and distinguishing this from evidence which bore a direct relationship to real facts and events. In the midst of the complex pattern of Hellenic rivalries, it would have been easy to give way to emotionalism and take sides, but he retained his impartiality, pursuing the line of truth even in the most confused events. He did not share Herodotus' desire to show the mysterious workings of the supernatural woven into the strands of history, nor had he much time for the many rumors and legends circulating in the Mediterranean world.

His method of research was remarkably modern and showed extreme awareness of the essential problems of community life and a natural inclination to look under the surface in order to distinguish fundamental causes from the merely incidental. His care in collecting evidence and in evaluating it sometimes foreshadows the methods used by modern historians. Even when he had to appeal to his own imagination for help in reconstructing an event, he always set the situations and quoted the speeches of his characters with proper respect for realism and verisimilitude. There was nothing ambiguous in his way of treating his material. On the contrary, he made a point of achieving clarity and consistency, just as he aimed, quite overtly, at instructing politicians so that they should draw from history models for their future behavior.

All this did not make it possible, even for an historian of such broad grasp, to avoid distortion and misrepresentation completely, for the influences of an environment soaked in mythology and imbued generally with strong religious feeling were strong. The fratricidal war which was rending the Hellenic world, foreshadowing civil and political serfdom, was bound to prompt in him painful reflections on the mainsprings of human behavior and on the relationships between individuals and between communities. The consequences of war and of peace and their power to determine how men must live—and die—proved too acute to be ignored by this observer.

There was no escaping the inference that at the root of the ills of existence lay a primeval collective frenzy, against which no people, whatever its origins, possessed an effective defense. And even if a case could be made out for war against a foreign people, particularly a foreign aggressor, civil war—the most harmful of all—brought with it the worst calamities. Now the Peloponnesian War, the narration of which was the main achievement of Thucydides' life, constituted the most wide-ranging and costly civil war the Greek world had ever known. Although there had always been a state of tension between the Greek cities, the Greek world had never divided itself so firmly into two opposing camps, yielding only to the logic of terror in a never-ending spiral of violence.

The struggle between Athens and Sparta for hegemony in the Hellenic world involved peninsular as well as insular Greece, and also distant Sicily, where ancient rivalries were reawakened. No one appreciated more than Thucydides the value of the lessons taught by these events. He wrote to keep alive an awareness of the danger threatening a community abandoned to the forces engendered by the irrational part of human nature. The Peloponnesian War was appalling evidence of this. There was no need to refer to religion or mythological warnings to show that the war was nothing more nor less than a ritual obeisance to the power of unreason, merely aggravating the ills of Greece. The metaphysical element plays no role in Thucydides' story. Events are described in their earthly immediacy, and he feels no need to heighten their impact by introducing characters from the next world. He shows a great sense of *relevance,* seldom allowing himself to be sidetracked into secondary questions: " . . . but whosoever shall wish to have a clear view both of the events which have happened and of those which will some day, in all human probability, happen again in the same or a similar way—for these to adjudge my history profitable will be enough for me."[151]

When Thucydides allowed himself a personal comment, he showed his sympathy with those who recognized the gravity of the evil caused by war and argued that an honest man must strive to curb its harmful effects. In a famous digression on the consequences of the war, he noted above all how the fighting robbed the factions of every patriotic feeling, so that every issue was weighed in terms of its usefulness as an instrument for reconquering political power in the respective cities. Hence, in every Greek polis the traditional conflict between democrats and oligarchs went beyond political controversy and became an appeal to the Athenians or the Spartans, according to the political party in which one was fighting. The ideal of the polis had therefore changed into a complex question of primacy within each individual community.

> And so there fell upon the cities on account of revolutions many grievous calamities, such as happen and always will happen while human nature is the same, but which are severer or milder, and different in their manifestations, according as the variations in circumstances present themselves in each case. For in peace and prosperity both states and individuals have gentler feelings, because men are not then forced to face conditions of dire necessity; but war, which robs men of the easy supply of their daily wants, is a rough schoolmaster and creates in most people a temper that matches their condition.

Civil war had deprived the Greeks of all proper awareness of reality. They adapted themselves to a conception of politics and even of economics based on the idea that war, and not peace, was the normal condition of mankind and that everything else must be subordinated to its laws. The passage continues:

> Reckless audacity came to be regarded as courageous loyalty to party, prudent hesitation as specious cowardice, moderation as a cloak for unmanly weakness, and to be clever in everything was to do naught in anything. Frantic impulsiveness was accounted a true man's part, but caution in deliberation a specious pretext for shirking. The hot-headed man was always trusted, his opponent suspected. He who succeeded in a plot was clever, and he who had detected one was still shrewder; on the other hand, he who made it his aim to have no need of such things was a disrupter of party and scared of his opponents.[152]

These reactions do not necessarily refer only to the Peloponnesian War but apply to conflicts of every age, when soldiers and those holding power adapt themselves to the idea of the inexistence of moral principles. The Greeks had cut themselves off from a moral heritage which, though still closely attuned to primitive heroics, constituted a barrier to and a restraint on explosions of bestiality.

In the Greek world an old morality was dying, and although this helped, with the support of Sophistic teaching, to kill off conventional ideas and emancipate culture to some extent from the bonds of the past, it also destroyed a way of being and of thinking and a pattern of moral conduct peculiar to tradition. Thucydides was struck by the fact that bonds of consanguinity could be dissolved under the pressure of a new type of solidarity: that generated by the community of ideas and party discipline. The following passage seems to show up severely a state of affairs which even a realistic mind like his own found it difficult to accept: "Furthermore the tie of blood was weaker than the tie of party, because the partisan was more ready to go to any extreme; for such associations are not entered into for the public good in conformity with the prescribed laws, but for selfish aggrandizement contrary to the established laws. Their pledges to one another were confirmed not so much by divine law as by common transgression of the law."[153] The words betray a sadness that is no literary flourish.

What were the reasons underlying men's acts? What induced them to make certain choices rather than others? Perhaps the quest for serenity and peace in the awareness of the futility of a life spent in fighting? Thucydides had no illusions: He was aware of the reality and judged facts and life in general for what they were worth. After listing in some detail the moral absurdities engendered by war, he posed the key question of why wars break out and formulated his reply.

> The cause of all these evils was the desire to rule which greed and ambition inspire, and also, springing from them, that violent fanaticism which belongs to men once they have become engaged in factious rivalry. For those who emerged as party-leaders in the several cities, by assuming on either side a fair-sounding name, the one using as its catch-word "political equality for the masses under the law," the other "temperate aristocracy," while they pretended to be devoted to the common weal, in reality made it their prize; striving in every way to get the better of each other, they dared the most awful deeds, and sought revenge still more awful, not pursuing these within the bounds of justice and the public weal, but limiting them, both parties alike, only by the moment's caprice.[154]

A clearer picture of political and administrative anarchy would not be easy to find. Without universal conclusions and relying only on facts, Thucydides is nonetheless peculiarly sensitive to the ills caused to his country by war, in terms both of material damage and of the corruption of public and private life. His words imply a judgment of the weaknesses of men, congenitally malevolent and prone to evil actions if only they can gain some personal benefit for themselves and can be certain in advance of escaping punishment. Where there is no police or efficient judiciary the baser part of man escapes control and achieves dominance, chaos results, and the advantages of civilization, consisting first and foremost in security, are lost. Events seemed to bear out the views of this careful observer, who based his judgments on facts and not on preconceived ideas. His aim was not only to show how much harm is caused by fighting but also to assess the causes of the ills which oppressed men. Man is born a captive, Thucydides is in effect saying; he is strongly subject to feelings of hostility towards his fellow human beings, but sound laws can control his evil instincts and keep him on the path of virtue. War in general, and particularly civil war, is therefore to be condemned, precisely because it tends to dispel man's inhibitions and suspend the apparatus of restrictive rules which make up a moral system.

The climate of war was a barrier to the development of a community, for it so distorted man's thinking as to render impossible certain legitimate and necessary advances. By contaminating the seeds of civilization, it left life completely infertile. The problem arose, then, in serious terms.

> So it was that every form of depravity showed itself in Hellas in consequence of its revolutions, and that simplicity, which is the chief element of a noble nature, was laughed to scorn and disappeared, while mutual antagonism of feeling, combined with mistrust, prevailed far and wide. For there was no assurance binding enough, no oath terrible enough, to reconcile man; but always, if they were stronger, since they accounted all security hopeless, they were rather disposed to take precautions against being wronged than able to trust others.[155]

This passage is not just a moralizing assessment of the consequences of one of the most serious crises in the history of the Mediterranean basin. By the concision of the style and its profundity, it constitutes a genuinely pacifist document, in which, under the guise of historical enquiry, the author appeals to his contemporaries and to posterity to think more about the corrupting effects of war and to acknowledge the need to oppose any measure liable to divide mankind and thus set in motion a series of events leading to unhappiness. For centuries, he argued, Greek culture had been dominated by an unduly narrow view of politics. He implied that the old attitudes should be reviewed so that a society based on the solidarity of the Greeks could be built, since man was not yet ripe for the adoption of universal solidarity. Man must acknowledge his own mortality and the precariousness of life on earth, and find his *raison d'être* in the respect of brotherly love, the only possible source of his material and moral prosperity.

Thucydides is also pointing out the implications of a system under which the power holding the Greeks together is not derived from a collective effort of self-discipline but from an imperial hegemony. It was to be foreseen that the threat would arise beyond the frontiers of the Greek world (for example, among the Persians) or on its edges, as in that Macedonian monarchy where certain elements of language and culture, common to the Greek inheritance, were overlaid with a centralized notion of authority. Events in Greek politics and the formidable rise of the Macedonian monarchy later showed that the danger was all too real.

The warning contained in Thucydides' history is not to be sought in passages explicitly condemning war and exalting peace but is indirect and must be inferred from the historical material presented and from comments such as those quoted. Some of the speeches which Thucydides puts in the mouths of his generals or politicians are not to be read as verbatim renderings of what was actually said, but as a literary reconstruction based on the reports of witnesses. These reports were not always accurate or reliable, and Thucydides therefore did not hesitate to work into the orations his own ideas and those shared by most Greeks on the war and its political and moral implications. In these passages he takes every opportunity to praise peace and emphasize the ills of war. He argued that the outcome of war was so dependent on imponderable factors that neither party in the struggle, not even the stronger and militarily better organized, could be certain of victory. He makes the particular point that man, despite all the arguments of logic to the contrary, uses force *first* and parleys afterwards, when arms have already reaped their tragic harvest of suffering and blood. For he is essentially a creature of impulse.

Reflections on the benefits of peace, showing awareness of the gains to be won from a cessation of hostilities, were included in the speech attributed to the Spartan plenipotentiaries who had traveled to Athens to offer peace (427 B.C.). Their words make it clear that Thucydides was very conscious of the need to repair the damage caused by war.[156]

But the most significant document in this connection is almost certainly the oration of the Syracusan Hermocrates at the conference of the Sicilian communities held in Gela in 424 B.C., which may be considered as a message handed down by Thucydides to posterity.[157] His aim was to draw attention to the harm caused by fighting, to its illegal, inhuman, and arbitrary nature. Thucydides can hardly be refuted when he argues that only in peace can abundance and security flourish. The evils of war, he claims, are known to all. And yet they are taken very lightly, as if they were unknown. There comes a time when men suffer a kind of mental blackout, and there is no way of preventing them from running absurd risks. This is the situation on the eve of war, when "to one side the gains seem greater than the terrors, while the other deliberately prefers to undergo the dangers rather than submit to a temporary disadvantage."[158]

A politician, Thucydides says, believes that war is a calculated risk. In fact it is always a leap in the dark. A calculated risk may only be based on a certain balance between the danger, the foreseeable result, and the price to be paid. But all parties involved are bound to emerge from war severely damaged. This becomes clear only when the war has already reached an advanced stage, when it is discovered that none of the problems has been solved, and everyone is forced to admit that a tragic mistake has been made. Then people begin to talk more of peace; peace parties emerge in the belligerent states. Hermocrates describes the situation: "For each of us began the war in the first place because we desired to promote our private interest. So now let us endeavour by setting forth our conflicting claims to become reconciled with each other; and then, if we do not after all succeed in securing, each of us, what is fair and just before we part, we shall go to war again."[159]

It is clear in the speech that Hermocrates is deeply disappointed at the failure of the Siceliots to sink their differences and make common cause. That they are doing so now is not because they want to forget ancestral struggles but because Sicily has been the victim of an Athenian aggression and the peoples of Sicily must unite if they are not to succumb. "For it is an instinct of man's nature always to rule those who yield, but to guard against those who are ready to attack. If any of us, knowing how matters really stand, fails to take proper precautions, or if anyone has come here not accounting it of paramount importance that we must all together deal wisely with the common peril, we are making a mistake."[160] And if the Athenian aggression were to lead to permanent peace between the peoples of Sicily, this would already be a substantial achievement:

> And if we follow this course, war will not end in another war, but without trouble quarrels will end quietly in peace . . . but as to the question of peace, which all men agree is a most desirable thing, why should we not make it here among ourselves? Or, think you, if one person now enjoys a blessing and another labors under adversity, is it not tranquillity far more than war that will put an end to the latter and perpetuate the former? And has not peace its honours and less hazardous splendours, and all the other advantages on which one might dilate as easily as on the horrors of war?"[161]

War could only aggravate the plight of mankind. In every age of history rivalries and conflict had deepened the sufferings of men. At the end of the speech Hermocrates stressed that peace would have incalculable effects on the lives and the prosperity of the population. The accidental cause, the need to expel the Athenians from Sicilian territory, assumed, in the perspective in which he sees it, an importance going far beyond that of the incident itself.

A similar message is contained in another famous passage, the dialogue between the Melian and the Athenian ambassadors (Book V, 84-116) which precedes the conquest of the island of Melos by the armies of Athens. Here he exposes the logic of imperialism and the justification which is given, when a strong state—and only because it *is* strong—is compelled to overcome and enslave the weaker state. The Athenians are at great pains to show that it is in the Melians' interest to accept their domination passively. For one thing, they cannot escape it and secondly the Athenians must impose it to avoid dangerous precedents which might be imitated by other subject populations.

This is unmitigated cynicism in its purest form. All the ideals behind which generals and peoples commonly mask their warlike operations disappear in the face of a grand plan of expansion and conquest. War, and the calculations which are at its roots, are thus, by implication, exposed as evil.

In the larger perspective, Hermocrates' speech and the Melian dialogue are further evidence that Thucydides sympathized with the pacifist vision of life and of relations between states. His words enlighten us as to how the progress of peoples may be speeded up and equilibrium preserved between the quest for prosperity and the need to prevent periodic effusions of blood. As a consequence of this desire for balance, Thucydides felt that new bearings must be taken, on wider horizons, horizons including all the Greeks and not only single city-states. A new society would unify all the Greeks and be a source of cohesion and of creative experience.

Xenophon (ca. 444-ca. 357 B.C.) was the third Greek historian to make an interesting contribution to the idea of peace. His influence on contemporaries and on many generations of later writers was profound. His *Hellenica* formed a sequel to the *History of the Peloponnesian War* and were intended as a major contribution toward understanding the events which took place during his life. In fact, however, he showed less critical acumen than Thucydides and failed to match his standards of objectivity. He felt that history writing should not only keep alive the memory of events but also disseminate moral lessons.

Xenophon was really a polygraph, interested in all the fields of human knowledge; no subject was too abstruse for his inquiring mind. Hence his empiricism, and, in some cases, the approximation with which he tackled certain important questions. He felt that it was enough to warn and teach, resorting if necessary to the fulsome praise of his main protagonist. Whether he was concerned with Socrates, with Cyrus the Great, with Hiero, tyrant of Syracuse, with Agesilaus the Second, king of Sparta, or with himself, as in the case of the *Anabasis,* he tends to show the main character in the most favorable light possible, because this person is being held up as a model of perfection.

This is especially true in respect of his comments on war and peace. He appreciated the importance of peace in community life and regarded it as a factor in the regeneration of human relationships and as a source of wealth.[162] The following passage is interesting in this connection:

> If, on the other hand, any one supposes that financially war is more profitable to the state than peace, I really do not know how the truth of this can be tested better than by considering once more what has been the experience of our state in the past. He will find that in old days a very great amount of money was paid into the treasury in time of peace, and that the whole of it was spent in time of war; he will conclude on consideration that in our own time the effect of the late war on our revenues was that many of them ceased, while those that came in were exhausted by the multitude of expenses; whereas the cessation of war by sea has been followed by a rise in the revenues, and has allowed the citizens to devote them to any purpose they choose.[163]

Nonetheless he took part in famous military campaigns and accompanied captains in the field of battle, acting as friend and adviser, not only out of natural curiosity but also in response to a personal bent. He is full of warlike fervor when assessing undertakings like the expedition of the ten thousand. His dislike of the activities of artisans is famous; he believed them to form a class of men incapable of defending themselves because by nature they were too docile. On the other hand he praised agriculture, the noble art which taught men how to resist fatigue and coordinate their strength in ways useful also in battle.[164] He condemned the coward, deriding him as a despicable creature, unworthy of living and working in a community.[165] His ideal was the man who sought to protect society from external dangers and to stimulate its sense of emulation, the key to progress and prosperity. (This was why he admired a general like Agesilaus II, king of Sparta, a courageous and just man who possessed the gift of inspiring his subordinates with the enthusiasm necessary to face the dangers and discomforts arising from war.) Xenophon felt that the good man should also be endowed with an acute critical sense, should be able to size up situations quickly, and should have a wealth of expertise, whether as to ways of conducting a war or as to life in general. Only on these conditions could an army captain call on his soldiers to forget themselves and show the abnegation which enables men to face the dangers of battle.

However, not all captains could attain this moral stature. Some were not equal to the task set them and their incompetence made no small contribution to the failure of campaigns: "Generals, too, differ from one another in this respect. For some make their men unwilling to work and to take risks, disinclined and unwilling to obey, except under compulsion, and actually proud of defying their commander: aye, and they cause them to have no sense of dishonour when something disgraceful occurs."[166] These reflections were a source of disenchantment to Xenophon, as he discovered that reality did not correspond with the ideal.

But in his judgment of war there was also a sentimental factor which led him to admire fighting for its sheer excitement. In some passages he even celebrates the joy of the victorious soldiers and their enthusiasm born from relief at danger escaped, from lust for booty, and from the emotion of being able to avenge oneself on the enemy at last defeated.

> For, you know, when states defeat their foes in a battle, words fail one to describe the joy they feel in the rout of the enemy, in the pursuit, in the slaughter of the enemy. What transports of triumphant pride! What a halo of glory about them! What comfort to think that they have exalted their city! Everyone is crying: "I had a share in the plan, I killed most"; and it's hard to find where they don't revel in falsehood, claiming to have killed more than all that were really slain. So glorious it seems to them to have won a great victory![167]

These and other extracts inspired by the same feelings are the author's tribute to his past as a soldier and to his knowledge of the psychological temptations of war and of victory. It could be objected that a more balanced judgment of the relationships between communities could have been expected from a historian brought up, as he was, on Socratic ideas. If even the men of culture, the historians, and the moralists are unstinting in their praise of the soldier and of war, then there can be little hope of a genuine renaissance or of saving mankind from its passion for strife.

But Xenophon is not always logical and consistent in his thinking, for he is also often at pains in his writings to emphasize the scale of the evils caused by war. This joins with the moralistic tendency of his works, in which there is a definite leaning toward the good and a desire to attain humanitarian objectives and mutual understanding. In the writings influenced more directly by Socratic doctrines and probably, as Jöel argues, by Cynic teaching, he shows delicacy of feeling and a desire that man's behavior in general and particularly the behavior of those vested with political responsibility should be governed by a sincere desire for spiritual betterment.[168] This is especially true in the *Cyropaedia,* since everything seems to converge toward the exaltation of cooperation and concord. The work—a novel with a political and psychological background—summarized the youth and upbringing of Cyrus the Great, king of Persia. In fact it is a literary sketch intended to inform the reader on a number of episodes of Persian history and to develop certain ideas. Xenophon had no scruples about sacrificing historical accuracy to these ideas, as when, for example, he shows the Persian king dying in bed, peacefully philosophizing, though Herodotus reports that the king was killed fighting the Massagetae.[169] This kind of inaccuracy apparently did not worry him, for what was important in the narrative was the moral edification of the reader.

The influence of philosophical doctrines widely known in his time is revealed in every page of the story. The choice of subject was itself significant, the life of Cyrus the Great having already been the subject of an essay, now lost, by the Cynic Antisthenes. This is probably no coincidence, since Xenophon's account is—as we have noted—almost certainly of Cynic inspiration. It focuses on the idealized figure of the perfect sovereign, whose every action was governed by philanthropy, that is to say, by a genuine and generous interest in mankind.

Probably keeping fairly close to Antisthenes, Xenophon described the behavior of a monarch fully aware of the responsibilities deriving from the mission assigned to him by the gods and determined to behave accordingly. The entire narration is an exaltation of the $\phi\iota\lambda\iota'a$, understood not only as friendship between individuals, but as an attitude of the mind toward the human species. This merciful and humanitarian attitude provided, according to the Cynics, a rule of conduct for the enlightened monarch, applicable in all circumstances, whereby he could win the friendship of all and make everyone happy.

In their attitudes to the Persians, so near to the Greek world and at the same time so distant from it, particularly in spiritual terms, the Greeks had entertained mixed feelings of admiration and fear. The Persian wars had shown that the Greeks were determined to stay loyal to a way of life based on a civilization which they believed to be the best possible. But the position of the inhabitants of the Greek cities of Asia, with their backs against the fortress occupied first by the Anatolian monarchies and then by the Persian king, was still far from secure. The proximity of an oriental autocratic kingdom entailed a relationship of vassaldom that could not be shrugged off. This explains why a Greek from Asia like Herodotus, in recounting the vicissitudes of the wars against the Persians, adopted a more flexible attitude toward them than certain writers who had been born or lived in other parts and had continued to subscribe to the myth of the natural superiority of the Greeks over the barbarians. In Herodotus there is nothing of the haughtiness and of the rhetoric informing the *Persians* of Aeschylus or the songs of Simonides. A process of intellectual osmosis was now taking place in the political ideas of the Greeks of Asia Minor, so different from those prevailing in the peninsula and in the archipelago. These Greeks could not ignore the pressure of a powerful emperor on whose tolerance they had to rely for survival; the Greeks of the peninsula could act more independently, their strategic position being what it was. Even the polis differed in structure in Asia Minor from the polis in classical Greece and the other Mediterranean colonies, for example Sicily. In Asia, the Greek tyrant had a good deal in common with the oriental satrap.

This circumstance explains why some writers, judging the events of Persia in a context different from that adopted by Greek literature, chose the Persian Empire as a model of universal solidarity, destined to unify the thought and conduct of men. Was not the Great King the "sovereign of the world," whose empire stretched from the Mediterranean to India? Xenophon, widely read in the philosophies of the time, convinced of the natural brotherhood of men and of the opportunities open to them to achieve far-reaching cooperation in the cause of peace, actually succeeded in discerning evidence of the cosmopolitan character of the Persian Empire in the Great King's title. By a similar process European writers of the eighteenth century Enlightenment sought to prove the congenital goodness of man and his inability to create evil. He was, they said, corruptible only by the temptations of his environment. Their evidence was that of the "good" savages and the oriental potentates—for example in the Chinese Empire—evidence flagrantly distorted by their ignorance of geography and ethnography.

The φιλία as reflected in the words and the behavior of his Cyrus mirrored certain individual and family virtues which Xenophon hoped to promote by bringing home to the reader their value for building character. Cyrus stands out as a sovereign cultivating this type of virtue. Moreover, every conquest in the field of domestic and individual discipline, all resistance to the influences of evil and to the spread of empiricism in human relations led to forms of collective control which would widen in scope so as to include the relations between one people and another. On the other hand, every concession to intolerance in the individual and family environment led to the adoption of the ethic of *raison d'etat*, enslaving the statesman to the temptations of domination and violence. The link between public and private behavior and the transposition of individual and family ethics into the infinitely wider field of politics are apparent in every page of the *Cyropaedia*. The object of Xenophon's tale was to improve the conduct of politicians by appealing to the moral principles applicable to relations between individuals. An example is a passage in which gratitude is praised, being recognized as a virtue rarely practised by the masses but well-suited to the young, that is, to the least corrupt of human beings and, therefore, those closest to the original spontaneity of nature.[170]

Book II of the *Cyropaedia* also applies the principles of private behavior to public morality. The aim is to describe the process of formation and consolidation of the Persian state, which had taken place, according to the narrative, through friendship, deemed the surest way of guiding men toward virtue and inducing them to accept common objectives and intentions. "What sort of men we have then as our comrades; they are so easily won by kindness that we can make many of them our friends with even a little piece of meat; and they are so obedient that they obey even before the orders are given."[171]

This fraternal approach was valid both in time of peace, in the governance of the state, and in wartime, when the policy was designed to induce the enemy to cooperate and yield to overtures of affection and brotherly love. Thus it was possible to see war—conceded as inevitable, at least at a certain stage of human development—as a means of winning the friendship of men and bringing them to attitudes informed with wisdom and goodness. A good example is the speech made by the defeated king of the Armenians, who seeks the favor of the victorious enemy and is grateful for what had been done for his people: "How little of the future, Cyrus, we mortals can foresee, and yet, how much we try to accomplish. Why, just now, when I was striving to secure liberty, I became more a slave than ever before; and when we were taken prisoners, we then thought our destruction certain, but we now find we are saved as never before."[172] Book IV also contains accounts of military incidents having as their aim not the conquest of new territories but the conversion of all former enemies into "friends and allies."[173] Even in the most tragic moments, when the only form of political action was apparently violence, Xenophon's basic theme remains that of the power of goodness, his hope the regeneration of mankind, his narrative a succession of events too regular and balanced to be true. His message is that all things in this world must favor the brotherliness of man so that, guided by providence, their destinies may converge and good may triumph over evil.

The interview between Cyrus and Cyaxares, described in Book V, is an interesting example of Xenophon's approach to history. According to him, the meeting got off to a bad start. Cyaxares, annoyed by the imposing array of cavalry brought along by his nephew, was at no pains to disguise his ill humor. The conversations seemed certain to fail when Cyrus' skillful diplomacy was brought to bear. Having instructed his attendants to stand out of earshot, he began to speak with open heart, proclaiming himself ready to acknowledge and make good any harm he may have done. Immediately the atmosphere of the meeting improved and eventually facilitated general pacification, which benefitted not so much the leaders as the armies and the peoples.

Although it contained the summary of a military encounter which was to decide the fate of the Persian Empire and other nations of the Middle East, Book VII also describes episodes which bring out clearly the feelings of humanity nurtured by a sovereign heavily influenced by the Cynic doctrines. While recognizing his own inability to escape the cruel laws of war, Cyrus is depicted in this book as a man willing to follow humanitarian rules and to consider the foe as men to be defeated, if this is required by the logic of war, but to be treated with mercy if they surrender. This impulse guided him in his conduct toward the Egyptians enrolled in Croesus' army, whose lives— partly also as a tribute to their valor—he agreed to spare.[174]

The last book (VIII) of the *Cyropaedia* describes the organization of the Persian court and bureaucracy. Here more than anywhere else $\phi\iota\lambda\acute{\iota}a$ stands out in the behavior of the protagonist. To select the best talents and persuade them to rally to his support, in order to constitute an efficient administration, he also used means of moral and material pressure, going so far as to confiscate the goods of those who held back from the life of the court, thus showing lack of loyalty. In no circumstances could a man indifferent to the splendor of the king aspire to employment in public service.

Friendship, concord, reciprocity of feeling, affection, remained the key objectives, without which the sovereign's mission lost all value. In the moral edification of a person, love was the motor of action:

> 1. In the first place, then, [Cyrus] showed at all times as great kindness of heart as he could; for he believed that just as it is not easy to love those who seem to hate us, or to cherish good-will towards those who bear us ill-will, in the same way those who are known to love and to cherish good-will could not be hated by those who believe themselves loved.

> 2. During the time, therefore, when he was not yet quite able to do favors through gifts of money, he tried to win the love of those about him by taking forethought for them and labouring for them and showing that he rejoiced with them in their good fortune and sympathized with them in their mishaps; and after he found himself in a position to do favours with money, he seems to us to have recognized from the start that there is no kindness which men can show one another, with the same amount of expenditure, more acceptable than sharing meat and drink with them.[175]

This convivial aspect of his attachment to supporters also had a place in his system of brotherly love, from which the vanquished were to benefit no less than others.

To provide a contrast to Cyrus' personality the *Cyropaedia* describes another sovereign who was unable to win the friendship of men or of the gods. The example chosen is Croesus, whose behavior always prompted suspicion and distrust, even in the Oracle of Delphi, consulted by him on his hopes of male offspring: "At first," Croesus said, "instead of asking the god for the particular favour I needed, I proceeded to put him to the test to see if he could tell the truth. And when even men, if they are gentlemen—to say nothing of a god—discover that they are mistrusted, they have no love for those who mistrust them."[176]

The *Cyropaedia* is the work of Xenophon in which the influence of Cynic teaching is strongest and most effective and in which the protagonist interprets with authority the character of that type of leader who takes a personal interest in the well-being of the people and seeks to inspire a regenerated society.[177] Other writings by Xenophon gravitate around the figure of the philanthropic leader, aware of the power of love, the peacemaker, fostering harmony and equilibrium among those entrusted to his care by the gods. Whether he is describing Agesilaus II, Hiero, or Cyrus the Younger (in the *Anabasis*), friendship and brotherly love always dominate his narrative, shaping the story and establishing the moral setting which the leading character adorns and enhances. Philanthropy, a virtue practised and defended by the Cynic school, provided the great reserve of ideals from which Xenophon drew arguments to promote a certain mode of living.

Though Xenophon does not say so explicitly, war is always seen as an abnormal situation to which a sovereign should resort only if the aim was so worthy and meritorious as to justify such a grave exception to the law of love. The sovereign of the *Cyropaedia*, like the Cynic model of which he is the literary incarnation, is seen by Xenophon as the instrument for implementing a plan to reform society, in which peace is seen as the one great catalyst of human initiative.

Crisis in the Greek World. Hellenism and the Stoics

The Peloponnesian War left a deep scar in the minds of the Greeks, completely changing some of their ways of living and thinking. The consequence was the crisis of the polis, the pillar around which, from the earliest times, political thought had turned. Thus Plato had regarded the polis as a necessity, a view which subsequent Greek history went far to refute. In his system, the polis is seen as safeguarded by pledges and guarantees, checks and balances, which protected it from damage or deterioration. It seemed destined to last forever, to overcome all obstacles, a bulwark against the uncertainty of the human condition. A reaction and change of attitude were, however, set in train by the Sophists, who preached human equality and were opposed to all political fragmentation. Although they criticized the Greek situation, they could not wholly escape the pressures of the social climate in which they were working. Sometimes they conceded the existence of an unbridgeable abyss between Greeks and barbarians and agreed that the two parties could never communicate or achieve mutual understanding.

The bravest intuitive ideas of the Greek thinkers did not go substantially beyond abstractions inferred from reality and tending, in the attempt to win admiration for the polis, to ignore the dangers and weaknesses inherent in the structure of an institution whose very existence apparently depended on internal discord due to personal and party pettiness and to conflicts with other states. The most enlightened political minds could at most desire the end of hostilities and the attainment of a condition of peace, but always with the aim of maintaining the polis.[178] The spirit of faction dissipated and weakened the heritage of ideas handed down by the philosophers, whose error lay in their inability to substitute for the pattern of the polis that of a human organization set on broader bases. A characteristic failing of Greek philosophic and political thinking was the inability to foresee early enough the constitution of large states dominated by the Greek mentality and culture. The philosophers did not observe how deeply Greek culture had penetrated the outer world. The grandeur of the Greek contribution was to be brought home to the world by a man of the sword, Alexander the Great. Then the Greek community came to full awareness of its own merits and its own destiny, of a mission no longer confined to the centers of the Hellenic *diaspora* but extended to all peoples, who, it was felt, were bound to pay tribute to past masters in the handling of ideas. In this way, civilization, born and nurtured in the polis, broke down the barriers that had hemmed it in for centuries and conquered the known world. Ancient Greece gave way to Hellenism—that is, to a movement which maintained the vital impulse, the creative capacity, and the critical acumen of the Greeks, but in one way or another influenced the entire world. The traditional equilibrium was broken by a military power which had long remained remote from the center of the Greek world and which had changed in the space of a generation into an expansionary power spreading over Europe and Asia.

The question was no longer one of realizing the pan-Hellenic dream of achieving a union of all the Greeks, who were spread over many lands but linked by the same language, customs, and propensities. Alexander's plans were on a much greater scale. The desire was to bring about *oecumene* in the Greek world, give it a single imprint, give it a stake in higher forms of life and thought. The fatherland was no longer a modest township where the citizens wore themselves out in fruitless political rivalries on a Lilliputian scale. Now the fatherland would be the entire world, from which, so it appeared, all obstacles liable to hamper the Macedonian crusade had been removed.

It would be vain to speculate as to what might have happened to Hellenic civilization if the city-states, ending their natural tendency to fight among themselves, had embarked on a movement of unification guided not by the military pressure of Macedonia but by a collective effort in the field of political thought and matched by appropriate political decisions. Perhaps a huge Mediterranean state would have been formed, based mainly on sea power and capable of vying with, if not vanquishing, the Persian Empire. In a short period of thirteen years, Alexander did in fact succeed in giving political unity to the peoples of the eastern Mediterranean and the Middle East, using Greek civilization as a means of penetration and Greek culture as a guide for the subject peoples. This innovating ferment penetrated as far as distant Afghanistan and northern India, making actual a fantasy which no thinker had previously taken seriously. The dream of a cosmopolis, anticipated by the Cynics, seemed near to realization.

The Greeks did not give up the polis without a struggle. They knew all too well what would be their fate if a Macedonian hegemony was established, and they sought to stem the rising tide. But not even this (by no means the first) attempt to resist the stranger was enough to put an end to internal discord and bring about voluntary political unity. The struggles for influence and the rivalry of the Greeks came to an end at the battle of Mantinea (362 B.C.). The Macedonian element began to dominate the Greek scene and was the key factor in subsequent changes. The city-states—with some responsible men, notably Demosthenes (384-322 B.C.), as their spokesmen—appealed in vain to the doctrine of the balance of power. Even to imagine that the doctrine could be applied was in itself a factor of weakness. In every age of persistent instability, when states, normally aiming at hegemony, realize that they cannot prevail, they take refuge in the illusion that the right solution is maintenance of the territorial status quo and its institutional consolidation. This is what happened in Europe in the eighteenth and nineteenth centuries, when the European powers endeavored to stabilize their divisions, believing that states aiming at hegemony could nonetheless coexist. Although it was sustained by Demosthenes, who mobilized his remarkable eloquence in support of these ideas, any doctrine of the kind was bound to fail.

At this point it may be recalled that in the fourth century B.C. a new concept of peace and its legal implications came to the fore within the Greek communities. The Peace of Antalcidas (386 B.C.) has been mentioned as evidence that the legal concept of the peace treaty was already developing along lines having much in common with the modern concept. Peace loses, from here onwards, the meaning of a mere suspension of hostilities sanctioned by inviolable guarantees and takes on that of an agreement which obliges the parties not to reopen the conflict, thus giving the de facto situation a definitive status. The fact that these criteria were not respected does not affect the value and significance of the change in the psychological position of the parties. The Peace of Antalcidas was the first case of a "common peace" between the Greek cities and Persia. The latter state acquired the right to intervene to punish defaulters.[179] This was how the Greek world suffered from the Peloponnesian War, which had weakened its capacity to resist the Persians.

The inclusion of an authority which in some ways was higher than the contracting states (the Persian state, the Delio-Attic league, or the Delphic "Amphictyony") to ensure compliance with pledges was a device used in other peaces made by the Greeks in the first half of the fourth century B.C. The "common peace" entailed an actual transposition of responsibilities and obligations from the individual states to the Greek world considered as a whole. This was a peculiar characteristic of the peace treaties concluded in this difficult period of Greek history leading up to the triumph of Macedonia. In any case there is no denying the psychological, legal, and political change in the character of the agreements concluded in these fifty years.[180]

The Macedonian notion of "Greekness," professed first by Philip and then by Alexander, was a further development. The Greeks had always believed that they belonged to a chosen tribe and were assisted by destiny in reaching higher forms of life characterized by aesthetic sophistication and a capacity for critical reflection; they had also always refused to believe that the dissemination of their principles and teachings among other peoples was either feasible or desirable. All propaganda for Hellenism was alien to their spirit, precisely because the incommunicability between civilizations and cultures was a settled Greek principle and justified in their eyes rebellion against the Macedonian hegemony. A relevant document here is the *Philippics* of Demosthenes, in which the memories of the past inspired an attitude that was undeniably noble and glorious but was sadly lacking in vitality. Demosthenes called for a union between the Greek cities to resist the Macedonians, just as they had resisted the Persians a century and a half before. But any comparison between the two events was in fact impossible, both because Greece had exhausted itself in internal squabbling and because Philip of Macedonia, unlike Darius and Xerxes, came in the guise of the champion of Greek unity and as the interpreter of a spiritual expansion movement such as the peninsula had never before known.

For Demosthenes every profession of faith and every political plan was firmly rooted in a conservative conception of the past. Isocrates (436-338 B.C.) had seen the dawning and waning of many historical movements in the course of his long life, and had a different approach. He believed that the Greek nation was in the throes of a political and moral crisis for which there was no solution other than a unity which would put an end to internal strife. Hence he supported Macedonian tactics. Perhaps he failed to understand the formidable political implications of such a union in terms of increase in power and transfer of influence. Nor could he be expected to foresee, as a consequence of the activities of Philip, the utterly unpredictable success of Alexander. But he deemed it of capital importance to prepare for the day when the Persian Empire, having regained its old vitality (at the time weakened by the rebellions of the satraps) would once again attack the Greek communities of

Asia and Europe. To prepare the ground for resistance against Persia the Greeks should unite and accept the political hegemony of one who, respecting the existing autonomies, would speed up their unifying process and facilitate serious military preparation. Hence the quest for a force which might bring the city-states together—first the Athenian state, which even in his later works he described as a lover of peace, perhaps as a tribute to its opposition to the Persians;[181] then Jason, sovereign of Pherae; Dionysius I, tyrant of Syracuse; and lastly Philip of Macedon, at a time when his star seemed certain to go on rising for a long time.

The Macedonian hegemony over the other Greek states bore a relation to the Macedonian attitude toward the non-Hellenic tribes. According to Isocrates, Philip was to conduct himself as "the benefactor of the Greeks, the sovereign of the Macedonians and the lord of the barbarians." The results of Isocrates' reflections were set out in two essays published in 355 B.C.: *On the Peace* and the *Areopagiticus*. In the former, he called on the Athenians to abandon the old mirages of greatness and treat other Greeks as equals, to seek a condition of collective serenity, to remember that imperialism is a faithless lover, that its glory is after the prelude to disaster. Characteristic of this discourse are phrases of distinctly pacifist content: "I maintain, then, that we should make peace, not only with the Chians, the Rhodians, the Byzantines and the Coans, but with all mankind. . . ."[182]

Peace would restore those material and moral values which had been too long discounted in Greece because of the boundless imperial ambitions of some of the states:

> For I, for my part, consider that we shall manage our city to better advantage and be ourselves better men and go forward in all our undertakings if we stop setting our hearts on the empire of the sea. For it is this which plunged us into our present state of disorder, which overthrew that democratic government under which our ancestors lived and were the happiest of the Hellenes, and which is the cause, one might almost say, of all the ills which we both suffer ourselves and inflict upon the rest of the Hellenes.[183]

The same idea is expressed in other passages from the same essay. The advantages of peace are legion:

> But if we make peace and demean ourselves as our common covenants [of the Peace of Antalcides] command us to do, then we shall dwell in our city in great security, delivered from wars and perils and the turmoil in which we are now involved amongst ourselves, and we shall advance day by day in prosperity, relieved of paying war-taxes, of fitting out triremes, and of discharging the other burdens which are imposed by war, without fear cultivating our lands and sailing the seas and engaging in those other occupations which now, because of the war, have entirely come to an end. Nay, we shall see our city enjoying twice the revenues which she now receives, and thronged with merchants and foreigners and resident aliens, by whom she is now deserted.[184]

Certainly the lure of war was stronger than the appeal of peace, and those who spoke out for a peace policy spoke in vain. This did not prevent Isocrates from attacking violently, with all the strength of his aggressive eloquence, the past behavior of the Athenians and their imperialistic policy.[185]

The *Areopagiticus,* on the other hand, is concerned with internal policy, praising the old Athenian democracy. The Athenians are called upon to devote themselves seriously and unremittingly to the cares of the state, adopting a less superficial and dishonest line of conduct and respecting the views of their ancestors. Like *On the Peace,* this essay has a definite point of view. Pan-Hellenism is seen as closely bound up with the defense of a civil idea under which the individual will can develop freely, sheltered from the threat of coercion. However, the plan could be implemented only in accordance with the principles endowed by tradition, which were themselves based on the defense of liberty. For this reason Philip of Macedon's victory at Chaeronea (338 B.C.), although it meant pan-Hellenic unity, was a rude awakening for Isocrates, for his dreams had proved true in war but not in peace and had been realized at the price of the complete submission of the Greek people to a single center of power.

The position taken up by Isocrates—his desire being to free Greek politics from the agonizing dilemma which had beset them for centuries—had favored the execution of Philip's designs, since this helped to persuade the Greeks that their unity must be achieved through a leader. How could a people too intelligent not to be aware of its own weaknesses and inspired, despite internal struggles, by a strong desire for peace fail to welcome the message of one who had for decades kept alive, in writings of great authority, the dream of unity? But he had not foreseen that his work would be used by an unscrupulous captain like Philip, essentially concerned with the imperatives of reality and ready to lend support only to ideologies which would speed up the achievement of his objectives. One must perhaps concede that Isocrates had persuaded Philip to grant formal liberty to the Greek cities, federating them in the Corinthian league, and to play the role of agent responsible for a common external policy designed to implement military plans against Persia.

These projects, temporarily interrupted by the assassination of Philip in 336 B.C., were taken up again with greater determination, sometimes illuminated by sinister flares of megalomania, by his son. In a few years the pan-Hellenic program became the driving force behind one of the most sensational adventures in history, pursued by a sovereign convinced that he was reliving the Homeric epic. Alexander drew inspiration from the Hellenic heritage to realize the political and ethical unity of the ancient world in the name of common aesthetic and cultural ideals and with the objective of achieving a complete osmosis of civilizations and a fusion of races. The objective of unifying the *oecumene*—that is to say, the inhabited world—was not the result of a late vocation of the great captain, nor an attempt to justify the dazzling success of his military adventure, imprinting on it a special ideological stamp. It was perhaps already fermenting in his mind when as a young man he had studied under Aristotle. Because of him, the Greeks advanced beyond the polis, which itself had made no mean contribution to the life of the mind, even beyond the bolder pan-Hellenic ideas, and made the world their parish. In this way he transformed the political configuration and the cultural texture of the Middle East. On the remains of older states there arose first a vast empire and then, after the death of its founder, new states dominated by Greek culture. Isocrates, the great champion of Hellenism, would probably have denied responsibility for this development and for the unforeseeable forms it took. Having moved to new geographical areas and historical climates, Greek thinking underwent a profound transformation. It tended to fix the rules of human conduct in a universal framework, at the center of which the dream of a serene life cherished by the Stoic philosophers soon found a place.

Stoicism was a speculative adventure closely linked with the age of Alexander, with the decay of the polis and the disappearance of the belief that between Greeks and barbarians, as between slaves and free men, there existed an insuperable natural barrier. The Greeks felt harassed by the problem of how they should approach the new relationships between society and the individual, now that aspirations, the quest for knowledge, and fear itself had gained a world audience. In previous ages, the individual had had to submit to rules of conduct dictated by the narrow circle in which he lived; he now had to allow for the interpenetration of races and cultures. The Stoics made these facts the basis of community life, transferring the concept of citizenship from that of belonging to the polis to that of belonging to an ideal universal city (the cosmopolis), embracing every individual and every existing nation. Man was thus projected into an ecumenical society consisting of rational beings like himself and of supernatural beings like the gods. As a citizen of the cosmopolis, he was to take part in the framing of the laws, practising the virtues deriving from a collective will. Hence the condemnation of traditional institutions, regarded as conflicting with the collective will; hence the high place accorded to brotherly love, which changed men into individuals with the same rights and obligations; hence the proclamation of a universal republic, founded on peace and humanity, the constitution and organization of which was described by Zeno of Citium (322-264 B.C.), the founder of the school, in an essay entitled *The Republic*. Zeno not only appealed to his readers to consider mankind as subject to a single will and ruled by a collective soul, but he also saw his Republic as the earthly image of the cosmic reality, in which all things were guided by reason.

We have only fragmentary information concerning the views of Zeno and his followers on the nature and the features of the cosmopolis. It would be interesting to know whether the idea of a universal state, in which men and

THE IDEA OF PEACE IN ANTIQUITY

Gerardo Zampaglione

Translated by Richard Dunn

What is the origin of the idea of peace? Has this concept arisen in the heart of war-weary modern man, or does it spring from deeper, more ancient sources? This important question, long neglected by scholars, is examined fully in the present volume, a translation of Gerardo Zampaglione's widely acclaimed study.

The author has carefully examined the ideas which inspired the main philosophical and political doctrines, as well as a number of the most significant literary works, of antiquity. A desire for peace is widespread and can be found in the myth of the Golden Age, in the Old Testament story of the Paradise on earth, in the Jewish prophecy of the coming of the Messiah, in the hopeful expectation of a better world of the early Christians, in the prophecies to be found in Virgil's *Eclogue IV*, and in the cosmopolitan expression of Stoic philosophy.

The early Christians' opposition to war was firm and absolute—a tenet which has reappeared in the beliefs of latter-day conscientious objectors. As Rome became a Christian empire under Constantine, however, this intransigence waned, leading eventually to St. Augustine's concept of the just war.

Zampaglione's study leads to the conclusion that, despite violent warlike demands and encouragement to heroism which often inspired both writers and philosophers, peaceful undercurrents and tendencies were not only present but far more active than has been hitherto imagined. These show a continuity and relationship which point to the existence of a genuine pacific trend in classical and Christian antiquity.

Gerardo Zampaglione, a former official in the Italian Ministry of Foreign Affairs, recently served as the Director General of the Council of Ministers of the European Communities at Brussels. He was a member of the anti-Fascist Resistance in Italy and is a convinced pacifist.

UNIVERSITY OF NOTRE DAME PRESS   NOTRE DAME   LONDON

$12.95

gods were spiritually federated, entailed a condemnation of war or not. This is no easy matter; the loss of *The Republic* means that we have no direct access to the master's thinking on this subject, and his disciples (Stoic teaching lasted several centuries and went through three phases: the old Stoa, the middle period, and the Roman period) came to temper the rigor of the original teaching, forcing it into forms acceptable to the authorities of the time. Stoic philosophy penetrated the Hellenistic monarchies first and then the Roman world, attracting support and even enthusiasm among the cultivated public, councillors at court, and even sovereigns. Although the latter were prone to intolerant methods of government and ruled mainly in response to reason of state, treating war as a normal instrument of pressure and hegemony, they often claimed to be convinced followers of the Stoic moral philosophy, which was allowed free access to their courts.

This circumstance sometimes led the propagators of the Stoic message to compromises and restatements of their thinking, especially in an area which interested every sovereign: the possibility of using force. Zeno's original teaching was very precise on this point, as necessary if it was to be consistent. The cosmopolis rejected all distinctions of race, caste, and sex; it refused to entertain the notion of a difference between Greek and barbarian, and taught that every individual took part in the formation of a universal will; the Aristotelian doctrine of the division of men into those destined to command and those condemned to obey was rejected, as was the Platonic doctrine of the existence of a special class of individuals whose right to command should be nurtured and developed through culture and physical exercise. In these circumstances it is virtually certain that Zeno also condemned the use of violence. However fragmentary the Stoic literature that has come down to us, there is still some evidence as to how Zeno tackled and solved the problem. Let it suffice to recall Stoicism's emphasis on the virtuous behavior required of the individual by his rational nature.

Universal harmony could not be achieved unless it resisted forces hostile to it, particularly war, a tragic calamity both for individuals longing for serenity and for the cosmopolis with its predestined design of perfection. The Stoics believed that there was a single virtue of which the individual virtues constituted the external manifestations; the organization of mankind must therefore also be unitary. For this reason there was no doubt as to the urgency of creating an ecumenical state, working effectively as a day-to-day political reality. The traditional division of mankind into states and nations, each distinguished from the other by its own beliefs and its own constitution, was rejected by the Stoics, who argued that all men should be considered as belonging, in essence, to the same state. Since mankind could be compared to a flock entrusted to the care of a single shepherd (who must be a wise man endowed with good judgment and capable of curbing its instincts and passions), and since the ideals and the speculation of men must tend toward unity, the exclusion of war from the number of instruments vouchsafed man to help him solve his problems must be inferred as a direct corollary. The Stoics denied that men were destined to live in small autarchic communities. They now offered man boundless political and moral horizons, and dismissed as wrong every attempt to subdue one's neighbor and to consider him as an object to be conquered and enslaved.

Zeno believed that a universal society based on justice must obey only one divinity, love, to which no temples would be dedicated, no bulls slaughtered, and no gifts made, but which would inform the behavior of all. Through love, men would be brought up in the practice of justice, with the result that money, courts, and even the family—the basic institution in a fragmented and divided community—would be rendered unnecessary. The family would no longer be needed in an ecumenical community governed with serenity. Within the community the individual would not need to concern himself with his own defense, nor live in a condition of permanent fear.

The successor of Zeno as head of the school founded by him in Athens was Cleanthes of Assos (ca. 331-ca.232 B.C.), a thinker perhaps of less acumen than his master but holding similar views on the problem of mutual tolerance and the inherent universality of man. The key to his teaching was the need for all human beings to behave in accordance with the law of nature. Identifying the essence of life with the exercise of virtue, he inferred that only virtue can supply the necessary opportunity and impulse for the attainment of serenity and happiness. These are benefits very different from pleasure, which in the hierarchy of values was unattainable and in any case superfluous, because it did not respond to a natural law. But serenity and happiness became in their turn mirages when the attention and cares of men were drawn away from their logical objectives and directed toward those set by the practice of violence and war. Cleanthes believed that violence and war were the causes of the greatest anomalies and entailed a violation of the cosmic harmony linked with the "general law of God."

The sources of our knowledge of Stoicism are few in number, since nearly all the relevant discourses are lost. In general, we must make the most of secondhand evidence. In the case of Cleanthes, however, we possess a fragment of thirty-nine lines which reveals in a direct way this philosopher's judgment on the duties incumbent on man. In the *Hymn to Zeus* his mood is one of acute bitterness when he considers the destiny of humanity, incapable of respecting the law of love, the only law which would enable it to live according to its true vocation. We become aware here of the ferment of a religious feeling seeking the liberation of man from evil, which of all the serfdoms is the most humiliating.

For so hast thou fitted all good things into one with the bad, that there arises one rule for all things that ever exist; which rule all wicked mortals shun and neglect; hapless men, who, always longing after the possession of

good things, neither see nor hear this universal law of God, by wisely obeying which, they would lead an excellent life. But abandoning what is noble,
they rush in pursuit of different objects; some carrying on a bitter struggle
for fame, some turning to the unfair pursuit of gain, and others seeking after ease and bodily gratifications.[186]

The passage not only expressed the keen disappointment Cleanthes feels for
the perverted states of mind which are responsible for the disasters befalling
men, but points the way toward a new way of life governed by the law of
God, whose kingdom is the entire world.

Because of the volume of his literary output, of which only a few fragments have come down to us and because of his careful restatement of Zeno's thought, Chrysippus of Cyprus (ca. 280-ca. 208 B.C.) was regarded in ancient times as the second founder of Stoicism. In his teaching, too, the exist-
tence of a universal state was inferred from a natural law. It was true that
states existed which were often at war with one another, but the responsibility for this must be attributed to the insolence of men and to the lack of
trust and serenity in their relationships, due to corruption. On the other hand,
the law of nature shows the persistence of a rule of love. This rule was valid
and effective between men as well, who should have taken it as a guide for
their conduct. Chrysippus, like other authors, had written an essay on *Concord,* now lost. It probably embodied his reflections on the problem of peace
and war. That it was written is in itself proof of Chrysippus' interest in the
subject, although Plutarch, a relentless and not always truthful critic of the
Stoics, accuses him of laying responsibility for war at the feet of the gods and
of regarding war as one way of dealing with the population problem.[187]

Several authors (Diogenes Laërtius, Cicero, Seneca, Philodemus) bore witness to Chrysippus' opposition to the use of violence, which he believed to be
as unnatural as the institution of slavery. The fact that this philosopher was
honored, almost worshipped, for decades, that many leaders of the Hellenistic
and Roman governing classes were brought up in his school or on his works,
which were regarded as vying in profundity of content and force of anticipation with those of Plato and Aristotle, is an accurate measure of the prestige
enjoyed by his teaching. His basic universality transcended the empirical experience of the individual, necessarily limited and incommunicable. But this
attitude would have proved meaningless if it had not also exercised an influence on moral values and on the rules of conduct which men were required to
follow. Developed into a rule of living, it led to the condemnation of physical
violence, both in relations between individuals and in those between states,
and to an implicit encouragement of tolerance and moderation.

At times Stoic thought closely resembles a kind of religious instruction,
more concerned with feeling than with rational arguments. But even if the
problem is examined from this angle, the definite rejection of war is clearly
implicit and necessary. Failing direct proof that the Stoics condemned war (of

an indirect bias there can be no possible doubt), it is worth recalling that, following the example of Hesiod and Plato, they liked to hark back to a legendary Golden Age. Once, they said, there had been only chaos. Then—through an act of will of God, or of the Logos, the sublime ordinating intellect, or by destiny—chaos, lacking shape, light, and color, changed into cosmos. At the beginning, the universe entered into an era of innocent beatitude. Men lived grouped in peaceful communities without fighting and without coveting what did not belong to them, but spontaneously observing a principle of hierarchy which impelled them to obey the wisest among them. They were guided by a desire to respect the natural law, among whose rules a fundamental one was that of not destroying life around them, be it men or animals. Being vegetarians, they lived on wild fruit, milk, and honey. But an urge to draw profit from the natural laws, to improve their lot, slowly took the place of their primitive simplicity. They began to fabricate tools and build dwelling places, the arts progressed, the use of metals spread. The arms manufactured were used in the first conflicts, which were always the outcome of covetousness. Their primeval innocence disappeared altogether and with it peaceful community life. In its place were betrayal, envy, and the desire to prevail over others through force and coercion. Thus the conditions, without which the terrible wars could never have been fought were fulfilled.

But there was a remedy for so many evils. Universal government, for which mankind longed and which had been foreshadowed by the Empire of Alexander, the Hellenistic monarchies, and later the Roman state, was ultimately bound to pave the way to the formation of a peaceful society, in which disputes between groups would be seen as a macabre aftertaste of an era gone forever. The evolutive cycle had enabled mankind to move gradually from its original meek simplicity to the state of strife and lasting instability. At an unknown date in the future this cycle would turn full circle and man would win back his peace of mind and his purity. Especially in its earliest forms, Stoic philosophy was closely linked to the fostering of peace, as expressed both in the representation of the first ages of humanity and in their political vision. It is right to conclude that their political views implied a rational condemnation of war so that differences between men could be settled by peaceful means on the basis of universal brotherhood.

Stoic thinking offered the most valid contribution in Greek civilization to the formation of a collective morality, aimed at freeing the individual and society from the uncertain fluctuations of a world rent by armed conflicts. Proof that such a message had considerable importance is found in the discourses which have survived and in the influence of Stoicism on Roman society, on the doctrines of Christianity, and on other religions.

Epicurus and the Quest for Peace of Mind

Epicureanism was the most sharply criticized of the teachings of antiquity. The moralizing zeal of pagans and Christians, allied in condemning a doctrine apparently conflicting with every accepted ethical principle, found in it a most satisfying target for abuse. The Epicureans attributed to pleasure a central role in the behavior of the individual, regarding it as a means of escaping the mishaps and misfortunes of existence. This fact seemed to justify criticism, which was in reality facile and colored by the incomprehension of ill-informed teachers of ethics. The opposition is explained, at least in part, by Epicurus' own behavior. Perhaps partly to attract the public's attention to his philosophy, he adopted unconventional attitudes which reflected his thinking only in part but were bound to surprise and alarm his audiences. Certain statements concerning the priority of the enjoyment of the senses startled many pagans who cherished a less hedonistic vision of existence and later the Christians who regarded all celebration of pleasure as coming from the devil.

But the ancients themselves tentatively revised this very one-sided view of Epicureanism. It became obvious that, in posing the problems of life in an apparently bizarre manner and addressing himself to society's rejects (for example, the *hetaerae* and the uneducated)—an attitude which deeply upset those who regarded philosophy as essentially a gentleman's pastime—Epicurus pioneered a new approach for the wise man in his relations with society. While the Stoics had been content to view community as a conceptual abstraction. Epicurus studied it in its many components, thus including the persons whom pagan society ignored or excluded. A closer analysis of his thinking reveals the presence of certain reforming doctrines, designed mainly to offer the thinking man a rule of life, and at the center is placed the quest for pleasure, as a means of achieving rebirth and peace of mind and not as an invitation to indulge in the more sordid aspects of human nature. Epicurus was a practical man and liked to strip ideas of all rhetorical decoration, relating them to their usefulness to men.

A political pattern of conduct was derived from these principles, which in essence became an attack on conventional society, considered as the great corruptor. The problem was to establish how far the individual should take part in public affairs. The hedonistic premises entailed rejection of all activity of this kind. The wise man should be content to work with moderation if public duties were imposed on him, but he certainly should not seek such honors. Epicurus' Maxim No. 58 is explicit on this point: "One must free oneself of the serfdom of domestic occupations and of that of public affairs." Since participation in politics would be certain to lead to dangerous mental stress, the wise man should protect himself in advance, avoiding, as far as possible, occasions likely to involve him in political controversy. In exchange for Stoic cosmopolitanism the Epicureans offered a vigorous individualism. Epicurus and his school were prepared to cut down the rhythm of human enthusiasm to its lowest level, vegetating serenely, pending the advent of the unavoidable and the predestined.

There is something pathetic about all this. The Epicurean's desire for peace and tranquillity resulted in worldly renouncement. The good life is the life of the spectator. There was no active commitment of any kind, since it was accepted that life passed by, a spectacle for the senses and for man's reason, almost without its passing being noticed. The Epicureans were not therefore unbridled *bons vivants,* as their foes claimed, but silent spectators, waiting for an unforeseen event which, as in certain stage plays, would finally resolve the enigma of the plot.

The Epicurean feared war as harmful for the physical life and the moral integrity of the individual. Detached from reality, constantly in search of a kind of sublime listlessness, he disapproved of the enthusiasm which led to military campaigns and enabled soldiers to face death in battle. These spasms of enthusiasm would have been praiseworthy if they were the response to an impulse of the mind, but the mind was in fact overcome by emotion, which the Epicurean condemned.

Unlike the Stoic, the Epicurean had no special interest in the "cosmopolis." The absence of all enthusiasm explained why his intellectual existence was wholly devoted to the contemplation of a reality placed outside himself, a reality in which he refused to play any role whatever. It is difficult to document all this through the writings of Epicurus, for while there were a large number of these, almost all have now been lost. But it may be inferred from other evidence of the time and from the fact that this philosophical system helped to restrain man's impulses and to neutralize active life, otherwise fitfully disturbed by incidents to which the wise man was not expected even to react. War could not interest him, for his main objectives must remain the consolidation of his indifference and the defense of his own right to peace—including peace of mind.

The Skeptics

The coexistence of different doctrines, all seeking the truth but almost always conflicting as to method, led to Ciceronian Eclecticism (which we shall deal with in chapter 2). It also led some thinkers to a blanket rejection of all doctrines. These thinkers came to the conclusion that the truth could not be attained and that all attempts to do so were useless. Here we have the confirmation of a phenomenon which is not isolated in the history of human thinking, whereby, as a result of the clash of contemporary philosophic and scientific doctrines, man finds himself in a position to accept or reject them all indifferently.

This was what happened in the Skeptic school. The Skeptics, following the teaching of Pyrrho (365-275 B.C.), founder of the school, rejected the leading philosophical doctrines of the time and concluded that none of them, despite the profundity of their arguments, had succeeded in supplying a solution to the problems raised. How therefore was it possible to enter into possession of the truth and achieve an explanation of knowledge acquired through the senses? By accepting the subjectivism of the Sophists, who pointed to the multiplicity of individual elements of knowledge and denied the possibility of validly reducing them to unity? Pyrrho claimed that this synthesis could not be achieved and that human understanding could not penetrate deeper than appearances. All judgment must remain in abeyance, since to understand in depth was a gift not vouchsafed to man. The solution of all controversies was empirically and necessarily entrusted to the senses themselves. But they were manifestly incapable of playing the simultaneous roles of prosecutor, judge, and defendant in the court of philosophy. It is easy to see where this line of reasoning could lead. Since it was deemed impossible to penetrate beyond the knowledge acquired by the senses, it was also impossible to attain real knowledge of the nature of things. According to the Skeptics even Aristotle's syllogism was really no more than a trick.

When he denied the value of any research into the truth and advised the wise man to abstain from making judgments, Pyrrho was attacking not only the philosophies of Plato and Aristotle but also that of the Stoics and certain anomalies immanent in Stoic teaching. The Stoics, working in an atmosphere deeply imbued with cosmopolitical ideas and the appeal of universalism, opposed contemporary doctrines and customs, widening their horizons beyond the confines of the little states which had played such an important role in the emergence of Hellenic speculation. The Skeptics, on the other hand, starting from the same premises, denied the value of judgment, favored a limitation of the objectives to be pursued, arguing that it was right to refrain from all active commitment to community life. The basis of all this was an extreme form of subjectivism, but not of the kind defended by the Sophists.

The destructive philosophy of the Skeptics left the vital impulses of the individual sadly compromised, especially when it moved from the field of knowledge to that of ethics. Here the opposition of Pyrrhonism to all forms of dogmatism became really obvious in extreme and paradoxical forms. Not only must man suspend his own judgment but also curtail all constructive activity. Meditation and a spirit of profound indifference remarkably remote from the positive character of the Greek mentality were the key features of Skepticism. It also had an element of oriental fatalism, of the annihilation of the individual in the face of the mysteries of the universe, which rose before him like an impassable barrier, curbing his emotional impulses and restraining any urge to act.

The ancient historians believed that Pyrrho had visited India in the train of Alexander the Great. There, it is said, he met the Gymnosophists, who pursued a kind of speculative activity very different from that of the Greeks: Indian philosophy was influenced by Buddhism and by an attitude of mind marked by detachment from earthly things, by the withdrawal of the thinking intellect into itself, and by an indifference to community life.[188]

An oriental element was certainly present in Skeptical thinking. The detachment recommended to the individual as a means of curing himself of the

ills of the world and of avoiding the harmful impact of the environment unquestionably represented a departure from Hellenic tradition, which sometimes went to extremes in denying realities perceived by the senses and apprehended by the intellect but never took this tendency to the extreme of neutralizing man through inertia. The notion that every proposition can be explained indifferently by a given statement and its opposite is definitely in conflict with their tradition. It was the negation of the principle of noncontradiction, according to which a statement and its opposite cannot be equally true.
The Sophists had affirmed something of this kind, but more as a rhetorical artifice than as a speculative method, as often as not in an attempt to dispose of
the received ideas of the past.

The peculiar state of relaxation in which most Greeks carried on their debates helps us to understand Pyrrho's arguments. The Greeks felt that the un-
ending disputes of the philosophers had perhaps served to refine the intelligence and sensitivity of the participants but had not fully met the need for
truth, nor had they succeeded in ensuring peace and serenity for men tormented by conflict.

How far were the Skeptics convinced of the need to achieve and cultivate
peace by conducting speculative inquiries and making moral recommendations
in this field? We know that, in line with the premises laid down by the founder of the school, they advised the wise man to shut himself off from the outside, to hold off from active life and let the world pass by, to stand and stare,
but *only* to stand and stare, not to get involved. The refusal to allow oneself
to be governed by circumstances or to take part in controversies entered not
only into the logic of the system, but also into the new psychological outlook
of the Greeks, who by now were tired of the excesses to which philosophical
disputes had led.

The Skeptics found these disputes boring. They denied the value of inquiry into a field they believed to lie outside that of the human intellect. They
shut themselves off in the ivory tower of their own ideas, asking no questions
as to the nature of phenomena which they regarded as complete in themselves
and incapable of supplying information on universal principles. All this being
so, how much less could they attach real importance to futile incidents and
circumstances which lead to conflicts and bring about appalling disasters for
peoples and states? Pyrrho and his disciples denied the correctness of any
doctrine and considered philosophy as a disturbance of human existence and
a threat to the stability of the individual. They saw the discussions between
advocates and opponents of the various systems as words for the sake of
words, word wars reminiscent of the noise made by the warriors in Homer. It
was therefore inevitable that armed conflict, obvious evidence of human inability to reach agreement would arouse an even greater aversion among men
who sought only tranquillity and abhorred anything that could hamper the
serene conclusion of their research.

The above is the transposition of Skeptical speculation into the field of war and peace: The few fragments which have survived support only in part our arguments that the Skeptics, no less than the Cynics and the Stoics, were morally committed to the thesis that a condition of peace must govern human development and that an end must be put, not only to discord among philosophers, but to the far more serious and cruel manifestations of hate in the form of violence.

Although Skepticism acquired the status of a philosophical teaching which would actually find a place in the sanctum of the Academy, the Skeptics resorted, on occasion, to presenting themselves as the enemies and fierce critics of contemporary society. A good example is Timon of Phlius (ca. 320-ca. 230 B.C.), a disciple of Pyrrho, his successor as director of the Skeptic school, and a great enemy of philosophers. In a satirical poem entitled *Silloi*, of which only a few fragments have survived, Timon pillories the whole class, sarcastically describing his protagonists' descent to the lower regions and dialectical encounters with various thinkers. None of the great personages of the Greek speculative tradition, from Heraclitus to Zeno of Citium, emerges unscathed. They are represented as grotesque word-mongers, seldom believing in their own arguments and an easy prey to flattery. This satirical discourse at many points parodied Homer. A philologist—Wilhelm Wachsmuth—has attempted a reconstruction.[189] Not all Wachsmuth's ideas—ingenious but sometimes dangerously near the arbitrary—can be accepted, but he was probably right as to the nature of the composition. Peace of the mind, no less than that of body—that is to say, the cessation not only of academic controversy but also of armed conflict—must necessarily have been the ultimate objective of a line of thinking of this kind, deliberately rejecting the paraphernalia of public success and the widespread custom of adulating anybody who has achieved notoriety. The story probably ended with the intervention of Pyrrho, coming as the bringer of peace. Pyrrho rebukes the philosophers for the futility of their idle chatter and reestablishes harmony. Skeptical thinking thus used antidogmatic arguments and satire to clear the air of the conventional commonplaces which are the very origin of discord.

It seems probable that Skepticism condemned war and favored peace as a force catalyzing human energies, moderating the harmful influences and bringing out the more noble ones. Proof of this is discernible in the later developments of the doctrine. We know that Timon had no disciples and that, after him, the teaching ceased to exist as such. It transmigrated, however, into the Middle Academy, successor to that created by Plato, of whose philosophy the Academy was a faithful proponent and commentator.

The founder of the Middle Academy was the Skeptic Arcesilaus of Pitane (ca. 315-240 B.C.). A man of vigilant and sensitive mind, he distinguished himself in the difficult labor of reconciling the dogmatic tradition of the Platonic school with the fitful and individualistic style of Skeptic teaching. Background to this conflict was the quarrel with the Stoics. Arcesilaus, speaking from a position of authority as head of the Academy, opposed Stocisim to the utmost, not only using the expedients provided by Pyrrhonism in its various guises, but also making the most of his singularly elegant rhetorical style. The basis of his system remained the claim that speculation could never achieve possession of the truth.

But suspension of judgment led to a cessation of all action. How could one know what road to follow and what one should do in the various circumstances of life if he was not even in a position to formulate an opinion? This was the very point at which Skeptic philosophy proved inadequate. Obliged to persist in unstable equilibrium in relation to the problem of knowledge, Arcesilaus faced the problem of action. Under pressure from his public to provide moral guidance, he could not refuse to formulate a doctrine which would trace out a line of conduct for the individual. This was the Skeptics' weak point, and the Stoics put their finger on it when they argued that it was absurd for the individual to act if he could formulate no opinions. The Skeptics retorted that if practical life demanded a rule of conduct, they discerned it in the reasonableness of every attitude and every statement. Their argumentation was roughly the following: The ultimate end of existence is happiness; the key to happiness is prudence; prudence stems from the certainty of not deviating from one's own duty; duty consists in performing certain actions in compliance with principles of reason.

The principle of indifference fitted by the Skeptics into the apparatus of Platonic speculation certainly made the system safe from the temptations of war. The Skeptics attached no value to objects and treated tangible reality as useless and contemptible, not worthy of attention, much less enthusiasm. Now war derives from emotional fervor, which is the opposite of indifference. It also presupposes a special obstinacy in sustaining arguments and doctrines deemed objectively just and so true as to demand defense and support even with the drawn sword. Intolerance, which lies at the root of all war, has its *raison d'etre* in the certainty that one is right, while the Skeptics were certain only that there could be no certainty.

Their thinking was therefore the least likely basis on which to justify war. The fact that Arcesilaus and the Academy varied Pyrrho's original views as to the need to suspend judgment did not involve any change in their opposition to war. Further: although they refused to admit the value of general principles, Arcesilaus and his disciples eventually appealed to human reason to judge reality, ruling case by case on the moral content and appropriateness of a certain act or a certain situation. By this criterion war was to fail the test even more completely than it had done for the Pyrrhonians, there being nothing in the world less likely to fit into the proposed patterns of reasonableness. A tendency to depart from the doctrine of Pyrrho and to align on the Socratic-Platonic tradition is discernible here. This was predictable both because the elaboration of the original Pyrrhonian ideas was to lead to a more complex and mature rethinking of the initial Skeptic position and because Platonism was bound to influence those who, like Arcesilaus, had accepted its speculative heritage.

Among the successors of Arcesilaus at the Academy, Carneades of Cyrene (ca. 214-ca. 129 B.C.) is remembered as one of the protagonists of a famous diplomatic and cultural mission to Rome, which marked a decisive change in the evolution of Roman thinking. Carneades' forte was dialectic. In the field of knowledge his position was not very different from that of Arcesilaus, though he developed the latter's opinions in his own theory of probability, which took the place of the dogmatic certainty to which the Skeptics were so hostile. It is said that, for Carneades, probability corresponded, in the field of knowledge, to what the reasonable represented for Arcesilaus in the field of ethics. Probability was concerned with the question: "What is truth?"; the second topic was concerned with the question: "What is the right way to behave?"

To ascertain whether Carneades' system provided the logical and rational premises for a justification of war, we must examine this doctrine. Because he opposed authority and reduced the problem of knowledge to the mere acquisition of facts deemed probable (not certain), he implicitly took sides with the enemies of war. As an acritical certainty of the rightness of certain opinions, dogmatism is the very fundament of war, which can be defined as an axiom taken to extreme conclusions and imposed upon others by force. It does not seem absurd to infer from this, even without conclusive evidence, that Carneades' speculation contains a pacifist component. Those who affirmed (in conflict with the views of earlier Skeptics) that the wise man could profess opinions relative, not to abstract and universal principles, but to phenomena as such were implicitly supporting a system based on uncertainty and doubt, in which war has no place.

The disparity between the views of Carneades and of the Middle Academy, on the one hand, and those of the founder of the school, on the other, was to be thrown into relief by Aenesidemus (first century B.C.), who accused the non-academic Skeptics of dabbling in the very dogmatism of which they claimed to be the enemy. He pleaded for a reversion to the doctrine of Pyrrho, for whom all attempts broke on the inevitable realization of one's inability to attain a concrete result. This harking back to the origins used its own methodology: Aenesidemus ordered systematically in categories, known as "tropes," the arguments which would prove that man could not enter into the possession of truth. In the tropes were grouped the elements which, through their being repeated and through the action exerted on the senses and on reason, generate distortions and errors of judgment which prevent man from achieving the truth. The tenth trope included habits, laws, and opinions. These were not sensations, but moral beliefs capable of infinite variation and, more than all others, confirmed by ordinary day-to-day experience. Aeneside-mus, and with him the later Skeptics who adopted the tropes as an essential part of their teaching, started from the finding that in the field of individual and collective ethics different peoples have quite different habits, which they all believe to be necessary. As examples, they noted that the Egyptians em-balmed their dead, while the Romans cremated theirs, and some Macedonian tribes simply threw the bodies into the marshes. In the field of marital ethics, the Persians had no legal bar to marriage between sons and their mothers, the Egyptians permitted marriage between brother and sister, while the Hellenes abhorred all incestuous relationships. Other differences were noted, as be-tween religious beliefs, the opinions of the philosophers, and the discourses of writers. The differences were therefore substantial and showed that those who had started, from isolated observations in the field of ethics and law, to reach certain universal results had taken their bearings from impressions which were in no way necessarily conclusive. The tenth trope was regarded as a proof of the inexistence of universally valid principles even in the field of morality.

This trope was the foundation of the postulate that since nothing can be proved, man can make no judgments but can only feel sensations. It therefore had a strong influence on opinions relating to war. It summarized the argu-ments usually used to show the absurdity of conventional attitudes toward community life and the efforts men made to penetrate society, the vanity of "social climbing," the futility of attempts to make significant changes in soci-ety. But of these attempts war was bound to seem the most resolute, since it reflected the opinion (absurd, like all opinions) that the possessors of truth could and should impose it on those who languished in the shadows and who must be brought to see the light. War therefore took its place among the fol-lies of mankind, the greatest of which consists in believing that certain conclu-sions can be judged as universally valid and imposed on other peoples by any means, even including force.

Pyrrhonian Skepticism, in its original formulation, as restated by Aeneside-mus, and in the neo-academic version, showed, in the general approach to the doctrine of knowledge and ethics, if not a desire to oppose the periodic ex-plosions of warlike insanity, at least an intellectual attitude condemning war as the major obstacle to that imperturbability which the wise man could not forego without betraying his speculative allegiance. Though the Skeptics did not actually come out firmly against war, unlike other contemporary and ear-lier philosophers, their criticisms of dogmatism as leading to extremism and sheer absurdity would necessarily extend to armed conflict, the most formi-dable and the most terrifying form of *a priori* reasoning.

Cosmopolitan Features of Hellenistic Religion. The Amphictyonies

The old order gave way to the new philosophies and to the new historical influences. Following the civil struggles, the Macedonian conquest, and lastly the Roman conquest, the new developments brought with them lasting and important changes. We have followed this process through speculative thinking and the works of writers. It would now be useful to survey other expressions of cultural activity to establish whether they were or were not affected by the same influences. How far, for example, were religion and art touched by an idea which came to the fore periodically in the reflection of the philosophers? Did they keep the characteristic imprint of archaic Greece, rooted to the celebration of war in its heroic and emotive aspects, or did they also react positively to the values of peace, tolerance, and brotherhood?

We have already seen that religion had made of peace a divinity called Irene, who is mentioned in Hesiod, but it is difficult to ascertain whether this resident of Olympus was the object of wide veneration. Aristophanes records the existence of a cult, adding that cruel sacrifices were not allowed.[190] But this is more likely a case of "wishful thinking" on the part of Aristophanes than actual fact. A statue of the goddess, a bronze work by the sculptor Cephisodotus, father of Praxiteles, was erected in the Agora of Athens. A number of copies were made during the Hellenistic and Roman period. In addition to the religious and moral significance of peace, the statue celebrated the material advantages and the prosperity reaped from it: Irene was represented holding in her arms a child impersonating Plutus (wealth).[191] According to Pausanias, another statue of Irene existed in the Prytaneum.[192] The figure of Peace also formed the decorative motif of various coins still extant. Isocrates and Cornelius Nepos recall that an altar was dedicated to peace in the Agora in about 374 B.C. and that an annual festival was held in her honor. According to Plutarch, the origin of the cult was seventy-five years earlier, just after the Peace of Callias (448 B.C.).[193]

The adventure of Alexander encouraged the natural tendency toward religious syncretism. In particular, the Greek world welcomed certain foreign rites with which it had come into contact and which, more than its own, seemed to offer a plan for spiritual salvation in the next world and peaceful community life in this. The solution given to the problem of salvation—the search for salvation was to become an essential aspect of the Christian message—had strong cosmopolitan overtones. From this angle, it would be useful to consider the spread of certain cults, for example that of the god Serapis. This cult arose in Hellenized Egypt as the result of a fortunate and by no means accidental marriage of local tradition with the most vital elements of Greek religious feeling. It involved the fusion of liturgies, of mystical experiences, of escatological certainties and even iconographical figures, in conformity with the tastes of the peoples mingling in Egypt. It was taken up with much enthusiasm around the Mediterranean basin and in the Middle East.

An Egyptian divinity who achieved great popularity in the Hellenistic period was Isis, whom Herodotus thought to be the same god as Demeter. Devotion to Isis spread in Greece and throughout the classical world, as far as distant Britannia, and she took over many attributes and peculiarities of former local divinities. The resistance of the cult to the advances of Christianity (though the two religions in fact shared some symbols and practices) and its efforts to overcome the empirical and fortuitous by praising values not circumscribed by the religious convictions of a single people were clear evidence of a cosmopolitan turn of mind.

The decadence of the polis did not leave the local gods unscathed. Of the Olympian gods, Zeus, Dionysus, and Aesculapius in particular survived the religious crisis, not because their cult had greater authenticity and verisimilitude but because it succeeded in achieving more pronounced universality, responding to the spiritual needs of a wider society. For example, the cult of Aesculapius, known in Laconia as the "friend of the crowd," seemed to extend its objectives beyond the curing of the body to the health of the spirit, the key to the individual's internal peace and perhaps to harmony among peoples. The cults tended to lose their personal character and link up with certain general aspirations. They were concerned with the intervention in worldly things of external forces—such as fate, fortune, necessity, nemesis—embodying, in the shape of vague terrors and hopes of succor, the emotions of the faithful.

Other religions of non-Greek origin engaged in highly successful campaigns of conversion. Most of them also offered believers a road to salvation on the basis of closer relationships between human beings, irrespective of national traditions. We are thinking of the Sabazian rites which emerged in the East, whose initiation ceremonies are mentioned by Demosthenes.[194] They were designed to propitiate peace. Other cults were those of Mithra, Artemis, Astarte and Attis. These favored a general and real syncretism which, perhaps without giving unity to the world of religious experiences, at least would limit their number.

There was also a liturgy of magical, arcane, and prophetic character which had developed under the influence of Orphic and Chaldean religions. It too had a universalist bias. The mystery practices served mainly to bring home to men truths not perceived by the senses and by reason. They achieved awareness of these truths through a process of sudden and ecstatic illumination occurring through the aid of privileged souls. The practices made it easier for the faithful to call on the aid of the gods. There were sibyls and prophetesses all over the classical world, endowed, they claimed, with prophetic powers. Believers from far and near made their way to these famous sages in search of advice and comfort. Serving the same "market" were the oracles, whose work of prophecy was administered according to liturgical rules which masked a good deal of pure charlatanism in ritual solemnity. Famous oracles in various parts of the Mediterranean world were consulted by pilgrims from all countries. At Eleusis, Samothrace, Crete, Delphi, and other localities, oracles were accessible to all and, by mediating with the world beyond the grave, offered every mortal the benefits he asked for.

A significant episode is reported concerning Alexander the Great, who consulted the famous oracle of Jupiter Ammon in the Libyan desert. This oracle was greatly venerated both in African circles and by the Greeks and Phoenicians. The oracle of a remote African oasis, whose rites, although Hellenized, certainly reflected experiences occurring in historical circumstances different from those of Greece, strengthened Alexander's belief in his divine origin and in the universal character of the mission to which he felt himself called. This is further evidence of the mutual interpenetration of influences in the ancient world. For the ancient religions, the cosmopolis was very near to a reality.

All this leads us to examine an institution characteristic of Greek life, closely connected with religion and regarded by many as an agency of mediation and conciliation between the city-states. We are referring to the amphictyonic leagues, sacred associations between cities professing the same cult, with their center in a given sanctuary. Their task was to coordinate devotional practices, ensuring free access to sacred places, administering their finances, ensuring their safety and neutrality in time of peace and war, and organizing periodic festivities. This work was generally dealt with by an amphictyonic council, on which all member cities were represented, though not always on an equal footing. It was precisely its vaguely democratic and representative constitution which suggested that the agency had, or should have, the powers of a court; it was given judicial tasks, and this is the feature which many feel is the important distinction between an amphictyonic league and a religious association concerned solely with the administration of a cult.

The most famous amphictyonic league was that of Delphi, whose sanctuaries were the temples of Apollo at Delphi and Demeter at Thermopylae. Various cities of the Greek peninsula were represented on the amphictyonic council. In the course of its long life it saw many vicissitudes and fluctuations in the pattern of power, but it survived into the Roman epoch. During the Persian wars it failed to organize a collective effort in defense of Greek independence but did decree a ransom on the head of traitors and voted solemn honors to those who had earned distinction on the battlefield.

The only sacred wars proclaimed by the amphictyonic leagues took place on less notable occasions of resistance against the invader. In 595 B.C. the amphictyonic council declared war against the city of Crisa because it had imposed a toll on pilgrims travelling to the sanctuary of Delphi, and the city was razed to the ground. In 448 B.C. a controversy broke out between Athens and Sparta concerning the administration of the sanctuary. Athens claimed that this was the responsibility of the Phocians and Sparta that it was a matter for the inhabitants of Delphi. The problem was solved by recourse to arms. In 356 B.C. a sacred war was proclaimed by the council against the Phocians because they had seized the lands of the sanctuary, and they were compelled to pay heavy fines. In 339 B.C. the council once again declared a sacred war, this time against the Amphissans, entrusting to Philip the conduct of operations. At the battle of Chaeronea (338 B.C.), Athens, allied with the Locrians, was defeated. Enslavement to Macedonian imperialism was perpetuated under the young Alexander, and the amphictyonic league was reduced to carrying out solely religious and administrative duties. The extent of such decadence can be measured by the reorganization of the seats of the council decided on by Octavian. Ignoring the rights of the most ancient cities, he allocated ten seats out of twenty-four to the inhabitants of Nicopolis, founded by him in memory of his victory over Antony and Cleopatra at Actium. The association, still active in the time of Pausanias (second century), fell into abeyance some time thereafter.

The Delian amphictyony, centered round the sanctuary of Apollo on the island of Delos, was formed by the Ionian communities of the archipelago and Asia Minor. Its fate was different. It is probable that it was originally a real military alliance against external enemies of the federated cities. We have no reliable information on the activities of a council similar to that of the Delphic league, and we do not even know whether the association, at least in the early periods of its existence, described itself as an amphictyonic league at all. The occupation of the island of Delos led to a shift in influence in favor of Athens, which deposited the treasure of the Delian league in the amphictyonic temple of Apollo. The transfer in 454 B.C. of the treasure of Delos to Athens marked the beginning of the end of the league. After a brief renaissance when the island passed into the Spartan sphere of influence after the battle of Aegospotami (405 B.C.), it again declined, finally disappearing completely.

The writings of the ancients and epigraphs and stone cuttings provide information on other groupings of cities which may well have been genuine amphictyonic leagues and not mere associations for common worship. One of these had its own sanctuary on an island off the eastern coast of Argolis and another in Boeotia devoted to the worship of Poseidon. This god was also worshipped by the amphictyonic league of Calauria, a small island in the Saronic Gulf, while Artemis was the protector of a league in Euboea. Very little reliable information has survived on similar federations which once existed in peninsular Greece and in Asia Minor.

For the purposes of our inquiry it would be useful to know whether the leagues were vested with powers of arbitration and, in particular, with that of imposing peace on the member states. The evidence seems to indicate that the Delphic council did exercise judicial powers over the member cities and their citizens. Though judgments to which we have referred were the object of considerable suspicion on the part of contemporaries, they nonetheless had a basis in absolute legitimacy. Moreover, if the principal objective of the league was to ensure liberty of worship and the independence of the sacred places, it was logical to vest the supervising college with the power to pursue transgressors. It was therefore right that the city of Crisa should be tried for having imposed an illegal toll which disturbed the exercise of worship and that the Phocians should be condemned for occupying lands which should have been left fallow. Because of their judicial duties, the officers of the amphictyonic leagues were required to have a smattering of law.

But the wider problem concerning us here is whether, in addition to the religious and judicial competences conferred on it, the amphictyonic council also had power in the field of political relations between member cities, especially power to consolidate peace and forestall war. There are not many hard facts, but the evidence does not seem to confirm the view that the council was vested with arbitral powers relating to all controversies, including purely lay disputes.

On the other hand it probably had a right to issue binding rules in a field approximating the international law of war, with the objective of alleviating the sufferings of soldiers and the civilian population. We know that amphictyonic law forbade member states to burn down enemy cities as a reprisal or to stop supplies of water, and that the penalty for those transgressing these rules was total war until they were completely destroyed. There is no sign whatever in this set of rules of any desire actually to outlaw war or to establish powers of arbitration. Nor did the fact that a law was recognized as binding necessarily signify that it would always be complied with. The Phocians, ordered in 356 B.C. to pay a fine ignored the judgment and even indulged in sacrilegious acts of aggression against the Delphic sanctuary, appropriating the treasure and using it to pay mercenaries.

It is interesting to note that the peace of 346 B.C. between Philip of Macedon and Athens assumed the form of an amphictyonic proclamation. The Delphic council was recognized as having the power of declaring sacred wars against peace-breakers. But the expansionist drive of Macedonia soon made a dead letter of this proclamation.

If we may finally conclude that the Delphic league was vested with ruling authority in matters of religion and law of war, it is nevertheless true that it lacked the necessary means to impose its decrees and its judgments. It must be remembered that the council was democratic only in appearance, since in practice it was almost always dominated by the state with the strongest army or navy. Its decisions were not autonomous but resulted from the sum of those of the member states, over which, even if there had been no weighting systems, the most powerful state always prevailed. It is therefore wrong to imagine that there was an embryonic supranationality, since the decisions never derived from an independent will separate from that of the states. On several occasions the association was in fact an instrument of hegemonial pressure.

The leagues were a consequence of the political conditions in which Greece developed. No one sought to make radical changes in these conditions and the ideas thrown out by the most advanced philosophers found no echo in the halls of the mighty. The status of the leagues as sacred associations led them to react cautiously, almost suspiciously, to anyone arguing the case for bold innovations. Consequently they probably regarded war as an essential factor in Greek civilization. Its elimination, as a fruit of utopian visions, might bring perhaps more serious harm than war itself. This said, it cannot be denied that the leagues were an original experiment, which in different historical circumstances and under the pressure of a more vigorous will, would have led to political unity. There was nothing which Greece needed more.

2

PEACE IN ROMAN THINKING
AND IN LATER
HELLENISTIC SPECULATION

The Ideological Motives behind Roman Expansion

Roman history-writers based their records to a great extent on distortions and inventions dating from periods well after the events to which they related. Their writings generally attempted to present as mythical predestination the prodigious adventure whereby a modest hamlet that happened to grow up on the bank of the Tiber became an opulent metropolis and a rude and primitive clan became the governing class of one of the greatest of all empires. An almost complete lack of original documents and the partisan tone of many texts compiled in the later era render critical inquiry especially difficult, for we no longer possess the chronicles from which the historians of antiquity drew their narratives. But we know that they sometimes yielded to the temptation to flatter persons or families seeking to consolidate their prestige by linking it to the origins of the city itself.

It is difficult enough to establish and understand what happened in the original Roman community; it is virtually impossible to pinpoint the philosophical and political forces and stresses which impelled a city, similar to so many thriving at the same era in the Italic peninsula, to build up a state with universal ambitions and a universal destiny. In the last analysis the task would be that of studying the historical and sociological process critical to the evolution of the portion of mankind centered around the Mediterranean basin, in order to answer such questions as: In achieving their tremendous wave of expansion, were the Romans responding to specific ideological imperatives? Did they act on the basis of preordained plans or, rather, pragmatically, adjusting to circumstances? Was there a doctrine inspiring their military

131

expansion, or was it that as a result of the successive annexation of a large number of territories the need was felt to find an ideological justification of a *fait accompli*? But research brings to light no answers to these questions. Only from the second century B.C. onwards do we find a complete political doctrine and a systematic examination of the problems of power and of the governing classes and their objectives. All inquiries of the kind respecting earlier centuries are hampered by a negative but formidable obstacle: the complete lack of documents and valid sources.

The formation of the empire led to political unity of a geographical area achieved by force of arms and the subsequent total submission of the conquered peoples; in the eyes of the Romans, the Roman state had a different status from that of the foreign nations, for the latter were required to relinquish all claims to independence and sovereignty and to throw themselves on the clemency of the victor. The Romans were convinced of the impossibility of maintaining relations with other countries on bases other than that of subjection to their own power.

We must, however, distinguish the period of expansion—with the gradual formation of the empire—from that during which, once past her prime, Rome was held at bay and finally vanquished by the peoples living on her borders. When we speak of the warlike ambitions of the Romans, we are referring to the first period, which may be dated roughly from the earliest times to the end of the first century A.D. The psychological, political, and institutional outlook of the Roman people was at that time essentially military. The etymology of a number of words may help us here. Thus, *virtus* stood for military valor and only later acquired the meaning of moral virtue; *hostis* was at one and the same time the enemy and the foreigner, enjoying no civil rights but subject to the discretionary powers of the Roman state as laid down in a rule contained in the twelve tables. Roman citizenship was closely identified with military service, and the sovereign power was referred to by a term of military origin: *imperium*. The exercise of *imperium* over the provinces was equivalent to a consolidated occupation, which imposed on provincials the payment of a *stipendium*, a tribute.

Economically, the Roman state in the first centuries was kept permanently on a war footing. It was ready at any moment to embark upon wars of aggression. The wars were used partly as a means of solving the economic crises and neutralizing the recurrent discontent of the ordinary people by diverting attention to happenings abroad. The pattern is now all too familiar. This does not mean that the Roman people lived in a state of constant warlike fervor (as would perhaps be correct to say of some Mesopotamian peoples and of the Spartans), nor that the military campaigns undertaken at regular intervals by the governing families were always fully supported by all classes. In the writings of the historians we can sometimes discern a note of disquiet and weariness regarding a policy which conceded no truces and subordinated everything to its exigencies. The following expression of war-fatigue is attributed by Dionysius of Halicarnasses to Coriolanus himself: "How fine a thing it is for everyone to enjoy his own possessions and to live in peace, how important to have no enemy and no crisis to fear. . . ."[1] The poet Livy noted the spread of weariness among the populations at war. He pointed out that the Sabines had a peace party as well as a war party and that the Romans could play the one off against the other;[2] he records that after the battle of Lake Regillus the war-weary Sabines unlawfully arrested the Volscian envoys who had come to urge resumption of operations;[3] he recalled how unpopular with the Roman plebes were the wars against the Volsci[4] and against the Veientes,[5] remarking that the tribunes of the people were liable to oppose military undertakings decided upon by the Senate, regarded as diversions and pretexts for putting off, rather than solving, the most urgent and pressing economic and social problems.

The formation of the Roman Empire through a series of successful military campaigns was not, then, a completely smooth process. There was resistance from broad sections of the population, especially from the lowest, to whom every conflict, even if it were a victorious one, could only bring sorrow and often actual bereavement. But when the Romans, following the example of the Greeks, began to reason in philosophic terms and the inexorable decline of their state began, their war-weariness was to prove far greater.

Etymology and Meaning of the Word Pax

From the etymological point of view the word *pax* belongs to the family of words deriving from the root *pak-pag* (to determine, to conjugate, to return). The fact that this etymology links up with that of *pacisci* (conclude a pact) suggests that the idea expressed indicated a condition free of conflicts, being the fruit of an encounter of separate wills; *pax* meant either a certain state of relations existing between two or more subjects, or the agreement through which this state was achieved. But for the Romans a treaty was an institution very different from that known to modern international law. It generally meant, purely and simply, the unconditional surrender of the defeated state. It could, however, assume the form of an alliance or a pact of friendship, or sanction the subjection of a people, if that people were regarded as incapable of resisting political and military pressure. This explains why Latin authors adopted expressions like "to impose," "to concede," "to dictate" peace terms. It was recognized, with the use of such words, that the relevant situations were due not to the convergence of free wills but to the victory of the Roman army.

All this implies, therefore, a substantial conceptual difference from the Greek εἰρήνη, whose legal basis was also formed by treaty, but a treaty devised differently from the way in which the Romans negotiated theirs. As in modern international law, the contracting parties in Greece were regarded, in theory, as having identical rights, even if in practice the content of the agreements was dictated by a given political and military situation.

The differing premises had another consequence. While the Greek εἰρήνη referred directly to the cessation of hostilities and the introduction of a new system of relations, the Latin *pax* did not necessarily arise from the end of a war, although this was very often the case. Peace, in the meaning of deliberate action for the attainment of certain legal objectives, could also refer to international situations in which aggressive political pressure had not been used and in which the relations between Rome and the other subjects were still maintained ostensibly on the level of friendly negotiation. Given its less rigid content, it is not surprising that the word *pax* came to indicate a state of mind; every commitment between states had a religious content connected with the sanctity of oaths, and it was the religious content that gave the commitment its binding force. Among the philosophical teachings imported into Rome from Greece, the Stoic school gained fuller acceptance than others and played a leading role in the subsequent development of philosophy, until the advent of Christianity. But Stoicism, with its mystical bias, addressed to all men and calling them to reject the dominion of the passions, advocated a universal solidarity which could not be achieved without peace of the spirit. It tended to praise a state of mind indifferent to material interests and aiming at higher metaphysical objectives. Although, in the later development of the school, this indifference to the adversities of daily life assumed a more cerebral function and one less spontaneous than that attributed to it by the original teaching of Zeno, it was nonetheless evident in the new meaning given to the word *peace*, which came nearest to that state of conscious serenity encouraged by the school.

The expression *pax animi* thus acquired the meaning of a condition of tranquillity and security from which the wise man and the philosopher drew the most profit. To qualify the term in this philosophical and moral sense, *pax* was often accompanied by adjectives like *secura, tranquilla, placida,* words emphasizing the condition of mind already implied by the substantive. Thus Cicero was able to say: "The wise man is always free from all turbulence of mind," and "always in his mind there reigns the most placid peace."[6]

The consequences of peace—if the concept were not limited to individual preoccupations, affections, and interests—were of course reflected in community life, especially in that of the state: To maintain the mind free of disturbances and passion, free to aspire to the joys of the contemplative life, political and social stability must be secured. It will be understood, therefore, why the peace imposed by Rome became the principal ideological justification for the empire when it took the place of the Roman Republic, which had fallen prey to civil strife. The word *pax* gradually assumed the meaning of security based on a centralized system, in which authority occupied a position of primacy over liberty. In the celebration of the order and stability assured by the empire there was a sense of legitimate satisfaction for the tranquillity achieved, from which every citizen benefited, whether brought up on philosophy or not. We may quote, in this connection, Velleius Paterculus (ca. 19 B.C.-ca. 32 A.D.), a court writer who praises the benefits deriving from the pacification of the state and then adds: "The *pax augusta,* which has spread to the regions of the east and of the west and to the bounds of the north and of the south, preserves every corner of the world safe from the fear of brigandage."[7]

Pax Romana

The various shades of meaning which the word *pax* embraced were to lead to the formulation of a wider concept: that of the *pax romana,* which embodied the idea of external relations based on the great power achieved by the Roman Empire, that of the liberation of the body politic from the shadow of civil war, and the idea of the formation of an atmosphere favorable to the activities of the mind. But the background remained the formalized set of attitudes centered around the Romans' proud conviction that they had been vested with the mission of imposing their laws and way of life on the rest of the world. The expression was given currency by Seneca, who used it in his *De providentia* (IV, 14).

Almost all the Roman writers agreed that spreading peace among mankind meant subjecting other peoples to Roman dominion. According to various writers, the Emperor Probus (276-282), whose own background was purely military, remarked to intimates that one day "the soldiers would no longer be necessary."[8] The statement seemed curious, and the historian Flavius Vopiscus observes:

> What was he thinking of when he said that? Had he not subjugated the barbarian nations? Had he not given the whole world to Rome? Could he then say, "Soon we will need soldiers no more"? It was just as if he had said, "There will no longer be a Roman army; the state, guaranteed by its own security, will dominate everywhere, will possess everything. Supplies will not be accumulated for war; the oxen will stay harnessed to the plough; the horse will be born for peaceful work. There will be no more wars and no more prisons. Peace will reign everywhere, as will the Roman laws, as will our judges."[9]

It was implicit in the reasoning that the nonsubject peoples could not enjoy conditions of peace and tranquillity. This feeling was an aspect of the conviction among the Romans that they were the sole artificers of history and were free to ignore completely the reactions of the nations over which their dominion was exercised. None took the trouble to question the subject peoples, of whose views very little is now known, mainly because, even when expressed, nobody thought them worth writing down. A pertinent example is in the words of Florus: "Thus the civil wars came to an end; the other wars were waged against foreign nations and broke out in different quarters of the world while the empire was distracted by its own troubles. Peace was a new state of affairs, and the proud and haughty necks of the nations, not yet accustomed to the reins of servitude, revolted against the yoke recently imposed upon them."[10]

The episode of Boadicea, queen and priestess of the British tribe of the Iceni, to whom Dio Cassius attributes the following words spoken to the subject people, is eloquent evidence of the kind of resentment provoked by the *pax romana:*

> You have learned by actual experience how different freedom is from slavery. Hence, although some among you may previously, through ignorance of which was better, have been deceived by the alluring promises of the Romans, yet now that you have tried both, you have learned how great a mistake you made in preferring an imported despotism to your ancestral mode of life, and you have come to realize how much better is poverty with no master than wealth with slavery. For what treatment is there of the most shameful or grievous sort that we have not suffered ever since these men made their appearance in Britain? Have we not been robbed entirely of most of our possessions, and those the greatest, while for those that remain we pay taxes? Besides pasturing and tilling for them all our other possessions, do we not pay a yearly tribute for our very bodies? How much better it would be to have been sold to masters once for all than, possessing empty titles of freedom, to have to ransom ourselves every year![11]

Boadicea thought serfdom preferable to conditions under the Roman conquest, although the occupation was presented as the victory of civilization over barbarianism, serving the pacification of unsettled peoples and territories. Calgacus, commander of the tribes of southern Britain who were defeated about 85 A.D. at the battle of Mount Graupius, was even harsher. According to Tacitus, he summed up the Roman conquest in these famous words: "To plunder, butcher, steal, these things they misname empire: they make a desolation and they call it peace."[12]

The *pax romana* was no different from that imposed by the conquerors of all times, who always desired the cessation of hostilities, it is true, but only on terms dictated by themselves. However, there are two sides to every coin. The new equilibrium imposed by the conquerors in the conquered countries did in fact favor the consolidation of order and discipline, which the subject peoples had seldom enjoyed in the past. Opened to a wider world and stimulated by the Roman presence, the local economies began to develop. After the military conquest, which required painful processes of adaptation and conversion, the defeated communities, organized administratively according to a principle of municipal autonomy, enjoyed many material and moral advantages, including a considerable degree of religious toleration. The deep divisions caused by warfare soon disappeared; animosities and destruction were forgotten as living conditions improved. The *pax romana* thus became associated with good ad-

ministration keeping the peace between peoples subject to the same authority, a single law, and, after Constantine, even a single religion. This explains
why its memory was often evoked nostalgically when the empire waned and
the benefits of the *pax romana* had been lost as a result of religious upheaval,
economic crisis, or barbarian invasion.

Although the *pax romana* was the product of empirical ideas adopted by
occupying armies and by administrators brought in afterwards, its progressive
expansion made the Romans feel that it was the best way of life for the whole
known world. An individual conquest was never seen as the final objective of
a given political and military operation but as a transitional phase toward further goals, the last of which would be the unification of the inhabited world
under a single authority. Nor did such a target seem unattainable; since the
imperfect geographical knowledge at the time suggested that by far the greater majority of men and women lived in the countries around the Mediterranean, their military, political, and administrative unity was believed to be syn-
onymous, in effect, with that of mankind. As for the peoples who lived beyond these confines and whose incursions disturbed the development of the
outlying provinces, they were written off as *gentes non pacatae,* barbarians
whose assimilation into the Roman state, at the time of its greatest splendor,
was believed neither necessary nor desirable. In fact the Mediterranean peoples, so far from being alone on earth, were not even the most numerous or
the most sophisticated. For example, during the very same epoch the Chinese
civilization, thriving hundreds of miles to the east, protected the arts and implemented social and political reforms along lines which we would regard today as highly progressive and uncannily modern.[13] Occasionally travelers'
tales hinted of the existence of other peoples who had achieved high levels of
organization and progress, but there is no evidence that this affected the Romans' conviction that they were at the center of the inhabited universe and
that it was their manifest destiny to supervise its development. The same
blind self-confidence recurs in other empires—for example, those of Charle-
magne and Napoleon. They too aimed at consolidating military and dynastic
hegemonies with a view to achieving essentially universal objectives.

In the first centuries of the Roman expansion, all research in the institutional and political field was confined to choosing methods of governing the
subject nations, a choice made generally out of empirical and fortuitous motives, related to no real ideology. Respect for the local laws, especially the religious laws, was at best a matter of administrative convenience. To conquer
the known world meant to extend one's own range of influence, to become
stronger and to consolidate the legend of one's own greatness. The
pansion was therefore achieved according to ideas and principles which had
no place in any formal doctrine. Their implementation was sometimes left to
the whim of the local governor.

Greek Influence on Roman Thought

The Romans' dislike of any systematic theory of government disappeared, however, when Rome came into contact with the Hellenic world. It was in the second century B.C., following the annexation of Greece, that the Romans, or at least some intellectuals among them, began to take an interest in doctrines which the philosophic schools had begun to popularize. The first reactions to the spreading of the Greek ideas were ones of reserve and suspicion. The new way of thinking and reasoning, so different from the old ideas, was a challenge to a number of deep-rooted convictions. However, the Romans were not without a considerable degree of mental resilience. The two civilizations exchanged notes, as it were, and found that they had much to teach each other, so that ideas gradually converged and were mingled in an osmosis which enriched and changed both sides. The Roman culture was the offspring of this marriage of mentalities, experience, thought, and language. This explains why the ideas and theories of government and of relations between states which supplied the first ideological justification of expansion were Greek. It also explains how the Stoic philosophy—basically universal and peaceful—gained acceptance and won influence among the haughty and powerful families of Rome.

The first Greek philosophers to visit Rome were given a cool, almost hostile, reception. The Stoic Crates, head of the Pergamene library, made the journey in 159 B.C. and gave a number of lectures describing the principles of his school. Four years later, in 155 B.C., a famous Athenian embassy exercised a decisive influence on the subsequent development of Roman thinking, which finally abandoned its traditional isolation. Members of this mission were the exponents of the three main schools of thought of the time: Diogenes of Seleucia for the Stoics, Critolaus for the Peripatetics and Carneades for the Academy. Diogenes in particular impressed the Romans by the gravity and quality of his exposition, while Carneades shocked and scandalized by the refined but misleading subtleties of his argumentation.

The influence of Greek speculation on the political activity of the Romans and on their treatment of other peoples was at first small. This is probably because of the resistance of Roman realism, instinctively aroused by the dialectical skirmishing in which the scholars often indulged. The peasant and military origins of the race were still too recent for it to be able to accede at once to an entirely new vision of reality and to forms of reasoning often pivoting on sophistry and paradox. How could doctrines like that of Epicurus, who recommended abstaining from all petty activity and practicing pure cogitation, or that of the Skeptics, who regarded all initiative as the expression of a sterile activism utterly unlikely to benefit man, be of any use to the tenacious, self-willed, and headstrong Romans?

Only Stoicism apparently had something to offer the Roman mind, both because it provided a rule of ethics under which relations between individuals were interpreted in terms of mutual understanding and tolerance and because it appeared to suggest, in the field of relations between states, a system which could be used to justify Roman expansion. The Stoics had grouped in confraternities, governed by actual hierarchies which were already flourishing in centers like Athens, Pergamum, Seleucia, Rhodes, and Alexandria. It is not surprising that they sought to gain a foothold in the capital of the state which was about to complete the conquest of the eastern Mediterranean. Another more mundane reason why Rome was a coveted goal was that, having long lain outside the ambit of important philosophical thought, it appeared to offer prospects of easy successes and profitable careers.

A radical change was, however, already discernible. In the second half of the second century B.C., cultivated Rome was a forum in which, despite the resistance of the conservative classes, many masters of philosophy, particularly the Stoics, sought to guide the decisions of the governing class, exerting over it real moral power. The most brilliant and versatile minds of every province, but particularly of Greece, set out to conquer the administrative and governmental heart of a great empire. And despite political and military reverses, the Greeks retained a dialectical and inventive superiority which quickly cast a spell over the Roman intelligentsia.

Panaetius of Rhodes and the Scipionic Circle

One name comes immediately to mind in any consideration of the ways in which this process of cultural penetration took place: Panaetius of Rhodes (ca. 189-ca. 109 B.C.). Born into a leading family, he had been trained in Pergamum and in Rhodes in the practice of philosophy. In Athens he followed the Stoic teaching of Diogenes of Seleucia, the same Diogenes who, representing his own school, had visited Rome in 155 B.C. Having moved to Rome, Panaetius, perhaps as a tribute to the experience and advice of the master, very soon became associated with the Scipionic circle. This group of intellectuals, clustered around the noble Roman family, included the liveliest minds of the time, a group of men anxious to bring up to date the old-fashioned Roman culture, now manifestly behind the times. Panaetius became an intimate friend of Scipio the Younger, and Scipio took him to the East when sent on an official mission, keeping him for a long period at his side. Panaetius settled later in Athens, where he became director of the "Stoa," a post he held for the rest of his life.

Having grown up in the Hellenistic world, Panaetius represented the link between Hellenic and Roman thought. The fact that he could live and prosper in Rome shows that the climate was now already tolerant, and more than tolerant, of cultural experiences differing from the Roman ones. This is no reflection on Panaetius' merits as a thinker, but highlights the changes which had occurred in the Roman state, which from now on was to link its political and military decisions to a movement of reform and renewal in a more open and cosmopolitan direction than had been the case for many years in the past.

Panaetius' teaching was fundamentally opposed to a type of government which had lasted over many centuries and was based on the use of violence. People began to notice that the arrogance and intransigence of the military classes was mellowing as awareness of similarities between the various nations increased. This was because the problems of coexistence were being solved by methods other than those most loved by the man of arms, for whom "normalcy" was war, while peace was treated as a period of truce necessary while preparations were made for getting "back to normalcy." The Romans were becoming more aware of the fragility of existence, the role played in life by fate, and the impossibility of consolidating military supremacy regardless of the feelings and views of others. Stoicism could help those in need of these teachings only if it could adapt to certain practical requirements, and in particular to the Romans' distaste for pure abstractions. For this reason Panaetius, in stripping Stoicism of a good deal of decorative material imposed by later masters, used it to explain Roman expansion, justifying the empire by the argument that every individual has a need to spread a message. Hence the acceptance of the Stoic principle that virtue stems directly from nature and should guide man's actions toward higher objectives.

Virtue—a very special quality, imbued with humanitarianism, including mercy, and hence very different from the virtue traditionally praised and practiced by the Romans—would constitute the rule of the wise man. If he held to the line of virtue, he would be saved from errors otherwise inevitable. Panaetius' position was an invitation to compassion and to the quest for peace of mind. There was implicit in it a recognition, later embodied in Christianity, that the key problem of philosophic speculation was the containment of unreasoning impulses and of the irrational violence of human societies not informed with principles of justice, equality, and peace. Proposing a model of life centering on the study of the history of the world and of the influence of divine providence, Panaetius underlined the universal character of man and of the virtues which must discipline his acts. He thus emphasized the moral aspects of Stoicism, making them accessible to the Roman mentality and neglecting a large part of the complex, and often futile, cosmogony preached by the school.

The disappearance of Panaetius' essay *On Duty* is an obstacle to any full knowledge of this period of Stoicism and of the renewal of Stoic thinking. Although Cicero gives us a summary of Panaetius' ideas which helps us to assess their impact on Roman thinking, some aspects still remain obscure, especially in respect of their pacifist content.[14] Of him we may perhaps repeat what we have already said of Zeno of Citium. Panaetius could not have attributed merciful traits to the human soul, nor have sought to build up a moral system designed to guide the individual toward the practice of virtue, respect for one's neighbor, and a universal vision of community life, without implicitly recognizing the weaknesses and errors immanent in the opposite system, based on the irrational use of violence treated as the right way to solve disputes between peoples and individuals. An aggressive and irrational nationalism, of the Roman type, would certainly incur his disapproval or at least could qualify for approval only as a manifestation of the tendency for mankind to seek unity.

An explicit profession of pacifist faith would have been too much to ask of Panaetius; it would have forced him to attack directly views held strongly in influential Roman circles. Like the Stoic teachers at the Hellenistic courts, Panaetius was well aware of certain weaknesses of the surroundings in which he was working. Had he urged the Romans to mend their ways, this would have hampered the dissemination of his teaching. But it would be wrong to think of him as a Pharisee, practicing but not daring to preach. His aim was a prudent exposition of the implications of his system: No man could hope to find virtue as long as he condoned war.

Polybius and the Roman Constitution

Polybius (ca. 205- ca. 125 B.C.), a contemporary and compatriot of Panaetius and also a member of the Scipionic circle, was just as prudent in his approach to Rome and its institutions. In a context which was historical for Polybius and speculative for Panaetius, the two apparently agreed that the Roman social order was founded on a harmonious equilibrium between social classes and agencies of government.

Such reflections were included by Polybius in Book VI of his *Histories.*[15] Invoking a famous doctrine, he argued that, given the tendency of men to group around the strongest, the first form of government in order of time had been the monarchies. But as the monarchy had often degenerated into tyranny, the notables came to assume sovereign powers, thus founding the aristocracy. Their degradation led to the oligarchy, the cure for which was democracy. But democracy, growing corrupt, often led to demogogy, so that the wheel turned full circle with the reversion to monarchic institutions. There had therefore been a cyclical succession of forms of government, each of which had nurtured the seed of its own downfall.

According to an idea formulated by Zeno and Chrysippus, the best constitution was that stemming from a carefully measured combination of the three methods.[16] Polybius believed that the Roman constitution had achieved this ideal: The monarchic element (the consuls) was associated with the aristocratic element (the Senate) and the democratic element (the people). The case to be made out for the Roman constitution was, indeed, by no means a weak one. In the Mediterranean world, generally governed by absolute monarchies, the democratic form of government, once vigorously defended in a number of Greek cities, was little more than a memory. Now, although the Romans confined the actual exercise of power to a minority, they changed or reappointed their leaders once a year and allowed some measure of control by the people. Therefore it was by no means fanciful to regard their constitution as particularly enlightened. Strong Stoic influences affected the thinking of Polybius. The empire created by the conquests had, in his opinion, given the Mediterranean peoples a political unity of which universal unity must be the inevitable corollary. This view was allied to a conviction that the empire was fostering the achievement of a state of peace, in which conflict would be definitively a thing of the past. Polybius' opinions in this connection are clear:

> Peace is a blessing for which we all pray to the gods; we submit to every suffering from the desire to attain it, and it is the only one of the so-called good things in life to which no man refuses this title. If then there be any people which, while able by right and with all honour to obtain from the Greeks perpetual and undisputed peace, neglect this object or esteem any other of greater importance, everyone would surely agree that they are much in the wrong.[17]

As for the ways of behaving in war, Polybius' views are apparent from the following passage, praising Philip of Macedonia: "For by war and arms he only defeated and subjugated those who met him in the field, but by his gentleness and moderation he brought all the Athenians and their city under his domination, not letting passion push him on to further achievements, but pursuing the war and striving for victory only until he found a fair occasion for exhibiting his clemency and his goodness."[18]

Posidonius and the Role of Virtue

The effort to relate Stoic thinking to the circumstances prevailing in Rome was completed by Posidonius of Rhodes (ca. 135- ca. 51 B.C.). With him Stoicism appeared to revert to a number of religious, mystic, and prophetic themes, which Panaetius had deliberately neglected. This did not prevent him from influencing the development of Roman philosophical thought. Cicero, who traveled to Rhodes to meet him, was much impressed and often quoted him.

In the field of cosmogony and metaphysics, Posidonius kept close to conventional Stoicism, but his moral and political doctrines were new, being based on the recognition of a distinct line of demarcation between good and evil. Following Zeno of Citium, he inferred that the individual must allow himself to be guided by virtue in his relations with others and in his political choices. Therefore there could be no happiness without virtue. The inhabitants of the ideal state should adopt virtue as a rule of conduct, basing their relationships in society on tolerance and the desire for peace and aiming at recreating the conditions of life which had prevailed in the Golden Age.

We have already assessed the impact on primitive Stoic thinking of the original state of bliss, references to which recur again and again in Greek literature. In Posidonius it is used as a guide for the actions of men and a model to be followed. He discerned a contradiction between a past reality, in which men walked in the paths of virtue, and his own age, during which evil and its pursuit seemed to constitute the basis of every form of community life: God had informed amorphous matter with an ordering principle, imposing peace among living beings, and not only among men. The universe stemming from this initial creative act was innocent, peaceful, and happy. Natural societies were based on a hierarchy governed by wisdom and by the strength of the leaders, who were recognized as having an unchallengeable primacy.[19] Even ordinary human needs were reduced to the minimum, since nature provided for all, men lived in caves or in trees, on fruit, milk, and honey, the procurement of which caused no suffering to other beings. But progress had undermined the honest sincerity and the simplicity of mankind. The first manufacturing and attempts to render existence comfortable had been the cause of all corruption; the arts and crafts had not made men sophisticated but had sharpened certain harmful instincts, engendering envy, hate, anger, and war. Only for this reason, feelings like distrust, vengeance, and suspicion had been able to enter into an atmosphere formerly imbued with unselfish enthusiasm.

Posidonius believed that the Golden Age had survived in the customs of the peoples of the Mysia, vegetarians who lived only on milk and honey, and maintained peace and friendship with those around them. This was the myth of the noble savage, which came into its own once again in the eighteenth century when it was taken up by some of the great minds of the Enlightenment. The works of Posidonius have been lost and we must rely on accounts of his ideas from other hands. We therefore do not know whether he was concerned with bringing about an actual reform, and whether he wished to induce men to make the long journey back to the early simplicity. The legend of the Golden Age was an ideal on which men were exhorted to model their behavior, but Posidonius was not unaware of the pressures and stresses of his surroundings. His philosophy did not include the promise of a renewal of the Christian type, a palingenesis enabling the martyrs to endure torture and contempt in the certainty that their ordeal could only bring nearer the coming of the Kingdom of God. The system was a compromise between the exigencies of philosophic speculation, the limits of a cosmogony deriving mostly from oriental inventfulness, and the need to avoid challenging too overtly imperial methods of government.

Given these premises, it would be too much to expect the formulation of an organic doctrine of peace based on the conviction that men should return to the origins and restore a state of tranquillity similar to that of the Golden Age. And yet, the fact that Posidonius often evoked the legendary epoch, that he extolled it and searched for signs of its survival among less developed peoples is evidence enough of a manner of understanding and presenting reality that would prove useful to many contemporaries who were tormented by political upheaval and ceaseless civil discord.

Hecato of Rhodes and the Practice of Humanitas

Hecato of Rhodes (second century B.C.) was the last of the three Rhodian Stoics who injected greater substance into Roman thought and thanks to whom Roman society passed from indifference toward philosophy to a mature restatement of the principles underlying political action and institutions. Hecato was the author of works on ethics, quoted by Cicero and Seneca, of which only a few fragments have survived. In his system great importance was attributed to the subdivision of the virtues into "theoretics"—those founded on scientific intellectual principles, such as wisdom, justice, courage, and temperance, which were the treasured possessions of the wise man, accustomed to reflection—and "non-theoretics," peculiar, that is, to the common man who was incapable of working out any systematic line of reasoning and therefore in need of guidance and advice.

Hecato's speculative contribution was mainly concerned with the individual in his relations with the family, other relatives, and the fatherland. It led to the enunciation of a set of practical rules, designed to guide the individual in his day-to-day behavior and enabling him to avoid the dangers endemic to community life. Doctrines of this kind were also applicable in case of war. Since he urged men to arrange the priority of their choices on the basis of their own personal convenience, it was natural that he should advocate self-control and prudence when men found themselves involved in conflicts. As far as possible the damage caused by rash attitudes must be guarded against and the wise man would avoid taking sides altogether; a reversal of fortune could change the outcome of the war, upsetting the forecasts of those who had thrown in their lot with the side that once seemed stronger. Hecato's ethics had an unduly practical flavor and in this deviated from the traditional Stoic line, which ignored utilitarian considerations to concentrate on universal objectives.

In contributing to the intellectual atmosphere and ideology of the Scipionic circle, the three Rhodian thinkers set a fashion welcomed by political opportunists and others who were anxious to maintain links with persons likely to influence and guide future official policy. The dissemination of the Stoic philosophy was thus encouraged and with it the practice of *humanitas.* This term was taken to mean a dislike of foreign wars and of civil strife and the approval of certain models of good government and social equilibrium drawn from Greek history and models. Despite the military conquests and efforts to interpret community life in a new perspective, the society of the time had reached a low ebb. In Rome the middle-class virtues had been exchanged for proletarian vices and there was an increase in the numbers and power of the irresponsible factions recruited by rich patricians to enhance their prestige. It was, therefore, an attractive—though illusory—idea to suggest, as the Stoics did, that the Roman Empire was the forerunner of the universal state, a state free from wars and in which the citizens would prosper in the practice of kindness and mutual assistance. The reality, partly apprehended by Panaetius, amounted in fact to the enrichment of wealthy landowners and speculators, the exploitation of conquered countries by mean and corrupt administrators, and a defective administrative structure. All this was a far cry from the longed-for cosmopolis.

The Gracchi and the Influence of Stoicism

The Stoics could not remain indifferent to the situation as they saw it. This was probably why a campaign in favor of the poor was conducted by Tiberius and Caius Gracchus, who sympathized strongly with the message of peace-loving *humanitas* fostered by those around Scipio. They found the Roman state very different from the picture of it presented by apologists such as Polybius; it was no longer the harmonious combination of the forms of government described by Aristotle. The problem was to reform a defective and antiquated constitution manipulated by the patrician class. Therefore the two brothers worked for the adoption of laws that would make the state more democratic. Tiberius Gracchus argued that the *ager publicus,* wrongly handed over to a small number of persons, should be confiscated and redistributed among the poor classes in small lots. A political campaign of that kind, challenging so many vested interests, met with fierce opposition and cost Tiberius his life. He died in 133 B.C., struck down by a faction of the senate. His brother Caius died in a similar incident in 121 B.C., a victim of his courageous policy to widen the powers of the plebs and of the equestrian order. An indication that the brothers were almost certainly influenced by Stoic thinking is that the Stoic thinker Gaius Blossius of Cumae was one of Tiberius' advisers.

By stimulating public interest in philosophy, the trio of Rhodian philosophers had made it easier for other Stoic thinkers, of varying talents and capacities, to find a place for themselves in the capital. From the doctrinal point of view, some set about the reelaboration of the principles formulated by Zeno of Citium, while others confined themselves to restating the old formulae, now hallowed by tradition. The presence of a Stoic in the intellectual circles, in the patrician houses, and even among the plebeians, had ceased to be unusual, although these men were sometimes self-important preachers with little of real significance to say, a fact which did not escape the attention of the satirists.

As a set of philosophic ideas achieves general acceptance, it usually loses some of its edge and penetrating power. This is also true for new religious ideas, the initial vehemence of which is often weakened by contact with groups already organized. Thus the great success of Stoicism was bound to blur its outlines. In matters of cosmogony and religion, the teachers felt that it was wiser not to drift too far away from the faith of the fathers, for an imperfect understanding of Stoic principles would certainly have led to accusations of sacrilege. Thus parallels between traditional mythology and Stoic doctrine were established and it was argued that the universe had been desired by a merciful god, whose providential will was present in all existing things.

The reconciliation was to have unforeseeable consequences. Posidonius had already dealt with the subject, and it was taken up again by Cicero in his *De natura deorum* and finally by the Stoic Lucius Annaeus Cornutus, a contemporary of Nero. Cornutus' comprehensive approach achieved considerable success. The point at which compromise seemed most difficult, since it went to the very heart of Stoicism, was precisely in the field which interests us most: that of the notion of the universal brotherhood of man, whereby every individual reflects in his person and his behavior a moral law transmitted by God and translated into reality through the practice of virtue and mutual help. The condemnation of war, as the logical conclusion of this chain of argument, was still endorsed by almost everyone, although fortuitous and changing political circumstances were apt to discourage teachers from stating the case for peace too vigorously. The innate unity of mankind, foreshadowed by the empire unifying the Mediterranean world, was also a conventional aspiration.

Lucretius and Active Epicureanism

With the passing of several generations the penetration of Stoic doctrine into the austere and ancient Roman families had softened their more intransigent attitudes, which were bound up with the rough and simple origins of the city and reflected the governing class's instinct of self-conservation. After the changes which had occurred at all social levels, this instinct was by now completely irrelevant and was particularly alien to that overall vision of mankind which the Stoics had done so much to propagate. Rome had become a center where all the philosophic teachings and the political messages could win publicity, for in Rome there was freedom of communication, which bred an atmosphere eminently suited to freedom of expression and independence of thought. Following the first thinkers, other Hellenic teachers achieved public favor varying according to their capacity (possessed in a superior measure by the Stoics) to fit their speculative contributions into the general framework of the Roman state and match their ideas to the specific distribution of social classes. Among these systems, the Epicureans achieved particular success, coming as an antidote to the unduly pragmatic and realistic cast of the Roman mind.

We have already mentioned the doctrine of Epicurus and his detached and perhaps rather inert vision of reality. This philosophy, like others sponsored by the ancient Greeks, aimed at a communion of minds and the elimination of obstacles deriving from ambition, pride, and envy. The key to this state of felicity was conduct based on proper understanding of existence and of its essential futility; man must recognize that the really useful things lie in the fascinating and exalting world of spiritual experience. Perhaps the least understood of the thinkers of antiquity, Epicurus had advised man to seek pleasure, but by this he did not mean meretricious and ephemeral delights. Pleasures of the mind were the only ones which could restore to man the dignity taken from him by the petty daily round and by contact with persons of vulgar tastes and selfish purposes. The Epicureans sought to free man from the snares laid by a society which oppressed him with its prohibitions and corrupted him with its hypocrisies. They therefore took refuge in little oases where the enlightened grouped together. There was no hate, much less contempt, for suffering humanity; the Epicurean merely looked for an understanding that would enhance day-to-day life by means of universal communion. According to Diogenes Laërtius, Epicurus cultivated friendship and showed "benevolence towards all men."[20] The Epicurean played only a marginal role in life in society, for he considered himself mainly a spectator, sometimes a critic, but hardly ever a protagonist. The political system was given scant attention precisely because of Epicurus' detached and somewhat negative attitudes. Epicureanism could be used to justify every compromise, since objectively nothing matters very much and all that is really worth striving for is the elimination of harmful disturbance coming from outside.

In Rome the high priest of Epicureanism was Lucretius (ca. 94-ca. 55 B.C.), whose *De rerum natura* was a restatement, largely in personal terms, of the teaching of the school. The poem is imbued with new ideas not easily reconcilable with the traditional detachment from earthly cares: Lucretius was more willing to shoulder genuine commitments. He rejected or at least qualified Epicurus' advice to the wise man, full compliance with which would have meant a severe inhibition of vital impulses and only a limited participation by the individual in society's efforts and achievements. A more resolute attitude therefore replaces the original Epicureans' inert abnegation and contemplative, almost ecstatic, view of reality. The new Epicureans could not deny that they were part of the universe, even though they could, and did, refuse to take active part in it. While Lucretius took a deeply pessimistic view of the ills of the world and the foolish malevolence of the human race, and while he rejected in part the legacy of Epicurus, at least in respect of joy and serenity, he eventually came to terms with the moral problem which he felt bound to tackle and which was an incentive to him to inform his conduct with a kind of cosmic sense of the divine. The statement of certain principles of Epicurean ethics were given an active bias, in order to reform society along new lines. The *atarassia* (this was the word the Epicureans used to express the idea of indifference), which in the early Epicurean masters had implied a state of isolation and of nonparticipation in life in society, now ceased to curtail action and became a guide to choices. The result was a firmer attitude to war, which Epicurus had certainly opposed, but apparently only indirectly. Lucretius, on the other hand, put war on the same level as religion and superstition, i.e., as a major obstacle to the tranquillity of the wise man and to his work to reform society.

Lucretius saw the elimination of war as an important step along the road to higher forms of society, essential if the journey of spiritual ascension was ever to be accomplished. The best aim of the wise man was not to cut himself off from the disturbances of the world, withdrawing into the dark recesses of his own solitude, sheltered from all disturbing outside influence. If he was to achieve personal salvation, there were defenses to be adopted which *atarassia* could not consolidate: Lucretius believed that it was right to oppose war actively. He did this in literary as well as philosophical terms, allowing his thought to be colored by the diffuse sense of religious feeling present in all parts of his poem, although at the same time he condemns religion as responsible for the plight of mankind.[21]

In his introduction, he invokes Venus, calling on her to protect the work on which he has embarked. This is an opportunity to beg her to put an end to the strife which torments men:

> Cause meanwhile the savage works of war to sleep and be still over every sea and land. For thou alone canst delight mortals with quiet peace, since Mars mighty in battle rules the savage works of war, who often casts himself upon thy lap wholly vanquished by the everliving wound of love, and thus looking upward with shapely neck thrown back feeds his eager eyes with love, gaping upon thee, goddess, and as he lies back his breath hangs upon thy lips. There as he reclines, goddess, upon thy sacred body, do thou, pending around him from above, pour from thy lips sweet coaxings, and for thy Romans, illustrious one, crave quiet peace.[22]

This invocation must be read in the context of the whole poem, with special reference to Book V, where the poet gives an explanation of the origin of life in society and of the process of refinement of customs made possible by agreement and communion among men. The key role attributed to friendship is further evidence of the nature of his thinking, in which the bias toward peace is unmistakable.

Epicureanism was one of the most widespread philosophic doctrines of antiquity, and was influential for several centuries. Perhaps more as a matter of convenient classification than for reasons of substance, historians have ranked Lucian of Samosata (ca. 120-ca. 180) among the Epicureans. Lucian, a skillful satirist writing two centuries later than Lucretius, was a resolute enemy of myth, prejudice, and conventional wisdom. War, he felt, was a monumental imposture, yet another deified custom foisted on gullible and simple people by unscrupulous politicans.

Ciceronian Eclecticism

With the passage of the years and despite the increase in the number of those engaged in philosophic inquiry, speculative controversies seemed to lose some of their vitality. More and more thinkers were coming to the view that it was wrong to urge the individual to espouse any particular doctrine, and that he should be left free to adopt those concepts in which he could best express his intellectual capacities. Abstract ideas were losing their effectiveness and impact, many of them declining to mere mental artifices, necessary as a guide in practical life and as a means of overcoming its adversities. This is common in periods when men's critical sense is becoming more sophisticated. At such times the vanity of all intransigence is proclaimed, the inference being that all doctrines are acceptable, provided they allow men to adopt a moral rule in line with their tastes and mission in life.

The confrontation of various schools of thought suggests that nothing could be proved satisfactorily; any argument could be used just as much against a given contention as for it, and the problems of logic, metaphysics, and ethics did not need to be assessed in a single context but could also be studied independently of each other. This is the genesis of eclecticism, which brought with it a better understanding of individual schools but no original philosophy. Marcus Tullius Cicero (106-43 B.C.) was to be the most famous exponent of this approach. His treatises on philosophy enlighten us on the doctrines of various authors and present the criticisms and the comments of opponents. His eclecticism reflected the opinions of Roman contemporaries, imbued with Greek culture, who liked to travel abroad to visit the Greek schools of the most famous masters and who drew from philosophy, more than anything else, material and munitions for their speculative controversies. What began as a rapprochement became a thorough intermingling. Often citing persons prominent in society in defense of individual schools, Cicero set out to show that the pursuit of philosophy was no longer the purview of a few specialists only. This entailed the elimination, or at least the adjustment, of many attitudes inspired by doctrinal intransigence. In the *De legibus* Cicero took his campaign of conciliation to its logical conclusion, arguing, for example, that the concept of highest good defended by the Platonists and the Stoic concept of a sole good were substantially the same.[23] The old disputes between the two teachings thus concerned differences "of words, not of things."

The source of Cicero's thought is, however, essentially Stoic. Bearing this in mind, it is useful to inquire into the range of his conciliatory eclecticism, in regard to problems of community life. The bias toward peace among certain groups had been, as we have seen, a later development, the result of the penetration—in some ways artificial and indirect—of the new ideas into the Roman "establishment." Could the desire to harmonize, to reconcile opposites and eliminate contradictions also prevail here? Not wholly, because in dealing with the relations between men and between societies, Cicero apparently discarded the principles of Stoicism and fell back on the cult of Rome. There is a significant contrast between the manifestly Stoic proposition that the universe should be considered as a single society inhabited by the gods and by men and made to be useful to men and the view that, in case of doubt, precedence should be given to the fatherland and the family.[24] The other communities—and therefore also the universal one—were relegated to a world of abstractions having no practical implications. Nineteenth-century nationalists would have endorsed this kind of reasoning.

Cicero's arguments concerning war, which is condemned in the abstract but accepted and indeed extolled in cases of legitimate defense, retaliation, or revenge, were just as specious.[25] Nonetheless, the influence of Stoic humanitarianism is still perceptible when he states that the ultimate goal of all conflict is peace, arguing that negotiation is preferable to the use of force in solving disputes between peoples and that the objectives of peace are superior to those of war.[26]

> Most people think that the achievements of war are more important than those of peace; but this opinion needs to be corrected. For many men have sought occasions for war from the mere ambition for fame. This is notably the case with men of great spirit and natural ability, and it is the more likely to happen, if they are adapted to a soldier's life and fond of warfare. But if we will face the facts, we shall find that there have been many instances of achievement in peace more important and no less renowned than in war.[27]

This did not prevent him from condoning brutality where it hastened the victory of those fighting in a just cause. Justice, seen more in a legal context than in a moral one, thus inspired various attitudes in this famous author. And if there was no escaping the use of force, this did not exempt the warrior from compliance with the commonly accepted rules of law: "Those wars are unjust which are undertaken without provocation. For only a war waged for revenge or defence can actually be just. . . . No war is considered just unless it has been proclaimed and declared, or unless reparation has first been demanded. . . ."[28] And again: "The only excuse, therefore, for going to war is that we may live in peace unharmed; and when the victory is won, we should spare those who have not been blood-thirsty and barbarous in their warfare."[29] As to the technique of fighting, Cicero declared that the degree of violence used should vary according to the status of the foe: Less cruelty should be used against a tribe with which agreement was possible, but total war was appropriate when the final objective of the conflict was the extermination of the enemy.[30]

Thus two opposing attitudes are found in Ciceronian doctrine. This was not exactly a contradiction, but an attempt, in a field outside that of pure speculation, to reconcile various lines of thinking in relation to the same objectives. Despite its many weaknesses—which, incidentally, mar all systems based on compromise—Cicero's thinking heavily influenced the opinions of the future imperial society, in which races, nations, languages were compelled to coexist and to temper the asperity and intransigence of their respective attitudes. Although he sympathized with certain Stoic ideas which urged men to greater readiness to sink their differences, his ideas were too often blunted by expedience and by the need to adopt solutions dictated by political convenience, which meant war more often than peace.

As for the problem of the Roman Constitution, Cicero is broadly in agreement with Polybius when he declares himself favorable to a harmonious combination of the three traditional systems of government, with aristocracy enjoying some measure of predominance. The love of peace is also treated as an exclusive attribute of the aristocracy:

> What then is the mark set before those who guide the helm of state, upon which they ought to keep their eyes and towards which they ought to direct their course? It is that which is far the best and the most desirable for all who are sound and good and prosperous; it is "Peace with Honour." Those who desire this are all reckoned as "Aristocrats," those who achieve it as the foremost men and the saviours of the State.[31]

Varro and the Logistoricus de Pace

With regard to our subject the views of Cicero's contemporary and friend, Marcus Terentius Varro (116-27 B.C.), a versatile writer of extraordinary erudition whose numerous works covered almost all the fields of human knowledge, were probably more definite. His many books, on which pagan and Christian authors later drew, have almost all been lost; we possess only a treatise on agrarian economics and one on grammar, plus a few fragments. His encyclopedic compilations (for example the *Antiquitates rerum humanarum* and the *Antiquitates rerum divinarum*) have completely disappeared. Large *catalogues raisonnés* of the cultural and scientific heritage of the time, their discovery might well entail a thorough reappraisal of Roman history before the birth of the empire.

It is almost certain that in philosophy Varro professed an eclecticism similar to that of Cicero but inclined to favor a return to Platonic thinking. For the purposes of our study he is mainly interesting as the author of an essay, now lost, known by the title *Logistoricus de pace*. The term *logistoricus* stood for a philosophical and legal essay in which the general principles enunciated were supported by examples and other evidence drawn from history. The one concerning peace definitely occupies an important place among Varro's writings. The problem of its content is still open to debate since, in the absence of the text itself, all opinions must be based on conjecture.

Some writers believe that it was nothing more nor less than an essay on the theme of pacifism.[32] Developing concepts derived from his eclectic standpoint, he is thought to have condemned war because man belongs to two communities: the fatherland in the strict sense, which includes the more intimate and restricted circle of his relationships, and the universal home, made up of all living human beings. Varro, it is conjectured, must have found war a monstrous aberration, in flagrant conflict with the notion of a second citizenship. The defenders of this view see in the *Logistoricus de pace* the writer who inspired Book XIX of Saint Augustine's *De civitate Dei* and the pacifist ideas developed therein.

Other writers, on the basis of historical considerations and careful analysis of Saint Augustine's book, believe that the *Logistoricus* was a legal and political essay in which peace and war were not examined in philosophic terms.[33] The main evidence in support of this view is, first, a fragment drawn from Varro's essay *De vita populi romani,*[34] which can be construed as an essentially legalistic interpretation of the problem of peace, and, secondly, a section of the *Antiquitates rerum humanarum* having the significant title *De bello et pace,* which is known to have been mainly legal in content.

Perhaps this discourse, tackling the problem from both points of views, started from both moral and legal considerations. It is possible that the *Logistoricus* was a rendering in metaphysical and ethical terms of Varro's observation of contemporary political events.

Virgil and the Prophecies of the Sibylline Books

The end of the civil wars and the restoration of authority in the person of a prince, in fact an absolute monarch although outwardly complying with the ancient republican formalities, and the pacification, now complete, of the entire imperial territory—incursions from outside and the occasional internal rebellion were becoming steadily easier to handle—strengthened the conviction felt by many that mankind was really on the threshold of an age in which society would be governed by the love of peace. Wars would disappear and prosperity would reign supreme. This would, of course, be due to the *pax romana* and to the superiority it ensured for the Roman state.

This notion underlies the famous prophecy which Virgil (70-19 B.C.) puts in the mouth of Jupiter, referring to the closing of the Temple of Janus by Augustus: "Then shall wars cease and the rough ages soften; hoary Faith and Vesta, Quirinus with his brother Remus, shall give laws. The gates of war, grim with iron and close-fitting bars, shall be closed; within, impious Rage, sitting on savage arms, his hands fast bound behind with a hundred brazen knots, shall roar in the ghastliness of blood-stained lips."[35] Thus the disappearance of "impious Rage" would herald the return of the Golden Age, described by poets like Hesiod and philosophers like Plato.

The Fourth Eclogue of the *Bucolics* of Virgil proves that men had this legend in mind when they spoke of pacification in the Roman Empire even before pacification was actually achieved by Augustus. It was a new poetic version of an ancient story belonging to the mythological heritage of almost all peoples, bringing to everyone the comforting hope that one day mankind would achieve lasting peace. Through the allegory in the story, Virgil attempts to anticipate the course of events in the Roman state, after the conclusion of the struggle for power, already believed imminent. Thus the poet:

> Now is come the last age of the song of Cumae; the great line of the centuries begins anew. Now the Virgin returns. The reign of Saturn returns; now a new generation descends from heaven on high. Only do thou, pure

Lucina [the goddess of childbirth], smile on the birth of the child, under whom the iron brood shall first cease, and a golden race spring up throughout the world![36]

At this point, the prophecy has a more urgent and immediate note. The birth of the divine child is alleged to have taken place under the consulship of Pollio (40 B.C.), marking the beginning of a new Golden Age, which would not be very different from that described in preceding versions of the famous fable. The new era would see the regeneration of all men; their crimes would be forgiven, and an atmosphere of calm, serenity, trust, and above all peace would be created. This child "shall have the gift of divine life, shall see heroes mingled with gods, and shall himself be seen of them, and shall sway a world to which his father's virtues have brought peace."[37] The return to a right way of living, to the ancient communion of gods and men, would have moral and material implications.

But for thee, child, shall the earth untilled pour forth, as her first pretty gifts, straggling ivy with foxglove everywhere, and the Egyptian bean blended with the smiling acanthus. Uncalled, the goats shall bring home their udders swollen with milk, and the herds shall fear not huge lions; unasked, thy cradle shall pour forth flowers for thy delight. The serpent, too, shall perish, and the false poisonplant shall perish; Assyrian spice shall spring up on every soil.[38]

The story continued in the same tone, describing the abundance of benefits that the great event would bring to all men.

The Fourth Eclogue has ever since been a subject of argument: who was the divine child? Like other writers in times of political troubles, Virgil, a court poet in the service of the powerful, would have liked to be able to predict the eventual victor in the struggle for power. But who? The father of the child born to pacify the world might have been Octavius, the future Augustus, no less than his enemy Antony. The child himself could have been a lovechild of Antony and Cleopatra.

The great success of Virgil's poem and the strange obscurity of the passage in question stimulated the imagination of ancient and medieval commentators, who inevitably saw in it a prophecy of the birth of Christ. At the time of Constantine we find an interpretation of the allegory along these lines in the *Oratio ad sanctorum coetum*[39] annexed to the writings of Eusebius of Caesarea. The purpose of the discourse is to establish that Virgil's lines are an anticipation of Christianity. It was not difficult to construe them as a reference to the birth of Jesus and to the Christian message of salvation. It seemed obvious that the Virgin was the mother of Christ and the new Golden Age salvation itself. There is a tradition that this essay was written by the Emperor Constantine himself, but it is more probable that one of the Christian writers of his court like Eusebius or Lactantius was the true author. Others believe that the lines are apocryphal, not written earlier than the fifth century A.D. In any

event, it is clear that the early Christian commentators were anxious to establish links with classical literature, perhaps to strengthen the authority of their
new faith. Even a passage like Virgil's, pagan in content and obsequious in
tone, could be used for this purpose.

The real meaning of the passage will probably never be known. Virgil's poetry, as was often the case in the works of court authors, was seldom unambiguous, usually allowing of various interpretations, to fit forthcoming events.
The victor of the conflict, whoever he was, would have recognized in those
words a prediction of his victory and would be induced to reward the
prophet-poet accordingly.

In the quest for ideas likely to ensure him the favor of the influential,
Virgil used the myth of the Golden Age and the prospect of its restoration
through a child of divine origin. He did this both because of the fascinating
nature of the fable, and because it seemed to interpret the destiny of the Roman state, its mission, its ability to achieve universal pacification. Because the
achievement was expected to take place through an army commander, pacification was associated with the military tradition and vocation of the Roman
Empire, and peace when it came would be the *pax romana*. All this led Virgil
—partly, but only partly, because of the prophetic approach of the poem—to
endeavor to adapt to the cosmopolitan and pacifist ways of thinking stemming from the philosophical teachings which had been fashionable now for
centuries in the Roman world. As we have seen, these ways of thinking had
gained considerable influence in the governing class in Rome, modifying its
structure and to some extent tempering its old severity.

It is also legitimate to inquire whether Virgil may not have been influenced
by a particular text. There are strange similarities between the content of the
Fourth Eclogue of the *Bucolics* and certain passages of the *Sibylline Books*, a
collection of oracular utterances originally compiled in the East and then
passing into Greek, Judaic, and Christian literature. In the material, surviving
elements deriving from each of the three literatures are discernible. The third
book, generally attributed to Hebrew sources, contains references to a pacified world in which each people made an appropriate contribution to society
and in which a central authority of divine origin would ultimately ensure that
the nations enjoyed the benefit of coordinated policies and efforts. This
would be no easy achievement. "And then shall God send from the sun a
king, who shall make all the earth cease from ruinous war, killing some [obvi-
ously, the wicked] and with some making a sure agreement. Nor shall he do
all this by his own counsel, but in obedience to the ordinances of the high
God. . . ."[40] The prophecy goes on to announce the abrupt end of all who opposed the supreme designs of God by attempting to start another war. East
and West were to be brought together again, then, under the sponsorship and
encouragement of a divine person having the power to bring agreement among
peoples. For this reason, having condemned the behavior of Rome, a city en-

slaved to its warlike ambitions, the Sibyl announced the coming of an age of
complete pacification, unifying in works of peace all the men and women in
the world. ". . . and calm peace shall make her way to the land of Asia; and
Europe then shall be blessed, the air fruitful year after year, healthy, without
frost and hail, bringing forth beasts and birds and creeping things of the
earth."[41]

Other passages from Book III (lines 743-759 and lines 787-794) revert to
the theme of the prophetic celebration of a future world, in which the rules
of animosity which have dominated for centuries the existence of peoples and
of individuals would give way to discipline among men. This discipline would
be based, as in fabled antiquity, on mutual love and magnanimity. As in the
old story, concord and tranquillity will go hand in hand with a renewed material prosperity. Nature, placated and made more fertile as if by a miracle,
will provide in abundance all that man needs to live free of want.

The kingdom of myths and of the merciful (the concept of serenity and
peace took its place alongside divine benevolence, dispensing grace to all those
who deserved it by works and thought) will be free of the ills which burden
existence. The sovereign, vested with political power over a renewed society,
will no longer be the despot responsible for imposing vexatious dues and
heavy military obligations—all, in any case, the cause of poverty and bereavement. Indeed, he will be the loyal friend of his subjects, the guarantor of their
peace, which is not a short-lived armistice, but is consolidated and made lasting because this is God's will and that of man reborn. The mediator in this renewed world will be a woman, who will have the task of obtaining such benefits from the one who can dispense them, by speaking for men who have become aware of their state of abjection and seek universal renewal. We shall
not try to analyze the influence on the deliberately obscure text of the
Judaeo-Hellenistic ideas rife throughout the eastern Mediterranean. It will suffice to stress its pacifist nature and its strong cosmopolitan commitment, in
which classical, Judaic, and Christian elements seem to be interwoven in a
sort of religious and political syncretism, revealing various, and sometimes
contradictory, tendencies. Pacifism was a major component of Sibylline
prophecy. From this source and others unknown to us, Virgil may well have
drawn inspiration and material for the famous Fourth Eclogue. The poem exercised great influence on the early Christians, who sifted classical literature
carefully for anything that could be interpreted as foreshadowing the birth,
reign, passion, and death of Jesus Christ.

Imperial Society: The Longing for Peace

The problem of the best system of government became the key political issue in Rome. Having imposed unity over a wide area of the world, it was now
troubled more by internal difficulties than by any desire to pursue expansion.
Ideologically the Romans saw themselves at the center of society, according

themselves primacy deriving from their superiority in relations with all peoples, whether they were subject peoples or not. The evolution of the system was therefore studied closely, both by those belonging to the old republican governing class, for whom the ideal constitution was still that for which Polybius had supplied a theory, and by those who were aware of the scale of the changes which had taken place in the body politic and thought it right to accept their implications. Roman imperial society, in the last analysis, sought two types of peace: the internal peace of the state, for so long torn by civil strife, and that of the spirit, desired particularly by the philosophers.

Internal pacification was achieved in 31 B.C. at Actium. The state regained institutional stability, changing into what was in fact a monarchy, although the victor claimed to be the restorer of the Republic and was praised as such in official propaganda. The inauguration in 9 B.C. on the field of Mars of the *Ara Pacis Augustae,* a commemorative monument dedicated to Octavian, set the seal on his work by introducing religious rites in his honor.[42] On the other hand, it is not surprising that no change in relations with other peoples derived from the new situation and that official doctrine was also unaltered. Despite the desire of Augustus to be remembered in a monument dedicated to peace, this remained an order based on force, in which the fundamental reform was the attribution of imperial power to the prince by the will of the people.

The state was still influenced by Stoic ideals, while internal order, finally reestablished, seemed to satisfy the widespread desire for peace and tolerance which all men shared. Writers have left clear evidence of this, in works often marred by an excess of respectfulness. We may recall the lines of Horace in the Ode to Augustus: "Thy age, O Caesar, has restored to farms their plenteous crops and to our Jove the standards stript from the proud columns of the Parthians; has closed Quirinus' fane empty of war . . .",[43] those of the *Carmen saeculare*: "Already Faith and Peace and Honour and ancient Modesty and neglected Virtue have courage to come back, and blessed plenty with her full horn is seen",[44] and Ovid:

> Thanks be to the gods and to thy House! Under your foot long time war has been laid in chains. Yoke the ox, commit the seed to the ploughed earth. Peace is the muse of Ceres, and Ceres is the foster-child of Peace. . . . Come, Peace, thy dainty tresses wreathed with Actian laurels, and let thy gentle presence abide in the whole world. So but there be nor foes nor food for triumphs, thou shalt be unto our chiefs a glory greater than war. May the soldier bear arms only to check the armed aggressor, and may the fierce trumpet blare for naught but solemn pomp! May the world far and near dread the sons of Aeneas, and if there be any land that feared not Rome, may it love Rome instead! Add incense, ye priests, to the flames that burn on the altar of Peace, let a white victim fall with cloven brow, and ask of the Gods, who lend a favouring ear to pious prayers, that the house which is the warranty of peace, with peace may last for ever.[45]

A change was very soon to occur in the general view of the old republican constitution. With the passing of generations its memory faded until it became hard to distinguish myth from reality. The respect showed by some writers of the imperial time toward the virtues which, it was claimed, had prevailed during the first centuries of Rome was partly a matter of literary convention and reflected no real desire to revert to a past constitutional system associated in many minds with administrative anarchy and the civil war of the last decades of the Republic. Later Stoic speculation, however, could accept the new reality, under the illusion that it was an anticipation of universal order, which mankind appeared to be approaching and which would be achieved through the empire. True freedom was internal freedom, which allowed men, particularly wise men, to achieve superiority over their environment, to withdraw into themselves and to abandon life itself, if the surroundings in which they worked proved too different from those cherished in their ideals.

Stoic training thus helped the old governing class to find its place in the new imperial order. Internationalism, which Zeno and his disciples had done so much to foster, was achieved de facto in the Roman state, for within its frontiers peoples having nothing in common, historically and ethnically, were governed by a single authority. And yet, war, as a brutal means of expansion and subjugation of other nations, was not subjected to adequate criticism by the new governing classes, who failed, perhaps, to discern its true nature.

However, it would have been a mistake to tackle the problem too directly, not only because this might annoy the emperor and his entourage, but also because outspoken views on this subject might appear to reflect on the origin of the Roman state itself. The Stoics of the imperial age preferred to skirt the question and avoid the dangers of certain opinions by emphasizing the individual's membership in a community in which each was committed to contributing to the edification of his neighbor. The very existence of the empire confirmed Zeno's doctrine that the age-old struggles between cities and between countries must be ended so that man could become the free citizen of one state, governed by a single law and subject to a single authority. Zeno had stated the case for subjecting every man to the government of reason, so that disturbances engendered by lack of logic and discipline could be properly contained. This objective, with its natural implications—the first being the condemnation of war—seemed largely to have been achieved in the Roman Empire.

Seneca and the Two Communities

Lucius Annaeus Seneca (ca. 4 A.D.-65 A.D.) professed a greater detachment from material life than many contemporaries and constantly pursued the finest models in search of ideas that would facilitate a new analysis of the Roman state's historical background. The profession of Stoic faith was perhaps in his case a literary affectation or a concession to the fashionable views of the enlightened classes of the time. For there is a sharp contrast between his philosophic opinions and the methods he used to achieve policy objectives or to advance in the service of the state. What interests us here, however, is not his public conduct but the message contained in his writings, for these were to have a substantial influence on both contemporaries and posterity. Because their content was imbued with humility and a spirit of brotherhood, Seneca was called the *anima naturaliter christiana* (a naturally Christian soul).

In the last analysis, Seneca's Stoicism was eclectic, like that of Cicero; in his thinking nature held a central position, being chosen as a yardstick and model of all reasonable behavior proposed to men. His doctrine developed against the background of a pessimistic view of human motives. Mankind, especially the masses, he believed to be mainly corrupt and vicious. His view of war, which he knew to be evil in itself and evil because it made nonsense of the moral rules set for individuals, was just as negative:

> We are mad, not only individually, but nationally. We check manslaughter and isolated murders; but what of war and the much vaunted crime of slaughtering whole peoples? There are no limits to our greed, none to our cruelty. And as long as such crimes are committed by stealth and by individuals, they are less harmful and less portentous; but cruelties are practised in accordance with acts of senate and popular assembly, and the public is bidden to do that which is forbidden to the individual. Deeds that would be punished by loss of life when committed in secret, are praised by us because uniformed generals have carried them out. Man, naturally the gentlest class of being, is not ashamed to revel in the blood of others, to wage war, and to entrust the waging of war to his sons, when even dumb beasts and wild beasts keep the peace with one another.[46]

From this premise he derived, at least on paper, a total contempt for political activities, which, he argued, had little to offer the honest man, since they brought him to work in surroundings in which his honesty was threatened. This did not mean that the wise man might not work within a social body having specific allegiances, nor must he cut himself off from his neighbors. Seneca's doctrine was influenced by the view, later endorsed by St. Augustine, that man is at one and the same time a member of two societies: that of the state of which he is a citizen and that of the community of mankind, a community which is governed, or should be governed, by rules of solidarity and clemency. To be effective in the latter society, it was not necessary for a man to occupy political offices or official positions; it would suffice for him to dedicate himself to philosophical contemplation, seen as a vehicle of personal edification:

> Let us grasp the idea that there are two commonwealths—the one a vast and truly common state, which embraces alike gods and men, in which we look neither to this corner of earth nor to that, but measure the bounds of our citizenship by the path of the sun; the other, the one to which we have

been assigned by the accident of birth. This will be the commonwealth of the Athenians or of the Carthaginians, or of any other city that belongs, not to all, but to some particular race of men.[47]

In a certain sense this was an anticipation of the Christian heavenly city: the rift between worldly interests and those of the spirit is reflected in terms not dissimilar to those used by the early Christian Fathers. Stoicism acquired the features of a religion based on brotherly love, on the basis of rules unknown to pagan religion. The problems of community life were thus tackled with conscious feelings of mercy and love for human beings and in the condemnation of hate, cruelty, and intolerance toward one's neighbor. Clemency for the foe, even the most ferocious, was accorded the status of a specific rule of conduct and treated as a privilege of the wise man, as Seneca endeavored to show in his *De clementia,* a work dedicated to the young Nero, his disciple. The same approach is apparent in the following passage:

> The human soul is a great and noble thing; it permits of no limits except those which can be shared even by the gods. First of all, it does not consent to a lowly birthplace, like Ephesus or Alexandria, or any land that is even more thickly populated than these, and more richly spread with dwellings. The soul's homeland is the whole space that encircles the height and breadth of the firmament, the whole rounded dome within which lie land and sea, within which the upper air that sunders the human from the divine also unites them, and where all the sentinel stars take their turn on duty.[48]

Stoic teaching was moving away from more traditional ideas to concentrate on the refinement of the human condition, which had always been one of its objectives. Implicit in Seneca's writing was a fundamental judgment adverse to the society of the time though this was a society in which he had achieved distinction, first as Nero's teacher and then as his minister. "As for me, I shall always live as if I were aware that I had been born for service to others, and on this account I shall render my thanks to Nature; for how could she better have served my interest? She has given me, the individual, to all men and all men to me, the individual."[49] And again: "Human life is founded on kindness and concord, and is bound into an alliance for common help, not by terror, but by mutual love."[50]

To preach clemency toward one's equals, tolerance toward subordinates, to emphasize the harm caused by anger and the advantages of a life based on a correct appreciation of earthly values and of their utter pettiness in comparison with universal truths, to seek the satisfaction of the needs of the spirit, treating them as supreme over those of the body, to mould one's own conduct on examples of men able to distinguish the meretricious from the eternal—it was simply impossible to do all this and yet to espouse the ideals of the warrior or of the commander of armies, much less those of the politician, for whom the soldier is an instrument of personal aggrandizement. Seneca's glorification of the Roman state itself is clouded by a pessimism based on a profound understanding of the ways of this world.

Compelled to judge the political situation of his time, Seneca was inclined to take a realistic view of the transformation of the Roman state into an absolute monarchy. Recognizing that the source of all power was now embodied in the prince, whose will had the force of law, he expressed the hope that the sovereign's choices would be governed by wisdom, by the desire to act as father and not as tyrant, by an awareness of the need to obey the laws and not to regard himself as exempt from them. The aim of all this was to consolidate the peace which the empire had ensured for the peoples, given that the new constitutional set-up was identified with the *pax romana.* [51] Here Seneca is clearly drawing on his experience of administration to establish an overall philosophic judgment of the Roman order. Harking back to the basic rules of his Stoic training, Seneca recalled the myth of the Golden Age, when a tender and merciful nature had prevailed, to be corrupted later by the evils of progress. The reference to this primitive age is an opportunity for Seneca to praise the figure of the wise man working within society, and to express the hope that responsibility for public welfare should be placed in his hands. "Accordingly, in that age which is maintained to be the golden age, Posidonius holds that the government was under the jurisdiction of the wise. They kept their hands under control and protected the weaker from the stronger. They gave advice, both to do and not to do; they showed what was useful and what was useless." [52] He believed that the relations between the privileged, the rich, and the strong on the one hand, and the poor, the weak, and the downtrodden, on the other, was the essential yardstick against which the moral value of a method of government must be measured. In the same letter this concept is expressed as follows:

> Not yet had the stronger begun to lay hands upon the weaker; not yet had this miser, by hiding away what lay before him, begun to shut off his neighbour from even the necessities of life; each cared as much for his neighbour as for himself. Armour lay unused, and the hand, unstained by human blood, had turned all its hatred against wild beasts. [53]

Thus the perfect government meant no armed conflict and the rule of moderation. By his nature and training the wise man showed himself tolerant of opinions different from his own and sought to assert himself only through the art of persuasion. Among his qualities, he must possess strength and stamina and in adversity, especially adversity arising from war.

Seneca's doctrine was expressed in a set of rules of conduct rather than in conceptual propositions. The rules were a guide to the conduct of the individual in society, helping him to avoid its dangers and pitfalls. For example, he advised men to avoid anger, a grave obstacle to the conclusion of their earthly mission. He thus placed heavy emphasis on the spirituality of man, which must be freed from encumbering or corrupting influences liable to weaken its content and limit its influence on individual and on community life. According to his teaching, each man should consider his own life as a whole, not in parts, for a failure to take an overall view could lead to dangerous difficulties. The overall view was achievable only when the bonds between action and intellect had been proved close and effective. The organization of the individual's activities was of particular importance for Seneca, were it only because of its effect on the world of practical interests and on day-to-day behavior. Although Seneca's dislike of war is made manifest through allusions and in general terms, his rule offers neither explanation nor justification for a pattern of conduct which is the gravest in its consequences and the least reasonable in its origins.

Epictetus

While Seneca's Stoicism was essentially organic in approach, reflecting his moderation and maturity, that of Epictetus (50-130 A.D.) had definite Cynic undertones. Epictetus wished to take into account the spiritual needs of men of low estate, for whom Cynic thinkers had always shown particular solicitude. He neglects the material life deliberately, because he feels that what matters is the primacy of the spirit. The wise man must concentrate on things of the mind and achieve indifference toward tangible reality. Anything liable to arouse passion or appetite he will treat as an irrelevant nuisance.

Consistent with his premises, Epictetus was very severe in his judgment of the choices of the individual, since he saw ethics as a complex of actions designed to shelter man from disturbances liable to curb his inner freedom. Inner freedom and peace of mind were therefore the key realities. It was for man, as a being capable of reflection, to distinguish the good actions from the bad, that is, those meeting the requirements of freedom from those hampering it. Only the quest for freedom mattered for the wise man, who must be philanthropist, teacher, consoler and missionary. Nor should he lose heart in the face of failures, since perfection was always attainable, if the search for it were maintained with sufficient intensity.

In a system with perfection as its objective, there could be no defense of war, for it would be an obstacle to the completion of a mission and an offense to universal solidarity. The desire for a state of peace, meaning above all serenity of mind, "all passion spent," is clear:

> You see that Caesar hath procured us a profound peace: there are neither wars, nor battles, nor great robberies, nor piracies; but we may travel at all hours, and sail from east to west. But can Caesar procure us peace from a fever too? From a shipwreck? From a fire? From an earthquake? From a thunderstorm? Nay, even from love? He cannot. From grief? From envy? No: not from any one of these. But the doctrine of philosophers promises to procure us peace from these too. And what doth it say? "If you will attend to me, O mortals, wherever you are, and whatever you are doing, you shall neither grieve, nor be angry, nor be compelled, nor restrained: but

you shall live impassive, and free from all." Shall not he who enjoys this peace, proclaimed, not by Caesar (for how should he have it to proclaim?), but by God, through reason, be contented, when he is alone reflecting and considering; "To me there can now no ill happen: there is no thief, no earthquake. All is full of peace, all full of tranquillity; every road, every city, every assembly. My neighbor, unable to hurt me."[54]

The unremitting quest for calm, the desire to eliminate all disturbance, explain why the phenomenon of war did not preoccupy Epictetus unduly. The serenity of the wise man was achievable through isolation, even in the middle of the storm and violence of war. Here is a remark on this point: "These principles make friendship in families, concord in cities, peace in nations. They make a person grateful to god, confident at all times, on the ground that he is dealing with things not his own, with worthless things."[55]

It was the last frontier, attacked by a philosopher who appeared, but only appeared, to have rejected life and the problems of his time, a philosopher working in the atmosphere of the imperial court, which would have treated with misgiving attitudes it deemed unduly sanctimonious. So much prudence, if prudence it was, was not enough to keep him in favor at court, for he was one of the philosophers Domitian banished from Rome in about 90 A.D.[56]

Attitudes in the Imperial Bureaucracy. The Two Plinys,
Dio Chrysostom, Publius Aelius Aristides

At the beginning of the first century official state doctrine was still substantially that codified two centuries before by Polybius, the only credo regarded as providing a convincing explanation of the emergence of the Roman Empire and the centuries which had seen a single state forged from such a wide variety of peoples and traditions. Stoic doctrine had become the official philosophy of Roman unity and remained the most acceptable to the class of enlightened notables which had grown up all over the empire. For these the universality of the state was the basic premise underlying philosophical and political thought and every administrative measure. This was the attitude of the high bureaucracy, whose Stoic training very soon came to signify total compliance with imperial authority. (Much the same had happened in the Hellenistic monarchies.)

Although some external forms of the old Roman constitution had remained intact, although the senators retained certain powers and the offices of the republican order had not been abolished, the essentially monarchic character was unmistakable. Greek and oriental thinking supported this trend, for it accepted the principle of hereditary monarchy without demur. The development was a logical one. Accustomed to regarding his own dependents and assistants as the docile instruments of government, and ruling over a hierarchy with an increasingly rigid structure, the emperor—and with him the court, the administration, and public opinion—found it increasingly hard to accept that the politico-economic military powers deriving from the exercise of absolute authority could still be curbed by the interference of those social classes which were theoretically still vested with a measure of authority. Augustus had already given himself a halo, as it were, by allowing religious ceremonies to be performed in his honor. The principle of designation through the adoption of the successor to the throne remained inviolate, since hereditary succession was incompatible with the republican system, which was not to be overtly repudiated. Everything hinged therefore on the personality of the emperor. He was considered to be of divine origin—that is to say, endowed with supernatural powers. He was God's anointed; to offend him was sacrilege.

What the bureaucrats really admired in the new system was the atmosphere of diligent toil and the absence of major disturbances. Civil services have always had an obsequious respect for those in power, and have almost always supported authorities determined to elicit obedience, even if their position had been acquired in violation of the laws; bureaucracy instinctively favors any regime in which major responsibilities are directly assumed by the political power and the civil servant is not constrained to take decisions lying outside his purview. Precisely because of this quest for security, which reflected the anxieties of a very long series of civil wars, when the fate of the bureaucrat had been extremely uncertain, the civil servants appreciated the advantages of stability and they gave the imperial regime full credit for this achievement.

Security was particularly prized in the provinces, where the civil wars had actually been fought out and where trade and the crafts now flourished and religious, racial, cultural, and geographical differences tended to fade into insignificance in the imperial ideology, which claimed the merit of having consolidated the *pax romana* and of having generated an atmosphere of internal *securitas*.

Pliny the Elder (23-79 A.D.) warmly praises this new state of affairs several times in his *Natural History:* "For who would not admit that now that intercommunication has been established throughout the world by the majesty of the Roman empire, life has been advanced by the interchange of commodities and by partnership in the blessings of peace, and that even things that had previously lain concealed have all now been established in general use?"[57]

The enthusiasm of Pliny the Elder was only in part dictated by political opportunism and a desire to curry favor at court. More generally it derived from a sincere conviction that the empire was the best political system that could be hoped for, the only guarantee of peace and prosperity for the citizens: " . . . all owing to the boundless grandeur of the Roman Peace, which displays in turn not men only with their different lands and tribes, but also mountains, and peaks soaring into the clouds, their offspring and also their plants. May this gift of the gods last, I pray, for ever! So truly do they seem to have given to the human race the Romans as it were a second Sun."[58]

This enthusiasm for security and peace soon brought an end to the fiction under which a monarchic system was masked by a republican facade. This was understood by Pliny the Younger (ca. 61-ca. 113), who praised the imperial institutions and the emperor in the *Panegyricus,* and in even more obvious form by Dio Chrysostom (ca. 40-ca. 115) in his *Orations.* This famous orator was the spokesman of the provincial peoples, for whom the transformation of republican institutions into monarchic ones was already a *fait accompli.* He was the theoretician of this change. For him the emperor was no longer the mediator between the aristocratic and democratic components of the state but the sovereign vested with his powers by God. His decisions had the infallibility of their divine origin.

But this was no reason why Dio Chrysostom's Stoicism, though sometimes colored by undue reverence for the authorities, should lose its universal character. In fact it had noteworthy humanitarian overtones, and he showed tolerance for the opinions of others and a general desire that man should not yield to the combative instinct or to the impulse of anger. The use of violence, he felt, was absurd within a regime derived from the divine will. What violence and what wars could there be, since the empire included the greater part of the known world? New campaigns seemed unlikely, save to protect the borders of the state from the recurrent incursions of the barbarians. In Dio Chrysostom's system, war had been replaced by police operations to be entrusted to the prince, who, being divine, could not lose. It would be more correct to discuss the conflicts fought out in the minds of men or within the communities, apparent not as manifestations of physical cruelty, which the imperial authorities would not have allowed, but in the traditional forms of civil rivalry and political strife.

Dio Chrysostom's experiences had been gained in the provinces. Born in Prusa, a city in Bithynia, he well knew how harmful the factiousness among the Hellenic tribes had been. In the golden period of Greek civilization their quarrelsomeness had led to a long series of wars, and in the Roman period it turned to administrative anarchy. Those who suffered most were the individual communities, to which Dio turned in a number of inspired orations, calling on their citizens to remember the Stoic warning that the essence of community life is concord. Drawing on the lessons of history, he emphasized the evil of anger, seeing a remedy in the application of the rules in force in the universal community, governed by a sort of cosmic intelligence. He was concerned not with a condemnation of war in itself, but with encouraging men to resist the temptations generated by factiousness, itself due to a gradual weakening of love for God and to the strengthening of primeval instincts.

The idea of concord (ὁμόνοια), an individual and collective virtue associated with the personal interests and with the family and civil relations of the individual, superseded the idea of peace, which was associated with the external relations of the state and with internal security. Dio's warning was simple. In the families and cities torn by strife, harmony must be restored by the adoption of rules. The family and the community could be seen as evidence of the existence of a cosmic harmony which the individual must not challenge. Concord was a recurrent theme in Dio Chrysostom's elegant discourses. It should reign, he argued, in families, and above all between cities, bringing them to repudiate the old rivalries. "If my purpose on this occasion were to speak in behalf of concord, I should have a great deal to say, not only about human experiences but celestial also, to the effect that these divine and grand creations, as it happens, require concord and friendship; otherwise there is danger of ruin and destruction for this beautiful work of the creator, the universe."[59]

Concord, he believed, was affected by the influence of the stars, where universal laws reigned supreme, and by that of earthly interests. "Do you not see in the heavens as a whole and in the divine and blessed beings that dwell therein an order and concord and self-control which is eternal, than which it is impossible to conceive of anything either more beautiful or more august?"[60]

The same note of satisfaction with contemporary achievements is sounded by Publius Aelius Aristides (second century), a master of rhetoric born in Mysia. Like Dio Chrysostom, he was a great admirer of Rome, impressed not only by the sheer scale of the undertaking that had created the empire, but also, in respect of the recently annexed states, by the calm and serenity brought to their populations.

Among the works of Aristides which have survived, we possess a few "historical" orations which are genuine rhetorical compositions in which he sets out to re-create and render in literary form the speeches made in specific circumstances by historical and mythological characters. The exercise was not original, having already been attempted by Isocrates and in a certain sense by Thucydides, for although the latter presents generals and politicians in direct speech, he possessed no verbatim records and is in fact offering only remembered versions. Aristides wrote two orations called *De pace.* The first, following Thucydides,[61] is a version of a speech made in 425 B.C. by Spartan envoys in Athens. The second, inverting the roles, is a speech made on the occasion of an Athenian embassy to Sparta in 405 B.C., following a narration by Xenophon.[62]

The two discourses are of interest because they present the Stoic problem in terms of a convergence of interest and objectives between all the Greeks, a convergence which only peace could encourage. "Do not wait for the day in which it will seem that you desire peace by necessity," is Aristides' advice to his compatriots.[63]

The orations, compiled to illustrate contemporary events, are undoubtedly of great interest in that they reflect—and this time not indirectly or through mere oratorical exercise—the point of view of an author already famous in his time. The theme of the ὁμόνοια underlies the orations *To the Cities for Con-*

cord and *To the Rhodians for Concord.* In these the author discussed the animosities and antagonisms arising between the Greek cities of the eastern Mediterranean, they who had, he felt, quite failed to discern the advantages to be reaped from their membership of the Roman Empire. In these orations peace is seen as the greatest aspiration of mankind and Aristides pays tribute to the state which has established it. When these writings are stripped of their rhetorical content and heavy ornateness there is no mistaking the genuine enthusiasm on the part of the author for the condition of calm, finally achieved and consolidated, and for the monarch whose achievement it is. Peace and concord are the *raison d'etre* of this formidable political edifice, but at the same time they add a remarkable luster to it. "Nobody has ever denied," says Aristides, "that concord is the greatest asset of the cities."[64]

Aristides' writings are informed with a definite feeling for peace. He sympathized strongly with the spirit of the times and with the thinking of the senior civil servants, who had taken over the reins of government from the aristocratic class and in general took the view that the Roman Empire marked the beginnings of a true cosmopolis. By praising Rome and its successes, as Aristides did in his *Encomium of Rome,* he extended his thinking and judgment of reality from the limited world of empirical interests to cover a genuinely universal world based on peace. This was why he called on the gods to ensure that "this Empire and this city may flourish for all eternity."[65]

Plutarch and the Origins of War

The unification of the known world within one state, guided by a single will instead of the old senatorial class, made it easier for the schools to overcome the contradictions between the various traditional teachings, using, if necessary, religious feeling for the purpose. Plato, Aristotle, Pythagoras were regarded as the forerunners and prophets, through whom the divine spirit had made itself known to the world. Aristotelian doctrine tended to merge into that of Plato, which became in its turn Neoplatonism, a leading school of thought in the later era of classical speculation. Neoplatonism also contained mystical elements drawn from Eastern religions and philosophies.

This is where we find Plutarch of Chaeronea (45-125), famous as the author of the *Parallel Lives* and of a number of discourses on moral subjects. Plutarch was convinced that philosophy was man's only hope of betterment and salvation. God existed and was identical with the good. This was all that could be known about him. Nonetheless this was a truth accessible to the human intellect, despite the views of the Neoplatonists, for whom God was a being so far removed from corporeal life as to be perceptible only through forms of ecstasy or mysterious metaphysical forms of communication.

The problem of identifying God with goodness posed the problem of evil, which Plutarch solved by treating its essence as the malevolent soul of the universe. In the framework of this antithesis—which has a dualistic undertone—

he sets his judgments on the phenomenon of war, the worst calamity that man could be called upon to bear. Those who claimed otherwise showed little love for the truth and precious little sensitivity. Here was the nub of his quarrel with the Stoic Chrysippus, who had observed that warfare had the merit of lightening the pressure of population in the overcrowded cities. Devoid of any attribute of nobility, warfare, in Plutarch's view, derived from profound defects of character: "for no war springs up among men without vice but one breaks out from lust for pleasure, another from greed, and still another from a lust for glory or for power. Well then, if god induces wars, he induces vices too by inciting and perverting human beings."[66]

Plutarch based his system on these premises, relating his judgment on war and on the behavior of politicians to them. Although he opposed Stoicism, on which he had written an essay pointing out its inherent contradictions, he was sympathetic to the humanitarian and universalistic aspects of Stoic doctrine. His criticism was that they failed to match up to a noble vocation which should have led them to dedicate themselves solely to achieving Zeno's objectives. His interpretation of the personality of Alexander the Great makes this attitude clear. Although he narrated heroic deeds, he was impressed not by the captain-at-arms as much as by the unifier of peoples and the precursor of the Stoic cosmopolis. He related that because Alexander

> believed that he came as a heaven-sent governor to all, and as a mediator for the whole world, those whom he could not persuade to unite with him, he conquered by force of arms, and he brought together into one body all men everywhere, uniting and mixing in one great loving-cup, as it were, men's lives, their characters, their marriages, their very habits of life. He bade them all consider as their fatherland the whole inhabited earth, as their stronghold and protection his camp, as akin to them all good men, and as foreigners only the wicked.[67]

Everyone should feel part of and partly responsible for community life, the aim being to work toward higher objectives of pacification. War, on the other hand, whether in the form of a campaign for the conquest of new territories or whether as civil war, the most painful kind, was an appeal to the past. The Roman Empire was in a position to ensure serenity and prosperity to the human race under a single sovereign. It was therefore the task of the moralist to promote peace in the family and civil interests. In the last analysis Plutarch's plan was the same as that of Pliny the Elder, but it was developed along more consistent lines:

> For observe that of the greatest blessings which States can enjoy—peace, liberty, plenty, abundance of men, and concord—so far as peace is concerned the peoples have no need of statesmanship at present; for all war, both Greek and foreign, has been banished from among us and has disappeared; and of liberty the peoples have as great a share as our rulers grant them, and perhaps more would not be better for them; there remains,

then, for the statesman, of those activities which fall within his province, only this—and it is the equal of any of the other blessings:—always to instil concord and friendship in those who dwell together with him and to remove strifes, discords and all enmity.[68]

These words show a sense of satisfaction generated by the condition of the Roman citizen, living in a happy age, under the guidance of enlightened sovereigns, in disciplined order, where all disorders such as war were resolved in general harmony. Here were the premises for a more complete and systematic doctrine of peace, but this was something that Plutarch's eclecticism was not able to provide.

The Thirtieth Dissertation of Maximus of Tyre

Another thinker had reached the conclusion that the notion of divinity could not be expressed in human terms, and he shared Plutarch's views on war. This was Maximus of Tyre, an orator and philosopher who lived in the second century at the time of the Antonines. Strongly influenced by Plato, he was a precursor of Neoplatonism, of eclectic background but not unsympathetic to Stoicism. His idea of divinity was based on the impossibility of expressing God and on the consequent need to use special supernatural mediation to apprehend his essence and invoke his intercession; in the field of relations among men in society, he believed that intervening actively to prevent wars was a task for man himself. He was less convinced of the benefits of an imperial regime as the unifier of the *oecumene* than Pliny the Elder or Plutarch.

The phenomenon with which Maximus of Tyre was concerned was actual conflict. In discussing it, his notional setting is ancient Greece, dominated by the city-state, and he condemns, as if these were situations still prevailing, the conduct of governments unable to reach agreement and to save men from the sufferings and the damage caused by war. His *Thirtieth Dissertation* is in fact a pacifist essay. In it war is seen as an external activity of the state and not as the absence of peace of mind in the individual or serenity in the social environment. He ignores contemporary events, as if the peace of the empire did not exist or had not achieved enough credit to aspire to the status which other writers had conferred on it. It seems not unlikely that the reference to such a remote historical period may conceal a prudent and indirect criticism of a state of circumstances found after the advent of the empire.

The dissertation starts from the presupposition of the existence of good and evil men, among whom it is the latter who yield to the temptations of wrath and war. All praise of war was a mental perversion, since it was not right to praise something intrinsically evil.

Therefore, wars were caused because good men were unable to act independently against evil men, against men governed by passion, the key to men's misfortune. What better antidotes to war could there be than agriculture, the most serene and peaceful human activity, to which we are all indebted for our sustenance? The farmer is opposed to the warrior in that the need to comply with the laws of nature also forces him to respect those of men. "War led men to ignore the laws, farming to respect them. Men under arms are rapacious, they covet the possessions of others, the more evil they do and the more they achieve their own objectives, the higher the opinion they have of themselves."[69]

Few authors of antiquity have expressed their horror of violence more emphatically and have analyzed more perceptively the dilemma of the choices which face the ordinary man, caught between conscience and evil example. One is tempted to discern Christian influences in the dissertation: It is informed with a feeling of humanity and mercy, the origins of which are far removed from the world of the Hellenic cities for whom Maximus apparently intended his message.

We should feel entitled to rest with this conclusion if the *Thirtieth Dissertation* were not part of a collection of essays which include arguments opposing those so far described. It will suffice to mention the preceding dissertation (the *Twenty-ninth*) to show that Maximus could defend completely opposite opinions on the same problems. The title: "Of the soldiers and the farmers, which are the citizens most useful to the State?" In the form of a paradox, accepting a kind of conventional wisdom, he argues here that only war can ensure freedom to the citizens and that a flourishing agriculture only whets the foreigner's appetite. Therefore men were right to devote themselves to the trade of arms rather than to tilling the fields. A comparison of the two essays suggests that Maximus was following a dialectical procedure of an obvious Sophistic type. To argue one point of view and then its opposite was a fascinating exercise in baffling the reader. The contribution of the essay on peace is somewhat offset by the statements contained in the *Twenty-ninth Dissertation,* and its importance and its power of conviction must inevitably suffer.

Marcus Aurelius and the Double Citizenship of Man

The Emperor Marcus Aurelius, who reigned from 161 to 180, was by no means unaware of the evils caused by wars, though compelled to wage them throughout his reign. In his *Meditations* he too developed the concept of a physical and a spiritual world, of each of which man was a citizen and toward each of which he had obligations. What would happen if the two worlds came into conflict? Would man obey the laws of his earthly homeland or those of the spiritual world, the only one in which perfection was attainable? In the case of war, was he required to fight or should he not stand aside from the struggle, in obedience to a higher rule of love?

The philosopher-emperor provided no answers to these questions, although they were linked with his vision of life in society. His maxims in this field, as in others, were valid in their approach but disappointing and obscure as to proposed solutions. Since factors external to man—including war—exerted no direct influence on him (save through subjective opinions), by effacing the image of these factors in one's own mind, one could dispose of the problems of which they were the reflection. What would become of war if our senses and our intelligence no longer perceived it?

If Marcus Aurelius' notes had not been confined to ethics and if he had discussed the political and social questions with which he was so actively concerned as an administrator, he could hardly have avoided a condemnation of war. The following passage gives some evidence for this inference:

> All things are mutually intertwined, and the tie is sacred, and scarcely anything is alien the one to the other. For all things have been ranged side by side, and together help to order one ordered Universe. For there is both one Universe, made up of all things, and one God: immanent in all things, and one Substance, and one Law, one Reason common to all intelligent creatures, and one Truth, if indeed there is also one perfecting of living creatures that have the same origin and share the same reason.[70]

Other passages confirm the idea that all mankind shares a common destiny: "We are all fellow-workers towards the fulfilment of one object, some of us knowingly and intelligently, others blindly; just as Heraclitus, I think, says that even when they sleep men are workers and fellow-agents in all that goes on in the world." And again: "As thou thyself art a part perfective of a civic organism, let also thine every act be a part perfective of civic life. Every act of thine then that has no relation direct or indirect to this social end, tears thy life asunder and destroys its unity, and creates a schism, just as in a commonwealth does the man who, as far as in him lies, stands aloof from such concord of his fellows."[71]

In accordance with Stoic tradition, Marcus Aurelius founded his conception of power on solidarity, without saying exactly what was to be understood by "solidarity." The moral imperative, a guide for him and for the entire governing class, was based on unlimited devotion to the state, on a respect for conventional values, and on the conviction that materially men had much in common and what mattered was what they shared rather than what separated them. The renunciation of violence, however, held no important position in this system or at least was not explicitly recommended as a goal to be attained. In a certain sense the problem seemed already resolved, in that the rational order, the *cosmopolis,* had been transferred into the world, being achieved in the structure of the Roman state, within which even the use of violence was preordained.

The Limits of Later Stoic Speculation

If we read them carefully, we can see that while these later thinkers, whether a freedman like Epictetus or a monarch like Marcus Aurelius, had an overall vision of cosmic and earthly reality and refused to acknowledge differences of race and religion. (Most men now belonged to a single state whose inhabitants were given common citizenship by the edict of Caracalla in 212.) But they could not cross the frontiers of philosophic abstraction to move to more advanced positions from which war would be condemned as an outrage to divine mercy and as the negation of all human solidarity. Although, logically, force should have had no place in their philosophic system, perhaps a premonition of the tragic stresses which would soon rock the empire prevented them from rejecting, even in intellectual terms, any element that might help to consolidate the unity of the state.

Stoicism still exerted some influence on public opinion. In the first place, as we have seen, the imperial bureaucracy had Stoic training by which its loyalty to the imperial order, hinging on the person of the *princeps,* was encouraged and strengthened. Secondly, the rebellions smouldering among the lower classes (encouraged by the old senatorial class), also drew support from Stoicism, though with the adjustments required by recent experience and changes in customs. Precisely because the republican opposition flirted—and more than flirted—with Stoicism, at times the word *Stoic* was taken to mean *rebel.* In the time of Nero, Tacitus reports that the philosopher Rubellius Plautus was put to death for having "taken upon himself the Stoic arrogance and the mantle of a sect which inculcated sedition and an appetite for politics."[72] Despite this and other excesses, the rapidly successful careers of Seneca and Musonius prove that it was possible to embrace openly a philosophy inspired by Stoicism and still win office and honors.

On the other hand, the Stoicism of the senate class was beginning to look more and more like an elaborate theory essentially designed to buttress vested interests. The principles of equality, humanity, and mercy, of which Stoicism had been the standard-bearer for centuries, were of only marginal interest to the class of privileged citizens. Tacitus reports that the Senate was on one occasion required to judge the case of the murder of an urban prefect, killed by his slave. By a customary rule, not only the guilty person but all the victim's slaves, guilty or not, were liable to the death sentence. Such a ferocious punishment could have been avoided had the Senate wished it. But, while that august body consistently invoked Stoic ethics in defense of its prerogatives, it saw no reason to apply the same beliefs to concede an act of clemency, desired also by public opinion. Accordingly, it decreed the death of many innocent people, including infants.[73]

Only the Christians seemed to have understood and absorbed the message of Stoicism. This they showed through their faith in Christ's renewal of human relationships, through their faith in salvation beyond the grave, through their enthusiasm, through their certainty of achieving a redemption in which all injustice, including war, would be swept away, through their unwavering belief in one God, and through their determination to overcome barriers of race, language and culture in pursuing genuinely universal objectives.

Philo Judaeus. The Revision of the Biblical Message

The later Greek philosophical schools attempted in vain to offer a response to the questions raised by the new religion. In vain, the waning classical speculation sought regeneration in the old ways of thought, like Platonism and Pythagoreanism. The leading pagan thinkers of the time were illustrious masters like Philo Judaeus (30 B.C.-40 A.D.), Apollonius of Tyana (a first-century thinker who foreshadowed Neopythagorean doctrine), Plotinus (ca. 204-289), Iamblichus (d. ca. 330), responsible for the development of Neoplatonism, and, lastly, Proclus (410-485), who did much to restore philosophic teaching in Athens.

Their work extended over a period of some five centuries, and around them philosophy developed along complex lines which sometimes drew strength and encouragement from the most intimate needs of the human soul, so as to become religious faith, and sometimes was identified with total rationalism, basing all certainty on the intellect and rejecting out of hand all intuitive knowledge. From the crossbreeding of these lines of thinking there emerged the mystical ideas which became increasingly active within the Graeco-Roman world, a world which was more and more convinced that men, and particularly the initiated, could reach the truth directly, without recourse to the cognitive mechanism of reason. The mystics, who began as opponents of the philosophical schools, later took to philosophy, just as, through a process of mutual exchange, old religious faiths like Judaism prospered under the impact of Greek speculation. This complex change led to a new vision of God. Far removed from the old pagan ideas, the faithful were nonetheless determined to hold on to all that part of the religious heritage of paganism which seemed worth defending.

Philo Judaeus, a Graeco-Judaic philosopher of Alexandria, attempted to strip Judaism of its artificial elements and Platonic philosophy of the conceptual exaggerations that had accumulated around it. His aim was the harmonious fusion of the two fields of thought in a single set of concepts likely to satisfy the cultivated classes of the imperial Roman community and, in particular, the Hellenized Hebrews of Alexandria. Philo Judaeus saw in the prophetic messages of the Scriptures evidence of the validity and divine origin of the Greek philosophic systems. The logical conclusion of the system was that the law of Moses must be obeyed, but only because it was the most just of all possible laws and bore within itself the seed of its binding strength. Philo thus was guided by a cosmopolitan impulse of Stoic coloring, rejecting the view that the Hebrew people had been chosen by God to reign over others. This led him to praise the Old Testament, which his exegesis freed of the conceptual difficulties apparently conflicting with the institutional reality of the Roman Empire.

Philo's attitude to the problem of peace, in particular, showed a great change in respect to a number of intransigent statements in the Bible. In the

Old Testament the direct intervention of God in the Hebrew nation's internal affairs, and even in its military ceremonies, is treated as completely legitimate. Standing aside from the tradition of the chosen people, or at any rate assigning it completely new values and judgments, Philo wholeheartedly favored tolerance in relations between men, arguing that their choices should be made coolly, rationally, dispassionately:

> But if the unmeasured impulses of men's passions were calmed and allayed by self-mastery, and their earnestness and eager striving after the infliction of wrongs were checked by righteousness; if, in a word, the vices and the fruitless practices to which they lead were to give place to the virtues and their corresponding activities, the warfare in the soul, of all wars veritably the most dire and most grievous, would have been abolished, and peace would prevail and would in quiet and gentle ways provide good order for the exercise of our faculties. . . .[74]

Philo's explanation of the actual genesis of war differed from the traditional one given both in pagan and in Jewish literature. Some mystical aspects of his thinking, in which scholars have even thought they discerned Christian influences, could not be reconciled with the opinions then held on the nature of war. It would be useless to seek a doctrine like Philo's in Jewish tradition, for he believed that war often derives from circumstances outside man's will—for example, from "poverty and ill fame." At other times it was connected with the evils of the soul.[75] Here is a clear attempt to probe the nature of the phenomenon more deeply. War is considered not as an instrument for achieving domination, but as a consequence of the corruption of the human soul, which would be kept pure if people would not "even admit any heinous thoughts, but live with our fellow-citizens in peace and law-observance, that order of which justice is the guiding influence."[76]

Certain Stoic principles seem to underlie several passages in Philo, especially those concerning the impact of the passions on human decisions and those concerning appropriate ways to escape the pernicious influence of anger. Thus, referring to the teaching of Moses and especially to his imperturbability, Philo said that an inordinate desire for earthly goods was at the root of all corruption. Passions should therefore be subjugated, so that things might be "permeated with peace and order," realizing "those perfect forms of the good which bring the full perfection of happy living."[77]

Philo concluded that peace was single and indivisible, whether it be the internal peace of the mind, or the social peace which unites the men of a single nation, or that of which peoples are the protagonists. The first step on this ladder was that peace of mind which makes the beatific vision of God possible. The other steps in the peaceful ascension followed logically. On the day when man achieved complete indifference to passions, not only would he have armed himself against all external disturbance, but he would also have achieved felicity. The individual's liberation from enslavement to vice therefore became a promise of peace, to which Philo attached great importance as a means of spiritual renewal and as an instrument for containing the excesses caused by the use of violence. If there was a road to truth and a way of possessing it, it could only consist in a condition of peace and detachment from passions.

Apollonius of Tyana and Pagan Mysticism

Apollonius of Tyana lived in the first century of the Christian era. Nothing definite is known about his teaching; the details of his life are shrouded in mystery, both for lack of sources and because already in Roman times he was known as the founder of a religious cult rather than as a genuine philosopher. Perhaps to satisfy a known demand, Philostratus, his biographer, gave him a leading role in stories designed to strengthen the belief that he was a supernatural being. The following remark, referring to his possible immortality, is famous: " . . . for with regard to the manner in which he died, if he did actually die, there are many stories."[78]

Apollonius was a reformer who attempted to refurbish pagan religion in order to keep it abreast of changes in the body politic and in the economic framework of the empire and to stem the revolt stirred up by Christianity against traditional religion. Although little is known of his philosophic and moral system, we do know that he was regarded as a divine being, having the power to help reconcile the world of earthly interests and that of metaphysical values leading toward the establishment of a true communion between God and man. His teaching, which achieved great success among his contemporaries, attempted to halt, or at least slow down, the spread of Christianity, although it too showed signs of Christian influence. There were other influences, drawn from oriental religions or from ascetic sects. As absorbed by Apollonius, those doctrines laid heavy emphasis on peace-loving humility and the condemnation of violence. A perfect understanding with God and spiritual renewal could be achieved only if his religious message—a mystic synthesis of the various pagan cults—was heard by a greater number of the faithful. The outdated, disdainful indifference to human misery shown by the pagans must give way to merciful piety, working for the salvation of men and freeing them from ancient evils like inequality and injustice.

In his biography, Philostratus portrays Apollonius as an apostle summarizing in his teaching the travail of the philosophic schools. The elimination of contradictions in the various classical teachings was essential to a message which aimed to calm the disputes born of the passions and temper the animosity between men, families, and states. Thanks to the reestablishment of concord and the discovery of new forms of association, certain severe differences or inconsistencies would be resolved. He saw war, party conflicts, and political and religious controversies as so many obstacles to the development of society and to the affirmation of the new morality, which, unlike the ancient one, came to succour men and not to enslave them.

Discerning in every difference of opinion a potential source of disorder and an obstacle to the victory of the morality which he championed, Apollonius preached harmony and peace. His advice to the inhabitants of Smyrna illustrates his basic approach: "let us consider my meaning to be somewhat as follows: Far be from your city the factiousness which leads men to draw swords and to stone one another."[79] Here he proclaims—and this is noteworthy, for Apollonius was a pagan reformer not a Christian—the individual's responsibility for his own destiny, the importance of his choices, and his responsibility for the conquest of the future. Discord and animosity, frequent outbreaks of anger: these were due to man himself and not to any will outside him. Because of this attitude contemporary writers and others much later, like Voltaire, saw in Apollonius the pagan counterpart of Jesus, the apostle of a message different from that of the Christians, but one of equal spiritual content, a man who nurtured a deep aspiration for peace and justice.[80]

Plotinus and Neoplatonism

In the third century Alexandria was one of the chief intellectual centers of the empire and the focal point from which the philosophers propagated their ideas to an audience as large as the Roman state. The thinking of Philo, who sought to establish lines of convergence between Greek philosophy and biblical Judaism, was still influential there; the Gnostic masters like Basilides and Valentine, attempting to relive systematically the mystery and speculative experiences of oriental religions, taught there; the school of Clement of Alexandria and of Origen also flourished there, its objective being to bring some scientific order into the Christian religion, which pagan society thought of as a dreamlike and eccentric process of ascetic elevation.

Alexandria was also the cradle of the Neoplatonic school, the scene of the last splendid effort to save classical philosophy from the Gospels, Judaism, and the experiments in the realm of mysteries so dear to the Orientals. Neoplatonism was, in a way, an attempt to overcome Christianity and to revert to the old but still vigorous ideas of Plato and Aristotle. The school could count on the aid of Plotinus (205-270), who, though not its founder, was its most authoritative representative. Through a formidable effort in philosophic method, linked with mystic intuition, he sought to give new life to the most famous philosophic messages. Plotinus' ethics were linked to his logical premises. Platonic law, according to which the realities of the world cannot be dominated without the assistance and the mediation of ideas, was therefore seen as a rule of life. The cognitive process became an ethic rule and a principle of action. Understanding was a vital attribute of the wise man, whose task it was to encourage to the utmost the dissemination of ideas. From all this Plotinus argued that the wise man must strive to facilitate the enlightenment of those still groping confusedly in the dark.

The wise man, being aided by a special cognitive perceptiveness, must visit prisons and slums, in order to convey to their inhabitants at least something of the spiritual knowledge which he possessed. In other words, he must seek to convert his neighbor, though this should not be carried so far as to distract the philosopher from his speculative activity. He was required to adopt a way of life sublimated through divine revelation—that is to say, to be intensely wise. His work within the community would thus help create an atmosphere which would induce in others the desire to work toward the same degree of illumination. But how could all this pass from the level of pure speculation to that of ethics in society? How should a politician face the needs of government? There were many gaps in Plotinus' thinking: He failed to specify what should be the conduct of the wise man in circumstances of this kind—whether he might accept office; if, once he had accepted such office, he should remain within the empirical world of all politicians and whether there were not gray areas in which the wise man, too, might reasonably accept the compromises which statesmen cannot avoid.

Plotinus' political views are a matter of conjecture. He had planned to found in Campania a city inhabited and governed by philosophers, the name of which would have been Platonopolis, but despite the good will of the Emperor Gallienus, the project was never realized. Just how would the philosophers have governed this city? According to Porphyry, it was to be a kind of phalanstery and monastery.[81] Would the philosophers have accepted office? Would they have come down from their ivory towers to seek solutions to real problems in the life of the community? The answer to these questions, if they had ever arisen in practice, would probably have been that the wise man should take no interest in empirical problems, leaving their solution to others, that he should hold aloof from the fluctuations of events, and seek to live intensively his contemplative experiences, his contribution being the formation of a climate which would be reflected in the behavior of the community.

Whatever the precise answers, none of this could be reconciled with war, which was implicitly condemned in Plotinus' philosophy—especially in his ethics, where it was clear that Stoicism had gained a foothold in Platonic territory. However, an element alien to the classic tradition, stemming from a new mystic experience virtually absent from the systems of Plato and Aristotle, was also present in Plotinus. This was the effort to apprehend and embrace God, an urge owing more to exaltation and love than to reflection. Plotinus' God had something in common with the Christian God: he offered man a new vision of eternity. The main feature of the universe was unity, in relation to which "beings are."[82] War, at once the cause and consequence of cruel dissension, had no place in a system which appealed to enthusiasm and found expression in love.

These judgments are the fruit of inferences concerning Plotinus' philosophy rather than a description of specific attitudes. Seen as a whole, his philosophy leads to these conclusions, although at times his words, as handed down to us in the *Enneads,* seem to allow of a compromise with the phenomenon of war. War is certainly an evil, but why should one worry about it if, at most, it can cause untimely death, sending the individual to claim his real citizenship in heaven?

> And when men, mortal as they are, direct their weapons against each other, fighting in orderly ranks, doing what they do in sport in their war-dances, their battles show that all human concerns are children's games, and tell us that deaths are nothing terrible, and that those who die in wars and battles anticipate only a little the death which comes in old age—they go away and come back more quickly. We may conclude that tears and moaning are not necessarily evidence of real evils; babies cry and complain for no reason.[83]

These words show that Plotinus lacked a capacity for sympathy with the sufferings of others. This is suggested also by his views on community life and on the conduct of man in society. He was not made of the stuff of social reformers. Indeed, he went so far as to condemn those who thought the contrast between the rich and the poor immoral.[84] He also argued that earthly life imposed different rights and duties for the wise man and for the common individual. While the former aspired to lofty summits, the latter also had an important task to accomplish in proportion with his modest status, though he too could achieve some distinction. A movement to restore lost individual rights, or a movement produced by a religious faith (as in the case of the Christians), or the rebellion of subjugated peoples wishing to reconquer their lost independence would not have won his approval. Thus, he condemned uprisings, even if theoretically they were morally justified.[85] The order of the Roman state, within which he recommended that his disciples live in peace, was the best of all possible systems. Although he witnessed at least two persecutions (that of Decius, 249-251, and that of Valerian, 257-258), it would be useless to seek in his writings even the mildest condemnation of the highly unphilosophic treatment meted out to the Christians. The furthest Plotinus went was to state or hint that the fervent pursuit of truth by man, particularly by the wise man, should also lead to the conquest of a serenity having nothing in common with war.

Plotinus' philosophy attracted much support among the defenders of traditional paganism, for whom the rapid rise of Christianity was a grave threat. Although he avoided any outright attack on the Christians, he had nonetheless laid the foundations of a pagan theology. By reviving in allegoric terms the ancient myths and emphasizing them as the driving impulse in the greatest masters, he sought to synthesize a thousand-year-old tradition, submitting it to contemporaries as a stimulus to faith. Platonic doctrine filtered through later Hellenistic thought and was forced into the defensive by Christianity. Concerned now with the revival of discredited mythologies, it could not, in

Plotinus' hands, assume an aggressive form and lend moral support to those who lived by the sword.

Porphyry and Iamblichus. Julian and Themistius

Antichristian attitudes were nonetheless implicit in the teaching of Plotinus. Porphyry (232-304), disciple and biographer of the master, who collected his lectures in the *Enneads* and wrote among other things a treatise, now lost, entitled *Contra Christianos*, confirms this. Another element, already present in Plotinus' system, was to be given greater emphasis in Porphyry. This was the magic and prophetic element, through which the initiated could enter into contact with the supernatural world, invoking the intercession of the Greek and Roman gods, and that of the demons and angels of oriental mythologies.

Iamblichus (d. 330), summarized the conclusions of Neoplatonic teaching, restating them in completely personal terms. Of Syrian origin, he shared Porphyry's interest in oriental mythology. He was mainly interested in liturgy and was fascinated by the mysterious and the arcane in the ancient mythological legacy. For him Neoplatonism, in obvious competition with Christianity, had the natural attraction of the marvelous, the dazzling, the inexplicable. But apart from magical and prophetic ideas, Iamblichus' system failed to contribute new values in support of the traditional ones which had suffered so much from the Christian offensive. Even the moral rule defended by Neoplatonism was essentially artificial. The aim was not to apply a principle of mercy, based on the equality of men and on their identical right to salvation, but to defend an order now utterly lacking in internal vitality and in the impetuous and irresistible force of the Christians, who proclaimed man's liberation through a faith committed to defending a moral imperative and overcoming the barriers of race and class.

This, among other things, explains the failure of the Emperor Julian, known as the Apostate (he reigned from 361 to 363), to restore paganism. Julian reopened the temples and set himself up as a priest of the pagan rites, compiling antichristian discourses. Not even the imperial authority or the evident sincerity of Julian himself sufficed to inject new life into a congeries of beliefs which had lost their sway over the people. The Romans had tired of the old customs and looked forward eagerly to the realization of the "pale Galilean's" message.

The factors which were to prove determinant in Julian's behavior were a sympathy for human beings and a longing for peace which was certainly of philosophic origin. His upbringing had been guided by philosophers imbued with Neoplatonic culture. He was certainly familiar with the doctrines of Plotinus, Porphyry, and Iamblichus, and of their leading disciples. He had studied their philosophies and knew that they had tried to revive the pagan religion and its outmoded ethical heritage, now menaced by Christianity. The quest for peace of mind and inner calm, a feature of so much of Roman-Alexandrian thinking, had certainly influenced his education, as can be inferred from many passages in his writings. On several occasions he declares—and there is no reason to doubt his sincerity—that he regards the imperial power as a burden and would have much preferred to devote himself wholly to philosophy. The inner peace of the individual and the external peace of peoples were his main objectives. He opposed the Christians because he felt that the new religion had made the attainment of these objectives much more complex. And if he was constrained to undertake wars, he was careful to recommend humane behavior to the troops, as his words to them after the rebellion against the Emperor Constantius show: "This one thing I beg and implore: see to it that none of you under the impulse of growing ardor be guilty of injury to private citizens, bearing in mind that not so much the slaughter of countless foemen has made us famous as the prosperity and safety of the provinces, widely known through instances of virtuous conduct."[86]

It is in this light that we should consider his admiration for the Cynic philosophy, which denied the validity of hierarchies and obligations deriving from community life. In one of his writings, Julian has this to say:

> Their [the Cynics] main concern was how they might themselves attain to happiness and, as I think, they occupied themselves with other men only in so far as they comprehended that man is by nature a social and political animal; and so they aided their fellow citizens, not only by practising but by preaching as well. Then let him who wishes to be a Cynic, earnest and sincere, first take himself in hand like Diogenes and Crates, and expel from his own soul and from every part of it all passions and desires, and entrust all his affairs to reason and intelligence and steer his course by them. For this in my opinion was the sum and substance of the philosophy of Diogenes.[87]

This judgment referred not only to the motives of Cynic philosophy, but also to the social objectives which this school of thought necessarily implied. Such objectives, as we have seen, found their expression in opposition to a system of ethics based on the *raison d'état* and to the military class which regarded itself as their custodian.

In this defense of a civil ethic innocent of passion and subject solely to the dominion of the intellect, Julian seemed to neglect the history of his own rise to power, promoted by the legions stationed in Gaul under his command. There was in fact an artificial and literary element in his attitude, which may partly explain the failure of his short-lived and ill-starred attempt to abolish Christianity.

It is true that the perfect sovereign—of whom he has left us a portrait in the two panegyrics written in praise of the Emperor Constantius, his cousin— would not have had to achieve power through the insurrection of a mobilized army. In his view of things, the government should not be the product of accidental circumstances but should express a definite will to study and to organize, according to reason, the lives and behavior of individuals. Addressing his emperor-cousin, whose crimes and weaknesses were already notorious (he had been responsible for the violent deaths of eight relatives), he was in fact setting out a program for government. Informed with humanitarian policies and philosophy, the monarchy was praised as an achievement of Constantius. The sovereign should, in Julian's opinion, be honest, pious, a protector of his family, generous toward the suppliant and the destitute, clement, hardworking, impartial in ordering and in judging, skillful in the choice of his assistants. Here are some of his comments on the ideal sovereign: "Though by nature he is brave and gallant, he takes no pleasure in war, and detests civil discord. . . . After he has conquered by force of arms, he makes his sword cease from slaughter, because he thinks that for one who is no longer defending himself to go on killing and laying waste is to incur pollution."[88]

Such an elevated conception of power, having as ultimate objective the kingdom of peace, was undoubtedly influenced by a multiplicity of philosophical ideas. In addition to the Cynics, Dio Chrysostom probably influenced most the mind of the young student who was to become a commander of armies and a sovereign. The *Second Panegyric of Constantius* contains a number of passages suggesting very strongly the prose of the famous rhetorician, whose humanitarian and pacifist views we have already mentioned.

Of the other writers who influenced Julian's intellectual upbringing, most were Cynics or Stoics. Another influence was Themistius (ca. 317-ca. 388), philosopher and rhetorician, who had achieved distinction as a commentator on Aristotle and had risen, despite a pagan faith which he never betrayed, to high political and administrative responsibilities at the courts of several emperors, most of them Christians. Julian kept up an intimate correspondence with him. In a letter from the emperor to the philosopher, the only one extant of many which must have been exchanged between them, Julian claims to prefer the contemplative life to that of a sovereign and asks Themistius to write more often and give his advice.

Regarded as a Sophist because of his dialectical attitudes and certain contradictions, Themistius showed a kind of affected pacifism and was inclined to praise the farmer as a virtuous and praiseworthy contributor to general prosperity. This position was similar to that taken up nine centuries earlier by the Sophist Prodicus of Ceos, who had extolled farming as a means of consolidating peace. It was also like that of the *Thirtieth Dissertation* of Maximus of Tyre.

Themistius' ideal was a society based on tolerance, freed from major disturbances like religious conflicts (although a pagan, he intervened to curb the orthodox zeal of the Emperor Theodosius in his persecution of the heretics) and foreign wars, which had now become more common and more serious. He felt that a truly wise man should be able to live in peace, devoting himself to study and, if necessary, to public activities. Recruits to public office should include philosophers. He argued that farming should discourage warmongers by showing them that without the sustenance provided by the land, the whole economy of the empire would grind to a standstill. "On the one side, how many are moved by a will to peace: on the other, how many seek to foment conflict. The former reject war, precisely because of the need to protect farming; the latter stipulate that warfare can be allowed only on condition that nobody harms the farmers; others defend peace to enable the husbandman and the ploughman to live in peace and to ensure that their crops are shielded from damage."[89] Underpinning the economy, farming also helped to restore serenity to the spirit, to leave time for reflection, and to prevent hasty decisions which were the main cause of all wars.

Themistius was an expert student of government, not only deeply cultivated but of great practical gifts, who was by no means unaware of the important role played by irrational impulses and sudden outbursts of anger in the decision-making process. If war became inevitable, if an invasion or an enemy threat compelled recourse to arms, the consequences of the military operations must be circumscribed so that animosities, now aggravated, could be allowed to ebb away and disappear. Therefore it was right to show clemency toward the defeated, as he advised the Emperor Valens: "Peace is the ultimate end of war. How many of those who embark upon war are compelled to do so, have no desire to fight indefinitely, and desire only to live serenely and quietly?"[90] Themisitius was not unaware that war, when not imposed by the needs of defense, was generated by the boundless ambitions of man and in particular by his formidable lust for power. "How many there are who have within themselves no concept of restraint, and desire no such concept on earth, embarking upon war to satisfy naked ambition, being not remotely concerned with considerations of public interest."[91]

Here the writer is expressing the opinions of an individual brought up on philosophy but also well-informed as to the realities of the time. For many decades now the memory of the serenity and peace reigning in the Roman Empire until the end of the Antonine dynasty had been forgotten; the throne had become the perquisite of the great captains. And since nothing could be less stable than a civil power based on the strength of soldiers, whose attitudes were remarkable neither for their consistency nor for their durability, civil peace was all too apt to degenerate into civil strife and bloodshed. Another aggravating factor was the pressure of the barbarian peoples on the boundaries of the empire and the quarrels within the Christian religion, now the victorious ideology but torn by violent internal conflicts. The *pax romana* was only a memory. In these historical circumstances, the reflections on peace and war by a thinker like Themistius, vested with public responsibilities and living near the court, were bound to make very substantial concessions to realism. Therefore he could not ignore the changes that had taken place in the empire, whose governorships and other high posts were now in the gift of the legions.

End of Classical Speculation

After the collapse of Julian's attempt to stem the tide of history, Neoplatonism was forced out of the mainstream and ceased to actively propagate its religious propositions and practices. Not even Proclus (410-485), a thinker of a lucidity comparable to that of Hegel, was capable of injecting new vital fire into classical teaching. In 529 Justinian ordered the closing of the school at Athens which had drawn fame and prestige from the work and memory of Proclus. The banning, at the same time, of all teaching other than Christian teaching spelt the death of non-Christian philosophy.

Because of the difficulty for a pagan school to work in a Christian state, its doctrine on community life was eventually reduced to recommending moderation, resistance to passions, the control of anger, clemency toward the conquered. Efforts to define the nature of peace were confined to rational descriptions, generally referring to activities of the mind and often presented in a context spoiled by literary preciousness. Together with classical philosophy, the pacifist and humanitarian ideas spread by the Hellenistic-Roman schools also faded away.

Contrary to current opinion, as we have sought to show, classical civilization was not wholly on the side of armed violence but in some, not negligible, instances extolled peaceful community life. Wars, as such, were often regarded as abominable catastrophes. The societies that had succeeded one another from the times of the Greek polis to Alexandrian times, the time of the Rome of the kings and the empire had, it is true, waged war almost continuously and had glorified valor, regarded as the supreme expression of human virtue, but they had also encouraged intellectuals and mystics who argued that brotherly love was superior to violence. During this long era, a considerable number of writers, thinkers, historians, orators, essayists, and statesmen had denied that war was the normal situation of peoples and the only appropriate instrument for controlling human relations.

Adulation of heroism in the field, characteristic of the early centuries of Greek history, was already outmoded by the time of Pericles. Because it lasted so long, because it was a burden on the economy and sapped the strength of the cities, because of the more sophisticated military techniques it encouraged, the Peloponnesian War did much to rob war in general of its literary glamor. Pressing their destructive criticism of traditional values, the Sophists had spared neither the braggadocios and the warmongers nor war itself. They publicized the idea of a common origin of man, stressing the existence among citizens and cities of Greece of a common heritage. This meant that military valor was no more than a talent for liquidating fellow-men, whose only fault was that they had been born in an alien city. Since war escaped the control of the intellect, they rejected it, believing it to be dominated by irrational impulses and by a purely physical and almost muscular concept of the duties of man. They saw all praise of war as the deplorable consequence of that ignorance fraught with conceit which was a peculiar quality of men trained to the trade of arms. In the fifth century B.C. the Sophist Gorgias had already reflected on all this, concluding that peace was health for the mind of the individual as well as for the entire human society. War, conversely, was illness.

Stoicism was to take these premises further, including in a single embrace all men—whether Greeks or barbarians—giving them a single citizenship and laying the moral and rational fundaments for a leveling process that Alexander the Great had already implemented. Thus was born that humanitarian line of thinking which was to penetrate by various roads into the Hellenistic courts and then into Roman circles, becoming a feature of the ideology prevailing among the imperial bureaucracy and even the senate class. It was a constructive and concrete view which brought men closer by seeing them as members of a universal community.

Cynic teaching was different. Developing the corrosive criticism of the Sophists, the Cynics appealed to a superior idea of virtue, concluding that worldly values were without substance and the opinions of others of no consequence, since the only good was virtue and the only evil, vice. Military glory and love of the fatherland, incidental and precarious concepts bound up with the individual's membership in a body politic, were definitely second-rate ideas in the eyes of the Cynics, for they had no time for states or nations and believed that the wise man and the enlightened should reject them. The Cynics were therefore among the supporters of the idea of a cosmopolis,[92] though there was more than a hint of anarchism in an attitude which abhorred all kinds of dependence. The Cynic cosmopolis had no hierarchies and, unlike that of the Stoics, there was no subjection to a single authority.

The position of the Epicureans, though starting from different premises, was similar. The Cynics were driven by an extraordinary faith in the independent virtue of the spirit, which enabled them to ignore community life, to yield to a deep longing for personal freedom, while the Epicureans argued that utilitarian considerations had led to the decay of the customs and moral rules inherited from the old Hellenic tradition. The need to escape all disturbance led them to loosen the bonds with society. In their eyes the wise man should abstain from all public activities and not merely show indifference to them, as Stoicism taught. In this effort to free himself from the trammels of life in society, the Epicurean despised war, which added the sufferings of the body to those of the mind. Epicurean cosmopolitanism, like that of the Cynics but for different reasons, became an all-out individualism, a single-minded pursuit of serenity. Thus all moral substance and all importance was denied to community life, for the Epicurean believed that the happiness of the individual depends on his independence of society.

These three schools influenced the later ones, though to varying extents and with the adjustments entailed by historical situations and current circumstances. Where the social factor gained the upper hand, Stoic thinking prevailed; otherwise it was Cynic and Epicurean individualism which led to a more or less marked detachment from old warlike tradition. Equilibrium seemed to be achieved in the Roman Empire with the Mediterranean world under a single state and the internal pacification of that state after long periods of savage civil wars. This apparently justified the view that the Stoic cosmopolis had finally been attained, but it was a dangerous illusion and those who cherished it ignored the fact that world peace had been won at the price of the violent subjugation of many peoples. After the Antonines, war reemerged as the means by which succession was determined and as an instrument needed to defend the empire against outsiders. In both forms it was evidence of decadence.

The attempt made by Hellenistic-Roman philosophers to revive the old themes, were it only in mystic terms and in such indirect forms as were allowed by the times and by the political order, was doomed to failure. These themes had, as we have seen, lost their edge and power of penetration. In their weakened presentation, they could not prevail over the formidable moral force embodied in Christianity.

PEACE
IN THE OLD TESTAMENT

Šālōm. *Peace and War in the Old Testament*

Born in the second millennium before Christ in circumstances connected with the vicissitudes of peoples living in the Middle and the Near East, and developing under the influence of special historical events, the Hebrew civilization was remarkable in that its religious background and beliefs were entrusted to a collection of written documents (the Old Testament), all of which is still extant. Other peoples probably adopted similar methods to preserve the record of their historical and religious traditions, but the evidence of their faith has in only a few cases survived the disappearance of their civilization and in no case has it achieved wide acceptance as revealed authority. Only the Old Testament has this remarkable status, being a sacred book for two religions (the Jewish and the Christian), each of which has a wide following in the modern world.

We should seek in vain in the Old Testament for a precise and consistent definition of the concept of peace. This is firstly because the various parts of the Bible were written over a number of centuries during which the mentality and psychology of the Hebrew people changed to such a great extent that the meaning of certain key words was modified. Secondly, the Hebrews, particularly those of the earliest times, found it somewhat difficult to reason in abstract terms and summarize their experiences in conceptual synthesis.

Hebrew idiom used the word *šālōm*, which is translated with some degree of approximation as εἰρήνη in the Greek version of the Old Testament (the "Septuagint") and as *pax* in the Latin Vulgate. The two terms expressed only a few of the many nuances of the Hebrew word. If it referred to an individual, *šālōm* could mean, depending on the context, "integrity, lack of pettiness and

185

possession of one's own attributes," "Health and condition of well-being." If, on the other hand, it concerned life in society, *šālōm* could refer to an order free from dissension or disputes. On the one hand, therefore, it concerned internal peace, considered as an attribute of the human person, and on the other, it concerned peaceful relations between groups. However, its meaning grew to include the idea of wholeness, of the undivided, of the integral, but also good health, prosperity, calm,[1] the safety of one who had escaped from the dangers of battle.[2] In certain passages the term has a note of solemnity, implying a degree of perfection in relation with a superior objective—of the benevolence of the Redeemer and of a favorable disposition of men.[3] In other passages it referred to the calm of a dwelling, of a locality, or of a region.[4]

Certain passages give the word a spiritual meaning, suggesting intimacy, and this acceptance later gained currency in references to relations between individuals. In this case the concept of peace linked up with that of the origin of that state of happiness which only trust could engender. *Šālōm* then came to indicate a condition of abandonment of oneself to one's neighbor, a relationship of cordiality and friendship between persons feeling mutual attraction. This is the genesis of the word used as a form of greeting. Here, it was understood in the sense of peaceful enjoyment of the goods of this earth and serene communion with God. The twofold meaning is present, for example, in the passage in which the unhappy fate of the tribe of Joab is contrasted with that of the race of David: "but upon David, and upon his seed, and upon his house, and upon his throne, shall there be peace for ever from the Lord" (1 Kings 2:33).

The presence of God and his active participation in the well-being and prosperity of the Hebrew people thus became the distinctive elements of the peace sent by him. Anyone wishing to achieve acceptance as the vessel of prophetic enlightenment promised his peace, well knowing it to be "hard currency," as it were, widely accepted and in great demand. "Thus saith the Lord concerning the prophets that make my people err, that bite with their teeth, and cry, Peace; and he that putteth not into their mouths, they even prepare war against him" (Mic. 3:5). This aspect of the biblical conception summarizes the Hebrews' moral assessment of peace, considered the highest good to which man could aspire, and as the reward for all wise action.

Because the word *šālōm* had many meanings, it is clear that its opposite could not be a single word. The word for war is the most obvious, but certainly not the only one. Thus in 1 Kings 2:5 it was said, in alluding to the behavior of Joab toward the two commanders of Israel's army: ". . . he slew them, and shed the blood of war in peace. . . ." And again: " . . . Ah, Lord, God! surely Thou has greatly deceived this people and Jerusalem, saying, Ye shall have peace; whereas the sword reacheth unto the soul" (Jer. 4:10).

The various nuances of the word *šālōm* emerge more clearly from an examination of opposites and antitheses. This kind of scrutiny shows that in the meaning of friendship and loyalty its opposite was deceit (Jer. 9:7), in the sense of serenity of existence: contrariness, obstacles, adversity (Ps. 119:165), in the sense of calm and moderation of feelings: terror and anguish (Jer. 30:5), in the sense of ordered prosperity: extermination (Ezek. 7:25), and in the sense of compliance with the law and internal peace for the people: injustice (Jer. 59:7 et seq.).

Another line of research consists in examining the words in conjunction with which šālōm was used and which were used to qualify it. In various cases it was used together with loyalty, luck, health, security, wealth, strength, joy, life, justice. Each addition to the meaning therefore touched the various fields of human activity very near those already indicated. Peace connected with the idea of justice (Ps. 72:3 and 72:7) recalled the vision of a society in possession of an equilibrium ensuring prosperity and order. If it was connected with the concept of wisdom (Prov. 3:17), it referred to individual equilibrium, attainable through maturity of character and the exercise of patience.

An important meaning is concerned with relations between peoples and nations. This does not differ from the meaning which the term *peace* possesses in modern idioms, covering, that is to say, both the agreement which has led to a certain situation together with the legal guarantees that surround it and the procedures imposed for its implementation.[5] A transposition of meaning of this kind led to the recognition of the compulsory character of, and the need for, the situation which was the subject of the peace agreement. A similar process took place in the Greek world in respect of the word εἰρήνη.

Šālōm therefore indicated the objective condition of calmness and the absence of disturbance in the relations of one people with another, confirmed legally by a meeting of wills among subjects having a legal status. The identification of a legal situation and the agreement leading to it emerges from several passages in the Bible. We may quote: "And Joshua made peace with them, and made a league with them, to let them live: and the princes of the congregation sware unto them" (Josh. 9:15). And again: "For let him take hold of my strength, that he may make peace with me; and he shall make peace with me" (Isa. 27:5).

The problem arose in much the same terms in other passages, in which, in respect of agreements between nations, it was recognized that peace was, implicitly or explicitly, the essential component of such agreements. "For the mountains shall depart, and the hills be removed; but my kindness shall not depart from thee, neither shall the covenant of my peace be removed, saith the Lord that hath mercy on thee" (Isa. 54:10). Thus peace was either the premise of the agreement or its objective.

The exegesis of a word from an ancient Semitic language, a word which developed in circumstances so different from those we know today, necessarily poses the problem of its use in relation to modern concepts; every word, like every idea, must be analyzed in the historical context and in the circumstances appropriate to it, and if these are ignored they are ignored at the risk of non-comprehension. The use of *šalōm* must therefore be related to an oriental civilization in which men were not yet capable of reasoning in terms of true conceptual abstractions and lived in the conviction that supernatural forces were constantly meddling in their world, changing and controlling it. In this primitive culture, where the main occupation was tilling the fields and tending the flocks, factors were at work which would be unthinkable in modern surroundings. This, among other things, explains the differences in, and the variety of, the meanings examined so far.

On the basis of the foregoing and on that of studies made by Caspari, the idea contained in the Old Testament regarding peace can be classified in three categories.[6] In the first place, there was the prospect of, or longing for, peace in the sense of a revolt against the oppression imposed upon man because of his belonging to the physical world. Here natural calamities were the target against which man's longing for peace was directed. He wished to free himself from the burdens placed on his shoulders by nature and knew that he could dominate nature and subjugate it, but at the same time he was aware of the weakness of his own situation, which forced him to turn ever to God, invoked as a liberating will. A vision of this kind was shared by other primitive peoples, who had become aware of their puniness before the great problems of nature and of being and who were resolved to free themselves from a state of permanent serfdom.

In the second place came the hope of achieving peace among peoples on earth in the not too distant future. This was to take more the form of a religious peace desired by the Lord than the form of understanding between countries which had decided to put an end to a state of war. Although in *šalōm* the meaning of a legally binding agreement was implicit, this did not mean that the prevalent feature of peace among peoples and among sovereigns was not that of a divine gift made to men in recognition of their good deeds.

In the third place, the word meant a process of development in the warlike temper of the Hebrews toward more cooperative attitudes. Of all the meanings, this is the one which it is most difficult to pin down; here, peace is a catalyst and at the same time a yardstick, aiding and providing a measure of the change in the characteristics of Yahveh. From Lord of war and protector of Hebrew arms, he became the dispenser of peace. We shall see below how this change coincided with the change in the destiny of the Hebrew people.[7]

Cruelty and Humanity in the Bible

Modern critics have gone over the Old Testament word by word in an effort to pinpoint, in the text which has come down to us, the various historical strata, sources, and versions which were the background to material assembled at a relatively late period.

The Bible as a book probably began at a very early epoch when a civilization of pastoral type came into being, strongly monotheistic, having significant anthropomorphic memories and a need to communicate with the supernatural. In those remote times the Hebrews were bound to feel nostalgia for a time when man lived at peace and in communion with his Creator (the heavenly paradise: Gen. 2:3), but another sentiment proved stronger and gained firm acceptance: the conviction that there was a pact between God (Yahveh), seen as a proud and vindictive divinity, jealous of his rights and privileges, and the Hebrew people, to whom he reserved his benevolence and to whom he entrusted the task of mediating with other men. The individual as such had no place in the dialogue between Yahveh and the Hebrew people. He took part in it only indirectly, as a member of a group which was the only true interlocutor of the divinity. Believing themselves to be the chosen people, the Hebrews had a rocklike faith in exclusive supernatural support, which would be vouchsafed them in all critical circumstances and particularly in case of war; the prestige and power of Yahveh would be reflected in success in battle and in their capacity to resist external dangers.

Now there is sharp contrast between this view of relations between God and man, considered as the primacy of a certain ethnic group over the others, and the Christian message, which brought to all men, without distinction of any kind, a message of salvation and hope. The concept of justice too, in the Hebrew interpretation, is different from that of the New Testament, in which, although ensured for all, even to sinners, it is nonetheless deferred to a world other than this world. For the Hebrews, justice was meted out by Yahveh, who struck down men in this life, acting according to whim, condemning them to physical pain and sufferings, killing at random and visiting his wrath even on innocent future generations: the Old Testament includes accounts of massacres and exterminations prompted by the contempt, rather than the justice of Yahveh. And the manifestations of his anger take up much of the dialogue with his people.

With the passing of the generations, the "contact" tended more and more to evolve into an abstract relationship that was spiritual in character. This did not mean that the Hebrews wavered in their belief that they enjoyed an exclusive form of protection and had a manifest destiny. Their relations with Yahveh were still expressed in terms of military triumph.

The tone changed gradually, when, toward the eighth century B.C., the trend in the fortunes of the Hebrews shifted sharply. Not only did they lose the expansive thrust and the aggressiveness of the early centuries, but they were caught in power struggles between states (Mesopotamia and Egypt), which led, after various vicissitudes, to the siege and capture of Samaria, capital of the kingdom of Israel, by the Assyrians (722 B.C.). Did this mean that the chosen people had been abandoned by its protector? This question was forced into the minds of a community which for too long had lived complacently in the certainty of his eternal succor. A new note now appears in the Old Testament. The Hebrews were now on the defensive. They feared that the support and the predilection of Yahveh had failed them, not because he had abandoned his subjects, but because they had not blindly carried out his instructions. The old passionate enthusiasm now gave way to the reflective attitude of a people whose very existence was at stake. The result was a mood of dark pessimism which brought with it a more subtle capacity for logical reflection and a sophisticated set of moral principles which marked the beginning of the prophetic age, an age also dogged by political and military misfortune.

It was a vital period for Hebrewism. The special relationship became virtually the exclusive domain of a class of enlightened men called prophets. Prophecy did not lead to a new structure of the faith of the fathers but to a restatement of the ideas which had accumulated over the centuries. The ancient beliefs threatened to collapse under the pressure of successive disasters. It would have been possible to argue that Yahveh, no longer able to defend his people, had allowed them to decline into slavery. It would be inferred from this that he was less powerful than he pretended and that his claim to remain in a state of exclusive isolation and to brook no rival around his throne from divinities worshipped by other peoples was as absurd and blasphemous as his refusal to enter into their pantheon.

But the prophets overcame this danger. Inverting the terms of the dilemma, they argued that Yahveh, so far from sharing the misfortunes of his people, had in fact caused them in order to punish them for their sins, the greatest of which was the worship of false gods. This confirmed the principle of the vindictive God, even if it changed the background against which his vengeance was wrought. In place of the certainty that divine protection would never fail and that it was not the errors they had committed which had prevented the Hebrews from achieving primacy, there crept in the nagging fear that the anger of Yahveh might prove lasting and universal and not, as had always been thought, mild and ephemeral.

This new biblical idea was the product of a changed attitude toward situations which, if they had occurred in the earliest period, would have provoked much more energetic and violent reactions. The pessimism of the prophets bore witness to a greater awareness of man's limitations, to a decline in the old aggressiveness, to an appreciation of the needs of other peoples. Though sadly ignorant of the power and the capacities of Yahveh, the heathen tribes were nonetheless entitled to live and to live in hope.

The prophets who lived before the fall of the kingdom of Israel and the destruction of Samaria felt that a grave catastrophe was imminent, since a powerful and expanding empire loomed near their frontier. This fact was enough by itself to destroy all optimism. The link which united Yahveh with his people has, in their writings, a more intimate and tolerant character.

The catastrophe of 722 B.C. was to deepen their despair, so that the prophetic messages referred to a reality and a way of life in which feelings of unity and brotherhood assumed increasing importance. While the rigorous interpretation of the bond between Yahveh and his people lost force under the pressure of these developments, the divinity came eventually to be considered as the personification of an idea common to all the Hebrews. The tone of prophetic literature became more subdued, expressing the attitude of one who asks but knows he cannot demand and who seeks to revert to the old alliance while realizing that he has lost the right to insist upon its implementation.

Thus a new religious awareness was born. Because of the misfortunes which had occurred or were expected to occur, the Hebrews reached the conclusion that the alliance had been broken through the fault of men, through their pride, vanity, and lack of faith. Expiation was certain and imminent. The scourge would descend on the people who had once enjoyed a protection and a superiority of which it had not proved worthy.

Fortunately, such dismal forebodings of impending doom called forth their own reaction and a mood of optimism. The day of regeneration and salvation would come. The old alliance would regain its past value because Yahveh's protective benevolence was once more available. Thus there began to emerge the promise of the Messiah, a savior soon to come among men, to help the people rise from the depths and bring back the favor of the Lord after the humiliations they had undergone.

Waiting for the Messiah became an essential element of Hebrew life. But who would this Messiah be? Perhaps a commander of armies, injecting new enthusiasm into his people, or the bearer of a religious message, offering redemption, not in this world, but the next, where redress would be obtained for the insults and injuries suffered and where men would be judged in terms of a rule of love and brotherhood? Initially men hoped for an uprising which would lead to a reform of the political institutions and the military order. Subsequently waiting for the coming of the Messiah became a spiritual and cosmopolitan attitude, in some ways comparable with that of later Stoic speculation. The Hebrews oscillated between the two extremes. Some clung to the ancient sources of inspiration, others adopted a more subtle viewpoint emphasizing the need to show greater respect for one's neighbor. The literature of this period reveals critical awareness and a deeper understanding of the importance of historical events.

Some of these features are also discernible in Deuteronomy, the fifth book of the Pentateuch, where the mildness of certain passages is in sharp contrast with the tone of the four preceding books, which are full of a sort of bellicose mystique in their approach to problems concerning peace and war, the rights of the individual in general and of the prisoner-of-war in particular. Deuteronomy implies in places the concept of an abiding justice which men should respect in fixing the limits of their conduct. The life of the individual was thus raised to a level of greater humaneness, though this is more often hinted at than expressed. The heroic vitality proper to the archaic period of Hebrew history gave way to a new spiritual set of ideas in which Yahveh appeared as the dispenser of rewards to the meritorious. Thus the number of those benefiting from divine assistance spread to include peoples other than the Hebrews. Those critics who reject the Mosaic origin of the Deuteronomy, believing that it was written much later than the date traditionally accepted, adduce the note of humility, suggesting significant analogies with the prophetic literature as evidence supporting their point of view.

The Sapiential Books (Proverbs, Ecclesiasticus, Ecclesiastes, Wisdom and the Song of Songs), mainly anthologies of popular precepts, were probably not compiled according to any fixed plan. But the thought of the compilers goes beyond individual rules, tending toward the formulation of principles of universal application. Wisdom, seen as a divine attribute, acquires an identity of its own. It has an aura of melancholy in the Ecclesiastes, which was almost certainly written in the Hellenistic period under the influence of new philosophies of Stoic and Skeptic origin. The sense of ennui and futility generated by earthly things, and particularly by science, which causes "so much harm" because "by increasing knowledge, one increases pain,"[8] is an indication of a fermentation of ideas and ideals diverging from tradition. The general tone of the book is meek and subdued. It urges moderation and stresses the vanity of things of this world and the advantages deriving from forms of ordered life, since men are always in thrall to somebody or something. A controversial passage would seem to hint that even the most powerful sovereign is subject to the call of the earth, whose gifts he cannot despise if he is to survive, for he too is "enslaved by the glebe."[9]

The same influences affected the Book of Wisdom, a book probably compiled in the Hebrew circles of Alexandria; from the teaching of the Hellenistic schools and particularly from Stoicism is drawn a refiguration of the divine principle which embraces the universe, directing its development according to a rational plan.

Of particular interest is an examination of the various writings to come to a better understanding of the ways in which pre-Christian Hebrewism reacted to the problem of peace. If the Old Testament were to be examined as a whole, leaving aside its background and the various factors inspiring it, it would have to be conceded that it is essentially a violent book with an obvious bias toward strife: how could one challenge the evidence of certain episodes of blood-chilling ferocity, in which not only are the Hebrews incited to make war, but their worst instincts are encouraged, the aim being to stifle all feeling of humanity and mercy?[10] We may consider for example the chronicle of the war fought by the Hebrews against the hosts of Midian.[11] This is once again an atmosphere of genocide, organized by Moses with the assent of Yahveh. The tone is exactly the same as that of the Homeric epics, feature excesses similar to those in which Agamemnon indulges in Book VI of the *Iliad*.

But, in contrast with the passages cited and with others of the same kind, it would be possible to cite extracts from the Old Testament (Deuteronomy, the prophetic literature, the Sapiential Books) imbued with mildness and a sense of humanity. Some of these, so far from inciting the Hebrews to war, urge them not to resist their foes and to surrender, since surrender is preferable to the serious disasters—death, hunger, pestilence—caused by conflict.[12] In the later books, almost certainly in the Hellenistic period, the same problem is even tackled in abstract and universal terms. Peace becomes a condition of the spirit, its aim being the moral edification of all. It satisfies a sacred desire of man and a requirement of society.

This brings us face to face with contrasting influences and opposing attitudes to the same topic. Their apparent contradiction may baffle the believer who turns to the biblical message in search of authentic and consistent evidence of the will of God on a certain problem, but it will not surprise those who remember that the Hebrew people had a history of many centuries in which, inevitably, environmental circumstances changed and ambitions and modes of thinking took new forms. For the purposes of our study, we shall consider below the most significant of these changes.

A Religion of Nomads

The record of the initial period of Hebrew history, a period of nomadism during which the Hebrews were searching for better places to settle, was preserved in the oldest books of the Bible and in the harsh warlike mentality which they express. A nomadic people is forced to keep on fighting if it is to survive. Continual changes of location and the quest for new pastures, to replace those ruined by a disorganized economy based on livestock, bring it into conflict with the peoples through whose territory it must travel—hence a permanent state of friction with its neighbors, interrupted only by short armistices.

The war of the nomads is also of a special type. Their campaigns, not being sustained by reserves in men and materials, tend to lose momentum quickly. They must therefore be rapid and conclusive and for this reason are often cruel. Success must be immediate because the very survival of the ethnic group is at stake, and the soldiers are all too well aware that quite near the battlefield are their families, defenseless, encamped in the open or in fragile tents, and at the mercy of the foe if things go wrong. A people settled permanently in a given territory can more easily risk a military reverse, since this may be a setback but not a disaster.

Because the nomad is compelled to carry his few belongings with him and live under canvas, he feels no real love either for a home of his own, since he has none, or for that of others which he cannot usefully plunder. Therefore he does not hesitate to destroy what belongs to the enemy and what he cannot carry with him. An obvious example is the fury of the Mongol hordes of Genghis Khan in twelfth-century China. The Hebrews behaved in much the same way at Jericho, where "they burnt the city with fire, and all that was therein: only the silver, and the gold, and the vessels of brass and of iron, they put into the treasury of the house of the Lord" (Josh. 6:24).

The type of war of which there is evidence in the Pentateuch is precisely that of nomad peoples. In Deut. 20:10-18, a distinction is made between the enemies living in distant countries, who did not constitute a serious threat to the safety of the Hebrews and the purity of their faith, and those living in the Promised Land. If the former surrendered without fighting, they were to be enslaved; but if they took up arms to resist, the men were all to be put to the sword and the women and children carried off into captivity. But no quarter must be given to the enemies belonging to the second group. Not one of them was to be allowed to survive. This was a primitive way of conducting war operations, characteristic of those who must win or perish. Even the immunity of envoys, allowed by almost all primitive societies, was not always respected by the Hebrews in the early times.

These defensive exigencies and this approach to strategy were reflected in the religion, which was founded on an exclusive cult and could not be blended with that of other peoples; what is generally needed to achieve an interpenetration of religions and a measure of syncretism is peaceful coexistence, based, for example, on cultural or trade contacts. This was completely lacking in the case of the Hebrews. This explains why Hebrew nomadism led to the practice of monotheism and the worship of a proud and wrathful God who forbade his people all contamination by other faiths. Absolute loyalty was demanded of the subjects, but the God of the Hebrew nomads also offered them total protection. Hence the concept of the chosen people enjoying the predilection of Yahveh, particularly in the one field vital to survival, that of war.

The relations between Yahveh and the privileged tribe as recorded in the most ancient books of the Bible seem to imitate this model. They became so close as to imply that the military victories of the Hebrews were solely due to Yahveh's protection. Yahveh himself ordered his children to embark on a certain battle, establishing its plans and even fighting himself: "For the Lord your God is He that goeth with you, to fight for you against your enemies, to save you" (Deut. 20:4). Yahveh enabled his people to prosper and to overcome the foe, provided the people remained loyal.

> If thou shalt say in thine heart, These nations are more than I; how can I dispossess them? Thou shalt not be afraid of them: but shalt well remember what the Lord thy God did unto Pharaoh, and unto all Egypt; The great Temptations which thine eyes saw and the signs and the wonders, and the mighty hand, and the stretched-out arm, whereby the Lord thy God brought thee out: so shall the Lord thy God do unto all the people of whom thou art afraid. [Deut. 7:17-18]

In the Psalms, too, there is a similar picture of man calling on God to help him in battle. "Blessed be the Lord my strength, which teacheth my hands to war, and my fingers to fight: My goodness and my fortress; my high tower, and my deliverer; my shield, and He in whom I trust; who subdueth my people under me" (Ps. 144:1). Although not always explicit, this kind of idea recurs again and again in Hebrew writings. It is bound up with their nomadism, with their faith in the future, and their conviction of achieving salvation. There is further confirmation of this in Num. 21:14, which makes a reference to the book of the wars of the Lord, perhaps an anthology of patriotic songs celebrating the age of nomadism. The songs had been drawn from the book by a later hagiographer and included in texts that have come down to us.

But after a time the nomads felt the need to settle in one place. This desire, kindled by the sight of the fertile Palestinian countryside, inspired the biblical passages concerning the land promised by God to Abraham and intended for the settlement and prosperity of his people. The pledge was to be fulfilled through the conquest of the Land of Canaan, the fall of Jericho, the driving out of the Canaanites, and the partition of the lands among the twelve tribes—in other words, the armed conquest of the territory, facilitated, as the Hebrews believed, by continuing divine help.

Men are inclined to see war from a very special point of view when they know that they can count on the benevolence of Providence, which will enable the few to prevail over the many and the better armed. It is quite possible that the most ancient biblical tests were designed not only to provide evidence of a revelation profoundly felt, but also to serve as rigid military instructions for the conduct of war.

> When the Lord thy God shall bring thee into the land whither thou goest to possess it, and hath cast out many nations before thee, the Hittites, and the Girgashites, and the Amorites, and the Canaanites, and the Perizzites, and the Hivites, and the Jebusites, seven nations greater and mightier than thou, And when the Lord thy God shall deliver them before thee; thou shalt smite them, and utterly destroy them; thou shalt make no covenant with them, nor shew mercy unto them. [Deut. 7:1-2]

And yet, the conquest of the Promised Land and the transition from a nomadic, pastoral type of economy to a mainly agricultural economy, were to cause fundamental changes of mentality in the Hebrews and in their attitude toward war and relations with other peoples. Their intransigent xenophobia was not tempered to a more conciliatory line of conduct based on the growing feeling that while it was right to worship Yahveh, there was no need to impose religion to the extreme of actual genocide. The mentality of the Hebrews changed as they changed from herdsmen to farmers and grew closer to nature and its seasonal variations. All this led them to invest their God with new qualities connected with tilling the soil and good husbandry.

Having settled on the land, the Hebrews also entered into direct relations with the indigenous peoples who had survived their fierce conquest. The religious practices of these peoples almost certainly included the worship of nature and fertility rites. This meant contact with a very different approach to the supernatural and these experiences may have helped to change Yahveh from a God of wrath and war and to confer on him other qualities of a less formidable nature.

The "pacification" of the God of hosts was neither quick nor easy. It prompted resistance from the priests who opposed innovation because they believed that it was causing degeneration of the race and encouraging contempt for tradition. Hence the confrontation of two tendencies, one of which was conservative and the other in favor of innovation: On the one hand, some adhered firmly to the old idea of divinity, while others adapted it to give a less rigid conception of the position of the Hebrews in the concert of nations and favor new forms of social life. In the period following the conquest of the Promised Land, when there were two Hebrew states, Israel and Judah, Hebrew thinking oscillated between the two extremes, with the latter gradually gaining predominance and later providing the foundation on which the prophets would build.

The Earthly Paradise

The severity and intransigence in the oldest books of the Bible were a consequence, as we have seen, of special historical and physical circumstances, and they were no bar to the emergence from the depths of the Hebrew soul of a longing for a state of serenity and peace, linked even to an actual geographical location. This nostalgia inspired the story of the earthly paradise, where the first man and the first woman had lived in conditions of absolute felicity. The description of Eden and of its loss because of the sin of the parents of man has something in common with the classical myth of the Golden Age, illustrated by Greek religious and philosophical tradition. True, there were substantial disparities between the earthly paradise and the Golden Age. The Garden of Eden reflected the active interference of Yahveh in human affairs. The classical tale, were it only because it was handed down by writers and philosophers and not by inspired hagiographers, was more a popular legend in which, even in antiquity, nobody really believed.

Plato treated the story as an allegory. In the Bible, on the other hand, it had spiritual import, the aim being to celebrate the work of Yahveh. In the creation Yahveh had given the measure of his perfection. He had created a sublime reality with peace as its basis and main component. When man had defied his Creator, thus meriting a tragic destiny of pain and ignominy, when his sin of pride had led to his downfall, when he had been driven out of the garden of bliss, it was clear that, of all man's assets, peace of mind was the most precious.

The conviction that there had at one time been an era of peace which would one day return is found in a number of oriental civilizations. In general, as J. J. Stamm observes, it lay not only in a distant past but was also cherished as an aspiration for the future.[13] Peace was included among the sacred riches of a happy kingdom and it was invoked on every accession to the throne. Hence a new sovereign was often represented as bringing concord and felicity to his people and only seldom as a man who would bring war.

For example, we have information from Egypt on certain ritual details of the investiture of the Pharaohs. It is clear that the keynote of the ceremonies was the praise of peace. The ascent to the throne of Tutmosis III, a sovereign of the XVIIIth dynasty who reigned from 1483 B.C. to 1450 B.C., was accompanied by the following invocation: "Horus has through you brought peace in the two countries [upper and lower Egypt], placing you at the head of all the territories." Peace was celebrated in this and similar passages as an inestimable benefit, which the Pharaoh—as the incarnation of a god, or the descendant of divine stock, or as the medium of a supernatural inspiration, but, in any event, as the possessor of exceptional faculties—would certainly ensure for his subjects.

A fragment of poetry preserved in the museum of the University of Pennsylvania suggests that the Sumerians were also convinced that at one time and in a certain geographical place there had been an earthly paradise in which all creatures lived in happiness and where the ills which later assailed them were unknown. In that perfect and happy world, men, who were simple and frugal, knew nothing of relations of life in society, the links of family, their exact place within created nature. All events took place against the background of unlimited serenity.

Another Sumerian text is of some interest in this connection. S. N. Kramer gives us the following translation:

> The spell of Nudimmund pronounce unto him:
> 'Once upon a time there was no snake, there was no scorpion,
> There was no hyena, there was no lion,
> There was no wild dog, no wolf,
> There was no fear, no terror,
> Man had no rival.
> Once upon a time the lands Shubur (and) [Ha] mazi,
> Many-tongued Sumer, the great land of the decrees of princeship,
> Uri, the land having (all) that is appropriate,
> The land Martu, resting in security,
> The whole universe, the people in unison,
> To Enlil in one tongue [gave praise] ....'[14]

Behind the religious legend and the memory of a time in which the same God was worshipped, we can find evidence of man's longing for peace and of his former capacity for mutual understanding and friendship, to which only external causes and a deterioration of human nature had put an end.

Similar ideas are found in the vestiges of other civilizations of the Near and Middle East (for example in that known as Ugarit, which flourished in the second millennium B.C. on the Syrian coast).[15] Even in the Mesopotamian warrior civilizations, on which we have so much information because of their diligence in keeping records, it is possible to discern evidence of a longing for peace and for the establishment of a state of widespread serenity to take the place of intense warlike fervor. An example is the prologue to the Code of Laws promulgated by King Hammurabi (eighteenth century B.C.), the unifier of the Mesopotamian kingdoms.

Just as in the other oriental cultures, then, we find in the Bible a narration of the past existence of an earthly paradise, connected with the notion of a creation, and the memory of paradise is associated with a longing for the proscription of war.

The Alliances between Yahveh and the Chosen People

The word *peace* took on the meaning of a condition such as would ensure for man what was necessary for life, without violence of any kind to other living beings, even animals. The diet of the first man in the earthly paradise had been wholly vegetarian. "And God said, Behold, I have given you every herb bearing seed, which is on the face of all the earth, and every tree, in the which is the fruit of a tree yielding seed; to you it shall be for meat" (Gen. 1:29-30). There is in the story which follows that of the creation a simple and instinctive unity, illustrative of the peace and tranquillity existing in Eden, and the perfection and the goodness of God, from whose will all is derived. The punishment inflicted by Yahveh on Adam was to be inexorable precisely because it stemmed from God's realization that his trust in man had not been properly reciprocated.

From the time when man had shown clearly the pettiness of his ambition, proving unworthy of the benefits vouchsafed him, his relations with Yahveh began to change; the disappointment felt by the Creator meant that these relations must be clarified. Yahveh was ready to assume new commitments with regard to man, but on condition that man complied absolutely with His will. Man was to promise not to squander in sterile fervor the prodigious divine grace and to prove his right to divine favor by constant observance of the law. Renewed at least three times, this alliance tended on the one hand to supply a logical system for the relations between Yahveh and man and on the other to mark the gradual drift away from the state of perfection and serenity once enjoyed in the earthly paradise.

In Gen. 9:3-4, the renewal of the pact concluded by Yahveh and Noah led to an increase in man's food resources, so that these were no longer limited to the vegetable world but also included animals, which men were now allowed to slaughter on certain conditions.[16] This event had marked the end of the initial period of human society, which, though it fell short of the respect for the sanctity of all life that had prevailed in the Garden of Eden, nonetheless retained that respect to a large degree. However, the ban on killing men—whose lives were sacred because they were made in the image of God—remained in force.

This rule was later to be changed when Yahveh renewed with Abraham his alliance with the Hebrews, thus intimating that he had chosen them for the execution of his design.[17] Until that time, although experiencing the consequences of the changed diet and of the authorization now given to kill animals, the men peopling the earth and all descending from the same founder of the family could consider themselves equal. The situation changed when Yahveh, having assumed an obligation toward Abraham, recognized the Hebrews as having a primacy over the others and a right to occupy the Promised Land.[18] In exchange for this pledge, which suspended the old rule against killing men, Yahveh demanded absolute submission. Thus began the third period, during which the use of force was allowed, provided it was used in the service of God. Promising dominion over a land belonging to others signified to all intents and purposes legitimizing wars of conquest.

The fourth period began when Yahveh had handed to Moses on Mount Sinai the Tablets of the Law, prescribing liturgical rules and a rule of conduct.[19] There had then begun for the Hebrew people, as for entire humanity, a phase distinguished by a more careful understanding of the reality of the world, of its fundamental evil, of its flaws and weaknesses. An attempt would be made to provide absolute protection—and this was the meaning of Yahveh's pact with Moses—through a set of rules designed to discipline individual and collective life.

The subdivision of Hebrew history into several epochs, each of which began with a pact, lends itself easily to a comparison with the eras in which classical mythology usually subdivided prehistorical times. Although it would be dangerous to press too far this comparison (argued by J. J. Stamm), there are unquestionably substantial similarities between the two stories.[20]

Some conclusions may be drawn from all this. According to the Bible, the creation was a peaceful phenomenon and was therefore guided by the desire to do good and to achieve the happiness of living creatures. This peaceful approach, revealed through successive manifestations of benevolence, was however thwarted by the spread of sin and the sinfulness of man. The memory of the original state of perfect concord was still alive in the first generation, although it witnessed one of the most heinous of crimes: fratricide.[21]

The consequences of the crime of Cain were to spread, causing the deterioration of the conduct of man in individual and collective life. Yahveh was forced to acknowledge a reality in which the impact of sin was proving stronger than had been foreseen. His intervention was almost always designed to help man, solving problem situations in which the use of violence seemed to be a constant factor which could not now be eliminated. War and not peace thus came to the fore as Yahveh sought to help a people for whom ferocity and destruction had gradually become the normal means of attaining their objectives of conquest and expansion. The problem of war and peace was inherent in the decline which had begun with sin and had continued with the gradual corruption of the human race.

Yahveh, who had been the Lord of peace when he had created the universe, had become the God of war, the protector of armies, the fomenter of conflicts, when he concentrated his active benevolence on a single people, authorizing the Hebrews to invade, to conquer, and to subjugate. To all intents and purposes he lost his peaceful attributes. War had become an inevitability from which there was no escape.

Tolerance of the Foreigner

The memory of the earthly paradise was not the only evidence of the existence of congenital brotherly love among men. Hate and violence did not always dominate relations of the Hebrews with other nations. The cult of Yahveh, for example, was not confined to the Hebrews. Foreigners also could be admitted, especially if they lived in the Hebrew world. "One ordinance shall be both for you of the congregation, and also for the stranger that sojourneth with you, an ordinance forever in your generations: as ye are, so shall the stranger be before the Lord. One law and one manner shall be for you, and for the stranger that sojourneth with you."[22]

This sentiment—vaguely cosmopolitan, at least in regard to religious matters—extends in some passages to the actual status of the foreigner, who could claim parity. Deuteronomy, in particular, contains references to this humanitarian spirit, to a wider and more enlightened vision of the interdependence of men and of the need for each man to assume a humane attitude toward his neighbor.

This was a genuine change of mentality, giving more room for feelings of mercy, a sentiment conspicuous by its absence from so many older biblical passages. "[The Lord] doth execute the judgment of the fatherless and widow, and loveth the stranger, in giving him food and raiment. Love ye therefore the stranger: for ye were strangers in the land of Egypt" (Deut. 10: 18-19). And again: "When thou cuttest down thine harvest in thy field, and hast forgot a sheaf in the field, thou shalt not go again to fetch it: it shall be for the stranger, for the fatherless, and for the widow" (Deut. 24:19). The succeeding verses confirm the rule that something should be given to those who have nothing, and the passage concludes with the following words: "And thou shalt remember that thou wast a bondman in the land of Egypt: therefore I command thee to do this thing." The order to consider the foreigner as worthy of the generosity of the faithful is also found in Deut. 26:11-13. This becomes a genuine right to join the community as a full member. So much liberality toward individuals who were always considered foes to be eliminated if they opposed the expansionist objectives of the Hebrews was related to the theory of the single origin of the human race and to the genealogy of the nations and of the peoples as set out in Gen. 10.

Nonetheless, in matters of faith Deuteronomy showed the same rigid intransigence as of yore.[23] But, as regards the foreigner and the weaker sections of the population, the fifth book of the Pentateuch was more tolerant and showed a greater spirit of sociability and sympathy for the needs of others. This circumstance is evidence of the greater value accorded to certain aspects of the human personality and shows an inclination to seek in work done for one's neighbor the satisfaction of essential spiritual needs. Beginning to emerge was the possibility of the individual working toward God and complying with his rules—no longer burying himself in the ethnic group and considering himself significant only as a part of a greater whole, but living as an individual working out his own salvation. Certain idealistic factors favoring a humanitarian and less egoistic vision of power began to take on substance, exercising a beneficial influence. These factors, admittedly, were not strong enough to govern the thinking and the political choices of the Hebrew people or their leaders. Ps. 72, the "Psalm for Solomon," leaves no doubt on this score when, praising the person and the virtues of the monarch, it says: "They that dwell in the wilderness shall bow before him; and his enemies shall lick the dust" (Ps. 72:9).

Under the pressure of changed historical and material factors, these new ideals were to evolve toward greater tolerance and more humane attitudes.

Prophetic Literature—the Coming of a Messiah

We have already noticed that the prophetic writings subsequent to the fall of Samaria, the end of the kingdom of Israel, and the deportation of a number of its inhabitants by the Assyrian army (721 B.C.) reveal greater respect for the individual and the rights of others, related to the prospect of the imminent advent of the Kingdom of God and of a Messiah. Comparing the various prophetic messages, we can summarize the doctrine of the messianic kingdom as follows: a scion of the house of David, of nature partly divine and partly human, would rule over a pacified kingdom (Isa. 9:5-6); he would be inspired by divine wisdom (Isa. 11:2); his kingdom of peace would extend throughout the world (Mic. 5:3-4); his behavior would be governed solely by a love of justice (Jer. 23:6); his dominion would be eternal (Ezek. 37:25); through his work he would wash away the sins of the world; because of this he would be subjected to endless humiliations, taking upon himself the anguish and the distress of mankind. God would accept his sufferings in expiation of their sins (Isa. 53:3-7).[24]

From now on the prophets spoke of the Hebrews as a nation condemned to expiate its sins. The concept of sin ceases to be the fact of doubting the omnipotence of Yahveh (an idea suitable only for the Hebrews) and becomes the transgression of a moral rule, universally valid. Power was no longer considered solely an instrument of empire over others but also a means of regeneration.

The prophetic literature also tackled the problem of how to practice humility. Vanity and pride were appropriate to the victors and to the powerful. They were valid for those who had imposed their supremacy, but they were quite out of place in the weak, for whom, by logic and by necessity, humility and resignation were the right attitudes. The Hebrews were now the vanquished. The disasters of their nation had all been fully deserved. Their vices and those of their leaders had called down the wrath of Yahveh and cost them his protection. The only thing to do now was to expiate their guilt, awaiting rebirth with the coming of the kingdom.

In the context of our study, the prophetic message turns around these two themes: the coming of the kingdom and the salvation of society. The Messiah, when he came, would implement a principle of justice among peoples, breaking the chain of vengeance and countervengeance and the domination of race over race. He would be the immortal, impartial, inexorable arbiter. War would become impossible because its premises—dependent on injustice—would cease to exist. "And he shall judge among the nations, and shall rebuke many people: and they shall beat their swords into ploughshares, and their spears into pruning hooks: nation shall not lift up sword against nation, neither shall they learn war any more" (Isa. 2:4). And again: "For every battle of the warrior is with confused noise, and garments rolled in blood; but this shall be with burning and fuel of fire" (Isa. 9:5). A soothing sense of peacefulness would come to pervade the people, and enemies, however ancient their enmity, would be reconciled. "The wolf also shall dwell with the lamb, and the leopard shall lie down with the kid; and the calf and the young lion and the fattling together; and a little child shall lead them" (Isa. 11:6). Some statements might be taken from Xenophon's *Cyropaedia*, of which they have the ingenuousness and idealism: "His name shall endure forever: his name shall be continued as long as the sun: and men shall be blessed in him: all nations shall call him blessed" (Ps. 72:17).

Other remarkable analogies were drawn from a world reborn through grace, moved by tidings of peace and by the messianic message.[25] "They shall not hurt nor destroy in all my holy mountain: for the earth shall be full of the knowledge of the Lord, as the waters cover the sea" (Isa. 11:9). So much messianic happiness was not intended to be achieved in disorder and lawlessness because "then judgment shall dwell in the wilderness, and righteousness remain in the fruitful field. And the work of righteousness shall be peace; and the effect of righteousness quietness and assurance for ever" (Isa. 32:16-17). Promises of peace, security, humility and concord abound elsewhere, notably in Mic. 4:3, Hos. 2:20, Zech. 9:10, Ps. 46:9-10, 72:3, 72:14. They suffice to prove the existence within the prophetic movement of a real longing for peace.

In 701 B.C. another Assyrian expedition threatened the surviving kingdom of Judah and only a happy accident, attributed to the supernatural, caused the enemy to suspend military operations. The prophetic movement drew prestige and authority from this because Isaiah had foreseen this providential liberation. But the peaceful component of the message also received a renewed impulse.

There can be no other interpretation of the words of Isaiah: "I create the fruit of the lips; Peace, peace to him that is far off, and to him that is near, saith the Lord. . . . But the wicked are like the troubled sea, when it cannot rest, whose waters cast up mire and dirt. There is no peace, saith my God, to the Wicked" (57:19-21). The most simple explanation of this passage is that it alludes to the loss of peace of mind. But the idea expressed at the end, which also reappears in Isa. 48:22, cannot be separated from the certainty of the attainment of a condition of universal serenity, to be propagated "even to the end of the earth."[26] Men were judged equal before God, wherever they came from. This law was to stem from a movement of faith shared by the entire world and shown to be applicable to all human beings, united in obedience to the Lord and in peace. "Look unto Me, and be ye saved, all the ends of the earth: for I am God, and there is none else"(Isa. 45:22). This hope for peace and unity was indeed announced in terms of concluded agreements in the name of the Lord, by people once enemies. "In that day shall there be a highway out of Egypt to Assyria, and the Assyrian shall come into Egypt, and the Egyptian into Assyria, and the Egyptians shall serve with the Assyrians" (Isa. 19:23). (This means the Egyptians and the Assyrians shall practice the same religion.)

The Hebrew religion continued to develop under the pressure of historical events in the Middle East. The Assyrian Empire was followed by that of the Babylonians, who inherited certain political and strategic ideas, including the tendency to press toward the Mediterranean. Hence the need to renew their influence over the Palestinian territories and particularly over the kingdom of Judah, which, after the fall of Israel and possibly because of help given to neighboring Egypt, had retained a precarious independence, remaining the only living center of Hebrew religion and culture. There followed the military campaigns of Nebuchadnezzar II, the first conquest of Jerusalem, and the first deportation into Babylonia (597 B.C.), and, ten years later, the second conquest of the city, the second deportation, and the end of the kingdom of Judah.

These tragic events took place at the time of the ministry of the prophet Jeremiah, a ministry which strengthened the personalistic element in the relations between Yahveh and the individual. Jeremiah tends to represent man as part of a spiritual communion, presided over by his Creator. ". . . I will put my law in their inward parts, and write it in their hearts; and will be their God and they shall be My people. And they shall teach no more every man his neighbour, and every man his brother, saying, know the Lord: for they shall all know Me" (Jer. 31:33-34). Thus the intense religious feeling in the times

of greatest trouble was to involve God in the lives of the faithful and depreci-
ate the old Hebrew heritage inspired by heroism and a will for power. To the
Hebrews, divided into various political parties, living in a buffer territory between great empires and in slavery and exile, this religious and literary heritage must have seemed extremely remote in time, dispersed in a fog of memory and symbols which only the faith of each believer and the work of the
prophets could justify.

Many attempts have been made to explain the development of prophecy
as the result of pressure from certain foreign elements. The hypothesis has
been formulated that Jeremiah, the most powerful and authoritative of the
prophets of the time, who had spoken out for understanding with the Babylonians, might in fact be in the pay of the court of Nebuchadnezzar II. The
king would naturally seek to suppress any national revival of the Hebrew people by transforming a political ideal into a religious message. This view neglects perhaps the substantial natural changes in the Hebrew mentality and
the nature of the prophetic ministry. For centuries the Hebrew mind oscillated between two memories: that of the earliest period, ever more dimly recol-
lected, in which a model for the state and its religion had been outlined and
that of the prophesied messianic coming. This conflict was to be resolved in
Jesus and in the New Testament with an affirmation of the supremacy of the
spiritual order over the worldly order and the liberation of the Hebrews from
their long wait for a savior who would finally solve their problems.

In Jeremiah, the herald of new disaster, the quest for peace was associated
on the one hand with a reconciliation with the Babylonians and on the other
with the wait for the fulfillment of the will of the Lord. His message has deep
undertones of pain, and he looks forward anxiously to rebirth and salvation,
to an understanding with Yahveh.

Then the Hebrews returned from exile because of the new political situation of the Near East, now dominated by the Persians (538 B.C.). Jeremiah's
prophecies, which had accompanied the transition from the old mentality to
the new, led to further developments. They accelerated the process of change
from a creed of war to a genuinely religious faith. Yahveh stressed certain aspects, the background to which we have already seen. God is no longer a God
of wrath and vengeance, and is now seen as the provident Creator. His constant presence was discerned in all created things, a view suggesting panthe-
ism. As Creator of the world—this contrasted with contemporary Hellenic
speculation, which generally regarded matter as eternal and not as having been
created—his personality fitted into a system in which new values, vaguely cosmopolitan and mainly connected with the realm of ethics, were asserting
themselves with growing authority. The Lord of the Hebrews had become a
legislator, a custodian of moral precepts, a champion of understanding among
men. "In those days it shall come to pass, that ten men shall take hold out of
all languages of the nations, even shall take hold of the skirt of him that is a

Jew, saying, We will go with you: for we have heard that God is with you" (Zech. 8:23).

Besides longing for justice, man began to yearn for a redemption which would give him the means to escape the extreme penalty through a process of personal purification which would restore his original innocence. In this changed attitude, too, there is evidence of pacifist thinking.

This approach would not however have been enough to demand a revision of the oldest texts; if certain views concerning the date when the bulk of the Old Testament was compiled are to be relied upon, it was during the Babylonian exile and after the return to the fatherland that a great part of the biblical material in the version known to us was rearranged. We must infer that the Hebrew nation was unable, despite a change of mentality, to make a clean break with the past, and to jettison, for example, the documents attesting to its old warlike ambitions, which remained part and parcel of the Pentateuch. The influence of the conservative classes may well have prevented the exclusion of these texts: too firm a breach with the old times, too full a re-elaboration of the texts, a completely renewed vision of tradition might have led to rebellion and controversy which could have damaged the prestige of biblical literature and its revealed authenticity. If this change really took place, it was probably due to new ideas generated by growing awareness and the need to face religious problems in a dimension tending to the universal, a dimension in which peace is a quest for internal serenity and a yearning for higher things.

Thus the old idea of the chosen people and its mission gradually faded. The Hebrews after the prophets had come to accept that intransigence must give way to an enlightened vision of the future kingdom, over which they would preside, not because they were the possessors of political and military power, but as interpreters of a religious and moral message for all men. The frontiers of time and space were overcome, and a set of ideas vaguely foreshadowing the Christian message gained acceptance. In this context, peace was sometimes given an abstract character, close to the meaning of the Greek concord (ὁμόνοια). Nor was the aim solely to establish it as between nations: the objective was to consolidate the personal and internal peace of each individual. By virtue of his new attributes, God no longer demanded that man go forth in bold military enterprises, but advised him to orientate his existence according to a line of thought in which peace, even if not expressly invoked, remained the ultimate objective.

The political and military events that followed failed to distract the Hebrews from their new vocation. It is at this period that suffering became "the badge of all their tribe." On their return to the fatherland, they found themselves closely involved in the power struggles of the Near East concerning the Persian, Egyptian, Macedonian, Seleucid, Ptolemaic empires and ultimately that of the Romans. The succession of events was to cause the *diaspora* formation, in the countries bordering on the Mediterranean, of Hebrew communities in which the will toward understanding with other peoples consistently prevailed, partly as a result of contact with Hellenistic civilization and Stoic and Cynic speculation.

In some periods, and especially among the communities which had remained in Palestine, religious and national fanaticism was to rise again (for example in the Maccabean wars against the Seleucids and in the insurrections against the Romans in the years 66-70 A.D., 115-117, and 132-125). The hope for a political revival was kept alive, but it was associated with the hope that universal peace would be the final outcome. This convergence of feelings is discernible in a number of passages in the famous Dead Sea Scrolls, some of which show that there was a revolutionary movement against the occupying power, while others indicate that many of the Hebrews longed only for peace.[27]

These events did not affect to any great extent the general line of Hebrew thought, particularly that developed among the communities of the *diaspora,* who realistically pursued a policy of patient resignation to adversity, while waiting for justice and peace to descend upon the world, as had been foretold. The values of charity and grace, to which Christianity was to initiate humanity by means of the Gospel message, were partly anticipated in the feelings and reflections of a people cruelly persecuted by its neighbors and dogged relentlessly by events beyond its control.

$$\text{\textit{4}}$$

PEACE
IN CHRISTIAN DOCTRINE

The Message of Christianity and the Early Christians

From the very outset, Christianity taught an ideal of personal betterment which would eventually culminate in a world purged of all violence. Invoking the inalienable rights of conscience, Christians preached faith in a lasting justice to be meted out by God in a world beyond this one. Man's deeds on earth would be measured against the yardstick of charity and mercy, and he would be judged and appropriately rewarded in the everlasting kingdom.

Precisely because of this, the preaching of Jesus, though it seemed to fulfill a specifically Jewish prophecy, rapidly won converts among the Greeks and Romans. Jesus was at one and the same time the Messiah promised to the Hebrews and the bearer of a message of universal appeal: this dual quality was what gave his message its impetus, for Christianity condemned conventional ethics, whose deficiencies no spiritual force had previously overcome and to whose victims no religious faith had previously offered consolation or hope of any kind. The originality of Christ's teaching lay in the following circumstance: he taught no ascetic rule designed to separate those who adopted it from the life of the community, nor did he seek to inhibit the convert's natural aspirations; on the contrary, he asked the potential convert to abandon the idea of a reward in this world in return for happiness in the Kingdom of God, situated beyond man's caprice and governed by justice.

He promised salvation to all men, but especially to the weak and the lame —not only in body but also in spirit. These were the people who had been sorely neglected by the religions of antiquity, which tended to attach great importance to aesthetic perfection and earthly happiness. Thus there was a

207

communion between God the Savior and all living beings, among whom the poor seemed nearest to grace. The Sermon on the Mount shows that the message of Jesus was addressed to the poor, the despised, and the persecuted. Alluding to their sufferings, he consoled them: "Rejoice, and be exceeding glad: for great is your reward in heaven" (Matt. 5:12).

Christ called upon his hearers and his followers to react constructively to the ills and pains of earthly existence. The Savior whose intervention was invoked did not belong to the world of the existing religions, but to the supernatural world drawing on the secret vitality of the soul. A heightened awareness, informed with repentance for sins committed and a determination to yield to their temptations no more, took the place of the traditional pagan formalism. At the center of the system was the figure of a single God, Creator of a new experience made possible by the coming of Christ. He is thus depicted not as an avenger but as a father whose law is dictated by serene confidence in the destiny of men. The law must be obeyed because of God's infinite goodness. God's goodness was looked upon as a model of perfection—a model that would lead to the possession of God. The relations thus established between man and his creator and judge were direct and peaceful, for they sprang from fellowship in a community seen as a vehicle of salvation.

The Coming of the Kingdom of God

Hence the certainty shared by all Christians of belonging, in this as in the next life, to a great community, governed by a law of love and sacrifice and lying above the common obedience to primeval instincts. These circumstances explain the rapid dissemination of Christianity in a world yearning—then as now—for justice and peace, but living without hope. The result was a bond of brotherhood which no religion, civilization, or culture had previously known, much less propagated. Fundamental to the new system—which required men to perform good works for the benefit of all, since we are all united in the creation—was the expectation of the Kingdom of God, that is, of a blissful state of community life in which the practice of mutual love would no longer be an aspiration or a mere corrective to the pain prevailing in the world but a goal finally reached.

But where would the Kingdom of God be achieved? Perhaps in the world of tangible things and therefore at some location? Did the early Christians associate the object of their long vigil with a system of rulers to be established in earthly society?

It seems probable that in the years after the crucifixion, when the first apostolic communities were formed, their aims and hopes were concentrated solely on the values of the spirit and not on the organization of the world. At the time, the kingdom was felt to be near at hand, and it would have seemed pointless to embark on elaborate attempts to transform the current system of temporal hierarchies. The transcendent humility informing the Sermon on the

Mount, inducing the Christian to embrace a happiness separated from things human, sustained by faith and the practice of virtue, was mainly concerned with a supernatural world: the Christians *knew* that it was not on this earth that the ultimate object of this striving would be attained. The words of Jesus himself made it clear that the quest for perfection, though the fundament of a great communion, was a personal matter for the believer. The Christian could be saved without the mediation of the state.

The new message therefore came to deny the primacy of the civil power. The coming of the Kingdom of God and the disappearance of earthly kingdoms were believed imminent, as the warning contained in the synoptic Gospels implied: "Verily I say unto you, there be some standing here, which shall not taste of death, till they see the Son of Man coming in his kingdom" (Matt. 16:28; Mark 8:39; Luke 9:28). Such a ferment of spirituality, of principles and objectives so different from those of the many oriental sects of apostolic times, was bound to have a disruptive impact on social and civil systems.

Jesus' message must necessarily entail a condemnation of war, which had no place in his religious vision, though it had ranked high in pagan ethics as part of the cult of strength and beauty. The appeal of the Gospels to meekness and forgiveness could not be reconciled with the violent outbursts, almost always due to anger, which led to wars and other catastrophes and, moving the faithful away from the pursuit of their natural vocations, prevented them from drawing close in thought and action to God the Creator. God was the father recognized by men; men were all brothers in that there was no specific people elected custodian of the truth as in the Hebrew religion; all must submit to the precepts of the Gospels. Therefore, war was a flagrant denial of the Kingdom of God.

From some points of view the message of the Gospels suggested affinities with Stoic doctrine and the rules of certain religious sects of the time. In fact, the gap between them was unbridgeable. This was particularly true with regard to the condemnation of war, which was more than just an abstract principle or form of words. The Christians believed that only one thing mattered— the salvation of the soul. It was all they knew and all they needed to know.

Since they wished to form communities to implement a program of redemption and religious devotion, the first Christian churches showed little inclination to seek political solutions for their problems. Jesus, taunted by Pilate, had made a reply that was to ring down the centuries: "My kingdom is not of this world" (John 18:36). It was a simple statement that not only established a mystic way and a hierarchy of options but at the same time stressed the unimportance of life in this world and the overwhelming importance of life in the next. What could be the point, then, in using force to achieve results seen to be completely trivial when measured against the yardstick of the real—spiritual—values of eternity? Every war, even a defensive one, stems from a sin of pride in the eyes of God and is resolved in an expense of energy much more usefully employed in efforts to achieve salvation. Such a clear-cut view could subsist only in the climate of mystic exaltation characteristic of early Christianity, when the coming of the kingdom seemed imminent and some doubted even the wisdom of consolidating the religion in forms of association having an institutional character. This was the period in which the rift between the interests of the soul and civil life grew wider.

The New Testament

This atmosphere of dreamlike expectation and detachment from day-to-day reality favorable to attitudes of meekness and the love of peace is clearly discernible in the New Testament, in which accounts of the life and work of Jesus and of his first followers are interwoven with a set of ethical rules. For the faithful, the lives of Jesus and of the apostles give these rules their binding force. The individual documents in this complex of revelations, written during apostolic and subapostolic times, all agree on the same objectives. They condemn violence and urge forgiveness.

In the New Testament, the word *peace* has a number of meanings, the accurate analysis of which is no easy matter. Sometimes it signifies concord (Acts 7:26; Gal. 5:22; Eph. 4:3; James 3:18; I Pet. 3:11), sometimes the absence of conflict (Acts 12:2, 24:2; Rom. 14:19; Heb. 12:14). These are concepts which have much in common, but there are some discrepancies. Concord, a voluntary attitude of the individual and of groups in association, derives from an act of will of the persons involved in a given situation, a situation which could also justify their bellicosity. The absence of war, on the other hand, is a state of affairs existing at a certain time in an organized society, regardless of the circumstances which have led to it.

In other passages, the word *peace* signifies health—both of the mind and of the body. Here, it corresponds to the fundamental content of the Hebrew word *salōm* and is sometimes used jointly with supplementing words such as *reconciliation, salvation, eternal life.*

The New Testament, however, for the reasons already stated, is not concerned with peace between states, although the early Christians believed all violence profoundly wrong. The idea of a permanent and consolidated peace did not fit into their scheme of things: the first apostolic generations were awaiting a supernatural event which would realize the expectations of their faith, freeing them from suffering. The things of this world (necessarily linked with the idea of peace between states), seemed irrelevant to individuals living in intimate communion with God, emotionally alienated from the Roman Empire, although they were formally its subjects. Their opposition to violence did not necessarily induce a policy aimed at strengthening peace in this world but referred to the desires and the hopes to be fulfilled at the time of the Second Coming. The idea of pacification existed, then, but it was for God, not man, to implement it. Even the song of the angels announcing the beginning of the great redemption: "Glory to God in the highest and peace on earth to men of good will" (Luke 2:14), could not be understood other than as a call to men to seek salvation within themselves and in their conduct. The importance of salvation, accessible only to the pure of heart and the meek of spirit, could be apprehended in this sense alone.

What we must look for, rather than a definition, is an atmosphere of humility and forgiveness from which peace, in the abstract and universal sense, including peace between nations, is implied as a corollary. The main episodes of the Gospel story—Jesus' trial and crucifixion—contributed most to the creation of an ideology of forgiveness of one's enemies. As the Son of God, Jesus was vested with supernatural powers and could have escaped the agony imposed on him by the salvation of man, confounding his enemies. And yet he had chosen to suffer and to die. The first Christians were convinced that he had renounced force and had chosen among all the forms of redemption that of painful expiation because of the very nature of his message, which conquered souls by preaching love and preparation for the afterlife, where earthly injustices would be redressed and real peace would prevail over the animosities of men.

Thus the Christian teaching developed along complementary lines: on the one hand the law of justice, on the other that of forgiveness, the two dovetailing and interacting on one another. Violence had no place in a system in which a man who was struck was advised to turn the other cheek.[1] As Jean Lasserre observes in *La Guerre et l'Evangile,* the Jesus of the New Testament never resisted by force insults and threats proferred. When, in the course of his teaching, there was a disturbance caused by his enemies, he freed himself from it almost mysteriously, apparently using unknown powers.[2] Often he resorted to subterfuge, hiding, asking people not to make too much of the miracles he performed, or he withdrew into obscurity to avoid bloodshed or violence. This journey of meekness and acceptance culminated on the eve of the Passover, when he allowed himself to be taken prisoner, well knowing that this was how the great process of expiation would begin. His message provoked dismay and derision among those who failed to perceive its spiritual implications and who interpreted it in terms of earthly power:[3] it was not a manifesto for a social and national rebellion against the Jewish establishment, nor against the Romans who had subjugated so much of the world. The ancient world had known many conquests and the Christians were well aware that these had brought nothing but sorrow.

What was new was that Christ spoke to all men, bringing a message of comfort. Salvation was not in this world. This vale of tears could not bring felicity to anyone, but in the next justice would finally triumph, healing men's quarrels. The message was based on the conviction that what happens among men is important only to the extent that it affects our destiny in the supernatural world, enabling us to save ourselves or to damn ourselves for all eternity. This had repercussions on the behavior of the Christian in this life and fixed a hierarchy of values and choices for him. War, because it brought death and grief, but above all because it was generated by uncontrolled violence and imprudent impulse, was incompatible with redemption. Triggering off the worst instincts of man, bringing him to yield to passion and neglect the duties imposed on him by the Savior, it led to individual and collective patterns of behavior from which only moral and material ruin could ensue.

Another point which must be mentioned: the Christians of the apostolic period were disturbing the stable religious situation of the pagan world; for this they needed indulgence and tolerance, particularly when they first began to spread the Gospel. At any moment—as the persecutions showed—their work was liable to be suffocated in blood. Violence in all forms—therefore including war—conflicted not only with their convictions but also with their interests.

This explains certain aspects of the Gospel story. It is striking, for example, that Jesus and the apostles walked abroad despite the dangers their missionary work entailed. The complex political and religious situation in Palestine, the coexistence, as part of a system of indirect administration, of two authorities—the monarchic, nearest to the population, and the Roman, possessing real power—to which must be added the influence of the priests, enjoying ancient prerogatives not seldom in conflict with those of the state, should have suggested to the itinerant company of preachers following Jesus that they ought to be prepared to defend themselves from aggression, but this was not how they saw things. The only forms of defense they recognized were the justice of God and the punishments liable to be incurred by those who despised his moral law. Using no violence but announcing a severe justice to come, Jesus and his disciples believed they could forestall all danger. An exception to the rule is the incident when Peter, in a fit of rage, drew his sword against the guards sent to arrest the Master and cut off the ear of a slave of the High Priest.[4] The incident, not caused by Jesus, led him to perform a miracle but was also the occasion of a remark which, for the first Christians, must have been interpreted as an announcement of the coming of justice: "Put up again thy sword into his place: for all they that take the sword shall perish with the sword" (Matt. 26:52).

In the Gospel according to Matthew, Jesus makes it clear that he underwent so many humiliations not because he could not defend himself nor because the Father would not come to help him if ever he were to ask for help, but because his Passion was part of God's design, which alone could lead to the redemption of man and to which the death of the Son of God was essential.

It is true that Luke, a little before the episode concerning Peter, reports certain remarks by the Master which have been the subject of controversy for centuries.[5] Feeling that the last moments and the epilogue of his earthly vicissitudes were close at hand, Jesus urged his disciples to meditate on what was about to happen and bid them be prepared. Using figurative language he advised them to sell all they possessed (even their cloaks) in order to buy swords. These words, obviously allegorical, were designed to strengthen the disciples, whose weaknesses were often to be put to the test. The sword was a reference to the internal defense of the spirit, which each—and particularly the Christian—must carry inside himself. This was certainly not a call to arms —when two swords were brought by those who had taken his words literally, he cleared up the misunderstanding with a curt: "It is enough." This passage, which is too often cited by authors seeking to use the authority of the Gospels to defend vengeful justice and the legitimacy of war, must be seen as purely metaphorical.

There are no other examples of the use of arms by Jesus or his disciples in the New Testament. The Master lost his temper only once, when he drove the merchants out of the temple.[6] The episode is not concerned with the use of arms at all, but with the expulsion of intruders from a sacred precinct, and it merges harmoniously with the rest of the story: there was something sacrilegious about the exercise of commerce in a temple, and the first Christians, wrapped in mystic fervor, could not have reacted otherwise. The synoptic Gospels expressed their feelings on this point. Other cases drawn from the Acts, the death of Ananias and Sapphira as a punishment for having deceived the apostles as to the proceeds of the sale of a property,[7] and the blindness with which Paul struck the sorcerer Elymas, who was interfering with his preaching,[8] are to be seen as the just deserts of those opposing God's design and do not detract from the character of the story, in which the practice of humility is urged as a rule of life.

We must look further to ascertain whether the New Testament contains judgments and statements which could be interpreted as justifying violence. Although infrequent, passages of the kind do exist and may be grouped as follows: (1) those which, describing the itinerant life of Jesus or the work of his disciples, put them in contact with people exercising the profession of arms; (2) those in which Jesus uses examples drawn from the military life or the practice of war to illustrate his teaching.

The first category includes the account of the curing of the Roman centurion's slave at Capernaum. The Master expressed admiration of the centurion, whose virtue and faith he praised as superior to anything he had found among the Jews. The story contains a reference to military discipline and to the principle of hierarchy governing it.[9] A similar episode was the miracle of Cana, where Jesus cured the son of a nobleman, deploring the lack of faith of men who must see signs and wonders before they will believe.[10]

Some of the persons in Jesus' following came into contact with soldiers. John the Baptist, speaking to the crowds of the coming of the Messiah, was addressed by a group of soldiers who asked him on which principles their conduct should be guided. The reply, "Do violence to no man, neither accuse any falsely; and be content with your wages" (Luke 3:14), seems to refer not to the behavior of the members of an occupation army, such as Roman soldiers would have been, but to prison warders or the agents of the judicial authority, doubts as to whose honesty and sense of justice might well be entertained. The advice that they should not allow themselves to be corrupted would be particularly pertinent.

Another relevant episode is the conversion by Peter of the centurion Cornelius, stationed in Caesarea.[11] In none of these episodes, which at times, as in the curing at Capernaum, seem illuminated by a mystic light, do we find a condemnation of the military life. Jesus never tells us that the soldier's profession is wrong but speaks with soldiers on terms of familiarity, showing no signs of reprobation or contempt. Those who give the Christian message a military interpretation have inferred that the profession of arms and, accordingly, war itself, not only were not condemned by Jesus but actually enjoyed his approval. But this is a sophism. There were other cases in which Jesus took up a position of detachment with regard to human activities and, although he could have done so, expressed no opinion. Silence is by no means always consent. He also spoke on occasion of evildoers without directly condemning them. But it would be absurd to argue that he approved of thieves and bandits.

An episode in the second group, often cited, is described in Luke 14:32-33. To remind his disciples how hard and dangerous the journey of redemption was and that undertaking it meant accepting a harsh discipline, and also to encourage them to be prudent, Jesus told them that a ruler, before taking up arms against another, must carefully assess the power balance between the two armies, avoiding battle and opening peace negotiations if he realizes that his side would be bound to lose if it came to open conflict. His point is that the weak, in trying conclusions with the powerful, run a major risk. Hence, a prudent man will study the situation with care before committing himself.

In other parables Jesus used the image of the monarch hounding his enemies. We may recall the episode of the marriage feast in Matt. 22:16-24, which shows us a king whose messengers had been murdered by their master's guests. He avenges the insult by having them exterminated and razing the city to the ground. The story, by no means easy to interpret, closes with the famous words: "For many are called, but few are chosen." The parable of the ten pounds ends with the useless slaying, ordered by the nobleman, of all those who would not that he should reign over them.[12] In the parable concerning the wicked husbandmen, Jesus predicts their extermination in expiation of their sins against the servants and the son of their lord.[13]

There is no lack of references to military life and the use of force in the Epistles. Paul's Second Epistle to Timothy (2:3-4) calls on the Christian to shoulder the burdens and face the suffering deriving from his status as a

"good soldier of Jesus Christ." The Apostle stresses the image, urging Timothy not to allow himself to be distracted by earthly preoccupations: he must
imitate the soldier who, to gain his leaders' appreciation, concentrates on his
military activities, renouncing all other occupations. The idea that membership of a militia does not conflict with the rules of life in society is found in
Saint Paul's First Epistle to the Corinthians (9:7), where it is referred to in
the following words: "What soldier ever fought at his own expense?" Citing
this and other episodes, commentators favoring a militaristic interpretation of
the Gospel message have argued that, despite the atmosphere of humility and
the words of forgiveness pronounced by Jesus—clearly indicative of the ways
in which divine mercy manifests itself and of how the Son came down on
earth to save and redeem men—there survive in his message traditional views
of the relations between peoples and nations, which his coming did not
change. These must include the possibility of waging war. We propose, however, to leave on one side the long controversy between those in favor of and
those against the militaristic interpretation of the New Testament, most of
which hinges on a few well-known passages featuring soldiers and war. These
arguments are mainly of a theological nature and depend upon the interpretation of writings considered to be inspired. But in our inquiry, the New Testament can also be regarded as evidence of a way of feeling and reacting among
the first Christian communities which flourished at the time when the Gospels
were being written, a time of tense expectancy when Christians looked forward to the coming of the kingdom and of the Redeemer.

It is doubtful whether the first Christians ever intended to institute a religious way of living together, with a complete organization, since the coming
of the kingdom would require a fresh appraisal of the problems of community
life.

The first decades of waiting for the coming of God were to be a time of
anxiety and mental torment. The excitement and the mystical ecstasy at
times reached peaks almost of frenzy. It was believed that the great event
could occur at any time. Reports were received from various parts of the empire from time to time that people had seen signs of the Messiah's return to
earth. The missionaries' preaching was based on the coming event and on the
preparation of the faithful to receive Christ returning as the avenger and the
judge. Any circumstance or occupation whatever liable to distract them from
this focal point of their existence was necessarily regarded as harmful to the
process of salvation. Some of the early Christians abandoned family and other interests to concentrate solely on the obligations connected with this work,
so it can be all the more easily understood what aversion they must have felt
for events and objectives of an essentially worldly nature. Among the most
important of these was war.

If this had not been so, there would be no explaining the collective fervor
which made possible the heroic acceptance of martyrdom. We know that the

persecutions were not all pursued in the same manner. They were sometimes the outcome of arbitrary measures adopted by local authorities, or of popular movements, or again of general laws enacted for the entire imperial territory. Particularly in the latter case, the Christians could escape capital punishment by denying their faith and going through the motions of adopting the pagan religion and the cult of the emperor. The fact that so many of them refused to do this and chose the extreme penalty shows how great were the emotion and the faith of these early believers. In the more recent history of Christianity there are few parallels, save perhaps in missionary lands (Japan, Madagascar), where situations similar to those obtaining in the early centuries have sometimes occurred. The objective, then, was not to establish a new way of living together but to make preparations for the coming event through repentance and renunciation of the things of this world, tolerating and forgiving insults in accordance with the rule set out in the Gospel.

At certain key moments the New Testament uses the image of war to underline the importance of the final aims of life. War is used as a synonym of ruin, as when, answering the disciples who inquire of him for details, Jesus describes the premonitory signs of the end of the world.[14]

He refers mainly to war and the insurgence of "nation against nation and kingdom against kingdom." When he mourns the ruin of Jerusalem, his words are full of sadness, as he speaks of the ills which a tremendous conflict will bring to the Holy City. "For the days shall come upon thee, that thine enemies shall cast a trench about thee, and compass thee round, and keep thee in on every side, And shall lay thee even with the ground, and thy children within thee; and they shall not leave in thee one stone upon another; because thou knewest not the time of thy visitation" (Luke 19:43-44). God, then, will use war and the destruction of Jerusalem to punish those who have not answered the call. And nothing could be more terrible than the unleashing of a war, for which the guilty ones will be punished by the hand of the very enemies of God, appointed the instruments of divine justice. That war is a most serious calamity, indeed the worst of all, is confirmed for us in Revelation 6:2, where, among the symbolic beings given the task of executing the decrees of the Lord, there is a horseman mounted on a red horse, on whom is conferred the power "to take peace from the earth, and make men kill one another." The allegory evokes war and its consequences in dramatic tones when it predicts the struggle between heavenly and earthly powers, which will end with the victory of the former,[15] just as the monster which symbolizes perhaps the Roman Empire and is responsible for the persecutions against the Christians is able "to make war on the saints and overcome them, for power was vouchsafed him over every tribe, people, language or nation"(Rev. 13:7).

From a scrutiny of these passages we may draw certain conclusions. In the first place they seem to prove the meekness and spirit of tolerance peculiar to the early Christian communities, seeing love of one's neighbor as a vehicle of a solidarity which, in the name of Christ, would eventually unite all men, guiding them toward salvation. Unlike the prophets of the Old Testament, Christ does not indulge in the praise of warlike virtues, for war conflicts with the essence of the Christian message. The Sermon on the Mount contains remarks in the following tenor: "Ye have heard that it had been said, An eye for an eye and a tooth for a tooth: But I say unto you, that ye resist not evil: but whosoever shall smite thee on thy right cheek, turn to him the other also," and again: "Ye have heard that it had been said, Thou shalt love thy neighbour, and hate thine enemy. But I say unto you, Love your enemies, bless them that curse you, do good to them that hate you, and pray for them which despitefully use you, and persecute you; That ye may be the children of your Father which is in heaven: for He makes his sun to rise on the evil and on the good, and sendeth rain on the just and on the unjust" (Matt. 5:38-40, 43-45). When a document which the first Christians held to be divinely inspired speaks in terms as clear as these, what purpose can be served by further research into the limits of its pacificism and of the way of feeling of the communities which had adopted it as a rule of life? Attempts to force its meaning and make out a case from the New Testament justifying war are bound to fail despite prodigies of exegesis. Even the principle of the just war—by definition a defensive war—is difficult to sustain on the basis of a text like the Sermon on the Mount, which has elements of asceticism and spiritual undertones very close to those of modern conscientious objectors and of the pacifist sects arguing for its literal interpretation.

It was this message of peace which lay at the heart of the Gospel teaching as the real guide for the most serious choices and as the source of the convictions which the Christian nourished in his heart. The system rested on the idea of love of one's neighbor, graphically illustrated in the parable of the good Samaritan.[16] This idea engendered a spiritual relationship between the men of this earth: all those like us are our neighbors, even if they are our foes. We must respect the rules of mercy for them, just as we do for friends and brothers. Man's personality is thus enriched in a way which is impossible in the proud and egocentric isolation of the pagan, for whom the personality of the neighbor is important only if he possesses natural similarities and "elective affinities," but not because of any divine law of general application. The spiritual affinity unifying the faithful stemmed from the conviction that God was the Father of all and vouchsafed his infinite mercy to all, sending to earth a Son to expiate in agony the sins of all. War, armed violence, subjugation, the domination of one people by another found no justification or excuse in a system of this kind, which took as its rule the universal law of love and tolerance and taught that man will complete his mission not in this life but in the next.

But the law of love was not easy to apply and required of mortals a blind abandonment and the renunciation of all other interests. The bonds which it created were infinite like those for whom it was intended. In loving God one loved one's neighbor; the converse was also true. This rule involved no *quid pro quo,* for advantage or recompense. Everything was freely given, through an urge which was its own reward and looked for no other, save that held in the next world for those who had believed and acted virtuously. It applied to all aspects of man's conscience. Here the New Testament conflicts with that element of the Old Testament which seemed to oppose such a new vision. Christ emphasized this conflict between a covenant formerly valid, when war was the actual evidence of God's love for his chosen people, and the covenant he had made with a view to the regeneration and the salvation of men. The law of love was not shown in external things, nor was it a device to enable man to achieve peace with himself, with his neighbor, and with God. It was a genuine rule to be applied in full, without reservations or limitations, in response to a need of the spirit, not to any artifice of the intelligence.

Peace, considered as spiritual serenity, without which no one could understand Christ's message, was not a passive condition which could in some way or other be aroused or stimulated. A benefit granted to the deserving, it had an outstanding position in the missionary instructions given by Jesus to the disciples when he told them to go forth and spread the good word. Hence, arriving in a house in the course of his itinerant missionary work, an apostle was required, if the house was worthy of it, to bring peace to it.[17] This confirms that the word *peace* meant above all that state of mind which alone can predispose man to embrace the message of God and to adopt it as a rule of conduct. The invitation to make of peace a means of moral betterment reflects the same idea as the phrase in the Sermon on the Mount: "Blessed are the peacemakers: for they shall be called the children of God" (Matt. 5:9). As H. Bietenhard points out, the individual is committed not only to rejecting any warlike conduct directed against his neighbor, but also to acting so that the divine message is realized without violence or intolerance of any kind.[18] In the Sermon on the Mount Christ is reported as listing patterns of human behavior likely to lead to holiness and defining the observance of peace as the origin of a relationship with God, of whom the peace-loving man is automatically the son, because he proves that he has remembered God's warning and is practicing his teaching. Nothing could illustrate more clearly the thinking of the early apostolic generations: the passage must be considered further evidence as to how early Christians believed they should behave in the community. They could not speed up the coming of the kingdom, for this was a matter for God alone. But, while waiting for Christ's return, they could endeavor to absorb more fully his message of peace.

The passage quoted may seem to conflict with that which follows a little later in the text, where Christ states that he has not come on earth to bring peace but to set "man at variance against his father, and a daughter against her mother, and the daughter-in-law against her mother-in-law" (Matt. 10:34).

In fact there is no contradiction between the Sermon on the Mount, imbued with meekness and a yearning for higher things, and this dramatic appeal, which aspires to achieve the communion of spirits and the exaltation of the good and of the humble, but imposes on man the duty of overcoming tremendously difficult and laborious tests. The strife which is referred to is not that of one nation against another, but the discord which necessarily arose in families and in states at the time of the spread of Christianity. In the passage in Luke (12:51) corresponding to that in Matthew, there is even a reference to the kindling of a fire which will burn everywhere that God's word is spoken and the flames of which will purge mankind. Here, too, the reference to war symbolizes dissent among individuals rather than strife among nations.

Whatever may be, then, the meaning of the word *peace* as used in the Gospels—whether it implies internal peace of the individual, or the concord which must preside over apostolic life and the community, or again the absence of war and the establishment of a communion between the peoples of the earth —and however much the exegesis of the Gospel may be stretched to confirm certain theses, the message remains one of harmony among men. It is a message designed to combat dangers which may impede the natural development of the work of God, and its ultimate objective is a point at which man, both as individual and as member of a religious and civil community, can achieve peace.

Mysticism and Pacifism in the Early Christian Communities

Expressed in terms of humanity and mercy, Christian love praised the sweetness of forgiveness and embraced all human beings without discrimination, considering them all sons equally entitled to join the ranks of the elect. This was one of the fundamental innovations of the Gospel message. Rejecting the ideas of the classical world and pagan religious doctrines, most of which preached punishment on this earth without appeal of any kind, Christianity recommended the law of love as a guide to human behavior, just as repentance, sincerely felt, was regarded as the key to the salvation of individuals and the regeneration of society. In the vision of Christ, Judaism had erred in overemphasizing compliance with the written law, ignoring the existence beyond man of a law of brotherhood, mercy, and sacrifice.

Contemporaries thought his message meaningless or even dangerous, reminiscent of those propagated by the mystery sects in the East and in Rome. These sects were often regarded as essays in collective hypnosis, having little to do with real faith. It was felt that as soon as the sudden flame which had brought them to life had burnt itself out, they would automatically disappear.

The religious awareness of Judaism, which we have traced in its gradual development from the arrogant warlike fervor linked with a limited vision of the relations between God and man to a definite, though ill-defined, search for a place in a universal system including the needs of peoples other than the Jewish people, was enriched in Jesus by a remarkable gift for proselytism. No one would ever have dared to predict that a message based on forgiveness would spread through an empire built up by the sagacious but resolute use of military force. For this message was sublimated by the expectation of a supernatural event which would transform the rule of the world. No one could have predicted that so many ordinary people would be ready to die rather than deny their new faith. All this is less difficult to grasp if we remember the sense of relaxation and love which the Christian religion was able to give to those who could understand it and follow it. Not only did the convert find in it a means of spiritual regeneration and a way of withstanding injustices, but he also drew from it serenity and internal peace, which the military and administrative civilization of the Romans had never been able to give him and which only a few Greek philosophic schools had preached. The Christian neophyte—whether a slave, a beggar, or a social reject on the edges of the proud Greco-Roman society—found in it something which no one had been able to provide before: total imperturbability in the face of the folly of mankind, an indifference based on the conviction that at the time of the Last Judgment inequalities would be leveled out and injustices redressed. In the language of Christianity the word *peace* summarized this kind of serenity and hope. Everything to which the Christian could look forward on this earth was pinpointed precisely by that word.

Peace was his reward and at the same time his strength. Having achieved internal peace and asking no more of this life, save the right to pray to God while awaiting the coming of His kingdom, he could face every danger and every threat. The revolution brought by the Savior meant the transposition to a supernatural world of the bliss which pagan religion sought and valued here below. This is the context, then, in which to interpret certain passages of the Gospels reflecting the inner serenity summarized in the word *peace*. The greeting: "Go in peace," found in the episode of the curing of the "issue" or hemorrhage,[19] indicates desire of concord and harmony, or release from internal turmoil in the individual. Understood in this sense, *peace* takes on poetic overtones where Simeon recognizes in the child Jesus the Savior of mankind and, turning to the Lord, declares his famous canticle: "Lord, now lettest thou thy servant depart in peace, according to thy word" (Luke 2:29). This ejaculation has psychological nuances worthy of note. In it, *peace* has the meaning of liberation from the state of frustration which pagan morality could easily arouse in sensitive souls longing, but at the same time unable, to rebel against the external world. Spreading the message of mercy and transferring to some future time the coming of justice, Jesus freed the downtrodden and the broken in spirit from the consequences of their weakness. And they drew from this the certainty that their travail would not go unrewarded. This explains why the conquest of inner calm appeared to the early Christians as one of the most important results of the spreading of Christian faith. Paul makes this clear when, speaking of the Savior, he says: "And [he] came and preached peace to you that were afar off, and to them that were nigh" (Eph. 2:17). The message then was addressed to all peoples, just as to all is extended the benefit of inner serenity finally achieved. Although developing the meaning to cover the emancipation of the individual from complexes of inferiority and disappointment, Paul correctly interprets certain lines from Isaiah (57:19) as an appeal to inner serenity.

These reflections on the significance of the allusions to peace could lead us to conclude that the problem of the pacifist content of the New Testament can be solved in religious and moral, but not political, terms, being related only to individual Christians. This would be too hasty a conclusion, in that every psychological attitude has political implications when it is referred to a community. On the basis of the Gospel teaching, the principles which should govern the reasoning of the early Christians may be approximately summarized as follows: If the prospect of the coming of the kingdom places us in a position of advantage vis-à-vis our neighbors, even those who apparently are our dominators and persecutors; if the regeneration we await is to be in a spiritual world; if the triumph of justice must be put off until the final event has taken place, what point can there be in clinging to attitudes of intransigence, pride, and insolence? A dangerous antithesis was thus established between the prospects for the future and the attitudes to be adopted on earth. An overappreciation of the former resulted in a denigration of the latter, were it only because Jesus, though avoiding the attitudes of arrogance of the oldest books of the Old Testament, though showing man the road toward rebirth through repentance, did not conceal that, once the last choices were made, once the point of no return of the individual's physical death was passed, it would be too late to repent and each man would be judged on his past behavior. The material and tangible life, community life itself, was thus reduced to a transitional phase on the road toward the super-tangible life, the final objective of every man and woman. The awareness of this hierarchy of values, of which the early Christians were deeply conscious, was the determining factor in the minds of those who preferred martyrdom to apostasy. It was a question of choices. They felt they had to place the eternal and the stable above what they felt to be transient and meretricious, and this they did by sacrificing their lives but keeping their faith intact.

The religious approach introduced by Jesus obeyed a rule of spiritual utility which required the believer to place the salvation of the soul above and beyond all other considerations. If salvation could be better ensured through opposition to certain forces which the classical world regarded as vital, the Christian must adopt this as a rule of conduct and accept the consequences. Hence the quest for serenity came to mean opposition to war.

The offer of peace of mind, the basis of the Christian revelation, and the consequent transposition of justice into a future world thus became an incentive to put up with insults, leaving the punishment of the offenders to the sure and incorruptible justice of God. The Christian adopted a pattern of behavior informed with humility and forgiveness and remembered that what mattered was the next life, ignoring anything liable to prevent, or even delay, the happy conclusion of his earthly vicissitudes. Love of one's neighbor was, as we have seen, the ultimate phase of this process, which led the believer to love even his enemy; Matthew emphasizes the importance of the love (at first sight unnatural) of one's own enemy, highlighting the contrast with the Old Testament. Love in the Gospels knew no frontiers and covered all men. There was yet another reason for avoiding war, the negation of all impulses of love.

We must not forget the atmosphere of vigilant expectancy in which the Christians worked and which separated them from the things of this world so that they could concentrate on the mystery of the next. You cannot wage a war, declare a war, or for that matter even love your neighbor, without attaching at least some importance to the things of this world. But this was the opposite of what the Christians believed right and necessary. What really counted was future life, and the present world was at most a prologue. The problems besetting it were minor difficulties. This was a further reason for avoiding participation in conflicts, even as mere foot soldiers.

Consequently it is hard to see how the peaceful nature of early Christian teaching can be denied. (1) Christ brought a message of meekness and peace; the moral system which he devised and the apostles preached took its place in a spiritual framework which transferred all ultimate aims to the next world, where all human injustices would be redressed. (2) Political pacifism followed logically on the moral pacifism advocated by Christian doctrine, partly because in the particular atmosphere in which the early Christians worked religious views on the honest life were bound to lead to political views on the good society, and partly because an attitude of submissiveness in classes pressed to the margins of society, vulnerable to charges of sedition and disloyalty to the state, was an alibi and a defense: how could those who preached submission and peace be guilty of subversiveness? (3) Apostolic Christianity spread among the humblest classes, for whom Jesus' message constituted a promise of salvation only if sought in the next world. This fact led to a devaluation of the things of this world, and of the objectives and interests to which life was related. (4) The Kingdom of God, which Jesus had said was imminent and which the early Christians impatiently awaited, would entail the triumph of justice and peace, otherwise unattainable.

Apart from their origin, which could be attributed to man's excessive attachment to material things, wars entailed the permanent division of mankind into enemy nations, all competing among themselves, all seeking means of affirming their supremacy, and none in the least concerned with the idea of a perfect justice. War harmonized, then, with the climate prevailing in certain books of the Old Testament but certainly not with that of the New Testament, wholly devoted to a prospect so much greater than anything that had ever before taken place on earth. The men living and working in this atmosphere formed a communion of the faithful among whom the very concept of state and fatherland had lost all temporal meaning and had given way to that of universal brotherhood.

Saint Paul

How did it come about that the preaching of a Palestinian martyr could take on, within a few generations, the features and the impetus of a universal message? Deriving from an ancient religion which had no missionary vocation, Christianity spread through the Roman Empire, altering thought processes, changing structures, superseding the pagan rites which were the empire's connective tissue. How was this possible? The very success of Christianity seemed so miraculous to the early Christian generations that they regarded it as a proof in itself of the truthfulness of the words of Jesus.

Our purpose here is to establish how far the love of peace could have influenced the change. The achievement was in no small measure due to the missionary zeal of Paul of Tarsus, who widened the audience of Christianity to encompass all the inhabitants of the empire, denying that the new message should be reserved to the Jews alone. Although references to a universal development of Christianity are already found in the work of the deacon Stephen, stoned to death in Jerusalem because he had preached in favor of the abandonment of the biblical law,[20] the Christianization of the empire is really due to Paul. Himself a Jew, he became the passionate and unwavering champion of ecumenism in the faith he had embraced. To him fell the task of defending this approach against those who claimed that Christianity had no role to play outside the Jewish tradition.

Saint Paul thus moved toward the conquest of the classical world, uniting through a single bond Jews and Gentiles and offering to both the fruits of his labor as a preacher. The Jews of the *diaspora* were out of sympathy with the intransigent views of their coreligionists who had remained in Palestine, applied the liturgy along somewhat free lines and were almost more familiar with Greek than with Hebrew. It was natural that they should welcome a way of thinking the aim of which was to overcome the diversities separating them from the pagan environment.

Paul is the key to the transformation of the message of Jesus into a new religion. Without making a clean break with tradition, the new outlook necessarily involved innovation, being broader in scope and richer in content. It is no accident that the word *Christian* was used for the first time in Antioch,[21] where Hellenistic culture was active and which was the thriving meeting-place of many races. However, the interpretation of the Gospel teaching was hampered by serious difficulties among the apostles, although they agreed on the allocation of missionary work. Paul retained the task of converting the Gentiles and Peter that of preaching to the Jews.[22] The consequences of this decision with regard to the apostolic ministry were determined by Paul's teaching. Paul consistently interpreted the new religion so as to render its benefits available to all. Salvation meant the absolute equality of men before God, whose passion and death marked the beginning of a completely new concept in ethics.

Jesus came as the redeemer not only of the small and downtrodden Jewish people but of all mankind. In Paul's thinking, the figure of the crucified God changed in significance when seen as the center of a universal system rather than within the framework of the Judaic law. Death through crucifixion, regarded as a dishonor in antiquity, became the symbol of salvation attainable by all the inhabitants of the earth without discrimination as to race, sex, or social status. "There is neither Jew nor Greek, there is neither bond nor free, there is neither male nor female: for ye are all one in Christ Jesus" (Gal. 3: 28). This led to the miracle of the realization of the brotherhood of man through the sacrifice of a God incarnate, crucified for man's salvation. In place of the law rigidly applied, there came grace, the fruit of the Creator's generosity, of which Jesus' sacrifice was the most signal example. It was a sacrifice intended to bring men together in a spiral of love, canceling out hate and giving all men the certainty of redemption.

Sublimated by grace, the religion preached by Jesus and renewed by Paul not only achieved wide dissemination but fulfilled all the conditions governing the practice of tolerance: consistent with the premises set, grace acquired the value of a communion, the effect of which ignored, and thus overcame, the concept of nation, tribe, and frontier, leveling out the inequalities which divide men and create animosities between them. No justification for war was to be found in a system aimed at overcoming man's predicament by mobilizing the power of love, a system which, through the impact of a religious movement, aimed at ending the great earthly injustice. In the teaching of Jesus injustice was already defeated and overcome by the triumphant harmony of the next world, but through grace it was also mitigated in this life. If God's aid were invoked, it could reestablish equilibrium even in this world. So comprehensive and penetrating was the strength of divine justice that it could embrace the old biblical law in the new spiritual harmony. The old message was no longer opposed to the rule of meekness allied with a spirit of generous altruism as preached by the Master. This new interpretation had to overcome a good deal of resistance in order to prevail over the interpretation defended by those Christians most sympathetic to traditional Judaism. In this connection the synoptic Gospels supply evidence, apparently contradictory, but throwing some light on the divergences of view and the uncertainties of the apostolic communities.

Thus the Gospel according to Matthew makes out a case against preaching to the Gentiles. Preaching to the disciples and laying down the principles of their apostolic ministry, Jesus, in his lifetime, is reported as saying: "Go not into the way of the Gentiles, and into any city of the Samaritans enter ye not: But go rather to the lost sheep of the house of Israel" (Matt. 10:5-6). Which does not prevent the Evangelist from attributing these very different words to Jesus after the resurrection: "Go ye therefore, and teach all nations, baptizing them in the name of the Father, and of the Son and of the Holy Ghost" (28:19), and again: "And I say unto you, That many shall come from the East and West and shall sit down with Abraham, and Isaac, and Jacob, in the kingdom of heaven" (8:11).

In Luke's Gospel the influence of Hellenism is stronger and familiarity with the ideas common in the classical world more obvious. Perhaps the cosmopolitanism peculiar to the Cynic and Stoic teachings had gained ground even in Christian teaching, taking root in a soil propitious to its development. Here we find a more marked interpenetration of experience, a less rigid interpenetration of the law and of tradition, an effort to understand a society different from the Jewish society.

Conciliation is the keynote of the Gospel according to Mark. The indication of a union with the Gentiles is found in the story of the Syrophoenician woman—not a Hebrew—whose daughter Jesus freed from the devil, approving her argument that between Jews and Gentiles there are in fact relations and bonds.[23]

In his discourse on the Areopagus of Athens, Paul makes a synthesis between Jewish and pagan elements and achieves a reciprocal integration of views and opinions.[24] This is a response to the wishes of the Stoic and Epicurean philosophers, who were doubtful as to how far the new message could be reconciled with the teachings dispensed for centuries in their city. Paul's sermon is mainly concerned with reflections acceptable to Hellenistic speculation, which had become eclectic with mystic overtones, accepting the existence of a single animating principle which took the place of, and in a certain sense synthesized, the old pagan mythology. Speaking to a cultivated public, he lacked neither eloquence nor skill. Referring to the Athenian cult of the "unknown god," Paul claimed to be his herald. By means of this stratagem, though sowing in the earth of the Greek world a completely new seed, he found there a link with the past. Paul also met a requirement of the old philosophy, that of clarifying the mystery of the creation: in respect of the person of God the Creator, he emphasized not only God's power to imbue things with life and strength but also His right to fix physical and moral principles with which living beings must comply. Seldom in the long history of Greek thought had anyone spoken with such authority, using arguments so valid. The essentials of the Christian message, however new and revolutionary their implications, were thus already clearly indicated, though in terms related to the authoritative past. The ideas of brotherhood among men and of the earthly homeland extending to all nations were here openly taught, but in relation to what "your poets" had already proclaimed. What poets? Paul was referring to the mass of Hellenic literary and philosophical production as a whole and to its quest for a principle of brotherly relations among human beings.

This gives us a glimpse of the reasons underlying, and the limits of, the new covenant. God the Creator was becoming the father of men, drawing away from the things of this world, becoming a nebulous and distant concept. He rarely interfered in the world, and never directly. The need for mediation was felt. This was provided by Jesus, whose position, expressed in universal terms, acquired features acceptable to Hellenistic speculation, which had never been preoccupied with the idea of a messiah. The introduction of the religious principle, understood as a guarantee of salvation and justice, took place at a time in which the need to extend the benefits of salvation to all was asserting itself.

Paul's intention was therefore to emphasize the inevitability and the urgency of the reconciliation which had begun with the Passion of Jesus. Jews and Gentiles now found themselves sharing the same hope of salvation, and nothing separated them in the new religious idea introduced by Christ. Peace between individuals and nations, even if the New Testament did not say so explicitly, thus became a foreseeable and inexorable corollary. From the communication of His message there stemmed the reconciliation of men with God and of men among themselves. War was a tragic reality, bound to delay the realization of the great design of salvation.

The process of pacification was supervised by God: "And all things are of God, Who hath reconciled us to Himself by Jesus Christ, and hath given to us the ministry of reconciliation; To wit, that God was in Christ, reconciling the world unto Himself, not imputing their trespasses unto them; and hath committed unto us the word of reconciliation" (2 Cor. 5:18-19). The missionary work of the apostles became the vehicle of universal concord, the key to liberation from sin.

The message was amplified in another passage of the Epistles by an urgent call to the faithful to consolidate the bond of communion with a view to achieving in the world that state of harmony of which peace, understood in the universal sense, would be the logical outcome. "Therefore being justified by faith, we have peace with God through our Lord Jesus Christ: By whom also we have access by faith into this grace wherein we stand, and rejoice in hope of the glory of God" (Rom. 5:1). If peace was to be considered as a means of salvation and communion was it not obvious that it must cover all relations concerning the individual without exception?

In the Pauline system the idea of a peace between man and God extended to a wide scale and encompassed analogous relations which joined other individuals to God. These flowed together in an atmosphere of peace which could be realized on earth only in virtue of the Christian message. The coming of universal peace was not limited to the spirit but embraced all of the relations among men and reached out to include nature and everything found in created reality: "For it pleased the Father that in Him should all fullness dwell; And, having made peace through the blood of His cross, by Him to reconcile all things unto Himself" (Col. 1:19-20).

The universal character of this teaching, the aim to unite men in the acceptance of the same bond, that of introducing a peace of men with God, and consequently, of men among themselves and with nature, acquired an ecumenical dimension. The situation was summarized in the statement that Christ, who through his coming had engendered this full system of salvation, was the embodiment of peace. "For he is our peace, who hath made both one, and hath broken down the middle wall of partition between us; Having abolished in his flesh the enmity, even the law of commandments contained in ordinances; for to make in himself of twain one new man, so making peace; And that he might reconcile both unto God in one body by the Cross, having slain the enmity thereby: And came and preached peace to you which were afar off, and to them that were nigh. For through him we both have access by one spirit unto the Father" (Eph. 2:14-18).

Going further, the message concluded, on the basis on these premises, that all the inhabitants of the earth—Jew and Gentile—would be joined in brotherhood in a universal citizenship, participating in a single plan of salvation, which found its guarantee of achievement in peace. "For God is not the author of confusion, but of peace" (1 Cor. 14:33).

The consequences of this were of key importance for the dissemination of the Christian message. The age-old machinery of the pagan religion, for which official protection and consolidated material advantages continued to ensure survival, was shaken by the new religion. The Christians, having shown a road to salvation valid for all, set out to harass their foes with the intransigence peculiar to reformers convinced of being inspired by a supernatural will.

In imperial Rome there were situations which assisted the dissemination of Christianity. The pagan cults, now in the throes of crisis, were fading into a vague syncretism which could generate moments of passing fervor but no real religious rebirth. Not even the philosophers could solve a problem having origins too deep and repercussions too far-reaching for speculation based on intellectual propositions. Moreover, the philosophers did not present a united front. The solutions proposed reflected a variety of inclinations and lines of thinking. The schools fought among themselves in a scramble to win the favor of the political class and the cultivated public. The pagan environment dominating philosophic thinking, had traditionally concentrated on the powerful and neglected the poor and the downtrodden. The result was that it had only a weak hold on the broad proletariat which had grown up as a result of the protracted civil wars and the progressive devaluation of farm incomes. And as a result of recurrent wars, conscription, and crippling taxation, too many peasants had been compelled to sell their land and move to the cities to eke out a less precarious existence. The urban masses lacked any religious impetus or urge to action. But they did feel the need for a faith that could offer spiritual and moral nourishment. The new religion gave them a hope for a new and better life, for justice.

More even than the educated class, for whom Christianity seemed little more than yet another cult, and perhaps even more than among the Jews of the *diaspora*, the proletariat welcomed the new message and was tempted by Paul's refusal to abandon the Greco-Roman cultural tradition and speculative heritage. The poor man almost certainly knew nothing of philosophy, but he knew that there was such a thing, for he had frequent contact with people deeply versed in it. Perhaps he felt an instinctive and bewildered admiration for abstract thought, a circumstance which may well have facilitated his conversion to Christianity. For the new religion, although announcing the early coming of a kingdom of justice and of peace, recognized the authenticity and the value of tradition and accepted unhesitatingly all that part of it reconcilable with its own doctrine.

The Gospel according to John—chronologically the last of the canonic Gospels, almost certainly compiled when the controversy between supporters and opposers of the propagation of Christianity among the Gentiles was over—reflected the mode of thinking of those who saw in the message of Jesus a continuation of the most valid and lasting part of classical speculation. There can be no full understanding of this Gospel without sufficient knowledge of Hellenistic thinking.

Like some of the Epistles of Paul, this Gospel reflects the penetration, now profound, of Greek speculation into Christian teaching, the re-elaboration of the story in terms which are not hagiographic but convey the understanding of Christ in a system which tends to transfigure it, emphasizing more the divine features than the human ones. The historical Jesus is less to the fore than in the synoptic Gospels. His existence was no longer an issue, whilst the problem of his mediating action, of his ability to shoulder the tasks and possess the attributes of the Hellenic demiurge—linking it with a new experience, the outcome of the pain and sorrow and suffering of Jesus—had become more intractable.

The figure of the Savior had been given to an abstract and universal context, separated from the biographical episodes. A profound transformation in the manner of thinking of the first apostolic generation had taken place.

The aim was neither to conquer the masses nor to find a meeting point between opposing attitudes, favorable or hostile to relations with the pagan world. All this already lay in the past. The coming of the Kingdom of God was now a more remote idea and people were beginning to doubt and to question whether it would in fact be achieved in the near future. John's Gospel concerned a religion and a Church already consolidated. Christ, their maker and founder, is now transferred beyond the earthly environment, identified with the *Logos,* charged with the task of mediation between mankind and God the Creator. The faithful are to be kept united in a single bond. Thus in the prophecy of Caiaphas the death of Jesus is deemed a vehicle of salvation, both for the Jewish nation and for the Gentiles, who are also "sons of God."[25] In Jesus' prayer to the Father (John 17:21-23), the unity of mankind is a consequence of Christ's faith in God as savior.

The greeting: "Peace be unto you," which John the Evangelist uses at two key points in his Gospel (20:19 and 20:26), must be seen in this light. These were the moments in the Upper Room when Christ appears to his disciples and entrusts to them the task of saving mankind. This instruction begins with the words of the traditional Hebrew greeting, which in this case lose the conventional meaning to assume a special significance as part of the plan of salvation. In the first case they precede the statement relating to the mission of preaching the faith transmitted by the apostles; in the second they take their place beside a message understood to emphasize the value of the faith. The reference to peace is a vital part of this message. It is designed to highlight the fact that a work of proselytism distributing such a rich harvest of spiritual goods would be worth nothing if peace among men were lacking. On these two occasions the idea of peace, although included in a conventional form of greeting, has a place in the context of salvation, of which Jesus had become the herald, and of its inevitable charismatic implications. Given a new context, these words are set apart, as in so many other cases, from the Hebrew tradition from which they derive. Peace becomes the fundamental objective. It is a special peace, the "my peace" invoked by Christ at the Last Supper[26] and indicated by the apostles as a basic element of the system deriving from the ordeal of Calvary.

The Gospel according to John reflects the aspirations of the early Christian generations, whose main aim was to eliminate the conflict between men and to achieve full communion with God. In John (16:33) we are concerned with "my peace," that is, with the legacy of ideas brought only by Jesus, a legacy which is the counterpart, though infinitely more important, of life on this earth. In this passage peace is seen as a determinant of the new communion. No reconciliation between the two realities seems possible, precisely because the objectives to be achieved are so different. Faced with the prospect of being abandoned by the disciples at the very moment of greatest need, Christ summarizes in a single expression the reasons for his coming and clarifies the mystery of his mission. This synthesis he enshrines in the idea of peace. "These things I have spoken unto you, that in me ye might have peace. In the world ye shall have tribulation: but be of good cheer; I have overcome the world" (John 16:33).

Every plan for the regeneration of mankind, every design for salvation, starts from the peace instituted by the coming and the sacrifice of Christ and

must be understood both as the foundation of the communion between believers and as a rule of conduct designed to eliminate from community life the
evils which stand in the way of mutual understanding. Of these evils war is the
most harmful. In the passage quoted we can perceive the duality between the
Christian conviction on the one hand, and on the other the sad reality of
man's society, with its vices and its disputes—including war.

The text in John is founded, then, on the antithesis between the two concepts of life. The two worlds are seen as different and independent. Man as
guided by the will of the Savior lives in the warmth of holy grace; man alone
is a slave to the burdens of day-to-day life, life in which human nature is expressed by sin. The problem of the relations between these two worlds arises
again in the complex of problems dealt with in later Christian speculation and
in particular in the *De civitate Dei* of Saint Augustine. And yet, it already
emerges as the key issue in the theology of the fourth Gospel. Every solution
is governed by the fact that the peaceful influence of the Christian message
has spread to the field of community relations, the aim being to eliminate all
reason for disputes and, above all, war.

Christianity and the Roman State

In the fourth Gospel the coming into being of the Kingdom of God is not
seen as imminent but as an event which will certainly happen, though at no
foreseeable date. It may be inferred from the Gospel that certain pre-requi-
sites for salvation are already being fulfilled. Thus the triumph over sin and
the existence of a rule of goodness are stated as realities ensured by Christ
himself through his Passion. Victory over the forces of this world is already a
certain and accomplished fact, as Christ makes clear (16:33), freeing the faithful from any uncertainty in this respect. There was more. The mere coming of
the Savior had sufficed to effect this transformation. Jesus had announced
through his own person the accomplished victory, without putting it off to
the next world. He himself began a new historical experience, represented as
the continuation of the one preceding his descent on this earth.

The quarrel between those sharing Peter's views and those sharing Paul's
was thus a thing of the past. Men no longer waited in fear and trembling for
his return and the early conclusion of his work which was not regarded as lying in the uncertain future. The problem no longer consisted in encouraging
the conversion of the Gentiles but in consolidating a tradition which now had
its influence on the conduct of Christians in their relations with one another
and with the civil authorities. For the reasons set out, but particularly because
it had always been awaiting the imminent return of the Redeemer, the apostolic generation had been forced to oppose manifestations of violence and
hence war. If disputes had in fact broken out within the Christian community
as well, they were almost always the consequence of the impatience and ner-
vousness of the faithful awaiting the return of the Redeemer. The sharper the

differences between supporters and opponents of Paul's interpretation of Christianity, the keener must have become the aversion to war among Christians, who were solely concerned with day-to-day living, neglecting anything liable to delay their salvation. But conditions changed completely when it was no longer the sense of expectation which prevailed but the conviction that salvation linked with the beginning of the kingdom had already begun.

How did the Christians behave when their faith became a religion of universal scope and range? Were they in rebellion against the constituted order? The problem of relations with the Roman state became a live issue for them as a direct consequence of their need to live and work in an organized society. Paul, for example, was aware of the advantages deriving from the possession of Roman citizenship when he appealed to Caesar to ensure that his trial should take place at Rome.[27] With the passing of the years and the succession of the generations, the advantages Christians drew from working in a society which had conquered an enormous geographical area, and which had imposed the same political order on profoundly dissimilar peoples, became steadily clearer. The unity imposed by Rome might well seem intolerable to certain subjugated peoples (for example, the Palestinian Jews) among whom the nostalgia for a lost independence had remained strong, but it acquired a different significance for the large majority of the converted. During the apostolic period the message of Jesus had sometimes been interpreted as an incitement to rebellion against the order imposed by the military power of Rome, but this idea was dropped when Christianity had become a religion open to all. The constitution imposed by Rome was then seen as a divine instrument which would favor the coming of the kingdom and facilitate the dissemination of the faith.

Despite persecutions, the Church desired to be judged not as a foe but as a victim of the administrative machine, which would one day come over to the Church's point of view. Hence the New Testament urged the faithful to respect authority, arguing that it was of divine origin.[28] When considered carefully, it seems strange to claim legitimacy for the acts of an earthly institution guilty of persecuting the Christians. The most famous admonition in this connection was Christ's ruling that one should give to Caesar what was Caesar's and to God what was God's.[29] But Paul was just as firm on this point: "Let every soul be subject unto the higher powers. For there is no power but of God: the powers that be are ordained of God. Whosoever therefore resisteth the power, resisteth the ordinance of God: and they that resist shall receive to themselves damnation" (Rom. 13:1-2).

Here, Paul is proving to the civil power the inconsistency of the accusation often leveled against the Christians that they were plotting against the state. This is, incidentally, not the only example of loyalty to the state, since it inspired other passages in the Gospels and in the Epistles, whose authors were aware of the dangers besetting the new religion and of the need to bring it nearer to agreement with the civil power. Thus Church leaders came to feel that an accommodation with the imperial authority should be reached. The sole governance of a certain sector of earthly activity would be conceded to the emperor while the Church reserved for itself all power in spiritual matters. There was a tendency to develop the practical aspects of religious life, avoiding all intransigence and all undue mysticism. This same tendency was to gain momentum and to prevail in subsequent Christian tradition.

Emphasizing that the wait for the coming of the kingdom should not distract the faithful from their work, nor bring them to rebel against the state, the Epistles spelled out the new ideas. Admonitions that the faithful should respect the authorities were interwoven with those calling upon them to act with moderation in their relations with other peoples. This reflected the transition which had taken place from the difficult beginnings of evangelization, with the aversion from the pagan view of earthly order, to a maturer and more stable phase in which, of necessity, the Christians adopted positions nearer to reality, tending to favor an agreement with the world of earthly interests.

The call to moderation was repeated in the Epistle to the Colossians (3:18-23), in which Paul warned the faithful to be obedient, actually instructing slaves to continue to comply with the will of their masters. Here he was amplifying the rules regarding authority that were contained in the Epistle to the Romans, in which the rules of hierarchical dependence between members of a political community were fixed. The call to Christians to accept the constituted order endowed Christianity with an actual doctrine of political power. An acceptance of relative submission now took the place of the idea of community life as a time of restlessness and expectancy. In the latter was implicit the recognition that civil power was of diabolical origin: the former view depended on the notion that community life had a divine nature.

But how could a religious society based on moral rules regarded as secure and immutable recommend subjection to a civil authority without recognizing at the same time the legitimacy of its precepts and the sanctity of its aims? By the very act of favoring an understanding with the Roman state, the legality of its claim to make laws was admitted and Christians were compelled to comply with them. On one point, however, agreement was not possible, and this was the key issue in the struggles between Christians and the imperial power in the first three centuries. The real stumbling block was the cult of the person of the emperor. Christians refused to recognize the divinity, not so much of the political and administrative system represented by him, as of the religious experience which he claimed to embody. On this, Jesus' teaching had been utterly unambiguous and allowed no compromise. The gap separating the two systems was symbolized by the grain of incense which the pagan magistrates ordered Christian prisoners to burn at the altar of the monarch. This they steadfastly refused to do, believing that it must inevitably cost them eternal happiness. The Roman state tended to adorn itself with religious and hieratic forms and symbols. The more the empire lost in compactness and solidity, torn asunder by disruptive forces like the army or the praetorian guard, the more the nominal holders of power sought to conceal their weakness behind the shallow facade of liturgy. This explains why the pagans pursued Christianity so relentlessly, for the Christians, though respecting the civil power, could not accept the divinity of its highest representative. The opposition to the Christians of a state traditionally tolerant in religious matters was not so much a matter of law, since in fact the legal basis of the persecutions was never very sound, as of instinct, aroused because the Roman "establishment" —led by the emperor himself—could see that the Christian message was incompatible with the old civil and administrative system. Thus the anxiety of Paul and the communities set up under his teaching to prove that the Christians were loyal to the constituted order was partly prompted by a desire to constitute in advance a defense against the accusation of fomenting rebellion.

This situation, due in part to a natural evolution in Christian thinking, in part to the rise of new generations of Christians with differing requirements and backgrounds from those of the apostolic period, and in part to the need to prepare a line of defense against accusations of disloyalty, influenced certain attitudes of official Christianity and its behavior with regard to war and armed conquest. If a *rapprochement* with the state was favored, with Christians asserting the sanctity of imperial institutions, some of the needs of the state, beginning with those connected with armed defense, would have to be satisfied.

The Christians and Military Service

The Roman Empire, the outcome of a formidable feat of military organization, remained faithful to its origins, despite the absorption of ecumenical and humanitarian ideas spread by Stoic and Skeptic teaching. The aim of Christianity was to become the single religion of a world governed by a universal state, and there was a tendency, at least on the Christian side, to seek an understanding between religious and civil society. Nonetheless, the new faith had to yield on a number of points in respect of which the position of the state remained completely firm while the Christians felt they could afford to be less intransigent. In consequence, the early professions of antimilitarism weakened. Once it became possible for a Christian to respect the civil order and its hierarchy, there was inevitably a change in the original attitude toward the state, whose fortunes had always been bound up with war and the enforcement of war's inexorable laws. Therefore baptized persons could not be prevented from bearing arms and accepting army discipline.

In the early apostolic communities, however, there had been no doubt as to the impossibility of reconciling detachment from earthly life—essential for the baptized—with the obligations deriving from the military life. Soldiering was wrong because it was governed by worldly values and because it exposed men to temptations which they were unlikely to resist. The expectation of the coming of the kingdom was at that time so strong that some Christians even made arrangements for disposing of their possessions, withdrawing from participation in the life of the state. Material progress was of little interest to those wishing to enter the heavenly community and refusing to be distracted from the achievement of this fundamental objective. For this reason, and to speed up the dissemination of Christianity in every class, Paul exhorted the faithful not to abandon their state, but to make it a platform for the evangelization of the environment in which they lived. Thus the slave among slaves, the artisan among artisans, the merchant among merchants, the patrician among patricians, the plebeian among plebeians, and even the soldier among soldiers, should become agents for propagating divine revelation.[30]

This was a way of fulfilling the conditions on which would depend a change in the policy of the state toward the faithful and in their behavior toward the authorities. The violence of controversy must be tempered, the propagation of the message must be facilitated, and the rough edges of a religion which had begun by waiting for the return of the Messiah but was now acquiring a steadily stronger hierarchy and doctrine must be made smooth. This did not necessarily mean that the evangelical documents, and particularly those written by Paul, already reflecting the new mood, would be used at once by the Christians to embrace a new vision of the world and to temper their hostility to the military life: certain accidental factors helped to make the problem less urgent.

The work of the Roman army in the first two centuries of the Christian era had been mainly that of consolidating public order and, with it, the *pax romana*, which had been of such value to Christianity in its efforts to expand. Recruiting had at that time been almost entirely voluntary, and military service was open only to free men. So those not actually wishing to join the army were not compelled to do so and the slaves, among whom Christianity had made many converts, were exempt. Harnack argues that the problem of reconciling military service with baptism could not have arisen before about 170 A.D.[31] The earliest evidence of the existence of an issue of this kind does not antedate the reign of the Emperor Marcus Aurelius (161-180). This would explain the lack of a specific Christian policy in this respect. The sources being quite clear on many aspects of the conduct of the faithful, it would seem strange, to say the least, that there should be no equally clear policy with regard to such an important matter as participation in the military activities of the state. While the Christians ran into many difficulties among the pagan with regard to propagating their faith and their moral rule, they had no difficulties at all on account of their failure to join the army, precisely because it was easy and perfectly lawful for them to avoid the issue altogether.

Their resistance to army service was based on the following arguments: (1)

Christ's doctrine was opposed to violence and bloodshed; (2) soldiers could not, without insubordination, escape the severe discipline of the army, which imposed obligations conflicting with Christian morality, such as that of executing death sentences; (3) unconditional acceptance of the duties of the soldier was not reconcilable with that, no less absolute, of duties toward God; (4) for a soldier it was virtually impossible to avoid participation in the ceremonies connected with the cult of the emperor, observed more widely in the army than elsewhere; (5) military signs and emblems reflected or represented pagan rites and convictions; (6) soldiers who used them, as required by military regulations, were tainted in the eyes of fellow-Christians; the behavior of the soldier in time of peace, often unrestrained by normal inhibitions and all too prone to excess and violence (for example, against civilians) conflicted with Christian morality; (7) the way of life and the customs obtaining in the army were not in accordance with the rule of purity and moderation which the Christians had imposed upon themselves.

These are Harnack's comments with regard to the reasons why Christians avoided military service, deeming it a constant threat to their moral integrity and to their preparation for the early coming of the kingdom. And yet, the problem could not be avoided indefinitely, because Christian penetration into every sector of Roman life was bound sooner or later to take in the army, a most effective vehicle for disseminating the Gospel message, and because Christianity was to prove a stronger magnet to soldiers than to any other section of the population.

It should be noted that there was nothing in the missionary program of the early generations of the faithful concerning an infiltration of official government departments. However, the conversion of many pagans in important positions, often officials in the Roman administration, led to the constitution of Christian cells within the state. In the army, in particular, their influence was to prove of considerable importance in fostering the work of evangelization.

Of all the agencies of the government, the army was the most homogeneous. Through a discipline rigorously applied to all, it strongly influenced the thinking and behavior of individuals of varying social and national origins, thus absorbing and unifying differing customs, ways of life, and even religions. For this reason a cult or an idea which had gained acceptance among its ranks was propagated rapidly throughout the imperial territory, both because the legions were highly mobile and were often moved, and because they came into contact with the local population, to whom they communicated the ideas which they themselves had absorbed. Besides Christianity could be reduced to patterns of ideas of extreme simplicity, easily accessible to soldiers, who had little aptitude for philosophy but felt the need for answers to certain questions arising in their minds.

A Roman soldier tormented by religious doubt drew great comfort from the Christian God, whose message offered him in case of death the certainty of resurrection and a new life. In crises of despair, the soldier could not but perceive the harshness and the absurdity of his status. He was usually dependent on the ambitions of others, and even in the case of victory the benefits accruing to the soldier were generally negligible. He therefore easily projected all his expectations into another world, seeking beyond the grave a justification for his own condition. Christianity offered him all this, transferring to the next world, as it had already done for the poor and the social outcasts, the prospect of those benefits which he would never possess here below.

Certain aspects of the military life were attractive to simple minds. A life among endless dangers showed affinities with that heroic self-dedication which Christianity demanded of the faithful. The missionary life could be represented, in a certain sense, as a military campaign against deceit and the force of evil: in his writings Paul had used examples and metaphors drawn from the experiences and the lives of soldiers. He had called on the faithful to put on "the breastplate of faith and love; and for an helmet, the hope of salvation" (1 Thess. 5:8). The fact that these words were an allusion to the Old Testament in no way affected their aptness and relevance to the moral life of the Christians. He used a similar image in his Epistle to the Ephesians (6:13-17), where the Christians are exhorted to don the whole armor of God and take up the shield of faith wherewith to quench all the fiery darts of the wicked. The military life seemed to have a special hold over the mind of Paul, who showed an understanding of the loyalty which binds men in the heat of combat. The soldier is compared to the athlete trying his strength in a competition and the farmer laboring in the fields: these activities have something in common and require application, constancy, and loyalty. "Thou therefore endure hardness, as a good soldier of Jesus Christ. For no man that warreth entangleth himself with the affairs of this life; that he may please him who hath chosen him to be a soldier. And if a man also strive for masteries, yet is he not crowned, except he strive lawfully. The husbandman that laboureth must be first partaker of the fruits" (2 Tim. 2:3-6). The company of the Christian faithful was also a militia to be governed by the same criteria, fundamental among which were the clarity of orders given and the stability of the hierarchy. "For if the trumpet give an uncertain sound, who shall prepare himself to the battle?" (1 Cor. 14:8).

The content of this and similar passages is certainly symbolic. These are metaphors, designed to clarify the thinking of the author and make it more easily accessible to his readers. One therefore concludes that in the subapostolic communities the intransigent and almost mystical aversion to the exercise of arms and fighting had been mitigated, gradually, with the waning of the controversy between supporters and opponents of a broader dissemination of the new religion and of its transformation from a life of expectancy to a rule of community living. The language of the Epistles is evidence of the change in the Christians' thinking, of their new readiness to abandon their initial concept of history, based on the conviction of an early Second Coming, and to adopt a more down-to-earth view of life. The world of human relations was tending to include ever-wider interests, ignored by the early Christian generations because they thought outside interests might distract the faithful from their preoccupation with God. The organization of the state and the possibility of cooperating in its government assumed an importance they had never had in the past. The idea of certain salvation ensured to anyone whose faith was strong enough to bring him to make a heroic confession of his beliefs if necessary was now related to a more realistic sense of history. The intransigence of the early Christians, carried away by their simple faith and shunning all temporal activity, now gave way to a revaluation of history in the light of the new religious experience, at the very moment when the expectation of the heavenly kingdom was partly obscured by participation in the events of the earthly kingdom.

Evidence of this change is provided by that complex document of mystical fervor which is Revelation. Here the work of Christ is represented as opening the way to catastrophe and disaster, events of which war and suffering form a common denominator. The fact that the conclusion of this prophecy is ultimately optimistic, in that all will be resolved in the triumph of Christ over evil and in the glorification of the saints and of the martyrs who will reign with him over the earth, provides further evidence of the change in awareness. In Revelation, a real theological exegesis of the Gospel message in the form of a fantastic vision, it is clear that primitive Christianity has been replaced by a religion aware of its ability to achieve victory over its enemies and resolved to give them a clear warning of the fate awaiting them.

The Epistles sometimes used images drawn from the language of military life because such images were no longer likely to shock the faithful. This does not mean that Christianity had been converted to the cult of war simply because it had accepted and endorsed the ancient tradition of the Roman state. Pacifist leanings, emphasizing forgiveness and mercy, were still part and parcel of the heritage handed down by the preaching of Jesus. The Christians did not deny the Gospel warning that they that live by the sword shall die by the sword and continued to affirm that the salvation of the individual lay in forgiveness for insults suffered. They were, however, willing to make concessions when it came to judging the behavior of the state. They felt that they could no longer stand aside and take no part in the affairs of the empire.

The Epistles breathe a new atmosphere, favoring an accommodation with the civil power and some degree of understanding of its requirements. One feels that their authors are unwilling to be regarded as anarchists and rebels and would like the authorities and the public to judge the value of the Gospel message not on the basis of unreliable information or conventional commonplaces which past policy statements had partly justified but on the basis of a just, objective, and properly thought-out assessment, the main factor in which was the desire of the Christians to be seen as loyal subjects of the emperor, though they could not regard him as divine.

Development of Christian Thinking in the Second Century. Gnosticism

How did the passage of time and the emergence of new requirements and new ideas affect the original solidarity of the Christian faith? The conciliatory development of Christian thinking among the generations following the apostolic time went some way to weaken their mystic fervor, leading to contradictory interpretations of the Gospel. Throughout the first century the Gospel had been the very basis of their conversion campaign and a strong shield against internal weakness and the flattery of the world, but it lost some of its force of penetration and its cutting edge, while a tradition and a hierarchy were being established which advocated a more flexible line of conduct toward the state.

The missionary work benefited from this attitude. From the first to the second century the expansion of the new faith was prodigious. Consequently a major movement of theological exegesis was born. The doubts arising as to the meaning of Christ's message and the explanation of it provided by the Church authorities after Paul were to lead to dangerous rifts. In the face of an orthodox Church about to claim to be the sole interpreter of the revealed truth, some religious thinkers rejected all "authentic" interpretations to proclaim that the individual Christians, in their varied attitudes and inspirations, should cooperate in the quest for truth and the guidance of consciences. Hence the heresies which plagued the young Church. They arose mainly from a desire to resist the dogmatic attitudes assumed by the ecclesiastical hierarchy, naturally tending to transform the period of waiting for the Kingdom of God into a body of liturgical, disciplinary, and political rules administered with an eye to the need to strive unremittingly for equilibrium and compromise.

The first heresies were the Gnostic heresies, which attempted to interpret the Gospel in the light of classical lines of thinking and tradition: with the passing of the years and with the weakening of its early momentum, not a few anomalies had been found in the new religion. They impaired its prestige in comparison with the well-known and much-studied philosophies and with the contemporary religious experiences of oriental origin, sometimes fused with the mystery beliefs of the Greco-Roman world. The fundamental objective of the Gnostics was to reconcile the Gospels with the speculative systems through which Hellenistic philosophy explained the impact of a supernatural will on earthly things. They also attempted to clarify another problem: that of the ways in which salvation, governed by the intervention and the sacrifice of Christ, the mediator between the will of God and the tangible world, would be effected.

The heart of Gnosticism was a study of the origin of evil and of its pressure on the cosmos. From this there was derived a dualistic explanation of the creation and a tortuous speculative attempt to separate the dominion of evil from that of good, the two being regarded as constantly passing through a state of antithesis. The moral issue was studied deeply, and its repercussions on the lives of men and their mutual relations were analyzed carefully. Although the question of the cessation of war was not a direct part of the Gnostic problem, the main purpose of which was to discover the causes of creation, it was nonetheless relevant as an aspect of a set of rules naturally concerned with cooperation and understanding among men. Here, Gnosticism was complying with a rule which gave less attention to the creation and emphasized the need for man to devote all his efforts to regeneration and rebirth. In a passage by Clement of Alexandria, the thinking of the Gnostic Basilides (second century) is summarized in a way that highlights the unifying impact of Providence. "Basilides himself says, we suppose one part of the declared will of God to be the loving of all things because all things bear a relation to the Whole, and another 'not to lust after anything,' and a third 'not to hate anything.' "[32] This passage seems to point to an attempt to overcome the dualistic approach. Basilides was keenly aware of the consequences of pain, whether physical or moral. On pain he based his vision of the destiny of man and particularly of that of the confessors and the martyrs. An aspiration for peace was implicit in his thinking. Indeed, peace was one of the persons in his system of emanations proceeding from the uncreated Father. "Basilides says that justice and her daughter peace are contained in the ogdoad."[33] (This ogdoad was a group of eight divine beings.)

Another Gnostic master was Epiphanes (second century), who died at the age of only seventeen years and became the object of a full-scale cult. He was the author of an essay *On Justice,* which has unfortunately been lost but of which Clement of Alexandria preserved a fragment. It depicts God as the incorruptible source of a justice which places all men on the same level, rejecting all discrimination, pooling everything in a system of equality covering both material and moral values. The desire to achieve a peaceful settlement of disputes seems to have pervaded the writings of this young Gnostic, together with the conviction that justice could be realized only in an atmosphere of peace and agreement among men.

Another thinker, who has not been universally accepted as a Gnostic but who certainly worked in an environment rich in intellectual ideas linked with Gnosticism, was perhaps also sympathetic to the idea that there is a longing for peace immanent in human affairs. This was Bardesanes (154-222 A.D.), an Armenian who combined a poetic gift with a penetrating speculative lucidity. Some of his ideas are set out in the *Book of the Laws of Countries,* written in the Syriac language and of uncertain attribution but almost certainly compiled on the basis of his teaching. Composed in the form of a dialogue, it reassesses the subjective merits of the individual and his free will. Though his vision of the forces dominating created things contradicted the traditional Gnostic approach, it supported the aim of facilitating agreement among men and removing the sources of disturbance. The essay ends with the following words of vaguely prophetic temper:

> And there will be a time, when also this injury which remaineth in them shall be brought to an end by the instruction which will be in another association. And at the establishment of that new world, all evil motions will cease, and all rebellions will be brought to an end, and the foolish will be persuaded, and deficiencies will be filled up, and there will be peace and safety, by the gift of Him who is the Lord of Natures.[34]

Millenarians and Marcionites

A reassessment of the message of peace contained in the Gospels was an essential element in the Millenarian heresy. The Millenarians believed that Christ would soon return to earth to establish there his own kingdom and govern it for a period of a thousand years. Reflecting the yearning for justice which permeated primitive Christianity, they looked forward to the creation of a vaguely socialist system which would ensure equal enjoyment of earthly riches for all. But the thousand-year Kingdom of God would have made no sense if it had not been supported by absolute spiritual tranquillity for those deserving to partake of this highest testimony of grace. Second-century Millenarianism, like its medieval and modern forms, also involved a desire to overcome the evils of the world through the enjoyment of peace. In Gnostic speculation the pacifist impulse was often masked by absurd cosmogonic ideas, while with the Millenarians the prospect of universal peace was somewhat forced into the background by the quest for ways in which the Kingdom of God would be established on this earth.

Marcion (second century) was the founder of heretic communities which achieved considerable success in all the Christian world. Though they were no small threat to the solidarity and the stability of the young Church, they supported the humility and tolerance of the Gospels. We know of the main lines of his thinking through the refutations written by contemporary pamphleteers, including a burning denunciation by Tertullian. For Marcion, the condemnation of violence took on special importance, leading him to praise the New Testament and condemn the Old Testament, which he felt proposed solutions valid only for the Hebrews, who believed that they enjoyed the special predilection of God and felt it right to use war in case of necessity. All this, he argued, was in contradiction with the letter and the spirit of the new divine message.

Marcion set down these ideas in a literary work called the *Antithesis,* in which he established the existence of a profound rift between the generally selfish and violent approach of the Old Testament and the generous humility present throughout the New Testament.

Marcion was concerned not only with biblical exegesis but also to restore to Christ's message the purity of its origins, which a century and a half of religious work among the pagans had, in his opinion, diluted. This objective led him to subject the Epistles and the Gospels to a critical analysis designed to weed out interpolations and distortions which he felt had corrupted the original text and changed its meaning. He devoted particular attention to the Gospel according to Luke, perhaps because it was nearest to the temper of his mind. He eliminated the passages he felt to have derived not from the original inspiration but from a Judaic source which tended to inject into the new message an egocentric vision of the world based on the exaltation of violence.

Marcion denied that Christ was a human being. His presence on earth could not be due to an act of conception—even a miraculous one, such as that occurring in Mary. It was the consequence of God's generosity inspired by mercy. Moved by the tragic condition of suffering into which man had declined, God had sent his own Son to preach the Gospel, thus showing that He possessed a nature quite different from that attributed to Him by Jewish tradition. The Gospel was thus given a central place in the teaching of love and of nonresistance preached by Christ himself in his call to the faithful to forgive their neighbor "even seventy times seven" (Matt. 18:22), or in the order to Peter: "Put up again thy sword into his place: for all they that take the sword shall perish with the sword" (Matt. 26:52). This meant an abrogation of the ancient law.

Material goods had always been regarded by Gentiles and Jews as evidence of divine benevolence, but there was now a complete inversion of values. The really holy were the poor, indeed even the poor of spirit, who together with the hungry and the sick became the object of special favor. Sweetness and patience were considered essential virtues, in the place of anger and violence; even justice, pursued on the basis of human criteria and therefore necessarily bloody and cruel, yielded place to the law of forgiveness. Marcion wished to free Christian teaching from two elements he felt to be the expression of an inferior morality: the fear of punishment for those committing sin and the certainty of an otherworldly recompense for those applying the Gospel precepts. The system of rules preached by Christ should not be governed by utilitarian values but should be rendered in a law of love, freely practiced. The God of old was to be feared: the new God was only to be loved.

Marcion widened the gap between the interests, now being consolidated, of the official Church and the mystical impulses of the first Christians. Unfortunately, his interpretation made pure Christianity seem even more unrealistic than it was. The prototype of the perfect Christian was for him a man detached from the world. Acts involved in the procreation of the race were forbidden because their moral context was of this earth. From this teaching there was derived—as often happens in systems opposing an ethic based on community life and its utilitarianism—a rule of mutual tolerance and a love of peace. What was the use of wars, if all problems could be solved by love and self-denial? In a system of earthly relations (this meant the pagan or the Hebrew system) in which the successes of the world were counted as evidence of divine benevolence and where everything that mattered was measured in terms of wealth and political power, a strong case for wars could be made out. But they could not be justified in spiritual terms, with man aiming at the realization of a mystical perfection free of earthly contamination and at a reassessment of the most authentic impulses of the soul.

Although the Marcionite communities spread rapidly at first, they were attacked in respect to ideology by thinkers like Tertullian and persecuted by the imperial authorities. After the Edict of Milan (313) their influence waned and they soon disappeared altogether. Their teaching and the controversies they caused were, however, to become the model of a recurrent argument between the Church and the ascetic way of life often adopted by dissident communities. Official doctrine continued to seek closer cooperation with the civil authorities and a sympathetic approach to their requirements and their views with regard to peace and war. The Old Testament, whose place in the new religious vision was so vigorously challenged by Marcion, precisely because of the content of certain passages, was received as an integral part of the revealed word.

The Apologists and the Antimilitarism of Tertullian

It is not surprising that the Christian theologians, generally inclined to prefer the middle path, to oppose extremism and the eccentricities of the heresies, and to work for an understanding with the authorities, should hold different views from those of the early faithful on the problem of war and peace and on the Christian duty in this respect. Most of these thinkers had been trained in classical philosophy, whose tradition they followed, and they respected its authority. Their main objective remained that of defending a faith freely accepted against accusations from pagan sources. These accusations were of two kinds: they attributed to the Christians iniquities and immoral practices supposedly taking place during the holy agapes or ceremonies. They also reduced the Gospel message to a simplistic and popular story, to a *superstitio nova*, innocent of rational basis and of aesthetic quality, though a threat to the structures of the empire and the Roman way of life.

The object of Christian theologians was to prove to the authorities the falseness of these accusations. The Christians were not guilty of the abominable crimes of which they were accused (incest and cannibalism), nor were they spreading doctrines that could alarm the authorities. This was the burden of the message of the apologists of the second and third centuries, the first representatives of a current of thinking which endeavored to show the lack of substance of pagan mythology by using the very logical criteria which the Christians were accused of flouting. It is true that the apologists included men of various statures and capacities. A Hermias, for example, was content to deride the pagan philosophers in a tone of doubtful taste, while Justin showed his appreciation of classical speculation by tracing in paganism the—admittedly imperfect—anticipation of the Christian message.

The principal objective of the apologists remained nonetheless to defend the faith without provoking the authorities, keeping the discussion to the realm of ideas and of religious truths, that is, to a field in which the Romans had generally shown themselves tolerant. Where the problem of relations with the state arose, it was generally treated with the greatest caution, the apologists stressing the legitimacy of civil power, quoting Paul on the divine origins of the authority of the state, the Gospel on the Christian's duties toward God and toward Caesar, and protesting their unconditional respect for the person of the emperor.

The case put up by the Christians against the accusations of the pagans persuaded the authorities to change their attitude with regard to the new religion, which now spread virtually unhindered in the empire. It was therefore understandable that the early Christian rule with regard to war fell more and more into abeyance. It was a delicate matter, and the apologists tended to emphasize analogies and points of agreement between the Christian faith and state requirements rather than disparities and divergences. The mysticism and aversion toward war which had informed the apostolic communities and inspired the doctrine and the patterns of behavior underlying the early heresies were losing power, yielding place to a statement of the religious problem which was more realistic and more consonant with the social origin of the faithful, an increasing number of whom were now recruited among the more cultured classes and no longer, as at one time, only among the poor and the social rejects.

Among the apologists, Tatian (second century), author of an *Oratio adversus Graecos*, published about 150 A.D., may have been sympathetic to the ideas prevailing among the first apostolic communities. He passionately defended the Christian faith, assuming a mystical and peace-loving tone informed with evangelical humility but refusing all compromise regarding the primacy of Christ over the state.[35] It is not surprising that he abandoned orthodoxy in the later years of his life to embrace Encratism, a heresy teaching the need for ascetic concentration, the renunciation of violence, celibacy, vegetarianism, and the acceptance of substantially pacifist views.

The attitude of Saint Justin (second century) was different. In his *Apologia* he did not deal with peace in a mystical sense or even in the meaning of abstention from use of arms. Deeply influenced by Platonism and wishing to establish the exact function of the *logos* in respect of God, he believed that earthly peace was one with that imposed by the empire.[36] This *rapprochement* to political doctrines praising the *pax romana* was taken further by Saint Melito, bishop of Sardis and author of another *Apologia.* He argued that the spread of Christianity had only been possible because of the Roman Empire, the existence of which was no accident but the outcome of the will of God. Proof of this was that, from the beginning of the Christian era, the empire, favored by the protection of God, had suffered no major calamity.[37] Here was a clear attempt to fit the new religious experience and the longing for peace into the hallowed structures of Roman civilization.

Tertullian (ca. 155-228) adopted a different position from the rather uncritical ones of these authors. Instead of welcoming their attempt at rational justification of revelation, he emphasized the distinction between philosophy and theology. He thus helped to imprint on the Western Church a cast of thinking which would set it aside from the Eastern Church. In his early literary works he seemed to defer to the authority of official institutions. And yet, behind a superficial endorsement, his essential respect was solely for the precepts of a single God, Sovereign of the universe, to whose decisions all mortals, including the emperor, must bow. It was probably these ideas which were developed in later writings, especially in those compiled after Tertullian had drifted away from orthodoxy. This metamorphosis was probably due to his discerning that between the empire, an agency obeying earthly values of a type which a Christian must reject and oppose, and the world of the spirit, competences were distinct, and finalities and objectives divergent. From this conclusion he derived his hostility toward any participation of the Christian in the career of arms and in military activities. In the face of intransigent pagan nationalism, expressed in the cult of the emperor, Tertullian stated two fundamental truths. In the first place he affirmed in hyperbolic form that the real greatness of the sovereign lay in the fact that he was compelled to remember that he was not God.[38] Secondly he restated the concept of fatherland in terms of universal brotherhood, obviously including the barbarians.[39]

This apologist was not always consistent. But that is not surprising if we bear in mind his impulsive nature and proneness to outbursts of anger. His confutation of his foes was seldom confined to the level of ideas: all too often it degenerated into personalities. In the first period of his literary activity, wholly devoted to defending the positions of the Church, he proudly resisted all mystical suggestions. Precisely for this reason it would seem that the Montanistic wave—which started in Anatolia, the cradle of many heresies, and spread in the form of a rebellion against official Christianity—would be sure to antagonize him, since he had opposed a religious life based solely on an imitation of the virtues of Christ and on waiting for the coming of the kingdom. But it proved otherwise. The embattled controversialist, perhaps developing that hostility to the power of the state which was already discernible in his early writings, ended by joining a heretical sect which had reverted to the anxious wait for the return of the Savior and which was much occupied with the picturesque fantasies and inspirations of its three founders (the prophet Montanus and the clairvoyants Maximilla and Prisca). Obviously, only two centuries after Christ the Gospel message still retained its original fascination for minds like his, which were more easily receptive to the immediate intuitions of feeling. Montanus called on the faithful to remember their duty to make ready for the day of the Lord, neglecting the futile and precarious "reality" of the world. In confirmation of his teaching, he adopted only the testimony and the support of his own visions. If he could do this and still win the support of logical minds, it is clear that Christianity's mystical commitment to peace was not exhausted and still had a hold on the faithful.

Few of Montanus' ideas could at that time—or for that matter at any time— be harmonized with orthodoxy, which rested on the need to reconcile Christian feeling and intuition with existing cultural values and with the political requirements imposed by coexistence with the civil authority. Mysticism, like pacifism (which is sometimes its projection into the field of social relations), is bound to arouse suspicion, since it tends to upset the existing equilibrium for the sake of principles that are difficult or even impossible to enforce. This does not mean that, in the work of theological systematization, orthodoxy may not have sometimes benefited from the contributions made by currents of thinking lying outside its ambit, at the edges of its teaching or even in conflict with it. It is therefore not without significance that Millenarians, Marcionites, and Montanists, attempting to revive apostolic Christianity, never doubted that they were governed in their undertaking by the acceptance of a rule of conduct refusing violence, even in support of their rights. These movements began with the expectation of the early and certain advent of the Kingdom of God and emphasized the need to prepare oneself for the great day. War was necessarily banned, since it could only delay a process that would bring to all the happiness long sought after.

All this enables us to assess more accurately the personality and the work of Tertullian: the transition from the orthodox to the Montanistic position led to a change of direction in his thinking concerning the behavior of the Christian in case of war.

In the works belonging to the first period of his literary career, there is already more than a hint of hostility to the profession of arms. This is confirmed when, addressing the pagans, he claims that combat is usually a manifestation of the temptations and the flattery of the evil one. "That spirit of demonic and angelic nature, our rival because we are severed from him, our enemy because God gives us grace, battles against us with your hearts for his base—your hearts turned and suborned (as I said at the beginning) to perverse judgment and to savage rage."[40] Christians were ready to fight and die in defense of their faith, but not to cause the death of others. If they had been ready to fight, if their vocation had been that of combat and not a peaceful and vigilant waiting for the kingdom, who could ever have been able to resist them?

We are but of yesterday, and we have filled everything you have—cities, islands, ports, towns, exchanges, yes! and camps, tribes, decuries, palace,
senate, forum. All we have left to you is the temples! . . . For what war
should we not have been fit and ready even if unequal in forces—we who
are so glad to be butchered—were it not, of course, that in our doctrine we
are given ampler liberty to be killed than to kill?[41]

Christians therefore disliked war, but out of respect for an ethical rule
which they had imposed upon themselves and not from fear of danger. Those
who were ready to suffer martyrdom—who almost sought it out, in fact, regarding it as the most perfect road to salvation—had no fear of the perils of
combat. Addressing once again the pagans, Tertullian said:

"Then," you say, "why complain that we persecute you, if you wish to
suffer? You ought to love those who secure that you suffer what you
wish!" Certainly we wish to suffer; but it is exactly the case of the soldier and war: Nobody is glad to face it with all its inevitable anxiety
and danger. Yet he battles with all his might and, victorious in the battle,
he rejoices,—though but now he was grumbling about the battle—because
he achieves glory and spoil. Our battle consists in being challenged to
face the tribunals; that there, in peril of life, we may fight it out for
truth. Victory is the achievement of the thing for which you have fought.
Our victory means the glory of pleasing God, and the spoils are eternal
life.[42]

In the pamphlet *Ad martyres,* written before he went over to heresy, peace
was defined as the privilege of the faithful as they face martyrdom. It was
hated by the evil one, the bringer of strife and discord. "Your peace is war
for him."[43] Tertullian added that those who had never found it in the Church
found it in the example of the martyrs. Doubtless he was referring to the internal peace of the Christian communities. He wanted them to settle their internal differences out of respect for the sacrifice of Christ and in memory of
those who, following his example, had sought to practice his teaching. A metaphor drawn from military life is used in the same work. "Already in this
world we are called to God's banner."[44] In fact he was circling round the
problem, using similes and symbols, all tending toward a realistic assessment
of war and a responsible understanding of the great damage it can cause.
Whenever the problem was stated in direct terms, he provided a solution for
it, suggesting its irreconcilability with the profession of the Christian faith.
By the same token a Christian could not bear arms, since "by disarming Peter,
the Lord dismissed all soldiers."[45]

These are the bases of Tertullian's thought. He regarded war as the greatest
of evils and saw military life as unseemly for any man who had been baptized.
The fact that he sometimes used images drawn from the life and the vicissitudes of soldiers did not affect his antimilitarism, which became absolute
once he embraced the Montanistic faith. He then condemned war quite cate-
gorically because of the abject suffering it entailed. Thus, in the *De corona* he

denied all possibility of compromise on this question, entering into controversies with those who argued the contrary. The conflict between duties connected with the military life on the one hand and loyalty toward God on the other could not, in his eyes, be more obvious. This pamphlet was written to defend a Christian soldier who had refused to parade wearing a chaplet or crown, since he regarded this act as pagan and therefore conflicting with the faith. In defense of this Christian, who was accused of rebellion against the state and of insubordination, he raised once again the problem of the lawfulness of war and of the duties of the Christian forced to take part in it: "To begin with . . . I think we must inquire whether warfare is proper at all for Christians." The reply, characteristically vehement, comes in the form of a rhetorical question:

> Do we believe it lawful for a human oath to be superadded to one divine, and for a man to come under promise to another master after Christ, and to abjure father and mother and all nearest kinsfolk, whom ever the law has commended us to honor and love next to God Himself, to whom the Gospel, too, holding them only of less account than Christ, has in like manner rendered honor? Shall it be held lawful to make an occupation of the sword, when the Lord proclaims that he who uses the sword shall perish by the sword? And shall the son of peace take part in the battle when it does not become him even to sue at law? And shall he apply the chain, and the prison, and the torture and the punishment, who is not the avenger even of his own wrongs?[46]

In search of ammunition for his verbal battles, Tertullian reached beyond the Gospels and invoked consistent Christian tradition. This was, he claimed authoritative. The antimilitaristic theme culminated in a warning to those facing the dilemma of choice between the militia of Christ and that of the emperor. If they were wise they would choose Christ. With a vigor verging on the intransigent, he refused to entertain moral weakness of any kind, and therefore rejected military service and war. Of all earthly activities war was the one most influenced by evil. Even if a person was seeking to avoid the worst and his life was at stake, there could be no exception to this iron rule.

Thus Tertullian urged that the Christian message should be interpreted according to the intention of the Gospels and in a spirit of humility guiding the individual along the real road of salvation. Nothing else really mattered. Cooperation between Christianity and the Roman state was, as a result, less close and binding: the refusal to bear arms and to wage war was not only a matter of pure morality but also one of policy: Christians should avoid collaboration and maintain neutrality, as the first apostolic generation had done. The only reality remaining was faith, the meaning of which was bound up with the sacrifices which the Christian was ready to make on its behalf. Nothing could be lost by renouncing civil life. Therefore it was wrong to attempt to escape martyrdom, it was wrong to seek public office, since the essential fact was not participation in civil life but the safety of the soul. Provided this objective was achieved, all the rest could safely be neglected. As for war, a Christian had no choice but to refuse to fight.

Tertullian's rejection of orthodoxy left him isolated, for he failed to establish a school of his own, although his thought influenced the Western Church and particularly the African communities. Most of his direct successors were writers of modest talent, seeking a place for themselves in the dogmatic controversies of the time. Rather than continuing his work, they used his writings as models for a mode of pamphleteering relying far more on vigor of argument than on its inherent strength. For this reason a good many of Tertullian's ideas failed to achieve acceptance and did not receive the consideration they deserved. This is true of his defense of the antimilitaristic ideas, though these were taken up and debated vigorously in the heresies of the second and third centuries. Any attempt to pinpoint how far the heresies of the early centuries leaned toward pacifism would be bound to fail, since their speculative ideas have come down to us solely through indirect material compiled by orthodox—and therefore hostile—students. The disappearance of almost all the original writings prevents us from assessing the pacifist content which, beyond theological disputes, was one of their most remarkable features. However, we can say that the fundament of the heresies was very often the desire to reach back to the sources of the Gospel teaching, appealing to the humility and the sweetness which had inspired it.

Tertullian's thinking almost certainly influenced that of Saint Cyprian (ca. 200-ca. 258), recorded in ecclesiastical history as the organizer of Christian communities and as the protagonist of sharp controversies concerning the Church's right to grant absolution to those who had been guilty of apostasy during the persecutions. But he was also a writer of distinction. Through the descriptions in his Epistles, he gives us vivid glimpses of the Christian life of the time. It is in these letters that we must seek evidence relating to the problem of peace. One of them discusses the inconsistency between the judgment which society usually makes of a homicide committed by an ordinary citizen and the very different kind of homicide committed by a soldier who slays an enemy soldier in battle. "The world flows with blood, everywhere shed. Homicide is a crime when committed by the individual, but a virtue when it is collective. It is not innocence, but the scale of the harm they cause which ensures that rogues get off scot-free."[47]

Saint Cyprian's teaching was suffused with a sense of humility which set his message against a background of pastoral edification. Take for instance the following passage: "The son of peace must seek out and pursue peace; he who knows and loves the bond of charity must curb his own tongue from the evil of discord." And again: "The sons of God must show that they are peace-loving, humble of heart, simple in their speech, of one mind in their affections, loyally bound the one to the other by the chains of concord."[48]

Was Tertullian's warning successful in provoking the desired reaction among the faithful? It seems doubtful, since the Christian conscience of the time, under the pressure of a moderate current of thinking, and anxious to reach an understanding with the authorities, was tending, despite the persecutions, to avoid all dissociation of the Christian life from civil society. Although a Christian could not make sacrifices on the altar of the emperor, since this would be tantamount to denying his entire religious heritage, he could pray for the life and the victory of the temporal sovereign, thus acknowledging Caesar's right to rule in the areas which were Caesar's. Defense was plainly one of the areas. The problem of the incompatibility of military service and baptism became less acute as Christianity gradually penetrated the higher classes. The conviction that there was no real inconsistency and that it was right to temper the antimilitaristic intransigence of the early apostolic generation with a greater inclination to compromise with the requirements of earthly life gained more and more ground.

The School of Alexandria. Origen

Contemporary with the Latin fathers, among whom Tertullian was the central figure, a Christian school developed in Alexandria which worked hard to relate the intellectual ideas of Hellenistic speculation to the philosophical heritage of Christianity, thus helping to spread the new religion in the more culturally sophisticated and mature circles of the eastern Mediterranean. The work of this school must be seen against the background of activity in Alexandria, a city imbued with the cultural and illuministic thinking peculiar to a refined society. Here the message of Christ could be accepted provided that Alexandria's speculative requirements were not depreciated in the process. For its part, Christianity, brought into contact with a philosophically consolidated tradition, drew from an atmosphere rich in stimulating inspiration an intellectual energy which enabled it to raise its own tone and its own level. All this happened at a time when Hellenistic thinking was also—through Neoplatonism—showing a vigor which was to stand the test of time. With the benefit of hindsight we see Neoplatonism and Alexandrian theology as complementary patterns, generated by the same thirst for ideas and expressed in a superior cultural maturity. Both tended to renew philosophical thinking, the one in the line of classical speculation, the other following a religious message destined to supplant the pagan cult. It is precisely this quest for high intellectual standards which enhances certain characteristics of the Alexandrian school, one of which was the attention devoted to the study of the Bible.

Clement of Alexandria (ca. 150-ca. 210) made a major contribution to this movement, and Origen (ca. 185-ca. 252) continued the work, in particular in the fields of philosophical analysis and the study of the Scriptures. The allegorical interpretation on which this work of exegesis was based was part of a phenomenon which is recurrent in the history of religions: whenever mystic fervor and emotive impetus, from which the first dissemination of a religious message has drawn its origin, have lost momentum, the faithful come to study more carefully the truths accepted initially on the basis of faith, seeking a justification of them such as will satisfy their cultural requirements. In Alexandrian Christianity, the rational approach therefore acquired an importance which would have been unthinkable two centuries previously, when Christians, waiting in fear and trembling for the return of the Messiah, stood in no need of erudition, living by faith alone. Thus a complete transposition of values took place. The perfect Christian was now the cultivated believer, dissatisfied with an unsophisticated and uncritical presentation of the faith and in search of an explanation going beyond the literal story. If this was to be found, what was needed was a philosophical and philological study conducted along scientific lines by men able to draw syntheses. One consequence of this was that methods and ideas familiar to classical culture now penetrated Christianity.

The problem of knowledge was the main subject of Clement's research. Consistent with the thinking of the school, it was for him a matter of vital interest to reach rationally valid solutions, although, at times, he too emphasized the duty of the faithful to allow themselves to be guided by the momentum of faith. As for military service, he thought that the crux of the problem lay in the need for the Christian soldier to safeguard the heritage of faith and the moral principles handed down since Christ. Hence a general aversion to war which is unmistakable in many passages. It should not be forgotten that two voices were united in Clement—that of the Christian and that of the Greek—each of which was fighting to draw the other over to its side. While the former set the problem of peace in the context of the Gospel message, as is clear in particular in his *Cohortatio ad gentes,* the second reacted along the lines of traditional speculation. Stoic ideas may have influenced him, so that he saw peace as an entity suspended in time and in space, detached from any environmental situation, generating universally valid solutions. The process of coming closer to God, corresponding to this detachment from community life, also affected his conception of peace, which was associated with the desire to achieve the elimination of all factors likely to prevent or delay agreement among men.

Clement believed that the training of the individual and his Christian education could succeed only if they took place in an environment concerned with the achievement of peace and serenity. "We are educated not for war but for peace. In war, there is need for much equipment, just as self-indulgence craves an abundance. But peace and love, simple and plain blood sisters, do not need arms nor abundant supplies."[49] These considerations refer almost certainly to peace of mind rather than between nations. But from here it was a short step to achieve an overall vision of peace, related to all aspects of existence, through which man would reach at the same time a condition of bliss and a state of security. In the same context, Clement praised peaceful minds

which can dominate or avoid disturbances that contradict reason and facilitate the explosion of absurd passions.[50] Peace must, of course, always be
based on justice: "Justice is the peace of life and governs its stability and
tranquillity."[51] As for the arms conceded to the baptized, these must be confined solely to those reconcilable with the mystic solidarity which Christ had
preached.

> The trumpet of Christ is his Gospel. He sounded his trumpet and we lis-
> tened. Let us therefore learn to handle the arms of peace. Offering our
> breasts to justice, taking up the sword of faith and donning the helmet of
> salvation, let us take up as well the sword of the spirit, which is the word
> of God. These are our arms, and nowhere will they inflict wounds.[52]

The position of Origen, Clement's successor as the head of the school of
Alexandria and the celebrated author of a comprehensive philological work
applied to the texts of the revelation, was more direct and more deeply committed. The sophisticated thinkers of Alexandria were well aware of the inconsistencies in the Old and the New Testaments and demanded a systematic
exegesis, to which he devoted the whole of his life. He limned the main features of a great theological synthesis in which the instinctive religious feeling
of Christendom was transformed, by virtue of a methodical effort, into a rationally acceptable system that could explain the essence and the character of
that revelation which the more cultivated and mature Christians were now refusing to accept solely as a matter of faith. A combination of the kind could
not always be harmonious and perfect. This explains why in his thinking it
was sometimes the classical element which prevailed, while at other times
through Christian mysticism he appealed to the gift of love and the generous,
though uncontrolled, impulses of the heart.

Metaphorical interpretation and patient philological research prepared the
ground so that ideas coming from various sources could be assimilated and
brought together and the sharpest conflicts resolved. One of the most serious
difficulties stemmed from the occurrence in the Old Testament of passages
praising war and invoking divine assistance for the military campaigns of the
chosen people. All this conflicted with the inspiration of the New Testament,
which fostered the exercise of humility and peace. Through an allegorical explanation everything was made clear. There was no longer opposition between
the two messages, the two being the fruit of complementary religious experiences. They were symbols through which God had shown himself to man, revealing certain truths and using a metaphorical language with images whose
meaning had been transposed into a field different from that to which both
the divine inspirer of the texts and the hagiographer who had written them intended to refer. In this way all became clear. The wars of the Old Testament
were interpreted as struggles between the faithful and the world of sin, instruments to achieve the salvation of mankind in harmony with a design of God
to which the Gospels bore witness and for which they provided a blueprint.

In this method of approaching the Scriptures, influenced by suggestions and reminiscences of Greek thought, certain expressions generally accepted by exegetic literature and entering into common usage also took on a new meaning. For example, the words "soldier of Christ" lost those unpleasant overtones suggested by the appeal to the military life and were used to symbolize the moral stature of the Christian, committed to obeying the Gospel rules for the same reason as the soldier is required to respect military regulations.

The concept of peace was thus given a cosmopolitan dimension, extending both to the serenity of the mind consistently extolled by classical philosophers and to concord in the body of the Church and peace among men and nations. Origen has given us a definition of peace which is a marvel of concision: "You can say that there is peace when no one lives in a state of discord, when no one gives way to quarrelsomeness and there is no hostility or cruelty."[53] This definition covers all aspects of man's life in relations with his neighbor and as member of a national community having relations with other such communities. It is of interest to us in particular in this second circumstance, in that it raises the problem of war, of its lawfulness and of its compatibility with the duties of the Christian. It reveals an absolute faith in the harvest of salvation, which must include the establishment of peace in the world. "Even the angels are amazed that, by God's grace, peace can be achieved on earth, a place infested with war."[54] Peace became a condition of society and of the individual. It was a gift of the Creator as savior: "Charity is the fruit of the spirit, joy is the fruit of the spirit, like peace, patience, kindness, goodness, continence and the other sister-virtues."[55] War, on the other hand, was a gift of the devil.

Oriegen's thinking on military service and the duties incumbent on Christians was illustrated in the famous essay *Contra Celsum,* a synthesis of his opinions both in the theological field and in that of relations between religion, civil power, and national society. The controversy had been triggered by the *True Discourse* by the pagan writer Celsus. Written about 180, this discourse contained a sharp attack on the Christian religion. Most of the essay, the original version of which is lost, is known to us through Origen's refutation, which contains many quotations. Celsus accused the new religion of undermining the structure of the Roman state, which had in fact enabled Christianity to spread and consolidate.

In his attack Celsus had made no irrational or hasty accusations. Familiar with classical philosophy but also with Hebrew and Christian literature, he based his refutation of the Old and New Testaments on a detailed textual examination. He found them poor in inspiration and lacking in speculative substance. Christ's prophecies and miracles were given a critical evaluation and related to classical thinking, particularly to Plato. The aspect of the Christian religion which irritated him most was perhaps the anthropomorphic approach.

The idea of a God who had become man, with a body, subject to the humiliating necessities of matter and conditioned in his choices and actions by the things of this world offended his intellect and brought him to the conclusion that the whole story was a mystification.

As far as this point Celsus kept to the field of religion and the credibility of the propositions challenged. Despite a tone of condescension, he avoided moral judgments: it seemed legitimate to him that the Christians, in conformity with Roman religious tolerance, should also have the right to profess their faith. But his tone changed when he turned to a consideration of the status of Christians within the imperial community. Here he felt that the opposition of the Christians to the religious tradition of the Gentiles was really dangerous, not so much in itself as because it undermined the very bases of imperial power. He was not concerned at this point with mystical or religious needs, but that the completely political and worldly policy goal of the state and its authority over the citizens should not be weakened. His opinions with regard to animal sacrifices and religious festivities were a good example of this. He defended both by the following reasoning: either the gods and the demons did not exist and therefore there would not be any great harm in taking part in simple manifestations of joyfulness and the sacrifices which accompany them, or they existed as ministers of the supreme God and men must be allowed to propitiate them in the ways provided for in the traditional liturgy.[56]

Celsus had learned from Plato to believe in the existence of the soul and in the next world. He thought that men would be rewarded or punished for their behavior on earth. Since the Christian doctrine did not contradict this aspect of the received teaching, he could have accepted it here without difficulty. His opposition became sharper, however, and his criticism more severe in respect to relations with the state, for he felt that reason of state and the demands of state must override all other considerations and could leave no room for compromise. His probings therefore sought a reconciliation between the Christians and authority. This would not only benefit the empire but also enhance the security of the Christians, no longer forced out on the margins of society. What was the point, he wondered, in this spiritual and material segregation from others, as if the Christians were not part of the same community? Did they really believe that the afterlife was for them alone? Any withdrawal from the community, particularly a refusal to accept public office or to bear arms, was tantamount in his eyes to a kind of subversion and a rejection of the historical heritage of the Roman world. This brought him to the heart of the problem. To defend the emperor, to allow oneself to be called up, to take part in fighting, were not acts from which the Christians could abstain—as had at times been thought, even by the Gentiles, during the apostolic period—but specific obligations compliance with which was a measure of the citizen's loyalty to the state.

Celsus had also argued that if everyone had adopted the same attitude as the Christians, the problem of their faith would never have arisen, because the empire would have fallen under the dominion of impious and savage barbarians. Undoubtedly this was an intractable dilemma, to which one might have answered, as Origen did, that the Christians possessed the power to convert even the barbarians and to bring them to a sense of justice and humility.[57] Despite the declarations of loyalty made again and again by the Christians, the pagans were sure that the principle of the division of the kingdoms (that of Caesar and that of God) was a temporary arrangement aimed at winning the tolerance of the authorities in exchange for an apparent fidelity. In the pagan mind, resisting Christian penetration, the idea of a kingdom better than the earthly kingdom to which it was possible to accede, of a heavenly Jerusalem, of which one might enjoy citizenship on earth as well, provoked inextricable questions. Where was this kingdom? Where did it lie in geographical terms? This was the question which a governor of Palestine, as recorded by Eusebius of Caesarea, put to a confessor.[58] Faced with the civil order, the Christians were seen in a position of passive expectation imposed by the need to survive, as a community and as individuals, until the advent of the kingdom and by their concern not to dissipate their energies in undertakings such as military campaigns, which they regarded as an obstacle to the attainment of perfection.

Writing a few decades later, Origen endeavored, not unsuccessfully, to provide replies to Celsus's objections, demolishing the argument that the Christian religion was at most a collection of propositions acceptable only to primitive minds and that Christian beliefs were no less gratuitous and absurd than the pagan beliefs, while lacking the prestige which the centuries had conferred on the latter. Origen, too, had been trained in Greek philosophy, and he could see the importance of developing Christian thinking, not with an impassioned apologia based on professions of faith and totally unprovable assertions, but by developing the immanent rationality of the spirit in the sphere of the supernatural, the existence of which was confirmed both by Greek thinking and by Christian experience. Few possessed his sense of the duty incumbent on the Christian thinker, who must defend the spiritual heritage which came from the revelation without denying certain key ideas and certain conclusions in Greek speculation.

In the effort to find common ground, Origen was compelled, as a matter of consistency, to tackle also the problem of the participation of the baptized Christian in the life of the state and particularly in military activity. In these two fields no compromise with paganism was possible and, even at the price of being judged rebels, Christians must stick to the positions of intransigent rigor assumed in apostolic times or revert to them, if, as might have happened, they had departed from them for reasons of safety or worldly prudence. The offer of conciliation made by Celsus, which perhaps reflected the lines of thinking of certain influential pagan groups close to Marcus Aurelius, must therefore be rejected. The Christian religion would emerge victorious from the confrontation with pagan civilization, whose only choice was to surrender to the victor. Between the old religion and the new one there was no scope for reconciliation. Too many things kept them apart—in the first place, the Christian conviction that the supernatural life was superior to that on earth and the consequent devaluation of the things of the world, written off as ephemeral and irrelevant to salvation. Moreover, how could this compromise with the pagan religion be achieved in practice? The proposition implied, perhaps, that the Christians should renounce the spiritual content of their faith, abandoning their intolerant and contemptuous isolation and allowing a syncretistic communion with other cults? How could one reconcile the universal and classless Christianity, based on the opposition of Christ to the formalism of the scribes and the Pharisees and on the aversion of Paul to Judaic legalism, with the various national cults, conventional and priest-ridden, and whose liturgy and political attitudes were infinitely remote from the religion of Christ?

Here Origen was totally rigorous and totally consistent. He not only rejected all idea of compromise but also refused to accept that the old religion and the new could even coexist. The struggle must be resolved by the disappearance of the first and the triumph of Christianity. The passages of his discourse which have come down to us leave no doubt that Celsus perceived clearly the revolutionary implications of an attitude of this kind and understood that voluntary isolation and the contemptuous rejection of all compromise might lead the baptized to commit acts of treason against the state to which they owed allegiance.

The pagan cults formed the very basis of the civilization of the old world. On them rested the social structure which reflected and translated into legal institutions and political rules their vision of the world. To desire the disappearance of these cults was surely tantamount to preaching the destruction of the state, which was unashamedly their protector and was identified with them. But Origen, writing some decades later, at the time of cruel persecutions, found no reason in this to accept the compromise proposed and temper his own intolerance. On the contrary, his opinion remained that of a pamphleteer clinging to his original positions, pleading for a reversion to apostolic intransigence, opposing any negotiation. Celsus' argument that in the last analysis the Christians were conspirators was consequently not far wide of the mark. The pagan cult was a key aspect of the constitution of the state in that the divinity of the emperor was recognized, as was his right to be worshipped. The refusal of the Christians to bow to this false god and to take part in the sacrifices in his honor was interpreted as an act of rebellion. In the mind of the pagan this was not only a serious and blasphemous sin of omission. It also smacked of revolution. Origen moved further forward along this road, recalling that, in practice, the emperors in no way deserved the adulation of which they were the object. They were often tyrannical and cruel, utterly unlike the descriptions of them fabricated by obsequious writers in search of personal advancement. Examining the passage in Paul's Epistle to the Romans (13:1-2) in which the Christians are called upon to submit to the civil power, he argued that the problem was less simple than it appeared and referred his readers to his commentary on the Epistle, reminding them how many emperors had neglected their most elementary duties.[59]

The reference and the arguments are in themselves significant. They reveal that Origen was somewhat reluctant to accept supinely Paul's opinion concerning the duties of the Christians with regard to authority, considered sacred because it derived from God. The fact that so many emperors had not shown themselves equal to the task entrusted to them by Providence was evidence in his eyes of the futility of things of this world and of the unreliability of certain doctrines.

This did not lead him to deny the existence of an earthly society organized hierarchically, to the rules of which man must submit. The acknowledged superiority of the world of the spirit was no obstacle to the recognition of a manifest truth, for to admit that a national hierarchy existed did not necessarily entail the acceptance of an identification between Romanism and authority, an identity accepted by pagan authors like Celsus. The barbarians too, traditional foes of the empire, were grouped in national societies; and they also could aspire to salvation. The unity of mankind was not therefore that expressed in the empire, as its pagan writers claimed, but must refer to the entire universe and be accomplished in the name of Christ.[60]

Celsus' position with regard to barbarians had been fundamentally different. These peoples, whom he regarded as savage and lost to all hope of improvement, represented a permanent threat to the Roman state. Romans—Christian or other—were obliged to fight them: if the empire were to collapse, the Christians would be involved in the catastrophe just as much as everyone else. It was therefore in their own interest to defend the state, bearing arms in the field, showing civic spirit and loyalty. There was something to be said for this argument. Origen was writing at a time which was critical for the Christians and for their survival as a religion and community. The persecution of Decius (249-251) lay not far in the future, and dark clouds were already gathering on the horizon. Like revolutions, persecutions seldom come without warning. That of Decius was preceded by the growth of anti-Christian feeling, both in the governing classes and among the civil population, who blamed the impious and rebellious followers of the Gospel for the serious difficulties into which the state had run. In this circumstance it would have been prudent for a writer like Origen—who was much read and respected—to assume a wait-and-see attitude, covering any retreat that might prove necessary by statements which were less categorical and accepting at least some of Celsus' suggestions.

But this is not what he did. To the question put by Celsus to the Christians, as to where they came from—a cunning question obviously designed to comepl the Christians to admit that their origin, common to all the subjects of the empire, was identical with Rome itself—he replied that they descended from Christ, who had ordered them to beat their swords into plowshares and their lances into scythes. "For we no longer take up 'sword against nation' nor do we 'learn war any more,' having become children of peace, for the sake of Jesus, who is our leader."[61] A more explicit and direct profession of faith is hard to imagine. The question could arise in agonizing terms for less firm and resolute consciences, but not for one convinced that it was impossible for a Christian to undertake the career of arms because this was incompatible with his faith, even if the object was to defend the empire. The Christians, Origen said, could offer only prayers, which were the more effective the keener the piety and the religious fervor of those saying them.

This was as far as Origen could go to meet Celsus' desire to succour the Roman state. To bear arms, to join the army, was out of the question. Perhaps Origen thought he had made a major step along the road to reconciliation with the empire, with a view to the achievement of a *modus vivendi.* To pray for the state was like setting out on the road mapped out by Paul in the Epistle to the Romans. It was an implicit admission that Providence had willed the emergence of the empire in order to help Christ spread his message of redemption. For this reason, although they refused to accept that the physical person of the emperor had any divine attributes, the Christians recognized that he incarnated the authority which Paul had said should be obeyed. As for the military campaigns of the empire, by praying that they be crowned with success, the Christians were doing something much more likely to facilitate the achievement of its objectives than they would have were they to join the army and learn the use of arms.

While their qualified support was in line with the traditional position of the Christians, it tended perhaps to induce the authorities to accept that the cult was neither illegal nor impious since it allowed them to pray to God to defend the state. It is hard to say whether a view of this kind was prompted by conviction or prudence. In any event it appeared suspect to those, like Celsus in his time, who started from the idea that the Christian message was hardly more than a mystification and that, in showing humility and submission in the face of their persecutors, the Christians were only trying to win time and ensure a period of truce, to resume later their campaign of conversion. Besides, the actual value of their prayers was a matter of controversy even within the Christian community. While Tertullian believed that every prayer for the emperor delayed the coming of the heavenly kingdom, Origen thought that it was permissible and indeed a duty to ask God to vouchsafe the emperor his protection.

The Christian could not assume an attitude of indifference and accept passively everything the emperors did. Before it could be right to pray for them, a condition of key importance must be fulfilled, i.e., that both the war and the ruler who declared it were motivated by a desire for justice. Origen here put forward an idea which was later to be developed by Saint Augustine and in medieval speculation: that of the just war, a war having, that is, a moral justification and a legal basis. The condition was a vague one, and it generated suspicion and doubts among the pagans. Not only did the Christians refuse to fight for the emperor (though undertaking, after some hesitation, to pray for his success), but they even reserved the right to examine war aims and might refuse their prayers should their assessment show that the proper moral requirements were not fulfilled. Their refusal to defend the state, their persistent reservations and stipulations, and their support of a moral system which was not only unknown to the Gentiles but was philosophically alien to their tradition and historical heritage, were so many arguments for discriminating against Christians and their way of life. Quite apart from earning Origen's disapproval, Celsus' compromise proposal for what we should now call peaceful coexistence was judged impractical by many pagans. The ordinary Roman believed that the only possible universal fatherland was that established by the empire. No religious community could claim exemption from the rules of that great institution.

A scrutiny of the problem of military service brings out certain important features of Origen's thinking. He emphasized the historical meaning and the interpretative value of every biblical episode so as to penetrate its spiritual content, that is, its meaning in supernatural terms. This method was his guide in the difficult field of biblical exegesis, the aim being to understand the real content even of the most obscure passages. For however unclear, the Bible was revealed truth, and thus, he believed, even the most inscrutable verses must always contain a message or a lesson to be learnt.

The allegorical method had the advantage of making the texts of the Old Testament and of the New Testament, mostly written without speculative or literary aims, acceptable to the subtle minds of the Alexandrian intellectuals now trained in philosophical research. A number of enigmas were solved, enigmas which otherwise would have remained without answer or justification, and of which it might have been thought that their sole aim was to surround the hagiographic story with a mystic light. According to Origen, the spiritual meaning of a passage or of a biblical proposition should not necessarily be sought at the point where exegesis seemed most obviously to suggest it. So vast was his learning, so keen his memory, and so penetrating was he in discovering precedents, discerning similarities, allusions or contradictions that, sometimes, when a proposition seemed sufficiently proven, he refrained from drawing the conclusions from his evidence, leaving this to the reader. This is precisely what he did in *Contra Celsum*. Here, the need for a Christian to shun the military life, reserving the right to assess the merits of a conflict and therefore the case for or against praying for its success, was not taken to the furthest logical conclusions. There was no general condemnation of war, though it was, however, present and implicit in many passages of the pamphlets, as in other of Origen's texts. He makes it clear that peace—in the sense of serenity of mind, concord with one's neighbor, absence of strife among peoples and within a society—is the highest aspiration of man.

From this was inferred the conviction that peace could be achieved only through Christ and his message of salvation. The problem was not that of solving in one's innermost conscience a mental struggle born of the individual's incapacity to overcome adversity, but that of fitting a rule of mercy into individual earthly relations and into community life in general. Peace is identified with good, while war, disorder and discord are the allies of evil. They are therefore the protagonists of a conflict. Because of the ultimate fate of mankind as stated in the Christian message, this conflict would eventually lead to the total defeat of evil. The victory of the good would take the form of a universal pacification. This is how Origen interpreted the words of the angels spoken at the time of the coming of Jesus, when they brought the tidings of peace on earth to men of good will. Here peace is an aspect of salvation. The drama due to the sin of pride committed by Lucifer, who introduced evil into the lives of men, involving them in a spiral of pain and degradation, would thus find a solution and an epilogue. This confirmed the diabolical nature of war, caused directly by the sin of man against himself and his neighbor.[62]

Peace remained the background of Origen's speculation. It had a place in his philological research and was related to his ascetic interests and his mystic vocation. It was seen as a transcendent objective, but at the same time as a worldly reality, countering purely theoretical and mental abstractions and serving the effective interests of man. This is why Origen saw it as a whole, almost as a mental category, the measure of a method of thinking, dissolved from the bonds imposed by time and space, not bound to episodic acts or to historical circumstances, a parameter enabling men to think and act within a context of unity and universality. Commenting on the Epistle to the Romans (12:18), Origen urged his readers to regard peace as a single and indivisible reality.[63] Faith marked the limits of human behavior, limits beyond which an ethical system was unthinkable; in faith should be sought the conclusion of every Christian journey and the reward sent by God to him who had deserved well of Him: "If he who believes defends himself, having recourse to the virtue of the Holy Ghost, he will certainly enjoy to the full happiness and peace."[64]

After the Edict of Constantine. Donatism

With the promulgation of the Edict of Constantine in 313, the Church soon emerged from the underground and after some three centuries of proscription as a religious institution was recognized and protected by the state.

The original group of persecuted Christians, concerned only with the coming redemption and hostile to the authorities, now became an established church with a strong organization. It was natural that within this system moderate and middle-of-the-road theological ideas should prevail, providing a backbone to orthodoxy and opposing any extremism which might lead to a weakening of religious and civil discipline and reduce the Church itself to a disordered group of exalted martyrs. Nonetheless many Christians resented the understanding achieved between Church and state. For example, in proconsular Africa and in Numidia the Christians had always been conspicuous for their intransigence. Even when the cruelest persecutions raged and the temptations and encouragements to the Christians to proclaim their loyalty to the institutions were most pressing, many North African communities had been particularly resolute in their attachment to their faith. Under the influence of Tertullian their dislike of the military life had been keen: its harmful effects on the formation of character and on compliance with moral discipline were much feared. This aversion found expression more and more frequently, since for some time Christians were being drafted, either to provide for the defensive needs of the empire or simply under the rules concerning the recruitment of the sons of veterans.

However, the conflict between religious and civil duty was settled in the climate of tolerance fostered by Constantine. Various explanations have been given as to the reasons which led Constantine, a man of complex personality and contradictory attitudes, to adopt with regard to Christianity a pattern of behavior opposed to that of all the emperors before him. Certainly a contributing factor was the desire to restore its old compactness and discipline to an army weakened by the persecution of Diocletian and religious controversy. According to the story accepted by the Christians, Constantine's reconciliation with the faith was due to a military event, the victory over Maxentius at the battle of Saxa Rubra (312).

He therefore could not approve of the intransigence of the Christian communities of North Africa, especially when their position led to the movement of clergy and laity known as Donatism. The restlessness of these Christians, which was also partly racial and partly the expression of dissatisfaction with Roman dominion, led them to oppose the official Church, which they felt had strayed from the narrow path of virtue in order to obtain imperial support.

The behavior of the Donatists opened up dangerous rifts in the very field in which the state had always shown itself least tolerant: that of its own security and unity. The Donatists had inherited and taken over the antimilitaristic attitudes of pre-existing heretical communities and seemed determined to exacerbate them for the sake of safeguarding the purity of the faith as they saw it. And all this at the risk of reviving old controversies. The quarrels would now no longer be between Christianity and paganism but between groups of Christians. The Donatists were bound to incur the wrath of Constantine, whose policy was intended to end the religious controversies and who could not allow these to break out again. The Donatists were condemned in two councils, held in Rome in 313 and in Arles in 314. At the second council the problem of antimiliarism was tackled more directly.

Although we have no hard evidence, it seems likely that the emperor's representatives exerted influence on these decisions, among which we must mention Canon III of the Council of Arles, in which all persons abandoning their arms *in pace* were banned from the Christian communion.[65] This obscure wording has occasioned much controversy and even the substitution in certain medieval codes of the words *in bello* for *in pace.* Yet the political motives of the ban are clear. The aim was not to punish desertion in the face of the enemy, a crime automatically entailing very severe penalties: what the authorities wished to do was to discourage the widespread hostility to military service which led the soldiers to abandon the militia in time of peace to return to their civilian trades. The words *in pace* are therefore probably correct. Canon III remains a fundamental document in the history of Christianity. It reflected the general lines of the imperial policy. By legitimizing the new religion, Constantine forced its adherents to drop pacifism as a principle of doctrine and to keep within the structure of the unitary state. The Church itself now assumed a conciliatory attitude to the state and its hierarchy, adapting to the requirements of the times. Being threatened within and without, the empire needed every able-bodied man, Christian and pagan alike. The situation arising after 313 entitled the emperor to claim the assistance of the Church in the military field as well, though he paid lip service to peace by building a temple in its honor in Constantinople.

Donatism survived its condemnation in the two councils and persecution by the civil authority thereafter. Indeed it continued to thrive, particularly in those regions of North Africa where the people were more remote from the governing class. Donatism was a movement of protest. It expressed in religious terms the popular dislike for a conqueror who had for centuries ruled with a heavy hand. Political resentment strengthened the antimilitaristic attitude of the Donatist communities. Like those of the apostolic period, they considered pacifism as an arm of defense against the Romans. While orthodox Christianity used the civil power more and more often for support in the theological controversies of the time, and in this way justified imperial interference in the internal affairs of the Church, the Donatists rejected the alliance outright, regarding it as sacrilegious and in any case harmful to Christian interests. This was another way of showing hostility to the Romans, to their administrative machine and to the emperor, to the policy pursued for centuries, and to the type of Christian faith adopted and defended by the Romans. "What has the emperor to do with the Church?" was the proud question put by Donatus Magnus, the founder of Donatism, to the imperial envoys sent to persuade him to eliminate the divisions weakening the African Church.

Throughout the fourth century Donatism exerted a disturbing or confusing influence on the minds of the faithful in Africa, leading indeed to rebellions and bloodshed. It took the indomitable eloquence of Saint Augustine and a severe decree of the Emperor Honorius (405) to silence these exuberant congregations. The victory, like many such victories in the religious field gained through the help of the civil arm, was a Pyrrhic one. The Donatists returned underground, nursing their hate in silence, and later made an important contribution to the defeat of the Romans in North Africa and to the success of the Vandal invasion.

The Abandonment of Antimilitarism. Lactantius

Tertullian and Origen, two great Christian personalities of the third century, left the imprint of their speculative vigor on the thinking of the Latin and Greek fathers respectively. Significantly, despite the differences of background and of surroundings in which they worked, they both reached roughly similar conclusions on the problem of peace among men.

If we extend our inquiry to other authors of the time or to that immediately following, it is difficult to find equally clear attitudes. Some authors do, however, deserve mention—for example, Arnobius, who lived at the time of Diocletian. In the treatise *Adversus Gentes,* this writer gave a picture of the condition of concord and serenity which would result from the advent of peace on earth.[66] Arnobius had been driven toward Christianity by the deep pessimism which informed his thinking and by his total lack of confidence in human nature and its capacity to achieve salvation without external help. He regarded it as absurd that man should trust solely to reason in order to find his own road to perfection. Man must give himself over completely to the mercy of God. Arnobius saw community life as contaminated and contemptible, since in no case had society on earth succeeded in creating a system resting on justice. He therefore felt revulsion against systems of government based on tyranny, which naturally inclined toward war and aggression. The Roman Empire was the most obvious example. He could see no justification in glory for the sake of glory, certainly not in the cruelty of conquest, nor in the methods of government introduced into the provinces annexed. Most of all he felt it absurd and sacrilegious to attribute to divine assistance the emergence of an empire in fact born of an insatiable thirst for territorial expansion. His anger shows through when, in Book VII of the *Adversus Gentes,* he castigates those who confuse the divine and the human by attributing to God the responsibility for military events imputable only to men.

After Constantine, peace with the state having been achieved and official protection accorded to the Church, Christian writers no longer had any reason to oppose the authorities, or to withhold full and sincere loyalty. The new situation enabled the Christians to praise imperial policy as the realization of a divine design.

These were the bases of the teaching of Eusebius of Caesarea (260-337), Christianity's first historian. He saw the emperor almost as the incarnation of divine authority. Asserting that God reigned in the world through His Word, he extended the concept of delegation of His power to include in it a new element: the Christian emperor. The state was the reflection of the creation, the ruler the lieutenant of the Logos, the imperial court the image of the heavenly one. To worship and honor authority was the duty of every Christian. Wars were no longer diabolical enterprises engineered by rulers persecuting the faith in their ignorance of the early coming of the kingdom. They were now meretorious undertakings on which heaven smiled. The Christian God protected the armies enlisted under His banner and expected the pagan religion to be rooted out.[67]

Although it reflected a line of thinking shared by many Christians once the state became their protector and supplied an explanation, in apologetic terms, of the political and religious situation which arose from the edict of Constantine, Eusebius' views were not accepted unreservedly by thinkers less sympathetic to an automatic and oversimplified interpretation of the message of Christ. A case in point was Lactantius (ca. 260-ca. 340). For Eusebius the apocalyptic vision of the Kingdom of God had faded and given way to a complacent contemplation of the reality around him. But Lactantius resisted the interference of the civil power in the religious field and took an independent—and critical—view of the policies and the methods current in Constantine's empire. To this very day, Lactantius' opinions have a strong moral impact. He sees man at the parting of the ways. One road leads to the practice of good, the renouncement of the flattery of this world, and the enjoyment of heavenly bliss; the other, that of vice and the pleasures of the senses, leads to the torment of hell. The individual who despises earthly values and works toward eternal ones has achieved virtue. Such premises automatically led to the condemnation, though masked and indirect, of the military life, as shown in the following passage:

> I ask now whether they can be pious and just men who not only allow those who are set up under the mark of death and who plead for mercy to be killed, but who even demand it; and who, neither sated with wounds nor content with blood, bring to the death cruel and inhuman assent. Why, they even order those struck and lying prostrate to be sought again and have their bodies torn apart by blows lest anyone delude them by feigning death.[68]

Though he urges humility, Lactantius sometimes endeavors to guide the interpretation of the Christian message along lines acceptable to the civil power. Christianity had now become a pillar of Roman society. Tertullian's doctrine that the empire would never be converted, reflecting the view prevailing at the time of the persecutions, had now been proved wrong by the participation of the civil authorities in the life of the Church. Although Lactantius' warnings to the Christians to refrain from violence and to be guided by humility seemed to include a condemnation of war, they referred mainly to the day-to-day relations between citizens, the obligation to help widows and orphans, to succor the sick, to bury the dead, and to house pilgrims. In practice they were no more than a set of rules covering the minor aspects of community life. Lactantius did not deal with the problem of the great moral imperatives incumbent on the state, meaning the renunciation of force as a weapon of government, to be used to settle the struggle for power. Only a superior skill in rhetoric enabled him to overcome his own inconsistencies, developing arguments which he knew to be pleasing to the public and to the state which he served, taking care on the other hand not to defend other views disagreeable to those in authority. There is a reason for this too: he remained, despite everything, a man of the court, to whom Constantine had entrusted the education of his son Crispus. Indeed the conversion of Lactantius to Christianity may well have been no more than an act of political opportunism.

Though the new legal status of the Christians involved the support of the state, it also compelled them to accept its exigencies and to assist it in solving them. If the emperor was involved in a war, no one could escape the obligation to take part in it, much less object or hinder. Generally speaking, military life was therefore regarded as reconcilable with baptism.

Moreover, thinkers were tending less and less to treat war and murder as essentially identical. The old assumption had been the subject of acute observations by Cyprian and was certainly present in the thinking and in the mystical yearnings of the first Christians. But the two concepts drew apart to take on an identity of their own. The murder of a man was still regarded as evil, while people were no longer willing to regard war as a crime made up of the aggregation of a large number of murders. At the same time a war morality developed, deriving from the application of the Gospel principles to the behavior of soldiers. Christian literature was more concerned with preaching humility and mercy, so that these virtues should help to temper the sufferings caused by fighting. This approach did not differ in conceptual terms from that of the humanitarian associations set up in the nineteenth and twentieth centuries. They too were much concerned to mitigate the evil effects of war but neither condemned it nor sought to prevent it.

Cooperation between Church and state grew stronger in the course of the fourth century, causing far-reaching changes in every aspect of community life. Thus in the *Apostolic Constitutions,* a collection of liturgical instructions, religious customs, and prayers reflecting the conditions of the Eastern Church and the atmosphere prevailing in the empire after the reign of Constantine but before that of Theodosius, we find the text of a prayer invoking divine protection over the empire, over the holders of public dignities and over the army: "that so, leading the whole time of our life in quietness and unanimity, we may glorify Thee through Jesus Christ who is our hope."[69]

For the compilers of this collection, peace was generally not that between states, which would have been difficult to fit into the new religious situation established in the empire, but was the integration of individuals into the ecclesiastical union freed at last from internal struggles. "But this peace and haven of tranquillity is the Church of Christ."[70] "Let us pray for the peace and happy settlement of the world, and of the holy churches; that the God of the whole world may afford us His everlasting peace, and such as may not be taken from us; that He may preserve us in a full prosecution of such virtue as is according to godliness."[71]

An important principle was formulated in Canon XII of the Council of Nicaea (325). It threatened severe penalties for soldiers who, having spontaneously abandoned military service after their baptism, attempted to join up again.[72] Although the text of the canon was unclear enough (the penitent deserters were compared to dogs "who returned to their vomit") to lend some support to the assumption that the aim was to condemn military service altogether, it was in fact a rule designed—as in the case of the prescriptions of the Council of Arles—to discourage desertion.

The attitudes of the Church, now in line with those of the state, meant that as time went on it achieved growing autonomy. A noteworthy example is the episode of the excommunication in 390 by Ambrose, bishop of Milan, of the Emperor Theodosius, who was responsible for the massacre of Thessalonica. What bishop of the time of Constantine would have gone as far as this? As the Church gradually became the conscience of the state, its organizational and hierarchical order grew stronger and its opposition to military service and therefore to war declined further. Greater independence of the imperial authority could not dispel completely the distaste for strife felt by the primitive Christians. Despite the uncertain times and the need to stem the invasions, the old attitude to peace was deeply rooted. Ambrose's circle probably included a Christian poet whose work became so famous in the Middle Ages as to influence even pictorial art and iconography. This was Prudentius (ca. 348-410), a Latin-language writer of Spanish birth whose short poems were mainly of apologetic content and were addressed to the highest classes, which still tended to hanker after the old pagan religion despite the conversion of the empire. In the short poem *Psychomachia* (the spiritual combat), Prudentius described allegorically the victory of Christian virtues over pagan vices. Although he had no desire to displease the imperial authority (he was a senior official), he argued that the triumph of Christianity had coincided with that of a will to peace. "Then kindly Peace, the foe now put to flight, drives war away."[73] The conversion of mankind to Christianity generated peace, concord, order, which had always formed part of the mercy of God.

The Cappadocian and the Later Greek Fathers

An immense disturbance was caused in the Christian world of the fourth

century by the Arian dispute over the nature of Christ. The Council of Nicaea, though condemning Arius and establishing what came to be known as
the Nicene Creed, failed to settle the quarrel. Indeed, the great debate raged
thereafter with increased violence. The parties saw no reason to refuse the
support of the civil authorities in what they believed to be good causes. The
Eastern churches in particular suffered much from political interference and
court intrigue. But we owe it to the dialectical spirit of the Easterners and to
their insatiable appetite for inquiry that the Christological and Trinitarian
problems were discussed with such vigor.

The contest was so heavily concentrated on a few points that to all intents
and purposes there was neither time nor means for examining in detail the
problem of peace and war. The political and military situation was deteriorat-
ing on almost all the frontiers of the empire because of the pressure of the
barbarians. The crisis precluded indifference to the great events of the time
and ruled out neutrality.

The members of the clergy who were engaged in permanent doctrinal discussions were no longer pastors working underground, their existence constantly threatened and thus forced to defend themselves from the state. They
had become the great ecclesiastical officers, the administrators of the established religion, for whom the support of the emperor was the strongest weapon in their armory: men competing in the religious field often used friends at
court. The winner was more often than not the person who had the ear of the
emperor or of his advisers, whatever the real value of his views.

Against this background we must examine the work of three Cappadocian
writers who were of exceptional importance in the development of Christian
thinking. These were Saint Basil the Great (ca. 330-379), Saint Gregory of
Nazianzus (330-389), and Saint Gregory of Nyssa (ca. 331-ca. 396). They
have all gone down in ecclesiastical history as unwavering defenders of orthodoxy against the Arian heresy. For despite the judgment at Nicaea, the Arians
remained on the offensive and achieved, under the Emperor Constantius II
(who reigned 337-361), moments of special favor at the imperial court. Some
barbarian peoples were also being converted to Arianism because its theology,
more accessible to simple minds, was more in line with their modest speculative requirements.

Although they did so in a variety of ways, this trio of doctors brought the
theological controversy onto a rational plane, using definitions and categories
which were later generally adopted and are still in use today. To what extent
was peace an issue for them? In the first place we must remember how peace
was seen by proud and sensitive men engaged in serious religious controversies. They could have regarded it as a personal asset reserved to the just or as a
condition of great importance to the Church, torn by internal strife. Universal
peace, seen as the unity of peoples and a pledge by rulers to abstain from war,
could hardly be a major issue for them. This reservation made, we can state

that, despite the obvious need for the paladins of orthodoxy to win ground from their Arian opponents, in the depths of their minds they nurtured a yearning for peace and concord which was not to desert them even at the most dramatic moments of the struggle.

The writings of Basil the Great are relevant to our inquiry. The unity of the Church was Basil's principal preoccupation. Despite its inflexibility, his campaign against Arianism, which had gained power in the court of Constantinople, was always conducted in terms of a quest for peace and serenity, of a return to the apostolic gentleness which the fierce theological disputes had led people to neglect. The peace of the Lord, of which their Gospels had spoken and which the first Christians had regarded as their symbol, remained the right objective. God was the sublime herald of a message of peace dissolving all quarrels. The peace of the Lord, an objective of the life to come, would prevail in the future kingdom. It was for the believer to conquer it on this earth as well. "Seek, therefore, after the peace of the Lord and pursue it and you will pursue not otherwise than running toward the goal to the prize of the heavenly calling. For the true peace is above."[74]

The converse also applied. Those who sought God, it was said, would also find peace. But those who sought peace must necessarily find God. The identification between the two truths was complete. "He who seeks after peace, seeks Christ, because 'he himself is our peace,' who has made two men into one new man, making peace, and 'enforcing peace through the blood of his cross, whether on earth or in the heavens.' "[75] Peace was above all an inner feeling, an expression of character and self-control. "Peace, which is a certain stability of mind, seems to be the most perfect of blessings, so that the peaceful man is distinguished by the calmness of his character, but he who is attacked by his passions has not yet participated in the peace from God. . . ."[76]

Basil's homilies, from which we have drawn these quotations, were addressed to the faithful to urge them to heed their inner vocation by adopting a pattern of conduct informed with humility and avoiding all unduly rigid and rational approaches to earthly problems. This pugnacious champion of orthodoxy was convinced that his cause could not be properly defended with the arms provided by theology and politics alone: the inexhaustible resources of the spirit must also be used so that human solidarity illuminated by the grace of the Gospel could be achieved. Nor could spirituality be left to work alone: it must be guided toward the determination of real peace, such as to shelter men from the "tumult of instincts and confusion."[77]

The peace of the individual, that of the Kingdom of God to come, and that of the Church are seen in his system as separate aspects of the same aspiration. Peace became a means of strengthening Christian life. As for peace as an alternative to war, its place in his writings was only marginal. The reason for this is readily understandable. Basil was a citizen of a state committed to defend its territory against aggression from outside while affected by an internal crisis which could at any moment lead to rebellion and civil strife. How could he condemn defensive war when on its success depended the survival of the Christian state and the security of its citizens? The same problem was to exercise Augustine a century later. And how could one deny that a civil conflict could upset the equilibrium of the state and the order of succession to the throne and that, for the salvation of the Christian flock and of the truth faith, it was wise to avoid such clashes?

Basil's thinking relates to that of Gregory of Nazianzus, with whom he was bound by links of friendship and by their common struggle in defense of the Nicene Creed. The orations of Gregory, particularly the five against the Arians, are a monument of theological perspicacity and stylistic elegance. They reflect the character of their author, a studious man naturally inclined to spiritual reflection and the monastic life but forced by circumstances, against his will, to adopt aggressive attitudes. That he was defenseless against court intrigues is proved by the episode of his deposition from the bishopric of Constantinople, which he accepted without demur.

Endowed with such immense speculative acumen and so much personal modesty, impelled by a desire to settle the differences which were the bane of the Church, and compelled to take part in the theological controversies of the time, this master was bound to feel an inclination toward peace, seen in its triple meaning of serenity of the spirit in the face of the adversities of life, of faith in the coming of the Kingdom of God, and of the settlement of theological struggles which weakened the Church and were unworthy of men who had taken a vow of service to the Lord.

There is a specific reference to his conception of peace in *Oratio VI, De pace I,* a work dedicated to a few monks who had returned to the orthodox fold.[78] Here he defines the essence of peace and its importance in every system of human relations. The peaceful intentions which he felt should govern the conduct of men were sustained in his writings by the memory of the goodness of God, the most luminous of realities. To this reflection he added a second, that the hosts of heaven partaking in the vision of God because they were living in his light could not exist without liberation from discord.

Starting from the certainty that the will of God is boundless, he inferred that God's will could not even concede that fighting might sometimes lead to a solution of certain difficulties and the removal of certain obstacles. In the last analysis war was completely alien to the nature of God, whose desire it is to remain in communion with Himself and with all living beings. God expects that his peaceful nature should be seen also in the expressions "love" and "peace" with which he is commonly invoked and which correspond to so many virtues which he calls upon men to pursue. Peace is therefore the premise underlying a moral rule with which men are required to comply if they are to obey the will of the Creator. Peace also marks the line of demarcation between supernatural creatures, the angels on the one hand and the demons on

the other. The former live in a perfect order governed by unity and their desire for peace, while the latter exist in a state of anarchy and strife. Hence the
exhortation to the faithful to listen to the divine voices and their teaching,
guided by a desire for concord and aimed at improving the understanding of
the laws of creation. According to Gregory of Nazianzus this was the principal work of God and was built upon his greatness. The cosmos, governed by
rules which allocated a specific task to each part of it, was conceivable only in
the harmony of the whole. If it had failed to apprehend this harmony, it
would have lost the fundamental order on which its very existence depended.

The cosmogony submitted by Gregory to the scrutiny of his reader was a
strange one. In it the divine essence was communicated to created things
through ordering principles. The rules of unity and harmony underlying the
cosmos ought also to govern human actions. Using arguments and considerations drawn from physics, Gregory gave other examples of this magnificent
unity. Dominating the created universe, it should be taken as a model for the
behavior of the Christian.[79]

In another place Gregory studied the problem of concord and peace among
men. He was concerned not only with the attack on Arians and with theological problems but also with a struggle for supremacy within the ecclesiastical
hierarchy in which no quarter was asked and none given. The conflict between claimants to the see of Constantinople, of which he had been appointed bishop but of which he was deprived through palace intrigues, was the occasion which led to the writing of *Oratio XXII, De pace II.* This begins with
an invitation to peace, identified with the idea of God.

The Christians had lost peace through their obstinate aggressiveness. Un-
mindful of the example set by the Redeemer, they were allowing themselves
to be carried away by wrath, as if they were unaware of the scale of the damage this caused. The behavior of the sowers of discord (since it was these of
whom he was speaking) was the effect rather of carelessness than of the will
to evil. This did not prevent them from becoming enemies of religion, since
their refusal to pause and reflect was, by causing clashes, the origin of the permanent crises which were doing so much to harm the Church. Hence whoever
"preached until yesterday like an Elias or a John, today becomes a Judas or a
Caiaphas."[80] It was just this spiritual rift, their quarrelsomeness, the inability
of individuals professing the same faith to reach agreement that was having repercussions on the organization of the empire as a whole and was the cause of
its chronic weakness. Written almost certainly in 379, *Oratio XXII, De pace II*
contains a description of the wounds which disunion had inflicted on the
once completely healthy body of the empire.

> Exceptionally grave events took place which we saw with our own eyes or
> which were reported to us. The disintegration of the defeated fatherland,
> the many precious objects destroyed, the land drenched in blood and
> strewn with corpses, a foreign people overrunning and occupying the coun-

try. Nor can this be put down to cowardice on the part of the defenders, since these had subjugated practically the entire earth with war and arms. It must be ascribed to our ill-will and to our repeated impiety with regard to the Trinity.[81]

Quarrels among Christians became the source of political misfortune, shifting from the religious world to the civil one. The state and the individual citizens would suffer the backlash of each theological conflict. It was thus recognized that God would reward evil with evil and that heretics and sowers of discord harmed others as well as themselves. The consequences of their actions would not be confined to the Church but would have an impact on all community life, affecting even those who had no responsibility in the matter. The inference was the need to live in peace. According to Gregory's definition, peace is, above all, "dominion over the turbulent passions of the spirit,"[82] a gift which, at the time of leaving this earth, we are allowed to hand on to our heirs.

The third of the Cappadocian fathers is Gregory of Nyssa, Basil's brother. A less able administrator than his brother, a less stimulating orator than Gregory of Nazianzus, he surpassed them both in the acuteness of his search for the truth, which he devoted to the service of orthodoxy. In the quarrel with Eunomius, with whom Basil had already crossed swords, Gergory gave a remarkable example of the profundity of his thinking. Eunomius had, among other things, emphasized the difference between the will and essence of God. Gregory of Nyssa riposted that the distinction was unjustified, being no more than the virtually mechanical application to Christian thinking of certain principles of Greek philosophy.

He defined God as a closed circle which, having its origin in the Father, proceeded to the Son and ended in the Holy Ghost. This does not mean that it was a finite being and was therefore subject, like all created things, to the rules and conditions imposed by nature. Everything in this system could be reduced to unity, including the concept of man. As the most perfect of earthly beings, man realized in his own essence that cyclical character which summarized the phases of the Trinitarian process. But in the last analysis what could cyclicity mean if not oneness? Gregory's anthropology stated the human problem in terms of unity in oneself. Man reflected God and in a certain sense reproduced Him. If it was desired to know one's Creator, the first thing to do was to know oneself. The implications of this approach are plain. If God was the source of beatitude, if he was oneness in the Trinity and in communion with the most perfect of the earthly creatures, it followed that every act designed to disturb this harmony was an act against God. Discord was no exception to the rule, any more than conflicts between theological parties, any more than war. The first task of the believer was therefore to subdue the discord afflicting his spirit. If he was really respectful of God's law and wished to apply it, he must temper his passions and relax in inner serenity.

How was the law of God to be complied with? In a manner useful to the believer too, in a way which enabled him to enjoy the benefits of true sanctity, repressing warlike impulses and allowing feelings of concord and friendship to flow freely.[83]

The aim was not only to establish a moral rule. Gregory of Nyssa was informed with the desire to single out the process by which the pacifying mission of Christ became part of the Gospel system, came to represent an essential element of it. Gregory discovered the basis of this process in Saint Paul's Epistle to the Ephesians, in which the symbol of peace is identified with the salvation brought, through the advent and the Passion of Christ, to all people on earth. To this was added the desire to act in accordance with His teaching:

> Recognizing Christ as "peace," we shall exhibit the true title of Christian in ourselves through the peace in our life. For the One "has slain enmity," as the apostle says. Let us not, therefore, bring it to life in ourselves, but rather show through our life that it is dead. Let us not raise up against ourselves through anger and backbiting what has been rightly deadened for our salvation by God. This would destroy our soul and bring about an evil resurrection of what is rightly dead. . . . For that One "has broken down the intervening wall of the enclosure," and, out of the two elements in Himself, has created "one new man," and made peace. Therefore, let us also reconcile, not only those fighting against us on the outside, but also the elements at variance within us, in order that no longer may the "flesh lust against the spirit and the spirit against the flesh." Subjecting the spirit of the flesh to divine law, let us live peacefully, having been dissolved into the new and peaceful man and having become one from two. For the definition of peace is the harmony of dissonant paths.[84]

The desire for peace implies an active commitment. *Oratio VII, De beatitudinibus* is wholly centered on the praise of the peaceful virtues of the individual, seen both in their intimate and personal sense and in the wider one of community relations. Commenting on the passage in Matthew (5:9): "Blessed are the peacemakers: for they shall be called the children of God," Gregory defined as *peacemakers* "those who bring peace to their neighbor."[85] Another point was that nobody could procure for others the things which he lacked himself. From this it followed that the man of peace, intending to bring peace to those around him, must possess it himself. Moreover, if it was desired that peace should be the agent of a complete regeneration of society, agreement must be reached on the meaning of the word. "What can it be other than a mutual affection joined with love and given freely both to one's neighbor and to one's fellow-citizen?" One way of defining peace was to catalogue its opposites—"hate, anger, violence, envy, the refusal to forget past injuries, dissimulation, calamity, and the devastation procured by war."[86] How could it be doubted that peace, by being opposed to so many and such harmful evils, was in itself a good? The serenity of those who pursued the peaceful virtues and the dissatisfaction of those who yielded to impulses of wrath bore witness to this truth.

It was clear that Gregory was aware of the harmful effects of war when he compared the aggression triggered off by the forces of evil against the virtue of man to the action of an "army mobilized against an enemy fortress."[87] He was well-informed on the details of military theory and drew arguments from it to show how difficult it was to defend oneself against evil. His analysis of the harm caused by war and of its consequences, contained in *Oratio VII, De beatitudinibus* (1281 C-D), includes a vivid account of a battle in which no quarter is asked and no quarter given. We can almost hear the encouraging cries of the officers and the screams of the wounded, almost see the bodies of the fallen, foes bound in death in a tragic embrace. The implication is unmistakably that nothing in the world can be more desirable than peace. Gregory's eloquence is fired by enthusiasm when he lists the joys and the pleasures of earthly life. His inquiry leads him to the conclusion that peace is the greatest of all joys, not only because of the goodness and happiness it brings, but also because it helps to create an atmosphere in which the other joys of existence are enhanced.

In *Oratio VII* peace is treated not only as the background to a pattern of behavior which should improve the Christian soul tarnished by sin, safeguarding it from the dangers and evils of this life, but also in the more practical context of community life. War is no longer an allegorical component of the struggle against sin but a cruel calamity to be avoided at all costs.

Although in some ways inspired by Plato, Gregory's thinking is intertwined in the overall fabric of Christian religious feeling. In it man has a twofold being: the external one, in direct relation to the world, and the internal one, responsible for the initiatives on which his salvation will depend. His salvation is not to be separated from the pacification which the individual must effect in himself, making it the fundamental rule of his conduct. Gregory expects from each Christian a strong religious commitment, designed to facilitate inner serenity, the elimination of disputes and the mitigation of animosities against one's neighbor. The Christian becomes the artificer of a universal change which will confer holiness on all things. Matter, too, finally liberated from the effects of hate and of war, and above all of evil, responsible for its corruption, will once again enjoy that state of perfection and felicity which reigned at the beginning of the world.

In this way another Platonic element took its place in the system of Gregory of Nyssa: the conviction that there had once been a happy age, brought to an end because of the explosion of those violent instincts on which war feeds and thrives. This is a different picture from that of the earthly paradise presented in Genesis. It evokes a reality to which man will have to revert on the day when his blind impulses will have yielded to the feelings of forgiveness and resignation borne by the Christian message. "The resurrection is the restoring of our nature to its former condition. At the beginning of life, whose creator was God, there was neither old age, as is reasonable, nor infancy, nor sickness resulting from disease, nor any of the other bodily miseries. For it is not likely that God would create such things. Human nature was something divine before humanity inclined itself toward evil."[88]

Gregory thus appealed to the very essence of the Gospel teaching interpreted by him in Platonic terms. His principal aim was to persuade man, through appeals to the real values of the spirit, to root out evil, to ensure that peaceful impulses prevailed over aggressive ones, facilitating the beneficial development of the human community.

The work of the Cappadocian fathers marks a milestone in the history of the religious struggles of the fourth century, shining like a bright shaft of light through a fog of dissension. Although arising in a period of spiritual torment and from an earnest search for truth, the frequent quarrels of the time reflected the personal ambitions of the leaders of the ecclesiastical hierarchy, whose power and wealth were growing as the unity and authority of the empire declined. Each diocese—indeed it is almost fair to say, every single community of the faithful—mirrored the theological controversies which plagued the Christian world and was a microcosm in which the great ideological contests declined into vulgar diatribes and power contests. Especially in the East and in Africa, where the passionate temperament of the people, their leaning toward speculation, and their taste for controversy all played a role, the struggle became ruthless, leading to excesses quite out of keeping with a religion based on a message of mercy and peace.

This did not escape the civil authorities. Having now embraced Christianity with the purely political aim of ensuring the internal stability needed to hold off the barbarians, they saw that the struggles which had raged before the Edict of Constantine were not very different from those which had broken out since, now that the Church, having obtained a legal status, was free to act unhindered.

Peace for the three Cappadocian fathers was a *religious* issue. When they spoke of peace, they were thinking, in the first place, of the internal peace of the individual, linked with the acceptance of the Christian message. Then they were thinking of religious peace, the notion of which had been lost in the environment in which they were working and the absence of which was aggravating the already critical condition of a body politic, now steadily disintegrating. The authors of religious tracts, particularly those of the Eastern Church, were incapable of seeing the problems of peace outside these limits. The approach adopted by the philosophical schools, particularly the Stoics and Cynics, by which peace had been seen as something attainable on this earth, was abandoned, and became something to be looked for in the world hereafter.

Some pagan schools had discerned by intuition the existence of a link of brotherhood between all men, transcending geographical barriers, links of race and of religion, and they had hoped to envelop mankind in a single embrace, on which universal peace would have set the final seal; they had mapped out for the men of their time a road which would facilitate the attainment of a state of perfection; these ideas had penetrated and helped to shape the Christian heritage, but they were destined to lose momentum when the pressure of events showed that there was no real solidarity among peoples.

Peace was thus examined in a different context from that in which it had been considered in the first and second centuries. The aim was now to protect the theological and hierarchical unity of the Church, the safety of its institutions. This was an idea very different from that disseminated by Stoicism. The Stoics believed in the brotherhood of men, men torn by innumerable quarrels but united by the identity of their nature. The Cappadocian thinkers saw the problem from another angle. They placed the interests of religion at the heart of their philosophy, caring only to safeguard its unity and solidarity, which was so severely threatened. Their reactions were less strong when conflict between two peoples or a civil war broke out. They then felt themselves men of party, involved in the outcome of a struggle, and could not assess the problem serenely and impartially. This transposition of the problem to the level of theology and religious organization was to continue in the Middle Ages, when the unity of the Church stood in stark contrast to a military civilization rent by fierce and uninterrupted conflict. This was the foreseeable outcome of the way in which the Roman Empire had been converted: its administrative machinery and political institutions had remained largely unchanged even after the establishment of the new religion.

Other theologians of the Eastern Church behaved in the same way. Their attitudes, almost always based on arguments of little value and informed with less vigilant speculative acumen, did not diverge unduly from those of Basil and the two Gregories.

The problem of war and peace, considered in this perspective, was also studied by Saint John Chrysostom (ca. 345-407). It is often difficult to make out exactly what John is trying to say, so rich and opulent is his eloquence and so poorly matched with his doctrine. He tended to draw support from the mystical element in the Christian religion—and emphasized heavily the need to follow a moral rule in line with the Gospels and admitting of no exceptions, compromises, or yieldings.

He provides us with a classification of wars grouped into three categories: those fought against the barbarians, civil wars, and those involving man against himself. The latter he deemed by far the most harmful. "For foreign war will not be able to hurt us greatly. What, I pray, though it slaughters and cuts us off? It injures not the soul. Neither will the second have power to harm us against our will; for though others be at war with us, we may be peaceable ourselves."[89] He examined the problem from the angle of the damage done to the soul. The other effects interested him less. The third type of war seemed to him the most serious and dangerous because of its moral consequences. This was the conflict of mind against body, caused by the explosion of passions. It was the deliberate flouting of every rule of community life which drew men into vice. John saw the origin of evil in the defeat of the mind in its struggle with the senses.

In Chrysostom's theological system this conception of war enabled the individual to fix his attention on the struggle going on inside him, the most hazardous of all. The focal point was therefore an internal factor, which mobilized the individual's energies without however prompting any direct opposition on his part to armed conflict. This apparent inconsistency should not surprise. It was in line with the tradition of Christianity, whose historical vitality had often been a matter of innate flexibility in face of the requirements of the state. The cataloging of the wars reflected the application, confined to the kingdom of the spirit, of the evangelical principle, according to which men, all being brothers, must allow themselves to be guided by a will to peace. Commenting on Psalm 46 which celebrates the future greatness of the Jewish people, John Chrysostom attempts to explain the contradictions between promise and reality in the Christian message. "Before the coming of Christ, all men were skilled in the use of arms and all were required to fight. City fought against city and war was widespread. But now most people on earth live in peace and all can exercise their gifts for cultivating the land or navigating the seas in security." This passage is an attempt to clarify the statement made a few lines earlier in which John notes that God "made war difficult for demons and spread peace throughout the earth."[90]

The reference here must surely be to war between peoples and not to the conflict between conscience and the body of every individual. If, as seems likely, the work was written between 370 and 386, the assertion that the empire was enjoying an idyllic condition of peace seems truly excessive. The passage links up with the words of Isaiah (2:4), claiming that the coming of the Messiah would pacify men, compelling them to beat their swords into plowshares and their spears into pruninghooks. But at the end of the fourth century this had not yet come to pass. These were the years in which the pressure of the barbarians on the confines of the empire weighed most heavily, the years of the famous Battle of Adrianople (378), when the Emperor Valens lost his army and his life and the great invasions of Roman territory began. How could John Chrysostom claim that mankind had been pacified by Christ? He showed his understanding of the position of the early Christians, still naively buoyed up by the conviction that the coming of the kingdom would coincide with an age of peace on earth and with the disappearance of hate and anger from community life. But how could one reach conclusions of this kind when one was involved in a bitter struggle against the imperial court in defense both of purity of conduct and of orthodoxy? How could one praise peace when the empire was fighting for its very existence, seriously threatened by the pressure of barbarians? Chrysostom avoided the difficulties by relating his teaching to an imaginary society in which men were free to dedicate themselves to their occupations, where few served under arms and the unity of mankind was finally realized by a peace-loving government. None of this corresponded to reality, being merely a myth in which John pretended to believe.

His eloquence, the large number of his writings, and his analysis of the Scriptures from so many different angles, make it difficult to single out a consistent guiding line in his thinking. A careful exegesis of the texts brings to light a number of contradictions. Commenting in *In Matthaeum Homilia XXXV* on the famous statement (Matt. 10:34) that the Savior was not come to bring peace, but the sword, setting the believer at variance with his nearest and dearest, Chrysostom boldly claims that not all peace is desirable and that in given circumstances discord may be preferable to concord.[91] This is not the first time he expresses this idea. It is found in *In Johannem Homilia* LVII.[92] The comment on a very controversial Gospel passage was not inconsistent with the idea which impelled Chrysostom to call the attention of the faithful not only to the need for a repentance unknown to the corrupt circles of court but also the need to consolidate concord, taken in the Gospel sense as a way of facilitating the realization of the message of peace and brotherhood preached by Christ.

The mystical vision of peace as finally achieved within the Roman Empire (propagated for centuries by pagan writers)—a peace which almost all men had enjoyed and which, in a certain sense, had given shape and form to the postulates of Stoic cosmopolitanism—is revived with special vigor by a writer of the generation after Chrysostom. This was Saint Cyril of Alexandria (376-444), a prolific pamphleteer who combined great industry as a commentator on the Gospels with the aggressive impetuosity of a persecutor of heresies. His work in the great Christological debates at the beginning of the fifth century constitutes one of the major contributions to the history of the Church and had decisive importance in the formation of the orthodox doctrine on the nature of Christ. But the sheer quantity of his writings precludes any assessment of his work in a single context and it is not possible to discern in it any constant line of thought, since he is not always consistent.

From a mind not much inclined to mysticism and involved in theological controversy, it would be a mistake to expect anything other than special pleading. Cyril is concerned to avoid denying doctrine belonging to an ideological heritage; such doctrine is not to be challenged, even if, on close examination, it fails to carry complete conviction. Commenting on a passage of the Gospel according to John (14:27) in which the Evangelist states that the peace brought by Christ is not comparable with that of the world, Cyril compared the two concepts of peace to conclude that the first corresponds to the essential spirit of Christ, being indeed practically the same thing.[92] This argument was supported by a number of reflections touching upon the truth which the writer desired to prove without in fact ever tackling it directly: the problem of peace was seen by Cyril also from the external angle of relations between peoples. The same quotation from Isaiah (2:4) upon which Chrysostom had commentated, gave Cyril material for meditation. Guided by the empiricism dominating Alexandria, where much of the intellectual ferment that had spurred on Clement and Origen had now worked itself out, all Cyril could do was to turn again with renewed vigor to Chrysostom's comment on this passage, confirming the pagan thesis of the unifying and pacifying role played by the empire. His reasoning developed along two lines: on the one hand the representation of a pre-Roman society, not subject to a single government (or a single "yoke"), subdivided into a large number of small states squabbling among themselves; on the other, the reconciling mission of the empire, which had brought safety and stability where only anarchy and merciless strife had prevailed hitherto.

The will of God was definitely behind the formation of the Roman state. "Moreover, when the God of the universe subjugated the earth to the dominion of the Romans and when a single kingdom embracing the whole universe was finally established, wars ceased, battles and strife came to an end, and justice and the certainty of fair treatment prevailed."[93]

And Cyril goes on to demonstrate that the Roman Empire, pacifying the world, confining the use of arms to the state, forbidding it to private persons and ending the divisions and quarrels, had, through the will of God, made a reality of Isaiah's prophecy. The reasoning concluded with the following statement: "Under the empire of Christ, Who is peace, the peoples have been freed from all struggles and all dissension, from battles and every kind of greed. The evils deriving from war and the fear it creates, have been banished. Thus the will of Him Who said 'I give you my peace. I leave you my peace' has prevailed."[94] The same argument was put forward by Cyril with equal fervor and apparent conviction in his comment on a passage from Micah (4:4) but never very convincingly.[95]

These extracts reflect the empiricism of a vigorous writer whose life was to demonstrate his lack of faith in peace and in particular his inability to apply any such faith to the internal relations of the Church. The manner in which he presided over the Council of Ephesus, persuading it to condemn Nestorius, is a good example of his approach to problems of community life and the relations between opposing viewpoints. Unlike Chrysostom, who took a mystical view of the same question, Cyril saw in the argument of the pacification brought about by the Roman Empire a confirmation in historical terms of his instinctive belief that strength and decisiveness can resolve complex situations and that, to all intents and purposes, might is right.

So far from settling the theological controversies which were doing so much to divide Christians, the condemnation of Nestorius at Ephesus helped to exacerbate them. Even the way in which the condemnation was decided upon was certainly no evidence of love of peace, nor support for the claim that peace had been brought to mankind by the Roman Empire: Cyril was ready to use any expedient to ensure the triumph of his point of view. The twelve anathemas listed by him against Nestorius threw light on his approach to theological dialogue. The intransigent attitude, the acrimony, the use of temporal methods to force acceptance of theological arguments, all affected the Christian thinking of later centuries. The conflict between sects and doctrines was later to sound unbelievable depths of intolerance and polemic. The evangelical humility in the name of which the Church was working was often itself humiliated. All debates had to be resolved through irrevocable decisions, and every contribution must be made in an atmosphere of bitter extremism. The responsibility for all this was partly that of men like Cyril.

In the Christological controversies which followed the condemnation of Nestorius the factions seemed not to be seeking agreement but determined to fight on until one or the other gave in. At the heart of these disputes lay the dogmatic problem of the natures, of the persons, of the hypostases and of the wills, and of the relationships between them. The problem was brought to a head once again by the argument of the Constantinople monk Eutyches, who believed that Christ had only one nature, that of the Incarnate Word. A relentless struggle broke out over this doctrinal approach. Once again, temporal values, competition for influence and prestige between patriarchal sees, and the ever-widening rift between the Eastern and the Western Church all played a role out of all proportion to their true importance.

The controversy arose between a mystical interpretation and a warlike and aggressive approach of which the champions were mainly in the Alexandrian Church. After the battle had swayed to and fro for some time the Council of Chalcedon (451) condemned Eutyches and proclaimed that Christ had two different natures perfectly united in one person. This was the complex definition to which the bitter theological battles of the fourth and fifth centuries had led. These had come about for various reasons, the main ones being the penetration of classical speculation into theological exegesis and the obstinacy of certain churches.

Chalcedon settled a question which was never again to be raised in the Catholic Church. Despite the doubts entertained by some theologians in later centuries, the dogmatic proposition emerging on that occasion has reached us unchanged. The Church has endorsed it and championed it. At most, the authorities have classified or condemned inquiries made by restless minds who might wish to create new systems out of old ones or to consider past research the premises of new ones. The conclusion of the argument in a compromise solution, in which political realism prevailed, also weakened the heritage of humility linked with the message of mutual understanding that had inspired the early Christians. From the day of the promulgation of the Edict of Constantine, the old outlook had been gradually disappearing, to give way to a more hierarchical and mechanical way of thinking. For centuries the problem of peace was dominated by the conclusions, considered unchangeable, which had matured in the two great ecumenical councils of the fifth century.

At this point we meet writers who, without moving away from contemporary theological themes, carried out useful research and critical work foreshadowing the Schoolmen. They seldom tackled the problem of peace, and when they did so it was almost always only incidentally. In dealing with it, there was a certain confusion and no common approach. But there are no signs at all of the dreamlike mysticism of the early Christians. The distinction between the various forms of peace—between the inner peace of the individual, that of the Church, and that of the human community—remained nebulous.

Exceptions to this rule were provided by a few Eastern thinkers. Though keeping to the line of orthodoxy and under the influence of classical speculation, these theologians showed a more than marginal interest in the problems of peace and its impact on community life. One of them was Synesius (ca. 373-ca. 414), a pagan philosopher who had been converted to Christianity and who became bishop of Ptolemaïs in the Libyan Pentapolis. His eclectic mind, guided by a variety of practical and philosophic interests, betrayed his classical training. He is remembered for his skill on the occasion of a barbarian incursion on the territory of his diocese, when he organized effective military resistance. Since his work covers the end of the fourth and the beginning of the fifth centuries, he belonged to the age of the great theological controversies but seems to have taken no part in these.

His main work, the oration *De regno,* written in 397, preceded his conversion. He wrote it on the occasion of an embassy made on behalf of the cities of the Pentapolis to the imperial court to solicit tax abatements and other concessions. The oration, which shows traces of the influence of the works of Dio Chrysostom, concerned the art of governing. The inspiration is only partly Christian, and the work is strongly influenced by Stoicism. The ruler is seen and judged as a benefactor and as a father in whom the subjects should place their trust. Peace must be his objective, although circumstances might compel him to go to war. "Peace is a happier condition than war, since the preparations for war are made with a view to ultimate peace."[96] A king must also be able to assess situations calmly, weighing their advantages and disadvantages. He must refrain from aggravating disputes, always preferring peaceful solutions. This does not mean that he must be a coward or refuse to fight. "Only he who can punish the troublemaker and have his revenge of them is entitled to love peace. Moreover, I shall regard as a sovereign genuinely imbued in the things relating to peace he who, while avoiding insult or injury to others, is

ready to deal with those who hurt or insult him."[97] A defensive war was allowed, but with the objective of reestablishing peace, a condition which in
any case is always "happier than war." For him the government of a state was
to be pursued along lines fully in accordance with the views of Stoics and
Platonists of all time.

Essentially, Synesius was a minor theologian who left hardly any trace at
all in ecclesiastical history. But the same cannot be said of an anonymous
mystic who lived in the first half of the sixth century and who substantially
influenced later thinking, in both the Eastern Church and the Western Church.
Using the pseudonym "Dionysius the Areopagite" for the name of a follower
of Paul who is mentioned in the Acts of the Apostles (17:34), he wrote a
body of theological and mystical works which were to achieve enormous success. The first historical reference to these writings (ten epistles and four treatises) goes back to a synod held in Constantinople in 531 or 533. On that occasion doubts were expressed as to their authenticity. Their author was certainly an inspired theologian and must have been alive after the Council of
Chalcedon. He interpreted in mystical terms the message of Christ, which he
explained in vivid imagery.

Elements drawn from various currents of contemporary thinking flowed
together in his works. Christian, pagan, Hebrew, and oriental ideas in general
are fused into one by an intelligence capable of establishing unity in what,
otherwise, would have been merely the overlaying of disparate elements. His
work has been compared to that of Plotinus, and the comparison is valid in
the sense that both authors attempted to make the synthesis of a system. In
one case this system was Neoplatonic, in the other Christian, presented in a
mystic setting which injected new life into subject matter the quality of
which protracted theological controversies had done much to impair.

The main work of the pseudo-Dionysius was the *De divinis nominibus,* in
which he provided a Neoplatonic representation of divinity. He argued that
God's goodness could not be separated from his infinite love; this in its turn
was instilled into created beings, establishing their hierarchy as a function of
their ability to absorb divine goodness. A thinker inspired by such a passionate mystic impulse, for whom knowledge was mainly a matter of the urge of
feeling and the life-giving force of goodness, could not ignore the problem of
peace: Chapter 11 of the *De divinis nominibus* is wholly devoted to an analysis of its essence and to the way in which it can be fitted into a system of cosmic love.

The pseudo-Dionysius sought first of all to define divine peace. He saw it
as that good "that unites all things together and begets and produces the harmonies of all things. And hence it is that all things long for It, and that It
draws their manifold separate parts into the unity of the whole and unites the
battling elements of the world into concordant fellowship."[98] Peace is seen as
an ecumenical virtue, free of impediments as to the field of possible action

and of barriers as to effects on created beings. These beings, enjoying its benefits and partaking of its essence in the same way as in respect of divine love,
are separated according to a hierarchy of values. Divine peace was defined,
then, in relation to its origin, which was bound up with an attribute of God, a
peace-loving as well as a merciful being.

The peace of pseudo-Dionysius partook at one and the same time of three
worlds. There was the cosmic peace, that of the earthly world, and that of the
individual. As a created being, man had the attainment of peace as a constant
objective. Peace was a state of mind in which all reason for unease or restlessness was lacking and existence was always a matter of calmness and repose. It
was seen in the form of stability, contemplation, isolation from anything that
could distract or disturb.

A question springs to mind, but the pseudo-Dionysius had foreseen it. In
created beings there is a natural tendency to movement and diversity which
governs their acts. If therefore their movements tend not toward peace and
serenity but toward dispersion and disorder they contribute increasingly to
ensuring importance to divine peace, making it appear what in fact it is—a
sublime good, the pursuit of which, subordinated to the perfection of the
spirit, represents the goal of individual ambitions. He who does not love peace
is the exception; his attitude must not be taken as a model nor allowed to influence that which is the fruit of divine will. This is all the more true since
peace cannot be separated from compliance with a moral rule. It is attainable
only by a person who renders himself deserving of it through his own behavior. The moral and political aspects of the concept emerge from the entire
context of the work, in other parts of which the author links once again the
idea of peace with compliance with a rule of conduct, rejecting implicitly the
idea of an ethic based on war.

Every act aimed at the satisfaction of the passions was therefore hostile to
the peace of the spirit, as was every uncontrolled impulse, seeking to upset
the serene equilibrium of the mind, denying that divine goodness is above all
peace-loving, "wherefrom we must learn to cease from strife, whether against
ourselves or against one another, or against the angels, and instead to labor together even with the angels for the accomplishment of God's Will, in accordance with the Providential purpose of Jesus Who worketh all things in all and
maketh Peace, unutterable and foreordained from Eternity, and reconcileth
us to Himself, and, in Himself, to the Father."[99]

This was a new enunciation of that overall vision of peace linked with the
mission of Christ, from whom it received the force of authority and the certainty of achievement. Peace was identified with the primeval energies of creation, with the life-creating power of God, which in the pseudo-Dionysius
sometimes seems closer to the Platonic model than to the Gospel. Understood
in the threefold way we have seen, peace took its place in a spatial and temporal universe where the dimensions seemed to melt together in a pre-established

harmony, where all war, all dispute, every unforeseen movement, is a major disturbance. The influences of classical thought were obvious. The expression of absolute peace in universal terms, remote from the individual, although in the last analysis the individual partook of it, was a re-evocation, in some ways, of contemporary Platonic doctrine.

Although some propositions of the pseudo-Dionysius aimed at stating and solving the problem of peace against a purely mystical and transcendental background, apparently lacking points of contact with community life, in fact the problem of the latter was dealt with in full. The individual peace which descended by steps from the cosmos to the individual through the intermediary phases of harmony with God, with the angels, and with one's neighbor, did not neglect the peace of the state, in the twofold sense both of concord within the community and of avoidance of violence in relations between communities. This impressive edifice was considered from a single point of view, so that the various aspects of peace harmonized in a single context and were bound by a cause-and-effect relationship. Inward peace and peace between communities were stages on the road to perfection. The inference was that peace not only brought with it a tendency toward repose or a state of calm and stability. It was also identified with a perfect universal order.

The ideas of the pseudo-Dionysius may be summarized as follows. The cosmos is dominated by a divine peace, which also entails a universal coordination among created beings. The resulting order has a number of characteristics. It may at certain moments suggest the complete stillness to which creatures seem to tend. But in fact peace is not lack of movement but harmony, since it comes from God. Man forms an essential element of the system. Various forms of human association—states and religious communities—therefore constitute realities without which the goodness of God would not be perfect. These communities receive, at least as a broad aspiration, His peace, the prime origin of the harmony and of the serenity achievable by men. Although the writer does not say so explicitly, peace between states and within states is implied as an absolute necessity, failing which the entire edifice would lack a fundamental component. But all this can be considered only in close relation to a moral rule, which is essential to the attainment of peace, the supreme objective sought by everyone, even by those who claim to love disorder and disturbances and see existence as an adventure based on strife.

Thus, we can discern in the system of the pseudo-Dionysius a clear distinction between peace seen as a comprehensive entity which is achieved by following a road descending from the cosmos, and the will necessary to the individual to achieve it. From the first point of view, peace is considered an objectively existing reality in that it stems from God; from the second, it is seen as a conquest made by traveling a road of perfection and serenity. In this way two aspects of the problems are clarified. In the ideas proposed, Christian notions were colored by reflections reminiscent of classical speculation. Such a vision of peace came close to that of the Stoics. It was the result not of a gift but of a conquest to be made gradually through successive acts of will and the constant refinement of the spirit, seeking emancipation from all error and confusion. Any Stoic could have endorsed attitudes of this kind. From this point of view the unity of the universe, and therefore its peace, were seen as objectives which the individual should pursue through the constant refinement of human virtues in communion with those of God.

All this helped to strengthen the mystic vision of existence and to support a theology remarkable for its emotional vigor rather than its logic. The pseudo-Dionysius saw knowledge of God increasingly as resulting from the instinctive questing of the spirit in a world in which the most vivid and pertinent ideas of Christian and Neoplatonic wisdom seemed to flow together and melt into one. Peace, too, had its place in this evanescent world, in which values were obscured by a fog that could not be dispelled without a strong effort of will. Peace became an instrument whereby the spirit succeeded in returning into itself. To know peace, so complex because linked to a special impulse, you must also possess it; thus the one was the condition and premise of the other. Peace between organized societies—whether religious or civil—escaped this mystic road in appearance only: for the reasons given, the peace of the spirit became the fundament of peace between groups and its determining factor. It thus became possible to hope for the restoration of serenity in one's surroundings, failing which the human spirit would have little hope of improvement and salvation. The mystical journey, which the anonymous author thus defended, was complemented in the intellection of God and in peace, understood in the threefold sense. All this influenced later medieval philosophers, who drew heavily on the work of the pseudo-Dionysius.

Our analysis of the idea of peace among the early Greek fathers ends with Maximus the Confessor (580-662), whose orthodoxy, professed in rigorous terms, annoyed the imperial court, especially the Emperors Heraclius I (who reigned from 610 to 641) and Constantine III (who reigned from February to May 641), both uncompromising champions of the Monothelite heresy. Those of his writings which interest us most are the mystical ones, which were influenced by the pseudo-Dionysius. The Neoplatonic element in them caused him to adopt an almost pantheistic vision of existence, in which rational beings partook directly of the divine light. The mysticism of Maximus was expressed to the full in his conception of divine goodness, made incarnate to bring about the salvation of mankind through association with His grief and expiation. Peace of the mind, and with it also peace among men and among societies, was the catalyzing element in this stupendous miracle whereby God becomes man. War, whether that provoked vainly by the evil one against his Creator, that waged against mankind to bar him from the law of charity, or that which men, yielding to the worst side of their natures, caused between themselves, in contempt of Christ's mission, was always seen as the worst calamity. It brought into contempt the aims of good men and favored those of evil ones. It diverted human beings from their road to salvation and prevented them from escaping the flatteries of sin and the spiritual corruption which this caused. In the absence of peace, salvation might well be no longer attainable: how could this be achieved, if not through the participation of man in the glory of the Creator? And was this not bound to entail the disappearance of anything which might hamper our journey toward peace?[100]

Peace stated in terms of mystic contemplation was later studied by more than a few medieval philosophers and theologians. The overall vision in which it took its place crossed the boundaries of relations between the individual and his Creator to embrace the problem of relations between men and communities. All this derived from the explanation provided by Maximus concerning the meaning of the priest's invocation of peace in the mass. This is interpreted to mean: "O Lord, you offered us peace and mutual concord. Give us, then, peace and undivided communion with you, so that, pacified in your spirit, of which you made us partake by the fact of our creation, we shall never want for your grace."[101]

The Latin Fathers

While in the East the Christological and Trinitarian disputes were slowly dissipating the energies of a Church conditioned by the rationalizing propensities of Greek speculation, theology in the West was more practical and more realistic, being concentrated on problems designed mainly to overcome the difficulties between the civil and the religious powers. Since Constantine had promulgated his famous edict, the need to reorganize Church-state relations had become ever more urgent in the eyes of the Western bishops: on a solution of the problem depended the future of their Church, which in later centuries would be forced to maneuver in politically fluid situations fraught with unknown difficulties. This context, largely determined by historical and environmental factors differing from those in the East, also explains why the research carried out and the speculative approaches adopted by the most representative minds of the two Churches were so different. In the East, theologians and philosophers faced the increasing interference of the imperial authority in the internal affairs of the Church, while the Church itself sought official support. In the West, less importance was given to theological discourses, but the need to find an explanation of history which would refute, or at least mitigate, the Church's dependence on the state was emphasized.

None of this prevented an intense flow of ideas between the two Churches. Especially when the empires of the East and of the West were for a time reunited under the same ruler, during the reign of Constantius II, son of Constantine, the contacts between the sees of Rome and Constantinople were to become more frequent, and there was an ample exchange of information and influence. Re-reading the works of the Western fathers and examining the contributions of their thinking concerning relations between the political and the religious authorities, we can discern, together with a more or less manifest desire for autonomy, also greater sympathy for the early pacifist content of the Christian message. The only Western writer to tackle the problem comprehensively was Saint Augustine, who dealt with it fully in the *De civitate Dei.* All, or almost all, the fathers felt certain, however, that it was a mistake to endorse the ideas on the problem of peace entertained by the Eastern Church, whether these were negative or positive. This is not surprising if it is remembered that the rejection of the pacifist attitudes of apostolic Christianity is explained historically by the Church's need to come to terms with the imperial power and to meet the authorities halfway on points not conflicting with the central content of the Christian message. The problem of peace was one on which a compromise was deemed possible. The situation was to recur in subsequent centuries and even today. The more the Church was forced into the arms of the state for support, the more it was obliged to drop pacifism as doctrine. The more it defended its autonomy, reaffirming its own right to advise and guide the emperor, the more it had to appeal to the words of peace and humility flowing from the early teachers who had had such a wide following among the faithful in the apostolic period.

The relations between Church and state in all fields—and therefore on the question of peace as well—assumed in the West a character which would have been impossible in the East. The thinking of the Latin fathers kept close to that of Tertullian, who had denied that the empire could become Christian since it was incompatible with the ideal represented by Christianity. Although the revolution of Constantine had shown this to be unduly pessimistic, Tertullian's influence kept a hold on the Latin Church because of its desire to safeguard a degree of separation between the two worlds in which the faithful lived. This was the beginning of the rivalry between civil and religious powers that was to mark the development of the Latin Church, giving it its moments of glory and imparting a distinct character to Western Christian society. To this rivalry mankind is indebted for major conquests in the field of philosophic speculation and political thought.

The rift between the Western bishops and the imperial authority was very soon a wide one. It culminated in the exile to the East of some of the Church's most representative leaders, ordered by the Emperor Constantius II. This measure of persecution had some beneficial effects in that it enabled Western Christianity to obtain fuller information on the theological ideas prevailing in the East. The deportees included Hilary of Poitiers (ca. 300-367), a tireless opponent of the Arian heresy. During his exile in Phrygia, Hilary studied the Greek fathers, who then became the source of inspiration for much of his writing.

Hilary's thinking has an outstanding place not only in the field of Trinitarian controversy but also in that of the demarcation of relations between Church and state. There is a passage by Hilary in which he attacks the Arian

bishop of Milan, invoking the old purity of the Church: During the persecutions, the Church had not begged for aid and riches at the price of its dignity
and prestige. It had been content to sing the praises of the Lord at the very
time and in those places where its saints faced martyrdom. The discourse in
which these reflections occur was written as part of the anti-Arian campaign
to overthrow the heretic bishop.[102] Its words, however, were intended for
anyone subordinating his faith to the impositions, often sacrilegious, of the
civil power, choosing the easy road of acquiescence and material comfort. It
was a strong plea to the faithful to stand firm against violence and flattery,
particularly when proffered in the interests of heresy.

Hilary was a controversialist and a party man. He felt it right to give battle
when the defense of the faith left no other choice. His persistence with regard
to the Arians is proof of this. Moreover, concord between religious and civil
communities, though he always regarded it as an essential objective, was sometimes liable to harm orthodoxy: when, on the pretext of maintaining peace
among the faithful, the Church yielded to violent heretical pressures or stresses, it was not consolidating a peaceful objective already achieved but favoring
the anti-Christ. For it was the heretics who boasted of their peace, meaning
not the peace of the Church seen as a whole but "the unity of their depraved
impiousness."[103]

The practice of the faith derived from the degree of knowledge of it possessed by the faithful, a knowledge which it was the duty of the Church to
promote and spread. "The doctrine of peace must therefore be learnt," said
Hilary, and further on in the same passage: "Learning peace is the characteristic of those who listen of their own will."[104] Hilary's teaching assumed the
individual's readiness to act, as does the psalm on which he is commenting in
this passage. The meaning of the word *peace* transcended that of cessation of
conflict to reflect a state of perfection and a need of betterment. The idea implicit in the word referred not to idle and slothful calm but to the innermost
workings of the spirit, to the ceaseless longing for new knowledge and mas-
tery of oneself. This led to the odd conclusion, an idea recurrent in the writings of Hilary, that the persecutions had been necessary to safeguard the purity of the faith. "Peace is dangerous for a lazy faith, just as the dangers threatening the inactive sentinel are numerous. Deceits will not easily get the better
of an individual used to fighting, since a glorious struggle is needed before the
crown of victory can be won."[105] This is not a contradiction, as the reference
to the crown of victory might suggest, but a responsible appeal to the noblest
feelings of the individual, a reminder that peace of mind does not mean a lack
of vigilance. Every Christian must be alert if he is to be sure of achieving salvation. Moreover, earthly peace and peace in God are complementary: the latter cannot exist without the former.[106] If it had been developed further, this
conviction, a result of the greater moral freedom achieved vis-à-vis the civil authorities, would perhaps have led to a genuine doctrine of peace having a de-

gree of inspiration and an impact surpassing any in the writings of the Greek fathers. In Hilary the relations of man with his neighbor—community relations—were not lost in the limbo of abstractions to which the Greek fathers had often relegated them but were accorded their own importance and autonomy.

In fourth-century speculation and theology there are few minds more acute and few temperaments more vigorous than those of Marius Victorinus, master of rhetoric in Africa, his birthplace, at a time when the Emperor Julian forbade the Christians to teach this discipline. A deeply pious man, he preferred his faith to his profession, although apostasy would have allowed him to continue teaching.

His thinking was Neoplatonic in substance and reminiscent of Origen in approach. This circumstance may well explain his opposition to persecution: those thinkers having the most lively sense of the unity of God discern the need to achieve concord. The God of Marius Victorinus was therefore placed at the center of a compact speculative world which allowed of no flaws or exceptions. God emerged beyond all material things, isolated in his creative activities and therefore separated from the empirical world. Victorinus found this cause-and-effect relationship so complete that through it he succeeded even in explaining the origin of God through autogenesis. God had first created himself and then the world. We shall not follow this author in his Neoplatonic fantasies, as they wander over the field of Christian revelation. Let it suffice to note that, for him, being and doing coincided. The essence of God, though remaining enclosed in its splendid isolation, expressed itself through its effect on the tangible and empirical world, which also displayed qualities of cohesion and compactness. This cosmogony entailed in its turn a principle of unity in which three elements were discernible: being, doing, and understanding, differing aspects of a single divine reality.

It is not easy to establish how far this was verbal artifice and how far a real attempt to penetrate more deeply the problems of existence and of God in a context which, despite its Neoplatonic approach, took account of the Christian message, providing an appropriate explanation of it. Whether they were artifices or convictions, the fact remained that the unitarian vision, both of the nature of God and of the tangible world, allowed of no disturbances. God had impressed on the world his perfection and his unity. All events liable to affect them conflicted with the divine will transfused in the creative process. War was high on the list of actions which opposed the laws fixed by God. Quite apart from the material harm it caused, it was a negation of the law which controls the universe, the law which led to God and his nature. Thus aversion to strife and discord was expressed by appealing to the natural law, regarded as divine rule, rather than by referring to mystic behavior and the convictions of the early Christians.

In commenting the words of farewell in Paul's Epistle to the Ephesians

(6:23-24): "Peace be to the brethren, and love with faith, from God the Father and the Lord Jesus Christ. Grace be with all them that love our Lord Jesus Christ in sincerity," Marius Victorinus stressed that the ultimate goal and the conclusion of the divine will consisted in substituting the benefits of peace for the evils of the earthly condition. "In this way all is resolved. Peace concludes discord; grace, concord; faith is absorbed in God."[107] Peace and serenity, which allowed of the realization of the divine plans, were the terminal phase of a dialectical cycle working itself out in the exaltation of the unity of God and of His creative will.

Saint Jerome (ca. 347-420), who was for a time Victorinus' pupil, was completely engrossed in the theological controversies of his time, both by natural bent and as a result of his experiences in the monasteries of the desert of Chalcis. His greatest work as a writer is the translation of the Old and New Testaments. Much evidence of his work as a controversialist has come down to us in the shape of letters and theological treatises. At times he was influenced by Origen, whose writings were prominent in the debates of the time. Some of these Jerome himself translated into Latin. At other times, particularly during the argument with Rufinus, he rejected Origen's doctrines and, implicitly, also that relating to the duties of the Christian in the case of armed conflict. Jerome kept to the line of Origen tradition when he gave an elegant definition of peace and of the spirit—a definition imbued with mysticism, perhaps reflecting and incorporating his monastic experiences. "Who can die in peace, save he who possesses the peace of God? . . . To whom is it vouchsafed to withdraw in peace from the century if not to him who realizes that in Christ there was God, conciliating Himself with the world?"[108]

This vision of individual serenity, taking its place as part of an idea of collective pacification, had further implications; it led Jerome to praise the peace-loving, who would gain special spiritual rewards. But who could claim to be a peace-loving individual? "O man who first in his own heart and then among his brothers, out of raging discord shows his determination to make peace." Thus a link is established between the internal peace of man and the external peace of human society. "What is the use of pacifying others through you, when in your own mind the strife born of vices rages on?"[109]

Jerome's work was imbued with an awareness of the links between the peace of the individual and that of the community. They showed pronounced similarities in that they were considered achievable only on condition that one was in communion with God, that one lived according to His rule and that one sought Him in the ways specified by Him. It was not sufficient to believe in God, as did Jews and heretics, if one then strayed from the path laid down by Him. "Those who do not seek God in the right way cannot achieve peace."[110] Peace was a heavenly gift, the fruit of special divine favor. "If there exist benefits granted by God the Father and Our Lord Jesus Christ, peace is certainly not the least important of them."[111]

Jerome was by no means insensible to the evils of the time, and his letters bear eloquent witness to the concern he felt.[112] The empire was in the throes of a very serious crisis, and he did not believe that it could survive the state of degradation into which it had declined, largely owing to internal strife. The struggles between inhabitants of the same state were more terrible and their consequences more serious than those fought against barbarians, which served at least to protect the confines of the empire. Jerome classified as internal conflicts theological disputes as well as the quarrels between temporal leaders. Both must be settled if the empire was to be defended and Christian society to survive and progress along the lines laid down by its Founder. This approach, influenced by ideas of Origen, underlies his comments on the writings of the prophet Isaiah, the author—it should not be forgotten—of some of the finest passages in the Old Testament, full of humility and a will for conciliation among men. Commenting on the passage in which the prophet looks forward to the day when, thanks to the help of the Messiah, swords will become plowshares and spears pruninghooks (Isa. 2:4), Jerome recalled the Gospel promise that peace would reign on earth and all discord would be superseded by love of one's neighbor. This passage is an attempt to relate individual and community life—and therefore relations between individuals and between groups—to a system in which animosities and discord would melt before the warmth of harmony and love.[113]

For Jerome the fact that the prophecy of the changing of weapons into tools had already been fulfilled with the coming of Christ summarized the whole problem. A period of calamities and civil wars was over and a second, dominated by peace and brotherly love, had begun.

If we refer to the ancient stories, we shall find that in the twenty-eighth year of the government of Augustus Caesar (in the forty-first year of whose reign Christ was born in Judaea) discord prevailed throughout the world and the nations longed to try conclusions with their neighbors, so that man killed and was killed. But once our Lord and Savior was born, when under Quirinius, governor of Syria, the first universal census was carried out, the peace of the gospel doctrine was prepared through that of the Roman Empire. Then all the wars ceased, and men trained for war no longer in the castles and the villages, but turned to the tilling of the fields, the task of combating the barbarian nations having been entrusted to the soldiers and the Roman legions.[114]

Jerome argues the same point in the comment on another Bible passage, where, once again, the transformation of weapons into tools is predicted.[115] This explanation of the influence exercised on political events by the coming of Christ had correspondences with pagan writings and had already been endorsed by other theologians.

Jerome lived in a particularly disturbed and tormented period of imperial Rome, at a time when the great institutions were beginning to crumble. The wars which had afflicted the empire before the coming of Christ and which had ceased during the early imperial dynasties had now been raging once again for many decades. The division of the empire, so far from ensuring a more harmonious allocation of responsibilities for the better defense of the state, had led to a disturbing aggravation of rivalries and disputes for the succession. Not even the empire's conversion to Christianity had brought an age of lasting peace, as, denying the obvious, Jerome pretended to believe. Besides the internal strife, there were also barbarian aggressions and other external dangers. How could Jerome reasonably make such a claim? An examination of the dates of compilation of the commentaries on the prophecies of Isaiah and Micah may provide an answer to this question. They were written when Jerome, freed from all Origenian influence, chose to deny his past, his "salad days," as it were, rather than allow the slightest doubt as to his orthodoxy. It was the time of the violent controversy with Rufinus (ca. 340-410), previously his fellow student and companion in the pursuit of the ascetic life and for a time very close to him in accepting Origen's thought.

The quarrel between the two writers, traces of which have come down to us in some of their translations from the Greek, hinged on a number of the more controversial of Origen's themes—for example, on that of the resurrection of the flesh. Part of Jerome's repudiation of his past was a weakening of his convictions with regard to the participation of the Christian in the profession of arms. Though the theological controversies between the two writers did not directly concern the problem of peace, it is fair to say that this problem was implicit. Rufinus did not challenge Origen's writings and much less their pacifist bias, although when translating them he thought it right to make some corrections. Jerome emphasized, on the other hand, his own orthodox zeal, not only against Rufinus, but also against the Pelagians, the sect which placed the will of the individual at the center of the Christian doctrine of salvation.

In his dialogues against the Pelagians, Jerome showed unusual acrimony, taking to extreme conclusions his explanation of the emergence of theological conflicts. "Where do the wars and disputes among you come from? Perhaps from the passions that excite your limbs?"[116] Although he oscillated between support for and opposition to Origenism, and although he first drifted away from orthodoxy, only to return to the fold and defend it later with all the zeal of the convert, there is no denying that the problem of peace was present in his mind and determined, at least in part, what questions he tackled.

His opponent Rufinus, who influenced Western Christianity particularly through translations of certain works of the Eastern fathers, was a more consistent thinker. The translation of Origen's *De principiis,* published in 398-399, was an important element in the controversy with Jerome: it has a preface in which reference is made to Jerome's earlier sympathies for the writings of Origen. This was more than enough to provoke the sharpest reaction, especially because what Rufinus said was partly true. Rufinus showed great obstinacy in attempting to prove that his old companion in meditation and study had not escaped the fascination of the doctor of Alexandria, the only difference being that now he denied his wayward youth, excoriating a man tactless enough to remind him of it.

Rufinus himself lacks assurance in this field, for he could see its dangers as well as its attractions. His translation of the *De principiis* was mainly a re-elaboration of the text, designed to make it accessible to a Western public unused to the finesses of language which allowed theologians to express and differentiate even the finest subtleties of thought. The fact that Rufinus commented, translated, and glossed Origen, making his writings the center of a system, not accepting them passively but treating them as working documents, means that he understood their message and shared, at least in part, some of their main attitudes. Origen had assumed a firm position in his *Contra Celsum* on the participation of the Christian in the emperor's wars. Though his tone had been less violent and intransigent than that of Tertullian, he had argued with no less vigor for the existence of a line of demarcation between the world of earthly interests, the world of Caesar, and that of spiritual values, represented by the Church of God. He himself had emphasized the principle of the incommunicability of the two worlds, denying to the Christians the right to join the army and *a fortiori* that of partaking in wars.

Eastern theology was mainly concerned with questions connected with the life of the spirit. Where lay the salvation of the individual in relation to universal salvation and what place was taken by the work of Christ in this scheme? Had there always existed in the next world a distinction between the rejected and the elect, between the damned and the blessed? Would the consequences of earthly existence and of the behavior of individuals on earth last forever in eternity, or would they not be mitigated by divine mercy? These were some of the questions provoked by the studies of Origen. They were questions on which Jerome and Rufinus had once been able to agree.

Rufinus remained loyal to his old enthusiasm, so much so that he was compelled to deny an allegation of Origenism in a famous letter to Pope Anastasius. This document contains an inventory of his opinions in matters of faith contrasting with errors in the doctrines of Origen. The list does not include the view that Christians may not bear arms. The same judgment may be formulated of the more important works written by Rufinus to clarify his position with regard to Origen. We are referring to the *Commentarium in Symbolum Apostolorum* and to the *Apologia in Hieronymum,* where he set out in full his ideas on the doctor of Alexandria and the part Rufinus had played in encouraging their greater dissemination in the Latin world. Among the works of Origen which he translated we do not find (nor do we know that it was included among them) the *Contra Celsum,* which would have been the irrefutable proof of a special interest in peace. The translation of the *De principiis* is, however, sufficient evidence of his main line of thinking, under the influence of which he interpreted the Christian message as a contribution of humility and mercy among men.

Origen had endeavored to free Christianity from the accretions and compromises which the need to live in the world and to coexist with the imperial authority had imposed upon it. Origen's God was very reminiscent of Plato's. One of His characteristics was His indivisibility. That God, according to the information given in the Old Testament, could have created matter and the beings made up of it was a truth which Greek philosophy could apprehend only with difficulty. How could matter derive from the divine oneness? How could the disorder of all earthly existence derive from order? Although it seems to have cost him something of an effort, Origen supported the biblical theory of the creation, although it was repugnant to the mentality of a Christianized Greek to admit the possibility of so direct a cause-and-effect relationship between a being uncreated and perfect, and therefore unique and indivisible, like God, and created matter, divisible and manifold. Therefore he used an emanationist explanation according to which all rational beings partaking of God's divine nature derived their origin from Him. Below these beings—to whom the fact of belonging to the same matter as the Creator brought with it the enjoyment of His warmth—were disposed all the others, in whom the warmth had cooled all the more to the extent that they lacked intellectual vigor.

The unitarian vision of God did not allow, although this was not affirmed explicitly, that circumstances could subsist likely to disturb it. Everything in this eternal nature was harmony, light, and concord. It is therefore not surprising that in the created beings, the degree of whose perfection was directly proportionate to their participation in this divine light, there was an attraction no less direct toward unity and a natural aversion to anything that could hamper it or slow down the process. Book III of the *De principiis,* in particular, which deals with the human capacity for applying divine law, overcoming the pressures exerted by the world, by the flesh, and by the forces of evil in general, was a basic document instituting a moral rule consonant with the principle of unity and of respect for the work of the Creator which had been enunciated. This treatise set out the premises and specified the conditions according to which the Christian might refrain from the military activities dealt with in the *Contra Celsum.* The pacifist doctrine of the author drew its origin from his moral rule, of which Rufinus himself, despite mutilations and adaptations to the text, was the main champion. The translation of the *De principiis* was, then, a bold attempt to bring home to the Western public of the time a message of virtue and continence, with the ultimate objectives of peace of mind and that of men among themselves.

One of the contemporaries of Jerome and Rufinus was Saint Ambrose (ca. 330-ca. 397), bishop of Milan and a great ecclesiastical organizer. His sense of balance and ingenuity as an administrator made no small contribution to the consolidation of the Church in difficult times. He symbolized in his person a particular moment in the history of the Church, especially with respect to its independence of the state. The excommunication of the Emperor Theodosius, guilty of having ordered massacres in Thessalonica, is sufficient evidence of his moral sense, his courage, and the degree of independence achieved by the Latin Church.

His aggressive personality won him many enemies, particularly at the Roman see, whose jurisdiction he sometimes encroached upon and whose rights he was apt to ignore if he believed this necessary to his work. The natural hostility of Roman circles was to find expression in the criticism leveled at him by Jerome in connection with the treatise *De Spiritu Sancto*. In this famous book Ambrose drew heavily on the Greek fathers for guidance and material for his pen. Classical literature (for example, Cicero's *De officiis*) also provided him with ammunition. Because of their twofold origin, his many treatises were to have a substantial influence on Western ideas and theological research in the Middle Ages. A mind of this stamp could not remain indifferent to the problem of war and to the need to resist the warlike temptations coming from the civil power. Violence scandalized him in all its forms, as the episode of the Thesslonian massacres proves. In his eyes peace was the final objective of human actions and therefore also of war. "This is the objective of courage and of physical effort itself, to ensure that once war is over, peace is restored: the will to fight is a function of the longing for peace. Therefore let no one challenge those of peace-loving inclination."[117]

Peace was seen in an overall setting, including both that of the mind and that to be achieved in relations between men and between communities. Serenity—peace of mind and social peace—would lead to undreamed of achievements, generating a sense of greatness and nobility and a detachment from worldly things. "He who possesses peace—which is superior to any intellectual capacity—is a strong man and is not one of the army of mean men."[118]

The metaphor of the sword was used by Ambrose to symbolize the battle fought by the sinner against justice, also armed with a sword. The Scriptures suggested this image and the certainty of the dangerousness of sin, which the Christian must fight. "In battle you must be a diligent soldier since the struggle against you is not only against the flesh and blood but also against the innermost iniquities of the soul. . . ."[119]

In the same passage he explains that the peace he is describing is achievable only on condition that sin and its dominance are resisted. This requires clarification as to who are the peaceful ones. Commenting on the psalm in which it is said that the humble will inherit the earth and enjoy the fullness of peace, Ambrose asks:

Who then are the humble, if not they who refuse to be involved by dissension, who refuse to be carried away by anger, or be exasperated by ferocity, or tempted by cruelty? This is because, fortified within, they have no taste for debauchery, nor for feasting, nor for wealth, but seek only the peace of the Lord. In exchange for material pleasures, which they believe it right to forego to achieve eternal grace, they will enjoy the fullness of peace, which our Lord Jesus conceded in his time to mankind, as the prophecy—not disproved—tells: "In its time will be born justice and peace, as long as the moon continues to rise." What is peace, thanks to which the people of all the Church has been multiplied, if not that of which the Lord said, "Peace I leave with you, my peace I give unto you" [John 14:27]? He granted peace, he who put an end to the wars of minds.[120]

Here is, indeed, a strong and effective analysis of the peaceful mission of Christ and of the content of his message. The vision of the Kingdom of God—this is also how the first Christians felt—becomes part of the work of the Savior, of his generosity and of his mercy, which man can merit only if he rejects the temptations and the flattery of the world, allowing himself to be guided by Christ's message. Peace was still that of the spirit, a willing renunciation of the passions of this world, an awareness of man's puniness, and an adjustment of his aspirations to the limits imposed by his earthly nature.

The idea of peace, the supreme objective of existence lived according to the rules set out by the Lord, might lead the believer to imagine that many benefits deriving from it—serenity and calmness in particular—were freely given and involved no effort of will or concentration. Ambrose believed the opposite to be true, in that peace, because of its moral context, was achieved through the constant overcoming of obstacles and a tireless quest. It was not quiescence, but action; not a mindless abandonment to life's vicissitudes, but determination to dominate them. Peace was not only an objective to be achieved in the ascent of the spirit toward the goals set for it: it also represented an unknown should the believer stray from the path of virtue or slacken in the ardor of his faith. Ambrose could not examine this subject without recalling the times of the great persecutions. The term *peace* then meant a truce with the imperial power, often followed by even greater and more sanguinary violence than before. "The leisures of peace are dangerous. Many persecutions originated precisely in time of peace. Moreover even such disasters served some purpose, since they strengthened the moral fiber required of the faithful, whose faith was thus constantly put to the test. In time of persecution there was no flatterer to tempt the mind with insidious adulation."[121]

This concept of peace was therefore not passive nor simply receptive. It derived from a determination to reject sin, to show oneself equal to the goals to be achieved. The result of effort and tenacity, it could not be separated from the exercise of divine virtue so different from human virtue, based on sin. "One, therefore, is the peace of God and one the peace of the world: even the evil ones and the shameless possess peace, but the peace which leads to damnation. The peace of Christ is innocent of sin. It shuns perfidy, scorns deceit, feels repugnance for evil deeds. It is pleasing to God and is friendly to Him, but the devil hates it."[122] True peace springs from the profoundly pacific nature of God. "Our God is truly a God of peace."[123]

In several passages Ambrose attempted to define the nature of peace. He found that it emanated from God and was a central objective of the behavior of the Christian wishing to live according to the teachings of the Savior.

Another interesting writer in the Latin Church in the declining years of the Western Roman Empire was Saint Paulinus of Nola (ca. 353-ca. 431), whose ascetic practices and charitable work left him time and energy enough to write poetry and letters which breathe a spirit of renunciation and missionary enthusiasms. His writings show the impetus of the mystic disturbed by the tragedies of the world, particularly those generated by war. Here his reaction is to argue that, despite everything, only meekness and the complete abandonment of the self to God can protect one from the anxieties of this world.

In Poem XXVI, dedicated to Saint Felix, his patron saint, Paulinus thought it was of no importance that the barbarians should invade the territory of the Romans, killing and plundering, provided the Christians continued to believe in the Lord and to love him, nourishing faith in the fulfillment of his message.[124] One should live in awe not of the enemy but of God, whose designs were, it is true, inscrutable, but whose grace was infinite. His advice was that man should pursue peace of mind. It was the advice of a mystic who had not given in to hardship and had enough enthusiasm to call on the faithful to love God even in adversity. It was a message of peace in the form of an invitation to nonviolence and to nonresistance to the aggressions of the strong and of the barbarians.

Jerome and Rufinus, Ambrose and Paulinus belonged to a generation of thinkers who kept the debate on the great problems of faith alive. This dialogue among some of the most enlightened minds of the time often took the form of exchanges between persons living thousands of miles apart. The controversy between Jerome and Rufinus is a case in point. Although the former was living in Palestine and the latter in Ravenna or in Rome, the quality and vitality of the debate in no way suffered on this account. Diligent friends ensured that letters and learned replies were delivered on time. From this and other exchanges, there took shape a Western theology in Latin which grew increasingly independent of Eastern sources. Single-minded conviction canceled out the distances, but it was also on a plane high above the tragic political calamities of the age, this being the time when the Western empire was slowly disintegrating because of internal crises and the barbarian invasions. Various thinkers, essayists, and letter-writers associated with this Western group were studied and respected during the Middle Ages, when they were to enjoy a fame sometimes indeed exceeding their real merits. There were a number of reasons for this: the fact that Eastern thinking became arid, the ever more marked separation of the Roman see from Constantinople, and the conquest of North Africa by the Arabs. In the cloisters of the medieval monasteries, the last bastions of a vacillating culture, their writings were to be carefully examined and commented upon. Under the impact of peculiar historical circumstances, but also of the philosophic contributions handed down by the great minds referred to here, the Latin Church was to become in the West the sole custodian of forces sympathetic to spirituality, justice, and peace, in sharp contrast with a civil power which was becoming steadily more arrogant and prone to see community life in terms of the success of the strongest.

Saint Augustine and the Just War

Born in Africa, where the seeds of Tertullian's thought had not fallen on barren ground, and educated in part among the Milanese groups gravitating around Ambrose, Saint Augustine's personality and philosophic intellect reflected both influences. The outstanding characteristics of the great doctor (354-430) were his powerfully intuitive temperament and his ability to look inward and establish a dialogue with his own soul. This was his method of analyzing problems in depth and finding the best solutions to them. Augustine's approach appealed strongly both to medieval thinkers, who found in his writings a body of propositions interpreting revelation, and thinkers nearer our own time (for example, Jansen), who were struck by his formidable gift of anticipation and by his inspired insistence on the virtues of grace. The fascination he exercised on subsequent generations was also partly due to his technique of dealing with a point by first circling round it, as it were, solving the difficulties by treating them not as being outside himself but as being intimately bound up with his own ego.

As an indication of the stature of the great bishop it would suffice to mention his theory of knowledge, which anticipated by twelve centuries the findings of Descartes. A healthy realism informed his thinking. He was concerned not only to unveil truths, but also to present a complex of rules that could be of real use to those shouldering responsibilities of government. He also rejected all useless abstraction and took fullest account of the day-to-day experiences of pastoral teaching, his aim being to refute the heresies and to instill faith into his hearers and readers, keeping alive their hope and trust in the future.

Both his early Manichaean experiences and later the Christian faith transmitted to him by Ambrose contributed to these aspects of his thought. Bearing this in mind, it is easy to understand why Augustine tackled the problem of peace, both from the theological point of view and from that of individual behavior. For the purposes of our study, the Manichaean influences require a few words of clarification.

The Persian Mani (the "Ambassador of Light," ca. 216-ca. 276) had devised a new religious experience, grafting on to the old Zoroastrian core elements derived from Christianity and Buddhism. Manichaeism won many converts, mainly in the Near and Middle East, and preached a tragic vision of existence and a cosmogony based on the contraposition of the principles of good and evil, deemed to have existed before the creation of the tangible universe. The belief that the origin of creation lies in the principle of evil, the doleful doctrine that the good life must be based on the negation of life and that the faithful must abstain from procreation—since existence is not a gift from a God of love but an evil dominated by wickedness—explain perhaps the rapid dissemination of Manichaeism in an essentially pessimistic world which, then, as now, longed for justice and peace.

Manichaean mythology contained many references to the conflict between the two principles. For this reason a hasty judgment might suggest that, like some other religions, Manichaeism was based on the cult of violence or at least on its veneration as a rule of conduct and a basis for created life. Pressing further this erroneous interpretation, it might be inferred that war and not peace, violence and not forgiveness, determined human conduct and that the creative power of evil was so imbued with obscure forces as to rob man of any hope of salvation from pain and war. But this was not the case; rather, a yearning for peace permeated the system. Through a series of closely linked mythical cause-and-effect relationships, the ideas in Manichaeism converged toward an objective of salvation and regeneration.

The fragmentary literature of the cult which has survived the persecutions shows that the problem of peace had an important place among the moral rules which Manichaeism sought to propagate. In some passages we can see that on peace depended the attainment of an objective of perfection on the part of man as a created being. The eschatology is unmistakably pacifist. It treats war as a diabolical phenomenon which revived on earth the customs and the methods of the demons: the beings who from the beginning of creation had fostered persecution and slaughter. The believer was required to refrain from war, since the killing of living beings (including animals) was forbidden. Inasmuch as the soul was nothing other than the continuation of the eternal substance of the Father, whoever struck his neighbor was guilty of aggression against God. Consequently the profession of arms was completely prohibited.[125] In the permanent strife between the principles of good and evil a merciful being, Christ, was the protagonist of a process of salvation. The cult's deep pessimism, then, was mitigated by the hope that the destiny of violence and of war could be redeemed through supernatural mediation. After so much suffering, man would eventually achieve emancipation. A doctrine of this kind was to survive for centuries, to be woven into future mystical and religious experiences. It fascinated the young Augustine, though after a time he came to react against its restrictiveness and eventually freed himself from it to arrive, after flirting with Neoplatonism, at the final goal of Christianity.

And yet the memory of the doctrine he had once espoused was to remain with him throughout his life, coloring his philosophic writing. Dualistic influences dominated his vision of the world of earthly interests, clearly separated from that of the spirit, inducing him to formulate in his *De civitate Dei* the famous thesis of an earthly city contrasted with that of heaven. "The two cities then were created by two kinds of love: the earthly city by a love of self carried even to the point of contempt for God, the heavenly city by a love of God carried even to the point of contempt for self."[126] This idea had already been aired by Paul and in Origen, but Augustine emphasized it, giving it order and making it one of the bases of his interpretation of history.

Manichaean undertones were present, not only in his vision of the universe but also in his pessimistic assessment of strength and will, seen as keystones of the earthly city: he did not claim that the heavenly kingdom should follow in chronological succession the earthly one, as the Millenarian doctrines claimed. The two worlds, precisely as in the Manichaean system, had existed from the very dawn of time. The earthly city, founded by Cain, had its expression in the state with its political power, its exigencies, its ills. The heavenly city derived from Abel and was identified with the communities of the Christians—that is, with the Church—governed by a sublime rule of charity. Between these alternatives the believer of the fifth century had to choose the road of salvation. Before him stood the empire, a prey to anarchy and exposed to aggression from outside, and a religious organization which, especially in the West, was steadily consolidating its ascendancy over the masses. Faced with this tragic dilemma, he had no choice but to accept the second and to support its beliefs. This was because the preeminent objective of the heavenly city remained the attainment of a condition of serenity and of peace, while the earthly city was torn by war, the outcome of the dominance of evil.

These ideas, oscillating between the world of spiritual values and that of earthly interests, were to flow together into Augustine's vision of peace and of its ability to determine the fate of man, his development, and his choices. Augustine's reasoning did not develop along clear lines. Besides, his output was on a formidable scale, so that a summary analysis of his thinking is no easy matter. However, it can be said that in discussing peace he made a distinction between that relating to the world of the spirit, peculiar to each individual, and earthly peace between individuals and peoples. The first was supremely necessary, for without it man—that fragile creature, a prey to pressures so much stronger than himself—could not aspire to the benefits of salvation. This was because peace was the daughter of humility, and humility alone justified the possession of the earth and of the hearts of men, who are not, despite appearances, proud and violent.[127] "The very voice of Christ, the voice of God is an invitation to peace. It says: 'if you be not in peace, love peace; what can you hope to receive from me more useful for you than peace?

What is peace? The condition from which war has been excluded. Where dissension, resistance and adversity no longer exist.'"[128] Peace must be diligently sought.[129] "But what peace? True peace, full peace, firm peace, secure peace, fraught with no disturbance, opposed by no foe. Peace itself is the object of all good desires."[130] Peace of the spirit was identical with concord within the Church, to which, again and again, Augustine called the rebellious, the sowers of discord, the heretics.[131]

In reference to the earthly world, the idea of peace assumed in Augustine's thinking a meaning closer to that which interests us here. It sometimes meant an agreement between states and renouncement of the use of arms, as emerges from Book XIX of *De civitate Dei*, which is to some extent a pacifist essay.

On 24 August 410 Rome was sacked by Alaric's Goths. The event came as a profound shock, and many saw in it the harbinger of the collapse of Roman greatness. The Goths were not only barbarians: they were also heretics. Their quarrel with Rome and its tradition was not only a matter of expansion and conquest: it was also deepened by the hate which possesses the minds of peoples divided by an unbridgeable religious gulf. It would have taken very little to persuade the pagans that the responsibility for so many disasters lay with the Christians and their disintegrating influence on what had once been the completely healthy organism of the Roman Empire. Augustine had proposed to refute these arguments by proving that the events of the world, even the most dramatic ones, must be judged in the light of the final objective of peace. But what peace was he referring to? Perhaps to the agreement between the heavenly city and the earthly one? To that between Church and state, the two institutions created and governed hierarchically, institutions in which man's desire to live in society was realized and which seemed to him to embody the features of the two cities? To the internal peace of the individual, constantly seeking a serenity in which the spirit could find solace in the contemplation of God? Or to the peace between nations, to which at some times he seemed to attribute no importance, while at others he thought it worthy of a place at the center of a complex and involved web of speculation? In Book XIX these ideas are so closely interwoven that it is not possible to say which of them prevailed.

After recalling Varro's opinions concerning the existence of the many philosophical schools attempting to solve the problem of existence on the basis of the principles contributed by each of them, Augustine, yielding to an emotional impulse rather than to the power of reason, emphasized the evils produced by war, under the impact of which all human feeling lost its warmth. All wars—even those which had accompanied the emergence of the Roman Empire—were evidence in themselves of their diabolical nature. What could be more wicked and antichristian than war, the aim of which is to cause death, destruction and suffering? All conflicts, he declared, were harmful and tragic. Of all possible wars the most fearful were not those undertaken against the enemy outside, but civil and social wars among members of the same nation.

> Let every man, then, reflect with sorrow upon all these great evils, so horrible and so cruel, and confess his misery. But if any man has no sorrow in his heart either when he suffers himself or when he imagines such suffering, his case is certainly far more miserable, for he thinks himself happy precisely because he has lost all human feeling to boot.[132]

Augustine gave a fuller and more balanced statement of the problem in Chapter 11 of Book XIX of *De civitate Dei,* where he examined the place of war in community life. Could it perhaps be regarded as the truest expression of existence, as some philosophers had asserted? Certainly not, because peace was the perfect condition of mankind. Undoubtedly there had been wars in which specific motives and objectives could be approved, for example those fought by the Romans to give unity to the Mediterranean area. But in the last analysis peace was the highest good, to which all things must lead. "For so great a good is peace that even where earthly and mortal affairs are in question no other word is heard with more pleasure, nothing else is desired with greater longing, and finally nothing better can be found."[133]

At this point came a reflection which might be thought a sophism but which has often been referred to and repeated. If peace was the ultimate end of community life, even people provoking conflicts were in fact seeking peace. Even the evildoers, who endanger the lives of all, preferred in the long run to come to terms with their companions in evildoing rather than to fight on indefinitely. This line of argument was based on the somewhat farfetched identification of peace between peoples with the internal peace of a state or of any association—for example, the family, the fundamental unit of society, or even associations of criminals. Even men having no sense of sociability, the renegades and what we should now call "dropouts," were attracted by peace. Animals, too, showed in their mutual relations some respect for the principles of humility, always associated with a desire for peace. "What tigress does not softly purr over her cubs and subdue her fierceness as she caresses them? What kite, however solitary in circling over his prey, does not join a mate, build a nest, hatch the eggs, rear the young birds and maintain with the mother of his brood as peaceful a domestic society as possible?"[134]

Once again the use of the word *peace* was somewhat vague. It indicated a condition of serenity and sociability, imagined to exist in all living beings and not only in men. Augustine reached these conclusions through the observation, against a Christian background, of the rules of nature handed down to him by pagan science. His thinking was influenced by a guiding principle of mercy, the purpose of which was to balance the position, otherwise desperate, of the individual in his relations with his neighbor. His conviction that a natural law existed made him state that true peace must be discovered in ourselves and in the beings who surround us.

To complete the picture, he made a distinction between the peace of the just and that of the wicked. He began by declaring that men cannot be compared the one with the other and concluded that even the bad man, whose conduct lies outside natural and social laws, was subject to certain rules, which included the quest for peace. The wicked man was primarily a *perversus*—the victim of a distortion of principles born of an insufficient application of them. This did not mean, however, that he need not obey them. However great the perversion of an individual, it could not be so great as to make him overthrow the natural law impelling him to seek peace.

This reasoning is joined to that of Chapter 13, where Augustine agrees that no one lacks his own peace—that is, an internal equilibrium and a communion with the forces of good which preside over the course of existence. Even unhappy and wicked men dispose of a residue of serenity, without which their lives and their work would be impossible: the loss of peace could not refer to the whole of the life of the individual, but only to a part of it. The other parts, unaffected by the change, remained in accord with the rules guiding the conduct of men. It was possible, then, to conceive of nature in a state of quietness and repose, but not to imagine a nature entirely in thrall to war, from which peace and the ability to act in a harmonious way were totally absent. All this was valid even for the demon, the most disturbed of created beings. Tranquillity in order was also a characteristic distinguishing the position of the blessed from that of the miserable. The latter lived in disorder and upheaval, by which their choices were affected; the others aligned their conduct on the god of peace. This was why the lack of peace took the form of pain.

Precisely because he gave such a detailed statement of its impact on the various aspects of the individual's life, Saint Augustine was not able to propose a valid definition of the concept of peace. His definition varied depending on whether he was referring to the one or the other component of the soul/body duality or to the individual forms of community life. This explains why he gave a list at the beginning of Chapter 13 showing how peace varies in different contexts:

> The peace of the body, therefore, is an ordered proportionment of its components; the peace of the irrational soul is an ordered repose of the appetites; the peace of the rational soul is the ordered agreement of knowledge and action. The peace of body and soul is the ordered life and health of a living creature; peace between mortal man and God is an ordered obedience in the faith under an everlasting law; peace between men is an ordered agreement of mind; domestic peace is an ordered agreement among those who dwell together concerning command and obedience; the peace of the heavenly city is a perfectly ordered and fully concordant fellowship in the enjoyment of God and in mutual enjoyment by union with God; the peace of all things is a tranquillity of order. Order is the classification of things equal and unequal that assigns to each its proper position.[135]

A fundamental point here is the certainty that the universe comprises humanity and divinity, body and spirit. Under the influence of Christian religious feeling, the soul/body duality was lit with a new light, establishing, on the one hand, a completely original link between man and creation, and, on the other, sublimating and transforming its substance. As for peace, it is seen as the catalyzing element of all individual and collective existence, of earthly existence and of heavenly existence.

Discussing, in Chapter 14, the peace of the spirit, Augustine argued that if man lacked a rational soul and if all that living meant was the appeasement of elemental appetites, his happiness would be limited to the enjoyment of pleasures and of earthly goods. But the fact that he possesses it compels him to make it the principal guide of his actions. Every effort should therefore tend to the protection of his rational capacities from all external disturbance linked with the satisfaction of his appetites. Intellectual elevation thus became the motive power of, and at the same time set the limits to, his conduct. All this, of course, could not be achieved without divine assistance and teaching, which alone could help him to keep to the road mapped out by the Creator and to avoid losing peace.

In addition to the love of God and of oneself, Augustine declared, however, that there existed a love of one's neighbor. Every believer was required to live in peace with those surrounding him, observing rules and precepts designed to make community life possible. The first aspect of this peace is its domestic form, to be obtained only through respect for a hierarchy of values which acknowledges privileges and authority for the man over his wife, children, and servants. However, he also had duties, since his power should not be the expression merely of a will to command but of a noble desire to provide for the needs of others. The family was thus seen as the cornerstone of the city, which is a wider community governed by the same principles. Upon peace in the family depends peace within the city.

Chapter 17 contains important reflections on earthly peace and heavenly peace. Augustine argued that one must bear in mind the diversity of aims between a community not imbued with faith and one which does have the faith and whose members would have their eyes always fixed on the life in the next world and its benefits. Both use the material things supplied by providence, but with different objectives, among which the enjoyment of peace prevailed: the first of the two communities was in search of an earthly peace and aimed, through the imposition of a hierarchy, at the establishment of order within the state; the second aspired for peace as communion with God.

In Chapter 18 Augustine pointed out that this converging approach to the problem of peace could provide an opportunity for the two cities to meet and work toward common goals. Although the heavenly city, expression of the world of the spirit, was concerned with the solution of problems that had nothing in common with the earthly life, although its glorious center was not on or of this earth, contacts with the earthly city, with all its problems and unknown difficulties, must be sought. The need for contacts was the reason for the link between the two worlds. How, then, was the problem of human happiness seen, given that happiness coincided with the condition of peace? Where did such happiness lie? Happiness could not be based on a precarious alliance between the two worlds. Man must therefore choose, remembering that the only true happiness was that relating to the heavenly city, where earthly realities melted into the vision of eternal truth and all things fitted into God's design. With regard to peace, an analogy could be drawn with the citizenship of the two cities. The heavenly citizenship must constitute the final objective of all believers, the earthly one the means of attaining it: earthly peace might seem of greater importance if one's eyes were on this life and the things of the physical world. But how quickly it vanished into nothingness if it was compared with the peace reigning in the heavenly city! The heavenly peace was indispensable to salvation, while the earthly one was identified, on the one hand, with a principle of hierarchical organization and, on the other, with a rule of conduct applying to men in their mutual relations.

Here Augustine was adapting to the problem of peace the old image of mankind permanently disturbed by strife and unable to reach forms of understanding and cooperation. It is as if the journey, the stages of which have been described in the preceding chapters of Book XIX, had been completed in the triumph of the heavenly city with its various attributes—the most important of all being peace—over the earthly city, incapable of rising above empirical reality.

Divine peace was thus the final objective of every journey toward saintliness. Chapter 20 of Book XIX is firm on this point.

> Since, therefore, the supreme good of the city of God is everlasting and perfect peace, not the peace through which men pass as mortals, by being born and by dying, but that in which they continue as immortals, wherein is no contrariety at all, who can deny that this is the most blessed life, or that in comparison with it the present life, however great may be the goods of soul and body and external things with which it is replete, is most wretched.[136]

Consequently, life in this world was lowered in status, since everything important had its place in the heavenly life. The tortuous dialectical road followed by Augustine, twisting and turning in previous chapters through many digressions, thus reached pessimistic conclusions, from which the earthly world emerged as an instrument, able to lead to God if the believer wished it, but which could not procure lasting benefits for man on this earth.

From this reasoning Augustine derived a practical rule of conduct. How must the individual behave in his relations with the two cities? If happiness coincided with the peace of the heavenly city, the empirical world must be used, not as an end in itself, but as a means toward the attainment of holiness. Augustine's thinking, having concluded by reducing the status of the earthly city, seemed to reawaken in a new vision and new dimension, destined to fix not a hierarchy of values and precedences but a pattern of behavior such as would benefit the individual. Whoever bent his desires toward earthly happiness alone was bound to be disappointed since he would not find what he sought. But if man hoped to rise to God and to his peace, this was enough to ensure lasting joy. If the individual succeeded in freeing himself from the ephemeral constraints formed by the world of empirical interests, he would achieve holiness, otherwise not attainable on this earth, where wisdom was most conspicuous by its absence. Everything was solved in a transcendent dimension through which the believer would succeed in obtaining the peace of the spirit, which was all that mattered.

In the same Book XIX Augustine paused to examine the problem of peace between groups of men. He began with an attempt to define the main features of the state in general, affirming that these were valid not only for the Roman state but for all the institutions which constituted associations among human beings sharing the ability to reason. Peace between states must be sustained and defended because it favored peoples and rulers, including the non-Christians. This led him to state clearly the problem of the participation of the believer in the life of the state, including pagan political institutions (Chapter 26). Man could not ignore the historical context in which he lived, precisely because of the problem of peace. Attainable in its perfect entirety only in the heavenly city, peace remained, nonetheless, always a central objective of the earthly city. This led to the idea of a peace between states, enabling mortals to prosper and attain a condition of harmony with their neighbors, even with pagans. And to support his argument, Augustine cites the prophet Jeremiah's appeal to the Jews, God's chosen people, to submit to the Babylonians and pray for peace.[137]

In Chapter 27 there is a return to attitudes similar to those which had guided the writer in the early part of his long discourse on peace, on its effects on the life of the individual, and in the field of metaphysics and ethics. Peace was indispensable if a place was to be found in the created world for that justice without which it was useless even to hope for salvation. After a brief discussion of the relationship between nations, peace was once again considered as a condition of the spirit, which of its own merit would escape external disturbances and internal dissidence. Here we are shown a state of felicity, remote from short-lived disputes, not only because strife is not permissible—nor for that matter possible—in the spheres of the spirit, but above all because human nature yearns to conquer a peace understood in these terms. Though corrupt, human nature would never be so corrupt as to invert its essential characteristics. Book XIX of *De civitate Dei* ends by predicting the day when the work of redemption will enable man to end the exhausting earthly journey upon reaching the supernatural peace identified with the vision and the possession of God.

In this long discourse, arguments of varying kinds, drawn from classical tradition, alternate with quotations from the Scriptures and all sorts of digression. All this is set in a concentric pattern turning around the subject of inquiry, examining it from every possible angle without exhausting it. The work is a mosaic which must be seen as a whole. In Book XIX a motley variety of assertions follow one another with bewildering succession, and we should seek in vain anything that, in the judgment of modern men, we could call a Christian doctrine of peace, or even a critical assessment of the problem.

Nevertheless Book XIX shows that peace is an objective common to the heavenly and the earthly city, that all men—even the perverted—tend naturally toward it, but that, in the last analysis, it remains only an aspiration. Augustine concludes, consistent with his premises, by acknowledging that peace is a utopia and that men will always have recourse to arms in the end.

Book XIX of the *De civitate Dei* is not the only discourse containing Augustine's ideas on peace and spelling out the criteria for achieving heavenly citizenship. In Book IV he dealt with the same subject, using, however, less grandiose themes. Turning to the question of individual interests, he examined the case of an individual forced to choose between a state of poverty sustained in tranquillity of mind, and a condition of wealth accompanied by internal instability and by the threat of dangers. Every man of judgment would prefer, in his opinion, the former. At this point, however, he extended the reasoning to political societies, since what is true for two men is also true for "two families, two peoples, two kingdoms."[138] The same criterion held good for the spiritual activity of the individual.[139] In compliance with the Christian message, man must maintain peace, not only with himself, but also with his neighbor.

This doctrine contradicted everything the imperial state had consistently supported both before and after its conversion to Christianity. In the religious thinking of Augustine the *pax romana* was not a factor of cohesion and unity, but a reason for deviation from the mystical road which man must follow to realize his destiny. The internal peace of the individual, as a stimulus to a process of improvement, found in a universalist state an almost insuperable obstacle liable to extinguish every other impulse.[140] This led him to the conclusion that peace could have been achieved in a world separated into several states, provided that their behavior was informed with a spirit of charity. "And so if justice is left out, what are kingdoms except great robber lands?"[141] Augustine asked, recalling the famous story of the pirate who had told Alexander the Great to his face that, from the moral point of view, the behavior of the two differed only in the scale of its consequences: both attacked the foe, Alexander for the profit of the state, the pirate for private interest. The reasoning concluded in praise of the benefits of peace, the supreme aspiration of man, but Augustine does not come out, as one might have expected, in favor of an absolute condemnation of war. Later, somewhat inconsistently, he shows leanings toward fatalism, which, incidentally, is by no means unusual in his work. Returning to the idea that without the Roman Empire mankind would have remained divided into small kingdoms unlikely to survive long and that the expansionist urge of the empire had been provoked by the injustice of its foes, he says: "Hence waging war and extending their dominion over conquered nations is in the eyes of the wicked a gift of fortune, but in the eyes of the good it is a necessary evil."[142]

The *De civitate Dei* includes various themes also dealt with in other writings like the *Contra Faustum* and the *Letter CXXXVII to Volusian*[143] in which Augustine endeavors to prove the legitimacy of conflicts. The reader senses Augustine's conviction that fate is irresistible. "Who can really say whether, in time of peace, it is a good or evil thing to reign or to serve, or to rest or die, or in time of war, to command or fight, to vanquish or get killed?"[144] War is an instrument used by the Lord to interfere in human affairs. Sovereigns and peoples were victors or vanquished according to the will of God. Not all wars were ordered by God, but they were at least authorized by him and were always part of his design, on the principle that "all power derives from God, Who sometimes commands and sometimes allows."[145]

Since everything in the earthly city combined to render the advent of peace impossible, given the baseness of the human condition, and since it was absurd to think that peace could prevail, though it remained the highest aspiration of man, war became a thing of necessity, which no one could escape. Despite the time that had elapsed since the preaching of Jesus and the change in official attitudes to the new religion, the controversy between supporters and opponents of Christianity as a message of peace had not yet died down. The intransigent interpretation still had a wide following in Africa and resolute supporters in a number of heresies, particularly among the Pelagians and the Donatists. These views were the cause of some scandal among the pagans, who were still numerous and all too ready to saddle the Christians with responsibility for the disasters that had befallen the empire. They felt that its conversion had let in the barbarians, who had been contained and repelled in the old days when it was the custom to sacrifice to the "true" gods and to persecute Christian "superstition." These criticisms, already made by Celsus, had lost much of their effect with regard to the faithful. They were now full members of the imperial system, many were in the army, and conscientious objection was not allowed. It was precisely the theory that pacifist Christianity had weakened the empire which led Augustine to develop his doctrine concerning the just war.

This is what happened. In 412 Volusian, formerly proconsul in Africa and a cultured official, began to speak publicly of the irreconcilability of public interests and the Christian faith. He declared himself dissatisfied with the way affairs of state were being handled, thus giving voice to the discontent spreading among the pagans, which was also being felt among the Christians. Speaking at Carthage among friends, he had declared his ideas, arguing that "the preaching and the doctrine of Christ cannot be reconciled with the exigencies of the state: this is so because of the [Christian] principle that evil should not be repaid with evil, but that he who is struck should turn the other cheek, and that we should give our cloak to the man who asks only for our tunic and should go twice as far as we would otherwise do for those who heap insults on our heads." All this he found in conflict with the customs of the state. "Who would allow the enemy to carry away his goods? On the news of the sacking of a Roman province, who would not wish to repay injury with injury, according to the law of war?"[146]

News of these discourses, sent to him by the tribune and notary Marcellinus, led Augustine to elaborate a Christian doctrine of war related to the political situation of the empire in the fifth century. Compelled to define the responsibilities of the Christian, Augustine denied—here contradicting previous attitudes—any incompatibility between the Christian faith and the interests of the state.[147]

The moral and political values on which religion was based were therefore the same as those which guided the most enlightened governors of the Roman state. Thus, he admitted the existence of a link—ensured by providence—between the work of the pagan builders of the empire and Christian principles. This served as a springboard for a further leap in his thinking: the conclusion that the Gospels were not to be interpreted literally and that the Gospel admonitions to the faithful to renounce violence really meant that the good Christian should work for the moral improvement of the individual and were not prohibitions on the use of force in case of need. Moreover, the use of force was necessary if the objective to be achieved was useful for the community as a whole.

In another discourse, dating from 398, the *Contra Faustum,* Augustine had also justified wars by invoking the authority of the Bible. Here he was fighting a Manichaean writer who denied that the Old Testament was the revealed word of God and pointed out that it was full of wars, citing in particular those fought by Moses, To praise a crime was, in Faustus' eyes, evidence of falseness and proved that there was no supernatural inspiration. Reversing the terms of the problem and taking for granted that the Bible, being of divine origin, could not err, Augustine argued that the conflicts were lawful, since they had been tolerated by God. It could therefore not be a sin to take part in wars. But God authorized them only if they were just.

Through various threads of thought Augustine develops the main points of a doctrine of war which forms the counterpart of the doctrine of peace set out in his *De civitate Dei.* They are roughly as follows: (1) War derives from

God, who uses it to guide and direct the actions of man and as a means of coercion and punishment: "every victory, even when won by wicked men, humbles the vanquished through a divine judgment, correcting or punishing their sins."[148] (2) Providence therefore controls wars, as those who escaped from the sack of Rome had certainly realized, and they should avoid attributing responsibility for their disasters to Christ, who is in fact responsible for their— perhaps undeserved—escape. (3) Providence controls the length of wars according to its inscrutable designs and always as part of a plan of intervention in human affairs.[149] (4) The passages of the New Testament which seem to condemn war are to be interpreted allegorically and not literally.[150] (5) Although to kill a man for private reasons is a grave fault, to kill one's own enemy in war is a meritorious deed, especially when the person who decides this is not a general, but the Creator.[151] (6) Military service is not only allowed for the Christian but is actually a duty. The best of armies would probably be made up only of Christians: "Do not imagine that you cannot be pleasing to God because you bear arms."[152] (7) If the Gospels had intended to condemn war, they would have made this intention clear, ordering the faithful to cast down their arms. But such an order is nowhere spelt out in clear and unambiguous terms. By authorizing soldiers to draw their pay, they were permitted to embrace the military life. If there was a prohibition, this concerned behavior in war, which must be guided by the natural law: "What is the reproach against war? That it brings death to those who must die anyway, so that the victors shall themselves be vanquished by peace? Objections of this kind would be typically those of mean men, not of virtuous ones. But the desire to hurt, the cruelty of revenge, the violence of uncontrolled rage, the fury of revolt, the desire for dominion and other similar phenomena, this is the objection—and a sound one—to war."[153] (8) The ultimate objective of war is always peace: "You ought to have peace as the object of your choice and war only as the result of necessity, so that God may deliver you from the necessity and preserve you in peace."[154]

Augustine did not propose, then, to condemn war but saw in it a manifestation of the will of God, who alone had power to authorize an otherwise execrable type of behavior. This rule applied not only to the conflicts which had broken out since Christ but also to those previously fought by pagans. In the hierarchy of legitimacy, the top of the list were the wars ordered by God, then those undertaken by the good against the wicked in defense of moral values, then punitive wars imposed by God and by civil authority to avenge insults, overcome rebellions, and exercise the powers inherent in sovereignty.

Augustine's thinking can therefore be summarized as follows. The happiness of man is found in a spiritual peace, free from strife and pointless rivalries, which are the bane of the earthly city. Some degree of happiness is, however, achievable in this world, where it too takes the form of a desire for concord and a search for serenity. War, the negation of peace, is part of the nature of man, who is in no way required to resist it but is in fact entitled to prepare the war and take part in it. All this, of course, provided that it is a just war and is therefore desired or at least tolerated by God.

Augustine thus rejected the pacifist attitudes assumed, for example, by the Pelagians, for whom mankind had once in very remote times lived in a state of peace, which would come again. Peace was not for him the echo and the memory of past realities, but the help and the promise of a future condition. Rejecting the view that the individual could isolate himself by retreating into indifference, this being a sufficient guarantee of salvation, he stated the problem of community life, and therefore of war, in terms of choices to be made in compliance with the principle of justice and legitimacy.

These ideas raised two perplexing problems: that of showing the faithful a road to salvation, to enable them to escape unharmed the vicissitudes of the times, using the teaching and the message of Christ, and that of acknowledging—rather than ignoring, like the Donatists and the Pelagians—the realities and the exigencies of this world. The inconsistencies in Augustine's thinking are partly explained by the two aims underlying his judgment of the historical function of the empire, seen, on the one hand, as the fruit of an immense larceny and, on the other, as the result of certain virtues of constancy and tenacity which the Christians should imitate. In formulating the first opinion, Augustine was guided by a conviction that war is the greatest obstacle to the coming of the Kingdom of God; in expressing the second, he was endorsing the doctrine that it may be right to wage war.

Medieval theologians and church lawyers found nothing baffling in this, for they saw the fundamental virtues of Augustine's doctrine in the firm logical structure of the arguments and in the conviction, passionately defended, of a justice to come which would put an end to the wickedness of the earthly city. The expectation of salvation in his writings took its place, for them, alongside the implicit advice to accept the earthly world with its evils, apparently incurable, and its enormous weaknesses: man must keep his eyes firmly fixed on divine goodness, which would bring a remedy to all errors, including, of course, war.

Peace in Pelagian Doctrine

Saint Augustine's complex personality, the range of his thought, and the inflexible impetuosity of his dialectic emerged in a famous controversy which is of interest for our inquiry and, in a certain sense, concludes it. We refer to the Pelagian dispute, which had such an immense impact on the Christian world of the fifth century.

The British (perhaps Irish or Welsh) monk Pelagius (ca. 360-ca. 420) had challenged Christianity in a body of doctrine conflicting with official orthodoxy, of which Augustine was the leading champion and fierce protector. Orthodox Catholics attached fundamental importance to the washing away of original sin. For this purification to take place, however, it was necessary to acknowledge the existence of a sin to be purged and to insist on the possibility of a redemption conceded to man by his Creator through the grace imparted by baptism. Pelagius and his followers saw baptism as an act of initiation into Christian life and not as a purification of the sin of Adam, who had stained only himself and not mankind. Children were born pure. The great thinkers of classical antiquity had remained incorrupt despite their ignorance of revelation. The salvation of the individual depended rather on his works. Pelagius insisted on the need to act in accordance with the Gospel message, but freely and individually, each man discovering in his innermost being the impulse to do good and avoid evil.

Given that human actions derived from the full autonomy and conscience of the individual, the individual must be the sole guide responsible for himself and was emancipated from that divine "prescription" argued for by Augustine in *De libero arbitrio*, which in practice was not appreciably different from what we now call predestination. By asserting that human actions are free, Pelagius was lowering the status of divine grace—considered no longer essential to man to do good—and indeed the significance of the Passion and death of Christ. A doctrine of the kind challenged a number of basic principles of orthodox teaching, as was to emerge clearly from the propaganda of Pelagius and his disciples, especially Coelestius, the Roman lawyer who became a follower and then the enthusiastic propagator of the rational implications of Pelagius' arguments.

But the will of the individual was strengthened and enhanced by this vision of the personality of man and of his place in the world. He freed himself from the harmful effects of original sin, but equally from that right of mediation of which the Church has always been so jealous. Liberation from the burdens of Adam's sin was achieved through the will and the initiative of man and not by virtue of any special divine predilection. The pessimism inherent in Augustine's doctrine was rejected in favor of a more optimistic approach, for Pelagius believed that it was possible for the individual to decide his own destiny, which was thus no longer overshadowed by fatalism of any kind.

In the times of Pelagius and Augustine, the problem of sin presented the following dilemma: either it was believed inevitable, so that the sinner, made aware of the state of ignominy into which he had fallen, had no choice but to yield himself to his Savior in the hope of obtaining forgiveness; or men imagined that it was possible for them to overcome the secret lure of evil behavior, provided they were assisted by divine grace. Pelagius accepted neither of the two hypotheses. On the one hand, he refused to accept the inevitability of sin, fatalistically—but not very objectively—asserted by the sinners of all times. On the other hand, he did not share Augustine's view that man lies in a state of impotence until baptism washes away original sin and the grace of God enables him to do good.[155] In Augustine's doctrine there were two forms of incapacity: one of general scope, to be eliminated through baptism, and another, specific to the individual, which only grace could remove. In keeping with his premises, Pelagius argued that man's faculty to do good, to escape the snares of sin and to reorder the means of his own salvation lay not in the performance of certain acts or in the enjoyment of certain favors, due to circumstances independent of individual choice, but in actions determined by his will, in free choices based on the conscious intention to keep to the road of virtue. His doctrine thus implied a commitment and a way of life, the two to be seen as a whole.

There was not much room left for the mediation of the Church. A doctrine of this kind ended by seeing certain fundamental truths as mere symbols, as aspects of a final perfection. This would reward the efforts of men, but they must strive toward it in full freedom, relying on themselves and on their inner capacity for regeneration. Ecclesiastical vows were accorded little importance: priesthood was a special gift of the Lord but did not imply an exclusive right to exercise the mission of teaching and guiding. Anyone who was capable of accomplishing this mission was, by the same token, entitled to do so. Arguments of the kind could not have been welcome to the ecclesiastical hierarchy, for it adopted a style and a line of conduct hard to reconcile with Gospel precepts. The laity was the object, not the subject of pastoral work. The conflict between Pelagius and Augustine, faced with so bold a definition of the nature of sin, took a very violent form, reflecting the irrepressible energy of the African bishop and the reasoning gifts of the British monk. After a number of initial successes achieved by Pelagius, who was able to persuade Pope Zosimus to concede the orthodoxy of his doctrine, victory was to go to Augustine, whose aggressive dialectic, generally supported by official theology and by the authority of the state, had a vigor and impetus which were not easy to resist.

It would be a pity to neglect the place in Pelagius' theology given over to the preaching of poverty and the need to revert to the austere life of the beginnings of Christianity. For the master and his disciples the Gospel teaching in regard to this was not a formal superstructure but a definite order complying with the will of God and the needs of society. One could not serve God and Mammon at the same time. Wealth brought spiritual ills, became an instrument of damnation and an obstacle to admission to the kingdom of heaven. Renouncement of riches must be total and final, since not even the use of wealth for ends reconcilable with the Gospels could suffice to ensure the salvation of the rich man.

Property ownership was also the source of the harmful discord which led men to stray from the path of virtue. "This is how they behave, how they argue, how they quarrel, those who have more time for their earthly possessions than for executing the orders of Christ, and who love money more than the glory of the Kingdom."[156] Speaking of wealth, Pelagius pointed out how

wrong it was to regard the possession of riches as evidence of divine predilection. What mattered was how the wealth had been acquired. If this had been
done by impoverishing others, it could in no circumstances be considered of
divine origin: it would then, in fact, be an instrument of perdition and in-
famy.[157] He was even less convinced by those who argued that the rich were
well placed to succor the homeless and those in need. This was another point
on which Augustinian orthodoxy—and, following it, the majority of the
Church—differed from Pelagius.

In a work of moral edification written on the occasion of a young novice's
taking the veil, Pelagius declared, as always, that we must rely on deeds and
on will to free ourselves from sin.[158] However, he did not rule out the possibility that the defenses set up by God for our salvation—principally our capacity to reason—could prove to be the expression of grace, although in his system the status of divine grace remained subordinate—or at any rate lower than
that accorded it by Augustine's pessimism.

By attributing to man a subjective vitality which could defend him from
the harmful effects of sin, Pelagius recognized man as a protagonist not only
in the life of the spirit and in individual behavior but also in community life,
to which many fathers had given insufficient attention. The little Pelagian
literature that has come down to us confirms that the master actually decided
to oppose certain compromises used by the Church hierarchy in order to ensure victory in its theological battles. He himself was to be its first victim—
first when he was condemned by the Emperor Honorius, at the instance of a
group of African bishops who managed to make their views prevail at the
court of Ravenna, and later when his condemnation was confirmed by Pope
Zosimus, although Zosimus had originally pronounced Pelagius' beliefs orthodox.

It was no easy matter to speak out against war at a time when the Western
Empire was fighting its last rearguard action against barbarian invaders who
were preparing to bring to a close a great spiritual and cultural era. Nor was it
possible—especially for those involved in theological and moral controversies
of such profound implications—to defend arguments which the opponent
would most certainly report to the imperial authorities as not only religious
aberrations but also incitements to rebellion. Forced underground after the
condemnation of 418, neither Pelagius, nor his disciple Coelestius, nor their
followers in various parts of the two Roman Empires could afford to provide
fresh ammunition for their opponents. It was not feasible for them to advocate a theory of international relations favoring the maintenance of peace
with the entire world and abandonment of the policy of aggression and conquest. This policy had become little more than a memory in a society which,
so far from embarking on aggressive campaigns, was reduced to defending itself from the pressure of the barbarians.

Pelagius, like Coelestius and so many others, had been compelled to flee from Rome before the Goths of Alaric, who put the Eternal City to fire and the sword in 410, spreading hunger and poverty among its inhabitants, but above all mortally wounding the dignity and pride of Roman citizens wherever they lived. In addition, the view (to which Augustine had made a reply in the *Letter LXXXVIII to Marcellinus*) that the virtues propagated by Christianity had undermined the empire's capacity to resist was too widespread. It would have been unthinkable to adopt a standpoint on this problem which seemed to have lost much of its importance at a time when the most urgent task was to stop the enemy.

Yet, there were people, especially in Africa, for whom the *pax romana* remained an embarrassing inheritance, a constant reminder of Roman ferocity in the past. In proconsular Africa and in so many other regions, the Romans had, it is true, endeavored to Romanize culture, the economy, and spiritual and administrative life. But they had not destroyed the seeds of national life. The local cultures were in a state of hibernation, ready at any time to emerge once again should the opportunity arise and should the oppressive efficiency of the occupation grow weak.

Six centuries after the fall of Carthage to Roman troops, there were still large sections of the Punic population who spoke no Latin and saw the Romans as foreigners in their society. The dangerous state of mind which lay hidden under the veil of administrative officialdom, only in appearance pacified, was to explode in the revolt of the Circumcellions. These were unemployed laborers and peasants speaking only Punic. They were Donatists, who looked forward to Christianity's return to the purity of its origins and the banishment of those whom they accused of ignoring the message of Christ as spelt out in the Gospels. In the name of their anarchic faith, they attacked and laid waste the homes of the landed proprietors, mainly rich Roman citizens. It was this protest mentality, not yet inured to Roman dominion, which facilitated the conquest of Africa by the Vandals. The Punic population felt closer to the barbarians than to the Roman occupiers.

There now prevailed in Roman Africa—and in other parts of the empire as well—a tendency to confuse the Roman world with orthodox Christianity and to regard both as differing facets of the same reality. The local governing class had no clear idea of the mainsprings of imperial power and could not see that the sack of Rome in 410 had foreshadowed the coming collapse of imperial grandeur. Proof of this is a letter from Augustine to an Illyrian bishop who felt that the prophecies concerning the end of the world were about to be realized, since the Gospels had been preached in every part of it. Augustine replied: "Here in Africa there are many barbarian tribes among whom the Gospel has not yet been preached. We have daily confirmation of those from the prisoners we capture. Some of them, living near the Roman confines, are beginning to know Christianity, as the Empire gradually replaces their leaders with its prefects."

A strange reply, in all truth, but real evidence of the lack of information concerning the progress of affairs among the outlying communities of the Roman state. Nonetheless, these communities, notably the African ones, showed much fighting spirit in the religious controversies. Augustine's reply was made only a few years before the Roman hegemony in North Africa was shattered by Genseric and the Vandals. The city of Hippo, made famous by its illustrious bishop, fell to the Vandals after fourteen months of siege. And yet, so soon before the fall of his city and the whole of Africa—events which were by no means difficult to predict—the great theologian could still express, in terms so remote from reality, his belief that the Roman dominion was still firmly rooted and even in a position to expand beyond its current confines.[159]

Various factors influenced Pelagius, then. Some tended to restrain him from adopting any position at all with regard to war. Others encouraged him, as a master of ethics, to seek to guide the Christian in this respect. No explicit and direct statement of view has come down to us. Too deeply involved in the exhausting controversy on the status of the will of man and divine grace in the process of salvation, compelled to defend himself against obstinate and aggressive opponents, Pelagius preferred to keep silent on a problem which would have opened a breach in his already difficult defensive position. And yet, the longing for peace is inherent in every line he wrote. His desire to draw man away not only from the fearful burdens of sin but also from the tremendous collective folly which is the most salient of all the world's defects is unmistakable. When he inveighs against wrath and its harmful consequences, against man's inability to settle his quarrels and to find common ground, he is expressing first and foremost a desire to restore the rules of peace which had informed the early Christians and their innocent, but firm and incorruptible, faith in the virtues of meekness, brotherhood, and concord. How could the words full of modesty which are found in every passage of this author be reconciled with the morality peculiar to men of arms? In his thinking, the elimination of violence becomes a specific moral imperative which is bound to prevail in the struggle against the other sins. And no sin is more harmful in its consequences than the failure to dominate wrath.

> We abstain from eating meat, but not from vindictive remarks; we take no wine, but get drunk on anger; we find it easier to eat less than our fill than to hate less than wholeheartedly. We are humble in our speech, in our gestures, in our dress, but we nourish in our bosoms a pride greater than that of kings. Nowhere will you find sincere humility, innocence, piety, pure and unadulterated simplicity. . . . From all sides comes news of war, strife, discord, quarrels, animosity, and hostility. Nowhere is there room for the alliance of true peace and the firm foundation of the pact of love.[160]

The significance of this message—closely linked with the praise of rationality and of the will of the individual, and opposed to Augustinian fatalism and its implications—was not confined to the intimate life of man nor to his relations with other individuals. It certainly applied to all the manifestations of human life, to all social phenomena, necessarily including war.

Beyond all argumentation and opinions concerning the organization and pattern of war, we find, summarizing all other truths, Pelagius' conviction, shared by the Christians of the apostolic period, that love among men is the vital factor in their relations. This was the view to which Augustine, utterly convinced of the majestic and transcendental immensity of God, gave little attention. Love, in Pelagius' view, was to be distributed justly and equally among men, discipline their relations with one another, govern their choices in all circumstances of life, induce them to opt for concord and understanding.

Much less was heard of the arguments reflected in Pelagian doctrine after the condemnation of the master and the banishment of his followers. Were it not for this, it is likely that they would have borne fruit in subsequent Christian philosophy and that, in consequence, meekness, humility, and peaceful understanding would have weighed more heavily with Christians down the ages. For the world of that time—no less than that of today and indeed of all times—was ready to welcome a message of love that could mobilize the extraordinary resources of courage and determination that all too often must remain dormant in the soul of man.

NOTES

NOTES TO INTRODUCTION

1. Carl von Clausewitz, *Vom Kriege, 1832-1834*, chapter 1 (the nature of war), nn. 1-6.

2. I use the expression "universal peace" to refer to a condition of society in which the **causes** and the risks of war between States would be eliminated. This would be done by efficient institutional machinery enabling international disputes to be settled through arbitration or other peaceful means.

The expression *pacifist* refers to a person who, being convinced of the possibility of achieving this objective, devotes his energies in one way or another to this cause. The idea guiding him is *pacifism*. The term seems to have been used for the first time in political language in the newspaper *Les Etats-Unis d' Europe*, published from 1867 to 1870 under the editorship of Emile Arnaud.

3. Bertrand Russell, *War, the Offspring of Fear* (London, 1915). *The Philosophy of Pacifism* (London, 1915).

4. *Principles of Political Economy with Some of Their Applications to Social Philosophy* (1848).

5. *Allgemeines Staatsrecht* (1852). *Die Bedeutung und die Fortschritte des modernen Völkerrechts* (1886).

6. *Essai sur l'inégalité des races humaines*, 4 vols. (Paris, 1853-1855).

7. Matt. 24:6-7; Mark 13:7-8; Luke 21:9-10.

8. *Soirées de Saint Pétersbourg* (1821).

NOTES TO CHAPTER 1
Idea of Peace in Greek Civilization

1. *History of the Peloponnesian War*, II, 37.

2. *Iliad*, bk. VI, lines 37-60.

3. *Odyssey*, bk. XXIV, lines 433-434.

4. *Iliad*, XIII, 636-639.

5. Ibid., VII, 350-353.

6. Ibid., IX, 632-636.

7. Ibid., II, 225-242.

8. Ibid., XI, 514-515.

9. *Odyssey*, VI, 180-185.

10. Ibid., XXII, 412.

11. *Iliad*, V, 889-891.

12. Ibid., III, 250-311; VII, 375-378, and IV, 86-222.

13. *Odyssey*, XXIV, 485-486.

14. *Iliad*, XI, 138-142, and VI, 215-231, and *Odyssey*, XV, 196-197.

15. *Odyssey*, XIX, 328-331.

16. Ibid., XI, 486-491.

17. *The Shield of Heracles*, lines 270-313.

18. *Works and Days*, lines 112-113.

19. Ibid., 185-193.

20. Ibid., 225-229.

21. Ibid., 213-217, 274-280.

22. Ibid., 11-26.

23. Ibid., 297-319.

24. *Theogony*, lines 901-903, 922-937.

25. Ibid., 226-232.

26. This and another fragment by Alcidamas are preserved in an essay entitled: *Contest between Homer and Hesiod*, written by a second-century grammarian.

27. Karl Brugmann, EIPHNH, *Eine sprachgeschichtliche Untersuchung* (Leipzig, 1916), p. 23. Paul Kretschmer, *Literaturbericht für das Jahr 1916*, in *Glotta*, vol. X (Göttingen, 1920). Bruno Keil, EIPHNH, *Eine Philologisch-antiquarische Untersuchung* (Leipzig, 1916), p. 90.

28. *Inscriptiones Graecae*, II[1], 34; 5, 14, 18, 35; 3, 10, 15, 103, 24 (Berolini, 1913).

29. *Works and Days*, 230-237.

30. *Politics*, II, 2.

31. *The Republic*, V, 471a.

32. Hesiod, *Works and Days*, line 653; Archilocus, fragment 54.

33. A. Raeder, *L'Arbitrage international chez les Hellènes* (Kristiania, 1912).

34. *History of the Persian Wars*, I, 170.

35. *De vita pythagorica*, 36, 267.

36. Ibid., 9.

37. Ibid., 7.

38. Mythical personification of tumult and uproar produced by armed conflict.

39. *The Purifications*, fragment 128.

40. Ibid., fragment 130.

41. Ibid., fragment 135.

42. Ibid., fragments 136 and 137.

43. Romain Rolland has thrown interesting light on the pacifist leanings of this philosopher in his *Empédocle d'Agrigente* (Geneva, 1917).

44. Fragment B 247.

45. Fragment B 251.

46. Fragment B 237.

47. Fragment B 44.

48. *Rhetoric,* III, III, 4.

49. *History of the Peloponnesian War,* III, 82.

50. *Protagoras,* 320c.

51. *Lives of the Sophists,* IX, 493.

52. *The Republic,* I, 344c.

53. Hermann Diels, *Die Fragmente der Vorsokratiker,* 6th ed., II (Berlin, 1952), 403, *Anonymus Jamblichi,* 89/7: lines 32-35.

54. *Memorabili,* II, III, 14; II, VI, 35.

55. *Apology,* 28 et seq.

56. *The Republic,* I, 334b, et seq.

57. *Tusculanae disputationes,* V, XXXVII, 108.

58. *Memorabili,* IV, IV, 15-16.

59. Ibid., III, II, et seq.

60. Ibid., I, II, 10-11.

61. *Lives of the Famous Philosophers,* VI, 63.

62. Ibid., 72.

63. *Protagoras,* 322b.

64. *The Republic,* I, 351c-352a; *Alcibiades,* I, 109, 112.

65. For an analysis of the Platonic theory of love, see Alfred Fouilée, *La philosophie de Platone* (Paris, 1889), IV, 108-124.

66. *The Republic,* V, 468c.

67. Ibid., VI, 484a, et seq.

68. *Protagoras,* 359e.

69. *The Republic,* II, 373a.

70. *Phaedo,* 66c.

71. *The Laws,* **VII, 803d**; see also I, 628c.

72. Ibid., III, 689d and 696b-e.

73. Ibid., 693b; 701d.

74. *The Republic,* V, 467c, et seq.

75. *The Laws,* VII, 813e-814a; VIII, 829a.

76. Ibid., III, 677a, et seq; IV, 713, et seq.

77. Ibid., I, 626a.

78. *The Republic,* VII, 514a-519a.

79. Ibid., V, 470b, et seq.

80. *Gorgias,* 469c, 470d, 471d.

81. *The Laws,* I, 628; VII, 803d.

82. Ibid., VIII, 829a.

83. *Politics,* VII, II, 10.

84. Ibid., I, III, 8.

85. Ibid., VI, XIII, 8 and 9.

86. *Nicomachean Ethics,* X, VII, 1177b, 6.

87. *Politics,* VII, II, 8.

88. Ibid., VII, XIII, 15.

89. Ibid., II, VI, 22-23.

90. *Rhetorica ad Alexandrum,* II, 1425, 27.

91. *Poetics,* IX, 1-3.

92. Fragment 1.

93. The third century historian Philochorus reports that the Spartan soldiers recited the poetry of Tyrtaeus during battle. *Fragmenta historicorum graecorum*, vol. I (Paris, 1841), Philocorus fragment 56.

94. Fragment 10.

95. Xenophanes, *Elegy* no. 1.

96. Solon, *Elegy* no. 4.

97. *Elegies*, bk. I, lines 885-886.

98. Ibid., lines 889-890.

99. Ibid., lines 1013-1016.

100. Fragment 101.

101. Fragment 94.

102. Fragment 4.

103. Fragment 110.

104. Fragment 109.

105. *Pythian Ode VIII*, line 1.

106. *Pythian Ode X*, line 42 et seq.

107. *Olympian Ode XIII*, line 6 et seq.

108. *Paeans*, XIII, 46.

109. *Medea*, lines 190-196.

110. *Agamemnon*, lines 63-65.

111. *The Persians*, lines 61-64, 532-547.

112. *Agamemnon*, lines 859-865.

113. Ibid., 437-455.

114. *Seven against Thebes*, lines 321-368.

115. *The Persians*, lines 103-105, 349.

116. *The Suppliant Maidens*, lines 661-665.

117. *Eumenides*, lines 858-869.

118. *Philoctetes*, lines 435-436.

119. *Ajax*, lines 1185-1210.

120. *The Women of Trachis*, lines 298-302.

121. *The Suppliants*, lines 744-749.

122. Ibid., 949-954.

123. Ibid., 481-493.

124. *Helen*, lines 38-41, fragment 1067.

125. *Gorgias*, 492c.

126. *Andromache*, lines 692-702.

127. *The Suppliants*, lines 229-237.

128. *Orestes*, lines 917-922; *Electra*, lines 386-400.

129. *Phoenician Maidens*, lines 531-537.

130. *History of the Peloponnesian War*, I, 70.

131. Hermann Vaerting Schultze, *Die Friedenspolotik des Perikles* (Munich, 1919), pp. xx-328.

132. *Peace*, lines 1210-1264.

133. *History of the Peloponnesian War*, III, 36; IV, 21.

134. *Acharnians*, lines 524-556.

135. Ibid., 509-523.

136. *History of the Peloponnesian War*, V, 16.

137. *Peace,* lines 292-300.

138. Ibid., 530-532.

139. *Lysistrata,* lines 1128-1135.

140. Ibid., 1143-1149.

141. *History of the Persian Wars,* VII, 149.

142. Ibid., I, 87.

143. Ibid., VIII, 3.

144. Ibid., VII, 9.

145. Ibid., I, 163-169.

146. Ibid., VI, 10.

147. Ibid., V, 28 and 97.

148. Plutarch, *De Herodoti malignitate.*

149. *History of the Persian Wars,* VIII, 132.

150. Ibid., IX, 52-57.

151. *History of the Peloponnesian War,* I, 22.

152. Ibid., III, 82.

153. Ibid.

154. Ibid.

155. Ibid., 83.

156. Ibid., IV, 17-20.

157. See Georg Peter Landmann, *Eine Rede des Thukydides. Die Friedens-mahnung des Hermokrates* (Kiel, 1932), p. 82.

158. *History of the Peloponnesian War,* IV, 59.

159. Ibid.

160. Ibid., 61.

161. Ibid.

162. *Hellenica,* VI, III, 15-17.

163. *Ways and Means,* V, 12.

164. *Oeconomicus,* VI, 5-8; V, 4-6.

165. *Symposium,* II, 14.

166. *Oeconomicus,* XXI, 4.

167. *Hiero,* II, 15-16.

168. Joel Karl, *Die* Φιλια *in Xenophon's Schriften.* In *Der echte und der xenophontische Sokrates,* vol. II, part 3a (Berlin, 1901), pp. 1030-1053.

169. *Cyropaedia,* VIII, 7, 1-28; Herodotus, *History of the Persian Wars,* I, 214.

170. *Cyropaedia,* I, 2, 7.

171. Ibid., II, 2, 10.

172. Ibid., III, 2, 15.

173. Ibid., IV, 5, 37.

174. Ibid., VII, 1, 41.

175. Ibid., VIII, 2, 1-2.

176. Ibid., VII, 2, 17.

177. There were many imitators. Another Cynic, Onesicritus of Astypalaia (fourth century B.C.), was the author of an essay—"How Alexander was educated"—which was a panegyric of the great captain. Now lost, it was written in praise of the constitution of the cosmopolis and the diffusion of Hellenic civilization.

178. See Andocides (fifth to fourth century B.C.), *On Peace with Sparta,* text of a speech made in Athens in 393 B.C.

179. Diodorus Siculus, XIV, 110, 3; Xenophon, *Hellenica,* V, 1, 31.

180. Xenophon, Πόροι, VI, 1; Isocrates, *On the Peace,* passim.

181. *Panathenaicus,* 241.

182. *On the Peace,* 16.

183. Ibid., 64.

184. Ibid., 20-21.

185. Ibid., 42, 44, 46, 68.

186. *Hymn to Zeus,* lines 20-29.

187. *On the Contradictions of the Stoics,* 32, 33.

188. Plutarch, *Life of Alexander,* LXIX.

189. Wilhelm Wachsmuth, *De Timone Phliuntis* (Leipzig, 1859).

190. *Peace,* lines 1019-1020.

191. Pausanias, *Description of Greece,* I, VIII, 2; IX, XVI, 2.

192. Bk. I, XVIII, 3.

193. Isocrates, *On Exchange,* XV, 110; Cornelius Nepos, *Timothy,* II, 2, 2; Plutarch, *Cimon,* XIII, 6.

194. *De Corona,* 260.

NOTES TO CHAPTER 2

Peace in Roman Thinking

1. *Roman Antiquities,* VIII, XXXV, 3.

2. *Roman History,* II, XVI, 3.

3. Ibid., II, XXII, 4.

4. Ibid., II, XXXIX, 6; II, XXXIX, 9.

5. Ibid., V, 11.

6. *Tusculanae disputationes,* V, XVI, 48.

7. *Roman History,* II, CXXVI.

8. Eutropius, *Breviarium historiae romanae,* IX, XVII. See also Sextus Aurelius Victor, *De Caesaribus,* XXXVII.

9. *Vita Probi,* XX.

10. *Epitome,* II, XXI, 12.

11. *Roman History,* LXII, III, 1-3.

12. *Life of Agricola,* XXX.

13. Take, for example, the level of civilization achieved by China during the four centuries of the Han dynasty (202 B.C.-220 A.D.), during which the Chinese people excelled in all fields of human activity and enjoyed the benefits of the *pax sinica.*

14. *De Officiis,* III, II, 7-14.

15. VI, 3, 10; VI, 11, 11.

16. Diogenes Laërtius, *Lives of Eminent Philosophers,* VII, 131.

17. *Histories,* IV, 74, 3.

18. Ibid., V, 10, 2.

19. Seneca, *Epistola ad Lucilium,* XC, 5.

20. *Lives of Eminent Philosophers,* X, 10.

21. *De rerum natura,* Bk. I, lines 62-145.

22. Ibid., lines 29-40.

23. *De legibus,* I, 55.

24. Ibid., I, VII, 23; *De officiis,* I, VII, 22 and I, XVII, 57.

25. *De re publica,* III, 23, 34; *Pro L. Murena,* IX, 22.

26. *De officiis,* I, XXIII, 80.

27. Ibid., I, XXII, 74.

28. *De re publica,* III, 23, 35.

29. *De officiis,* I, XI, 35.

30. Ibid., I, XII, 38.

31. *Pro P. Sestio,* XLV, 98.

32. Harald Fuchs, *Augustin und der antike Friedensgedanke* (Berlin, 1926), pp. vi-258.

33. H. Dahlmann and R. Heisterhagen, *Zu den Logistorici,* in *Varronische Studien* I (Wiesbaden, 1957), 52.

34. B. Riposati, *M. Terentii Varronis De Vita populi romani. Fonti. Esegesi,* a critical edition of the fragments (Milan, 1939), pp. x-320.

35. *Aeneid,* I, 291-296.

36. Eclogue IV, lines 4-10. For a eulogy of the kingdom of Saturn, see also Tibullus, bk.I, Elegy 3, lines 35-50.

37. Eclogue IV, lines 15-18.

38. Ibid., 19-25.

39. P. G. 20/1233-1316.

40. Bk. III, lines 652-656.

41. Ibid., 367-370.

42. The Emperor Vespasian, who reigned from 69 to 79, also built a temple of peace near the Forum (Svetonius, bk. VIII, Vespasian, IX). See also G. Moretti, *Ara Pacis Augustae* (Rome, 1948), p. 330, table 39. For a judgment on the civil war see Lucan, *Bellum Civile,* bk. I, lines 1-16.

43. *Odes,* IV, XV, lines 4-9.

44. *Carmen saeculare,* lines 57-60.

45. *Fasti,* I, lines 701-704, 711-722.

46. *Epistola ad Lucilium,* XCV, 30-31.

47. *De otio,* IV, 1.

48. *Epistola ad Lucilium,* CII, 21.

49. *De vita beata,* XX, 3.

50. *De ira,* I, V, 3.

51. *De clementia,* Proemium I, 3 and III, II, 1.

52. *Epistola ad Lucilium,* XC, 5.

53. Ibid., 40-41.

54. Flavius Arrianus, *Discourses of Epictetus,* III, XIII, 9-13.

55. Ibid., IV, V, 35.

56. Domitian was celebrated as the restorer of peace by Statius (*Silvae,* bk. IV, I, lines 11-16; bk. III, line 17).

57. *Natural History,* II, 117.

58. Ibid., XXVII, 3.

59. *Discourse XLVIII* (A political speech delivered in an assembly), 14.

60. *Discourse XL* (made in his home town and concerning peace with the Apameians), 35.

61. *History of the Peloponnesian War*, IV, XVI-XXII.

62. *Hellenica*, II/II, 19.

63. *First Oration on Peace*, 68.

64. *Oration to the Rhodians for Concord*, 376.

65. *Oration in Rome*, 399. '

66. *On the Contradictions of the Stoics*, 33.

67. *On the Fortune or the Virtue of Alexander*, Discourse I/6.

68. *Precepts of Statecraft*, 824/C-D.

69. *Dissertation XXX*, IV.

70. *Meditations*, VII, 9.

71. Ibid., VI, 42 and IX, 23.

72. *Annals*, XIV, LVII.

73. Ibid., XIV, XLII-XLV.

74. *On the Creation*, 81.

75. *Who is the Heir of Divine Things?*, 285.

76. *On the Change of Names*, 240.

77. *On the Special Laws*, IV, 95.

78. Philostratus, *Life of Apollonius*, VIII, XXIX.

79. Ibid., IV, VIII.

80. Voltaire, *Essai sur les moeurs*, chap. XXXIII.

81. *Vita Plotini*, 12.

82. *Enneads*, VI, 9, 1.

83. Ibid., III, 2, 15.

84. Ibid., II, 9.

85. Ibid., VI, 15.

86. Ammianus Marcellinus, *Histories*, XXI, 5, 8.

87. *To the Uneducated Cynics*, 201D.

88. *II Panegyric of Constantius*, 28, 86bc.

89. *Oration XXX*, the case for the farmer's life, 350.

90. *Oration X–On Peace* (dedicated to the Emperor Valens), 131A.

91. Ibid., 141A.

92. Diogenes Laërtius, *Lives of Eminent Philosophers*, VI, 63.

NOTES TO CHAPTER 3

Peace in the Old Testament

1. Ps. 37:3.

2. Josh. 10:21; Judg. 8:9; Jer. 43:12; Ps. 55:19.

3. Ps. 85:9-11; Isa. 9:6, 32:17, 55:12, 57:19, 60:17; Zech. 8:12.

4. Ezek. 7:25; Isa. 32:18; Jer. 34:4 et seq.

5. Josh. 9:15; Judg. 4:17; 1 Sam. 7:14; Isa. 27:5.

6. Wilhelm Caspari, *Vorstellung und Wort: "Friede" im Alten Testament* (Gütersloh, 1910), p. 26.

7. For further material relevant to this chapter, see J. J. Stamm and H. Bietenhard, *Der Weltfriede im Alten und Neuen Testament* (Zurich, 1959).

8. Eccles. 1:18.

9. Eccles. 5:8.

10. 1 Sam. 15:2; 2 Sam. 8:1; 1 Kings 11:16.

11. Num. 31:1-54.

12. Jer. 21:8-10, 27:8-13, 38:2, 38:17.

13. *Der Weltfriede im Alten und Neuen Testament,* p. 16.

14. *Emmerkar and the Lord of Aratta* (Philadelphia, 1952), lines 135-146.

15. H. Gross, *Die Idee des ewigen und allgemeinen Weltfriedens im Alten Orient und im Alten Testament* (Treves, 1956).

16. The rule against eating meat is confirmed in Leviticus 7:26.

17. Gen. 12:2-3.

18. Gen. 13:14-15.

19. Gen. 34:1-35.

20. *Der Weltfriede im Alten und Neuen Testament,* p. 18.

21. Gen. 4:8.

22. Num. 15:15-16 confirmed in Lev. 17:6.

23. Deut. 13:7-12.

24. C. H. Patterson, *The Philosophy of the Old Testament* (New York, 1953), p. 218.

25. Isa. 52:7.

26. Isa. 48:20.

27. Among the Dead Sea Scrolls, see in this connection: "Manual of Discipline," I, 16-18; "Book of Hymns," XI, 15-27; XV, 9-26.

NOTES TO CHAPTER 4

Peace in Christian Doctrine

1. Matt. 5:39.

2. Matt. 12:15; Luke 4:30; John 8:59-10:39.

3. Matt. 17:30-44; Luke 23:33-43.

4. Matt. 26:51-54; Luke 22:49-51; John 18:10-11.

5. Luke 22:35-38.

6. Matt. 21:12-13; Mark 11:15; Luke 19:45-48.

7. Acts 5:1-11.

8. Acts 13:8-11.

9. Luke 7:1-10.

10. John 4:46-54.

11. Acts 10:1-48.

12. Luke 19:27.

13. Matt. 21:41.

14. Matt. 24:6-8; Mark 13:7-8; Luke 21:8-9.

15. Rev. 19:11-21.

16. Luke 10:29-37.

17. Matt. 10:13.

18. *Der Weltfriede im Alten und Neuen Testament* (Zurich, 1959), p. 75.

19. Mark 5:34.

20. Acts 6:7.
21. Acts 11:62.
22. Gal. 2:7-8.
23. Mark 7:24-30.
24. Acts 17:18-34.
25. John 11:51-52.
26. John 14:27.
27. Acts 24:10-12.
28. John 19:11.
29. Matt. 22:21; Mark 12:17; Luke 20:25.
30. Harnack, *Militia Christi* (Tübingen, 1905), p. 49.
31. Ibid., p. 47.
32. *Miscellanies*, IV/217/P.G.8/1294C.
33. Ibid., IV/231/P.G.8/1371A.
34. *The Book of the Laws of Countries*, XXX.
35. *Oratio adversus Graecos*, 4/P.G. 6/813A.
36. *Apologia I pro Christianis*, 12/P.G. 6/341D.
37. *Fragmenta ex apologia*, P.G. 5/1212A.
38. *Apologeticus adversus gentes*, XXXIII/P.L. 1/509B.-511D.
39. Ibid., XXXVIII/P.L. 1/528A.
40. Ibid., XXVII/P.L. 1/494A.
41. Ibid., XXXVII/P.L. 1/525A.
42. Ibid., L/P.L. 1/598AB-599A.
43. *Ad martyres*, I/P.L. 1/695A.
44. Ibid., III/P.L. 1/697A.
45. *De idololatria*, XIX/P.L. 1/768A.
46. *De corona*, XI/P.L. 1/111C, 112A.
47. *Epistola I ad Donatum*, VI/P.L. 4/208B-209A.
48. *De unitate Ecclesiae*, XXIV/P.L. 4/534A.
49. *Christ the Educator*, I, 12/P.G. 8/369A.
50. *Miscellanies*, IV, 6/P.G. 8/1252C.
51. Ibid., 25/P.G. 8/1369B.
52. *Cohortatio ad gentes*, XI/P.G. 8/236C.
53. *Commentaria in Epistolam Beati Pauli ad Romanos*, **IV, 8/P.G.** 14/988C.
54. *Commentaria in Evangelium Joannis*, I, 13/P.G. 14/45C.
55. *Homiliae in Lucam*, XXII/P.G. 13/1858C.
56. *Contra Celsum*, VIII,24/P.G. 11/1552D, 1553A.
57. Ibid., 68/P.G. 11/1620.
58. *Of the Martyrs in Palestine*, XI/P.G. 20/1505C.
59. *Contra Celsum*, VIII, 65/P.G. 11/1614B.
60. Ibid., 68/P.G. 11/1620C.
61. Ibid., V, 33/P.G. 11/1232B.
62. *Commentaria in Epistolam Beati Pauli ad Romanos*, IV, 8/P.G. 14/ 989CD-990A.
63. Ibid., IX, 21/P.G. 14/1223BC.
64. Ibid., X, 9/P.G. 14/1266A.
65. J.D. Mansi, *Sacrorum Conciliorum Collectio*, II (Florence,1759), p. 471.

66. 1/II/P.L. 5/719B-720A.

67. Among those defending Christian intolerance of the pagans, we may mention Firmicus Maternus Julius (fourth century), who urged the Emperors Constantius II and Constans, sons of Constantine, to close the temples and prohibit pagan services. If they did so, he argued, the empire would obtain many advantages including peace. *De errore profanarum religionum,* XXIX, 4.

68. *Institutiones divinae,* VI/20/P.L. 6/707AB.

69. *Constitutiones apostolorum,* VIII/12, 42.

70. *Constitutiones apostolorum,* II, 20, 10. (A similar definition of peace is given in another collection of liturgical rules called *Didascaliae apostolorum,* XIX, 5-6: "In truth, peace is a quiet church. . . .")

71. *Constitutiones apostolorum,* VIII, 10, 3; we shall also find a more important rule, nearer the spirit of the early Christians, in *Canones Hippolyti,* a collection of religious instructions and customs derived in all likelihood from the uses and practices of the Church of Rome in an era preceding that of the *Constitutiones apostolorum:* "The Christian should not of his own will become a soldier, unless he is forced to take up arms by his commander. Carry the sword, but avoid making yourself responsible for the crime of bloodshed" (*Canones Hippolyti,* XIV).

72. J. D. Mansi, *Sacrorum Conciliorum Collectio,* II, p. 673.

73. *Psychomachia,* lines 631-632.

74. *Homilia in Psalmum,* XXXIII/10/P.G. 29/376B.

75. Ibid., P.G. 29/376C.

76. Ibid., XXIX/8/P.G. 29/304D-305A.

77. Ibid. 5/P.G. 29/320A.

78. *Oratio VI; De pace,* I/XII et seq., P.G. 35/737A.

79. Ibid., XIV P.G. 35/741A et seq.

80. *Oratio XXII; De pace,* II/V/P.G. 35/1137A.

81. Ibid., 1/P.G. 35/1133A.

82. Ibid., 424/P.G. 35/1149A.

83. *De beatitudinibus oratio,* VII/P.G. 44/1289A-B.

84. *De perfecta christiani forma,* P.G. 46/260A.

85. *De beatitudinibus oratio,* VII/P.G. 44/1284A.

86. Ibid., 1284B.

87. *In Ecclesiasten Salomonis, Homilia,* VIII/P.G. 44/744B et seq.

88. *De anima et resurrectione,* P.G. 46/148A.

89. *In Epistolam I ad Thimoteum homilia,* VII, I/P.G. 62/533 et seq.

90. *Expositio in Psalmum XLV,* 2/P.G. 55/207.

91. 1/P.G. 57/405.

92. 2/P.G. 59/314.

93. *In Isaiam,* bk. I; *Oratio,* II/P.G. 70/72D-73A.

94. Ibid., 73C.

95. *Commentarium in Michaeam Prophetam,* XXXIX/P.G. 71/700D-701A.

96. *Oratio de regno,* 16/P.G. 66/1100A.

97. Ibid.

98. *De divinis nominibus,* XI, 1/P.G. 3/948D-950A.

99. Ibid., V/P.G. 3/953AB.

100. *Epistola*, XXIV/P.G. 91/609D.

101. *Quaestiones et dubia, interrogatio,* LXVIII/P.G. 90/844A.

102. *Contra Arianos vel auxentium mediolanensem liber unus,* P.L.10/609-618.

103. Ibid., 609C.

104. *Tractatus in CXXI Psalmum,* 11/P.L. 9/665B.

105. *Tractatus in CXVIII Psalmum,* XI, 8/P.L. 9/575C.

106. *Commentarium in Matthaeum,* IV, 18/P.L. 9/938A.

107. *In Epistolam ad Ephesios liber* II/P.L. 8/1294CD.

108. *Translatio Homiliarum Origenis in Lucam homilia,* XV/P.L. 26/252CD.

109. *Commentariorum in Evangelium Matthaei liber,* I V/P.L. 26/34D.

110. *Commentariorum in Epistolam ad Titum liber,* III/P.L. 26/594B.

111. Ibid., Prologus P.L. 26/554A.

112. *Epistola,* LXI/16/P.L. 22/600; *Epistola,* LXXVIII/8/P.L. 22/695.

113. *Commentariorum in Isaiam Prophetam liber,* I, II/P.L. 24/25C.

114. Ibid., 46AB.

115. *Commentariorum in Michaeam liber* I, IV/P.L. 25/1187CD-1188AB.

116. *Dialogus adversus Pelagianos liber* II/19/P.L. 23/555C.

117. *Expositio in psalmum David* CXVIII, 17/P.L. 15/1509AB.

118. Ibid., 19/P.L. 15/1509D.

119. *Enarratio in psalmum* XXXVI, 24/P.L. 14/979B.

120. Ibid., 978AB.

121. *Expositio in psalmum* CXVIII/P.L. 15/1557D.

122. *Commentaria in epistolam ad Galatas,* P.L. 17/338A.

123. *Commentaria in epistolam ad Colonnenses,* P.L. 17/419B.

124. 607-622/P.L. 61/638-648.

125. *Contra Faustum,* XXII, 78/P.L. 42/450.

126. *De civitate Dei,* XIV, 28/P.L. 41/436.

127. *Enarratio in psalmum* XXXVI, 12/P.L. 36/362-363.

128. *Enarratio in psalmum* LXXXIV, 10/P.L. 37/1075.

129. *Sermo* XVI/P.L., 38/124.

130. *Sermo* CLXVIII, III/P.L. 38/912.

131. *Sermones CCCLVII De laude pacis c CCCLVIII De pace et charitate* / P.L. 39/1582c -1586.

132. *De civitate Dei,* XIX, 7/P.L. 41/634.

133. Ibid., 11/P.L. 41/637.

134. Ibid., 12/P.L. 41/639.

135. Ibid., 13/P.L. 41/640.

136. Ibid., 20/P.L. 41/648.

137. *Geremia,* 27/1-23.

138. *De civitate Dei,* IV, 3/P.L. 41/114.

139. B. Paradisi, *La Paix au IV et au V siècles,* p. 337.

140. *De civitate Dei,* IV, 3/P.L. 41/114.

141. Ibid., 4/P.L. 41/115.

142. Ibid., 15/P.L. 41.

143. P.L. 33/515.

144. *Contra Faustum* XXII, 78/P.L. 42/451.

145. Ibid., 75/P.L. 42/448.

146. *Epistola CXXXVI, di Marcellino ad Agostino*, 2/P.L. 33/515.

147. *Epistola CXXXVIII a Marcellino*, 9/P.L. 33/528-529.

148. *De civitate Dei*, XIX, 15/P.L. 41/643.

149. Ibid., V, 22/P.L. 41/168.

150. *Contra Faustum*, passim.

151. *De civitate Dei*, I, 26/P.L., 41/39.

152. *Epistola CLXXXIX a Bonifacio*, P.L. 33/4/855.

153. *Contra Faustum*, XXII, 74/P.L. 42/447.

154. *Epistola CLXXXIX a Bonifacio*, 6/P.L. 33/856.

155. *De natura et gratia*, XIX, 21/P.L. 44/256.

156. *Tractatus de Divitiis*, X, 2.

157. Ibid., VIII, 2-3.

158. *Epistola ad Demetriadem*, P.L. 30/13-45.

159. On the spread of the Christian religion in the whole world, see Prudentius, *Apotheosis*, lines 421-447.

160. *Epistola de malis doctoribus et operibus fidei et de indicio futuro*, XI, 1.

INDEX